Contemporary Literary and Cultural Theory

Contemporary Literary and Cultural Theory

From Structuralism to Ecocriticism

PRAMOD K. NAYAR

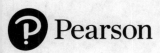
Pearson

ISBN 978-81-317-2735-5

First Impression, 2010
Sixteenth Impression, 2018
Seventeenth Impression

Published by Pearson India Education Services Pvt. Ltd, CIN: U72200TN2005PTC057128

Head Office: 15th Floor, Tower-B, World Trade Tower, Plot No. 1, Block-C,Sector-16, Noida 201 301, Uttar Pradesh, India.

Registered Office: 4th Floor, Software Block, Elnet Software City, TS-140, Block 2 & 9, Rajiv Gandhi Salai, Taramani, Chennai 600 113, Tamil Nadu, India.
Fax: 080-30461003,Phone: 080-30461060
Website : in.pearson.com , Email: companysecretary.india@pearson.com

Printed in India by Rahul Print O Pack

Contents

Acknowledgements

The usual suspects have been involved, to varying degrees, in the process of writing this book, and to whom I owe great gratitude:

My parents, alternating between anxiety and affection, but ever prayerful

Ai and Baba at Nagpur, who have now given up hope of hosting me;

My student friends who found the time to read the manuscript and offered their suggestions: Deepthi Sebastian, Saradindu Bhattacharya, Cecil John and Neeraja Sundaram; and

Other friends over the years whose work and affection (in many cases both) have been equally important to me: Narayana Chandran, Brinda Bose, Nandana Dutta, Colin Harrison, Lyn Innes, Elleke Boehmer, Kate Teltscher, Indira Ghose, Walter Perera, Anindita Mukhopadhyay, Brian Yothers, Maryse Jayasuriya and more recently, Akhila Ramnarayan, Joe Moran and Rita Kothari.

As for Anna, for suffering my high-decibel opinion-making and her affectionate friendship ('No, I *don't* think you need to do a book on …')—it's a privilege to thank you again.

The readers of the proposal and manuscript deserve a special mention and my thanks for their close reading and useful suggestions.

At Pearson: Urmila Dasgupta who initiated the project, Debjani Dutta and Arani Banerjee for taking it forward—thank you. Also, to Ashish Alexander and the production team: much gratitude for your fine job.

To Nandini, whose contribution to my work- and home-life is immeasurable, for her monumental forbearance, endless cheer and unstinting love—I owe an irredeemable debt.

To Pranav, who demonstrates how all 'Theory' quails before a 7-year-old's praxis, his pats on the back (mine) whenever he sees another of my books, and his joyous romps through the home—thank you.

Parts of the chapters on Postcolonial Theory and Critical Race Studies were delivered as 'Postcolonialism Now' in the form of the third P. K. Rajan Memorial Lecture, University of Kerala, Thiruvananthapuram, 12 February 2009. I am grateful to Dr P. P. Ajaya Kumar, the Center for Distance Education and the Department of English and *Litt Crit* for the honour.

Prefacing Theory

What is Theory and why are they saying such terrible things about it? (and who, to indulge in paranoiac criticism, are 'they' anyway?) To take the second part of the question first, 'they' say terrible things about Theory because much of it is admittedly jargon-ridden and incomprehensible, but also (and this is the uncharitable answer) because (i) it takes considerable patience and effort to understand the 'key' essays and most diatribes against Theory come from people who don't want to make the effort and (ii) it destabilizes authority over interpretation, and authority is what teachers (especially teachers of literary studies) seek to impose over texts, meanings and readers.

A preface is supposed to propose in *advance*, its 'pre' makes, as one philosopher put it, 'the future present', where the main text is *presaged*: it 'puts before the reader's eye what is not yet visible' (Derrida 2004 [1981]: 7–8). It also functions, according to another commentator, 'to ensure that the text is read properly', to provide the author's 'statement of intent' (Genette 1997: 197, 221). If these thinkers are correct, then 'prefacing theory' is a statement of intention, an introduction (a warning, perhaps?) to what this book does (as to whether there is a 'correct' way of reading—anything—I am not so sure). 'Prefacing Theory' is a defence, a justification and a manifesto.

*

Literary Theory is the organized, systematized analysis of literary texts, the institution of Literature (with L in upper case) and a reflection on the interpretative strategies 'applied' to these texts. Cultural Theory moves beyond literary texts and studies art forms, film, the superhero comic book, sports, fashion—all cultural practices, of which Literature is one. Contemporary literary and cultural theory, which is how this book positions it, has conceptual, general, political and methodological questions that it asks of cultural practices. It seeks to understand modes of *interpretation*, of how *knowledge* is formed and distributed, the *pedagogic*—i.e., teaching, classroom and educative—role of literary texts, the *philosophical* basis of metaphors or image-making, the *historical* location and sources of texts (by 'texts' we now mean any form of representation, from fiction to film to the Google opening menu) and interpretation, the *psychological* (individual or collective) roots of particular kinds of images or representations and the *political* consequences of literary and cultural representations. Thus, Theory now is not restricted to literary texts or literary approaches to, say, the novel, but has widened out into other domains. Such multiple roots of Theory in anthropology, psychoanalysis and philosophy in addition to traditional literary criticism, generates its complexity, its

political edge, its jargon, its agenda and (to its more sophisticated 'users') its rivet-
ing analytical rigour. The most sophisticated approaches to literary texts have, at
least since the mid-1960s, come from these diverse, non-literary fields. Studies of
anthropology, of history or of art have influenced the way we read literary texts.

Theory speculates on meaning-making, practices of representation and consumption, on the relation of social structures and meanings in films and books, on
the nature of knowledge produced, on abstract realities like dreams or desires,
on the visible effects of invisible forces like power or structures like class. But such
'speculation' cannot be taken as mere extended and random fantasizing. Theory's
speculation is based on close studies of words, images, sounds, structures and economics. 'Speculation' here gestures at the unquantifiable effects of words and social
practices, but it is also taken to mean a careful, considered reflection on how these
practices *work*, of the *language* in which power or desire operates in film or image
or words. Barbara Johnson's translator's introduction to Derrida's *Dissemination* is
a useful description of Theory itself:

> the deconstruction of a text does not proceed by random doubt or generalized skep-
> ticism, but by the careful teasing out of warring forces of signification *within the text
> itself.* If anything is destroyed in a deconstructive reading, it is not meaning but the
> claim to unequivocal domination of one mode of signifying over another. (Johnson
> 2004: xv, emphasis in original)

No doubt this is the kind of language that gives Theory a bad name, but the point
Johnson is making is a general one about the work of Theory itself. Theory works
to show how one meaning or meaning-practice ('signifying') has often been given
importance over another. The task of Theory is to reveal this process of rejecting or
marginalizing one meaning in favour of another and claiming that this privileged
meaning is 'natural'. Meanings of texts are never final or natural—they are formed
through practices of representation and interpretation. Theory shows how certain
kinds of representation and interpretation propose a 'natural' meaning.

'Theory' etymologically comes from the Greek *theoria*, which means con-
templation, speculation, a looking at, things looked at, and is linked to *theorein*
(to consider, speculate, look at) and *theoros* (spectator) and *thea* (a view) and *horan*
(to see). Theory thus gestures at several things at once: to speculate and contem-
plate but also to *see*. Theory—and this is the simplest explanation—is a way of
seeing, a way of looking very, very closely at texts. Theory is a way of *seeing* how
meaning emerges in any cultural practice whether film or fiction, architecture or
fashion. Theory is the *practice* of *reading* itself, but a *reading* of *how we read* build-
ings, road signs, dance forms, novels, newspapers or political developments. Theory
is the study of the production of meaning in texts, the distribution of this meaning
in various forms (genres of literature, but also in rhetoric, visual culture) and the
reception of these meanings. In its detailed analysis of meaning-practices, Theory
studies authors, readers, texts and contexts. It examines the genre, the medium,
the language and the register of films, novels, advertising, political speeches and
clothes.

Theory is an examination of meaning-practices. Theory is thus political because meanings—whether in 'classic' literature where Homer's male heroes become more important than his women or in popular films where the patriarchal family is praised as the ideal state—are always political, whether they deal with the politics at the level of the nation or that of the family.

Theory is political also because it unsettles and upsets established meanings of texts. It is political because it looks the *structures*—institutions—such as law, the university, the family in which representations are interpreted and meanings produced. It makes use of reviews, criticism, commentaries, responses, social events, awards, prefaces, legislation, market production as structures that inform, regulate and disseminate meanings. Theory is interested in exposing not simply the linguistic and rhetorical features that produce meaning, but in the very *structures* where these features are studied, the principles of these studies formulated and practices of these studies regulated by norms, values and systems of evaluation.

To return to the example used above, Theory (especially feminist theory) shows how the idealization of the patriarchal family (where the 'ideal' nature of the family is the common *meaning* of the concept of 'family') in films or novels is based upon a politics: the politics of silencing the woman, the politics of suppressing the value of her labour, the politics of equating her with an endlessly giving 'Mother Nature', the politics of rejecting her sexuality, among others. Feminist *theory* shows, therefore, how the commonly accepted meaning of the ideal family or the 'happy' family in 'common' readings of films and novel conceals or ignores deeper inequalities, injustice and oppression. Here Theory works to show how the commonly accepted, so-called 'obvious' or 'natural' meanings are actually masks for something else. This makes feminist theory a political device since it points out the material, economic and social basis for the textual (filmic, fictional) representation and our reading of the representation. Theory in this case links *social* practices with *textual* ones and reveals how meanings are produced and consumed.

Theory gives you a better, sharper way of seeing through the obvious. It is not abstract speculations in 'difficult' language (or rather, it is not abstract once you get the drift of the Theories): It is praxis—technically, theory that seeks social change or transformation, but here taken to mean any analytic method that refers to and seeks changes in the *social* realms of reading or the making of meaning in the law or even the acts of writing histories—in the sense it helps a reading practice, a political commitment and a mode of interpretation.

*

When I wrote my first introduction to literary and cultural theory almost 10 years ago, I was teaching in a small university where students attending my classes had problems even with basic academic English and, therefore, the language of Theory seemed wholly incomprehensible. Now, teaching in a wholly different setting (and perhaps having become, hopefully, a better teacher), I find that the English language may make sense to students here, the language of Theory still doesn't. This discovery led to the present book. But I would be dishonest if I didn't admit that part of the impetus for this book came from the mockery that I receive from no-doubt well-intentioned colleagues about Theory (I would have called it, for *their* sake, 'Monster Theory', but Jeffrey Cohen got in first with the title for his scintillating collection on the monstrous!).

The aim of this book is to explain rather than critique, to define rather than discern. The organization is based on schools of critical thought, with the assumption that students need a handle on a methodology or critical 'approach' (as these are often called). I have also eschewed the approach where individual or 'key' essays are discussed because I am deeply sceptical as to its pedagogic use: an essay does not summarize a school or indicate an entire 'approach'.

The use of definition boxes and occasional point-wise organization is meant to facilitate readability and easy comprehension. The list for further reading at the end of every chapter is a short one, and consists mainly of basic works. A detailed bibliography offers primary texts of theorists as well as secondary works and commentaries.

The chapter on Critical Race Studies demands an explanation. It was originally intended as a chapter on African American literary theory. The reviewer of the proposal, quite correctly, proposed that it could be expanded into addressing other race-related matters in Theory. Since there was already a chapter on Postcolonial Theory the *via media* was to look at other critical approaches that foreground race and ethnicity. The result is 'Critical Race Studies'.

*

This is by no means intended as a substitute for reading, say, 'The Death of the Author' or 'Shakespearean Bullets'. It also does not adequately locate schools of Theory within their philosophical, political and social contexts, nor trace every school's 'history of ideas' except as a short account called 'opening moves'. Every school of thought owes much to its antecedents with whom it agrees and quarrels—and Theory is no exception. But this book does not delve into intellectual histories of this kind, nor does it presuppose that the student would be familiar with them. The book also does not elaborate the newer critical theories being used in the interdisciplinary discipline called Cultural Studies.

It serves as an *introduction* to concepts, authors, approaches and ideas in the vast, turbulent reaches of Theory-universe. Having negotiated this introduction, armed with the alphabet (A for Adorno, B for Bourdieu, C for Chodorow ... Z for Žižek) of Theory I hope you will turn (return?) to 'original' essays, albeit mediated and contaminated by this book.

Pramod K. Nayar
Hyderabad

1 Structuralism

Along with its related field, semiotics (technically the study of 'signs'), structuralism is one of the most influential modes of critical and cultural analysis of the twentieth century. Structuralism's emphasis on the *language* or formal properties of texts, their structures and frames in specific genres like the novel or poetry, is an extension of the kind of work New Criticism practiced. Before moving on to structuralism, a short introduction to New Criticism will help us understand the context in which structuralism developed. New Criticism (the term was taken from John Crowe Ransom's 1941 essay of the same title), associated mainly with the work of Cleanth Brooks, Robert Penn Warren, William Wimsatt and Monroe Beardsley, R. P. Blackmur and I. A. Richards, set out to develop a 'science' of literary criticism and literary texts. They argued that the author's intention behind a work is far less important (and unknowable) than the meaning generated by the language, style and formal features of the text. What they proposed—especially in Wimsatt and Beardsley's key essay, 'The Intentional Fallacy' (1954)—was simple:

There is no need to bring in extraneous features such as author-biography or history to understand a text. All we need is the words on the page; and meaning is contained in the text. In other words, New Criticism proposed the autonomous existence and nature of the literary text, an *autotelic* text. This means, the contexts of an author's class, gender, sexual preference, race or economic conditions were deemed irrelevant to an understanding of the author's writings. New Criticism, therefore, paid close attention to the language of a literary text—the form, style, paradox, ambiguity, images and metaphors, meter, rhythm, sounds, etc. Since their focus was on the tensions and contradictions of the literary language, the New Critics turned readily and easily to poetry, for poetry embodied the most interesting uses of language. William Empson's *Seven Types of Ambiguity* (1930) and Cleanth Brooks' famous *The Well-Wrought Urn* (1947) are excellent examples of the work done by the New Critics. Empson's taxonomy of ambiguity moved from simple ambiguity such as double meaning to outright contradictions. He begins with words that seem to mean several things at once due to similar sounds. In the second type, two meanings merge into one. In the third, two seemingly unconnected meanings are given together. In the fourth, alternative meanings combine to confuse interpretation. In the fifth type, there is some confusion that the author has discovered as he went along, and is the result of the author not being able to 'hold' the entire work in his head when composing. In the sixth, irrelevance constitutes the ambiguity and the reader has to make a choice. Finally, outright contradiction and antagonistic meanings are deployed by the author (Empson argues, via Freud, that this indicates a split in the author's own consciousness).

Richards's *Practical Criticism* (1929), one of the most influential New Critical works of the age, was, along with his earlier *Principles of Literary Criticism* (1924), an attempt to formulate clear-cut approaches to a systematic study of literary texts. Richards paid attention to the form and language of the text, and excluded all biographical and contextual details as being unnecessary to the text. He handed out poems to students after removing all information about the author or the context in order for them to come to an understanding of the mechanics of literary responses unmediated by anything other than the text and the reader. His interest lay in the interpretive process—what he termed 'literary judgement'—and the way the text determined this process. Richards believed that when the students responded to the emotions and ideas in the text, they 'organized' and understood their own emotional and psychic make-up better.

The relevance of New Criticism even today—despite its problematic politics of excluding all context—is because of its attention to language and formal properties of texts. No criticism before the New Critics paid such close attention to the language of texts, or read them so closely. In fact, if we look at the work of the structuralists like Todorov or Barthes or even poststructuralists (see Chapter 2) like Jacques Derrida, we see the parallels with New Criticism in terms of their attention to language and form.

*

Structuralism believes that the world is organized as structures. 'Structures' are forms made up of units that are arranged in a specific order. These units follow particular rules in the way they are organized or related to each other. Let us see how units are organized in a poem.

A poem is a structure constituted by units such as sounds, phrases, pauses, punctuation and words. Every unit is connected to every other unit. The poem is thus the result of all the units put together. In order to understand the poem's meaning we need to read all these component parts together and see how the images generated by the words hold together with the rhyme scheme, the sounds, the stops (punctuations). The meaning of the text is not confined to or generated by any one of these units—it is the result of all the units working together. A word in a poem makes sense because of its specific location in the poem and its relationship with the other words, images and sounds in the poem. This is the *structure* of the poem. Let us move beyond the poem now.

The poem is situated within other forms of literature like the novel and drama. Thus, in order to understand the special features of a poem we need to relate it to other forms of literature. That is, 'literature' is a system, or structure, whose constituent parts include the poem, the essay, the novel and drama. In this structure called literature each form (or unit) generates meanings in particular ways. This is the larger structure within which we read a poem or a play. Hence, when we read a poem we are aware that it is one unit within a larger context or system of literary representation.

Expanding this notion, we see that literature is one system within a larger system of representation of culture. The system of culture includes other non-literary forms such as cinema, reportage, television, political speeches, myths and traditions. 'Culture' is a structure where these various forms exist in relation with each other. Meaning is generated when we understand the rules by which myth, literary texts and social behaviour are linked to each other. As we shall see, such a notion of linked elements informs the definition of 'text'.

Structuralism is interested in the relationship between the elements of a structure that results in meaning. Since it believes that meaning is the effect of the coming together of elements, it follows that if we understand the rules governing the relationship between elements we can decipher the processes of meaning-production. Structuralism is the study of structures of texts—film, novel, drama, poem, politics, sports—with specific attention to the rules, or grammar, of the elements.

Structuralism looks at the relationships between the various elements within the self-contained, well-organized structure of a text in order to understand the ways (the grammar or rules) by which the text produces meaning. It focuses on the form of a text by looking at elements like voice, character, setting, and their combination.

A pithy summary of structuralist literary criticism is provided by Jonathan Culler in his book on Barthes in which he says that structuralism

- is an attempt to describe the language of literature in linguistic terms so as to capture the distinctiveness of literary structures,
- is the development of a 'narratology' that identifies the constituents of a narrative and their various combinations,
- is an attempt to show how literary meaning depends upon the codes produced by prior discourses of a culture,
- promotes analysis of the reader's role in producing meaning.

(Culler 1990: 80–81)

Structuralism emerged as the most rigorous form of critical analysis in the 1950s. However, its origins lay further back, in the work of the early twentieth century linguist, Ferdinand de Saussure.

OPENING MOVES

THE LINGUISTIC TURN: SAUSSUREAN LINGUISTICS

Ferdinand de Saussure's 1915 work, *A Course in General Linguistics* (English translation in 1959), proposed that language was a system in which various components existed in relation to each other.

What Saussure was proposing was a radical rethinking of the nature of language. It is not enough to see how words acquire meaning over time (what is called a *diachronic study*). We need to see how words mean within a period and as part of a general system of language. This is the *synchronic study* where we look at words within the current state of the language and not at its history. This is now self-evident. When we listen to a sentence like 'The film star looks glamorous' we immediately understand what it means. We are not aware that any of those words had a different meaning before in history ('glamour' was in fact a term used to describe witches). We understand the meanings of the words as they are in use, as a part of the language system *today*.

Saussure makes three significant moves in his analysis of language. First of all, he divides language into two main components.

(i) The *set of rules* by which we combine words into sentences, use certain words in certain ways, rules which are rarely altered and which all users of a language follow. This he termed *langue*.

(ii) Everyday speech where we use words in *particular* contexts. This he called *parole*.

To use an example. *Langue* is like the mathematical tables. The tables are a system of rules and tools for use. The everyday calculations we do—from prices in shops to simple totaling—is an instance of *parole* where we employ the tables to get the calculations done. If *langue* is the system of rules and conventions that govern how we use words and meanings, *parole* is, then, *language in context*. In most cases we are not aware of the langue component; we use the system of conventions by habit, and are not always alert to the large structure of language in everyday use. Parole, therefore, is *live* language.

Then, in his second move, Saussure proposes a relational theory of language where

(i) 'words' existed in relation to other words and
(ii) the meaning of each word was dependent upon the meaning of other words.

Thus, meaning was the result of being able to recognize the *difference* between words—'cat' is 'cat' because it is *not* 'bat' or 'hat'. It is different in terms of the sound produced and the way in which it is written. Meaning thus emerges in the difference or opposition between words. We work with binary or paired oppositions to make sense of words and sounds in speech. 'Cat', 'bat' and 'hat' are all words in the system of language: They are related to each other because they belong to the same system, and because they make sense only in being different from each other. We would not be able to recognize 'cat' as a unique word if we did not have other words from which it is different.

What we, therefore, have is a principle. This principle is the *structure* of language itself: that of difference and opposition. Language imposes its structure (the recognized difference between 'cat' and 'hat') whatever be the individual contexts in which the sounds or words are being used. We are aware of this system that makes conversation and understanding possible. We learn to use the differences that generate meaning.

Finally, Saussure's third move. Saussure suggests that words and their meanings are not 'natural' but created through repeated use and convention. The word 'cat' does not naturally refer to a four-legged furry animal of a particular kind with particular habits. The pronunciation or writing of the word does not invoke the animal. We have come to associate the name or word 'cat' to the animal through long *use*. There is no real relationship between the word and its meaning. Meaning is attributed through its use by a community of language-users. The animal cat does not declare its 'catness', we *attribute* the 'catness' to it by giving it a name. The cat might very well see itself as 'man' or 'tiger'. But humans have given the name 'cat' to it, whatever the cat may think of itself. The word (or 'signifier') is connected to the meaning or concept (the 'signified') in a purely *arbitrary* relationship. Together the signifier and signified constitute a *sign*.

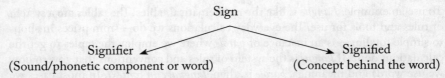

For Saussure the sound was a material manifestation of the abstract concept. Words are signs that enable us to understand the concept or the object. Words are like a form of transport that takes you to the object or concept. They help us construct the concept in our mind.

Saussure's move is apparently very simple, but its consequences are far-reaching. He was undermining the very notion of language by proposing the relationship between words and meanings as arbitrary. The structure of language ensures that when we use words, however arbitrary their meaning might be, we register certain differences and make sense of them. Thus, even though the term 'cat' is only arbitrarily connected to the animal, we still make sense of it because it is different from other words that are equally arbitrary in their relationship with things.

This means (and this is the consequence of Saussure's thinking on the nature of language) that words in a language do not refer to a 'reality' but to other words from which they are different. We are able to distinguish between 'real' things because the words for them are different. Language is, therefore, a system that constantly refers only to itself.

We can now summarize the three principles regarding language that Saussure puts forward:

(i) *Arbitrariness*: Words have no real connection to their meanings or the things they describe. The connections are established by convention.

(ii) *Relationality*: Words make sense to us, or have 'value' (Saussure's term) for us in their *relationality*: in their difference from other words. Words are therefore related to each other in the form of difference and have no absolute value of their own. As we have seen above, every word is opposed to, different from another word, and meaning emerges in this *difference*.

(iii) *Systematicity*: The structure of language, or the system, ensures that we recognize difference.

Later, Saussure's ideas about structures and rules were adopted by the anthropologist Claude Lévi-Strauss to analyse rituals, myths and kinships. This created the 'discipline' of structural anthropology.

In terms of literary and cultural criticism, Saussure's structural theory of language provides particular insights and approaches as follows:

- It suggests that content in a poem, a film or a play is dependent upon the form in which the themes are expressed.
- The effect of a poem or a film is the result of an effective combination of elements that have been arranged in a particular way.

> Saussure proposed that the link between the word/sound (signifier) and concept (signified) is based on the difference between sounds and our ability to distinguish between them, the relationship between sounds (a relationship of difference) and is purely arbitrary (where the sound/word does not describe the object, but is assumed to do so by convention and repeated use).

- Following from the above two we can say that there is *no content without form*.
- Content is a function of form.
- It is possible to uncover the basic principles of organization (or grammar) of a film or a poem.
- The grammar is the structure of the poem, and follows specific rules that function like language, based on opposition, difference and relationality.
- Culture itself has an underlying organization or structure where different elements are combined to generate meaning.

Saussure's ideas were also appropriated by the linguists and the literary critics in Europe and Russia. In Russia, a mode of literary critical analysis developed around theories of language and came to be known as Russian Formalism.

RUSSIAN FORMALISM

The Moscow Linguistic Circle of the 1920s and 1930s was at the forefront of formalist criticism. A related society was the Petrograd Society for the Study of Poetic Language. Russian Formalism is often associated with the work of Boris Eichenbaum, Viktor Shklovsky, Roman Jakobson and Juri Tynyanov. The major works that launched and popularized the Formalists include Osip Brik, Eichenbaum and Shklovsky's *Poetics* (1919), Jakobson's *Modern Russian Poetry* (1921), Shklovsky's *On the Theory of Prose* (1926, 1929) and later works like Vladimir's *Morphology of the Folktale* (1928).

Like the structuralists of the later decades, the Formalists believed in certain key assumptions:

- Literature, especially poetry, was a special function of language.
- It was possible to discover the underlying formulae or *structures* of literary texts by a study of its *devices* (a term they were fond of using to describe literary techniques such as symbolism).
- Literary analysis could be as accurate and precise as science.

Thus, literary language extended everyday language, used it in different ways. The purpose of criticism was to find out how a literary text generated or possessed a *literariness*. This can be described as the main concern of the Russian Formalists.

Literariness was a special use of everyday language. It was the effect of the formal and the linguistic properties of a text—and the purpose of criticism was to discover these underlying properties. What a literary text did was to use language in such a way that everyday objects could be made to look different, extraordinary or even strange. Literary and poetic language transformed everyday objects into something else by using words about the objects differently. A literary text represents the world in such a way that ordinary things appear different. This is what engages our (the reader's) attention. This process is what Shklovsky termed *defamiliarization*.

The formalists focused on poetry as a supreme example of the device of defamiliarization. Poetic language has the following features that make it different from ordinary or everyday language:

- It does not seek to convey information; it is an end in itself.
- It is *self-reflexive*, drawing attention to itself. Poetic language makes us aware that it is unique (for example: 'My love is like a red, red rose' by Edmund Waller alerts us to the fact that something unusual is going on. The quality of love is not an object, so the poet is using the two key words, love and rose, in an odd combination).
- It often uses a word to mean multiple things and thus *destabilizes* meaning itself. The words in poetry can mean more than one thing.

Together these features of poetic language produce the effect of defamiliarization.

However, what is striking is that the Formalists, by focusing on what makes a text literary, clearly negotiated the relation between literary and non-literary texts. In order to identify what 'literary' meant, they had to account for non-literary forms, which made their project historical because the question of form is related to the rise and development of that form in a *particular period*.

> Defamiliarization is the literary device whereby language is used in a way that ordinary and familiar objects are made to look different. It is a process of *transformation* where language asserts its power to affect our perceptions. Reality is thus modified for us through a special use of language. In short, the content of reality, story or theme is made to look attractive, ugly or good through the representation in language. Defamiliarization is therefore about *form* as it affects content and reading. Defamiliarization is what distinguishes poetic or literary language from non-poetic or non-literary language.

Later some of the formalists began to look at the poetics of fiction. Shklovsky, Propp and Tzvetan Todorov looked at the ways in which the language of fiction produced the effect of defamiliarization. They looked for the structure of a narrative and explored how elements like plot or characterization (form) contributed to the narrative's effects. Propp, for example, looked at what he called the 'morphology of the folktale', identifying the elements and their functions in the plot. Critics like Shklovsky were fascinated by formal properties that defamialiarized reality and earlier literary forms. Shklovsky's classic essay, 'Art as Technique', for instance, treated Laurence Sterne's *Tristram Shandy* as a novel that parodied earlier conventions of writing and thus drew attention to the very *act of literary writing*. Sterne, argues, Shklovsky, was testing the limits of realism (the established form for the novel during that time) by showing how literary representations of reality were only *representations* (or signification) of reality. In Shklovsky's beautiful and precise formulation, literature 'creates a "vision" of the object instead of serving as a means of knowing it' (qtd. in Bennett 20).

We shall look at Propp and the poetics of fiction in Russian Formalism under Structuralism and Narrative Theory later in this chapter.

THE PRAGUE SCHOOL

Closely aligned with Russian Formalism is the Prague School of structuralists. Roman Jakobson, a Russian immigrant, was one of the central figures in this school. The Prague's School central tenet was that *language is a coherent system fulfilling a range of 'functions' in society*. Jakobson's work on language built on this tenet. The Prague School believed that there was a poetic or aesthetic function of language. *Poetic language foregrounds its own use.* This means, poetic language does not seek to convey information. Instead it draws attention to its own utterance, to what and how it is saying/speaking. Jan Mukarovsky, therefore, declared that 'the function of poetic language consists in the maximum of foregrounding of the utterance … it is not used in the service of communication …' (qtd. in Hawkes 1997: 75). Once again we see the Russian Formalists' emphasis asserting itself: Poetic language is an end in itself, it does not seek to do more.

ROMAN JAKOBSON AND METAPHOR-METONYMY

Jakobson worked with aphasics, people with an inability to use language without difficulty. Observing the way aphasics use and understand ordinary speech, Jakobson developed a theory of language use. Jakobson argued that there are two major rhetorical figures: metaphor and metonymy. Both are figures of *equivalence* because they *substitute* a new term that is believed to be an equivalent for the main/original term. Let us use an example to understand what Jakobson termed the metaphoric and metonymic poles.

We often declare that on our roads the 'traffic crawls along'. Now 'crawl' is a term used to describe the relatively slow movement of creatures, like worms, snakes and insects, that stop and go, stop and go, inspecting various things on the way.

How does it describe the vehicular movement on the road? What the image does is to posit an equivalence between the pattern of movement of the vehicles with that of the insects. It assumes a *similarity* between the two. We could have picked 'bustles' or 'races' or 'goes', but we selected 'crawls' from this *vertical* list of possible descriptives because we think the movement of vehicles is *akin* to that of the insects. What we have, therefore, is a term that provides a *metaphor* for the vehicular movement. It is possible to visualize vehicular movement as the movement of insects through this metaphor. We have *substituted* insects for cars and vehicles. Metaphor is an act of substitution through *selection* and *association*, in this case the association or analogy between the movements of cars and insects.

Another form of language use is metonymy. Metonymy is when a part is substituted for the whole. For example, we say, 'the orders were issued by Rashtrapati Bhavan'. Now, the building, that is, Rashtrapati Bhavan does not issue orders. It is the President of India, who lives in the Bhavan, who issues orders. Here the building is taken to be the equivalent of its resident by the principle of contiguity. One word is placed next to another as being contiguous. Here we choose a word that is seen as adjacent to another. This is the principle of *combination*.

Selection and combination are the two ways of language operation. We can select any word from a storehouse of words, and then use these words in combination to generate a sentence. As an example, we can look at the following sentence.

I live in a	house
	cave
	shell

Now, we *select* the word house from a list of possible words. This list is a *vertical paradigm* of options where, technically, the sentence makes perfect sense even if we were to pick 'shell' or 'cave': 'I live in a shell' is *not* a wrong sentence. Selection from the paradigm enables metaphor: We can use 'shell' as a metaphor for 'house'. We can describe a dark house as a 'cave'. Just as we selected 'crawl' as a metaphoric equivalent of vehicular movement along roads, we can use 'shell' as a metaphoric equivalent for the 'house'.

Having picked words we need to organize the sentence. In the above instance we selected words from a vertical list of possible words. Here we have to *combine* the selected words in a *horizontal* sequence so that they make sense.

I house in a live

Or

Live a house in I

These are both options in terms of sequence or *syntagm*. But for the sentence to make sense we need to order the selected words in a different sequence: 'I live in a house.'

Language thus works on the dual principles of selection and combination.

Poetic language, for Jakobson, uses *both* selection and combination in order to produce equivalence. Let's go back to my first example. We *select* 'crawl' from a list that includes 'goes', 'races' and 'bustles' and *combine* it with 'traffic'. What we have is a poetic formulation: we have a *symbol* for the slow moving traffic on the roads. We have, in effect, produced a poetic symbol through a process of selection and combination where the usual description ('slow traffic' or 'traffic congestion' or 'traffic jam' has *not* been used). We have defamiliarized the description by providing an unusual poetic symbol—we converted vehicles into insects (i.e., provided a *metaphor* for vehicles).

As we can see Jakobson suggests a special use of language here. Now, the point is that ordinary, everyday language is used to communicate meaning, and poetry is only a special and unusual mode of communication. Or, in this case, the *aesthetic* function is greater than the communicative function of language. This is precisely what makes the language 'poetic' or 'literary'.

In order to understand this special quality of poetic language it is necessary to look at the ordinary modes of communication. Jakobson's model of communication is as follows.

Context
Message
Addresser ------------------------ Addressee
Contact
Code

All speech communication involves these six elements, and the process can be described as *narrative communication*.

Let us take an actual example. Suppose I write, in a letter to a friend who lives in a different town, the following sentence:

I work in a university that is at a distance of 12 km from my home.

We have the six elements as follows:

1. Addresser (myself)
2. Addressee (my friend)
3. The message
4. Contact (the letter, handwritten or e-mailed)
5. Code (writing)
6. Context (the language used in the writing, both of us understand English)

The process of communication as it happens above can be described as follows:

- An addresser sends a message to an addressee.
- The message requires a medium or *contact* (visual, oral, audio, and now electronic).
- The message is in the form of a code or process (speech, writing, numbers).
- Both addresser and addressee must share the same context of language and conventions of speech and writing in order to understand each other's speech/writing.

Now the meaning or the function of the utterance is dependent on which of these six components is dominant. We can get the same sentence to mean slightly different things depending on our emphasis.

The above model can be reorganized around particular functions of language. We now have a revised model:

Referential (context)

Poetic(message)

Emotive (addresser)   Phatic (contact)   Conative (addressee)

Metalingual (code)

If the *context* is dominant then the function is *referential*. Thus, in the above sentence the context would be the distance described: 12 km. The context here is only information-distribution because the sentence refers only to the distance and nothing else.

If I say: '*my* work place is at a great distance from *my* home' then the *addresser's* situation dominates. This is the *emotive* function.

If the *addressee* is the dominant the sentence would carry a *conative* function and become: 'Look, don't complain, you travel only 3 km as compared to myself'.

If the purpose is to simply set up a conversation then the *contact* is dominant. The whole sentence then serves a *phatic* function, where the purpose is not to exchange information but simply to start contact. In the example above if the purpose is to start talking about oneself or one's workplace, then it is simply an introduction. (Examples of phatic communications would include greetings like 'good morning', and conversation openers like 'how are you?' to which you only respond with a 'good morning' and 'I am fine' instead of taking the query literally and setting out to explain all your assorted ailments to the person.)

If the *code* of the message is dominant, where both addresser and addressee establish that they are using the same terms and discourses, then it serves a *metalingual* function. When we say: 'Do you understand what I am saying?', we are referring to the code of the conversation. In the example given earlier, if the addresser is trying to emphasize the enormous distance travelled to work, where the discourse and code involves distance and time spent, then the metalingual function operates.

Finally, if the *message* draws attention to itself, we have the *poetic* function. In the above sentence if the emphasis is on the message itself— 'See, *what* I am saying about distance to workplace?'—then we have the poetic function in operation.

> Jakobson argued that all meaning in poetic language is the result of a *metonymic* combination (syntagm, the horizontal organization as a sentence) and *metaphoric* selection (paradigm, the choice of one term from a collection of terms). In communication the meaning of the message is based on which of the six elements—code, address, addressee, message, contact, context—is dominant.

As we can see, structuralism is based on the formula for meaning-generation embedded in a text's form and language. Structuralism's interest in words, their combinations and meanings leads it to examine the text at various levels as follows:

- that of the *text*—where we look at the arrangement of words, the rules of combination;
- that of the *genre*—where we see a poem as an example of the genre of poetry itself, and compare the present case with that of the others;
- that of *culture* itself—where we see literary texts as part of a larger cultural text that includes film, television, sport, and other such phenomena.

Structuralism is also interested, since it draws upon Saussure's notions of language, in *signs* that constitute language and meaning. A specific branch of structuralism that developed modes of analysing signs is semiotics.

SEMIOTICS

Semiotics can be defined very simply as the *study of signs*. Signs include words, gestures, sounds, objects and visuals that generate meaning as part of a system of signification.

But how can objects be signs?

The arrangement of a traffic island, with a concrete structure, a central box mounted by a traffic light is a *sign* that generates meaning, asking us to look at the light above, move ahead only when it is green, and go around or past the island. A man with a gun is also a *sign*, since he signifies danger and threat or safety and security (if he is in a policeman's uniform).

There are two accepted origins of semiotics. One we have already seen: Saussurean linguistics. Saussure used the term *semiology* to describe the study of signs. The other origin of contemporary semiotics is the work of the American philosopher and logician, C. S. Peirce. Peirce preferred the term *semiotics* and today this term is more commonly used. Semiotics is popular among students of media studies, film studies and cultural studies, in addition to those of literary criticism. Semiotics provides them with the tools required to analyse the forms of a text and to read texts as part of the general social system of signs, where meanings are generated, accepted and subverted as part of a cultural process. Semiotics helps them relate the various elements of a text to each other and to the larger social system. In this it is similar to structuralism. *Structuralist semiotics* builds on semiotic theories of signs to read narrative (for a discussion of structuralist semiotics see below).

Since we have acquired some familiarity with Saussure's work we can move on to look at Peirce's contribution to the study of signs.

Peirce offered a three-cornered, or triadic model of the sign as follows:

- *Representamen*: The *form* the sign takes (material or immaterial, like sounds, writing, a painting, a gesture, a word). This is the equivalent of the Saussurean signifier. It is also sometimes described as a 'sign vehicle'.
- *Interpretant*: The sense made of the sign, that is, the sign created in the mind of the listener/viewer as a result of reading/listening to the *representamen*. It is important to note that 'interpretant' is not the person doing the reading but rather the idea generated in the mind when we see the sign.

- *Object*: That to which the sign refers. It is sometimes called the 'referent'.

All three make up the sign. The interaction between these three is semiosis.

Language is the effect of this interaction. For example, let us take a sign in a doctor's clinic: 'Doctor is In'. This is a sign that is inscribed as words and not as a picture. What semiosis occurs here?

- Representamen is the text itself: 'Doctor is In'.
- Object is the doctor referred to in the text.
- Interpretant is the idea generated in our mind upon reading this sign— that the doctor is inside and we must wait. The sign itself does not say: 'please wait'. But the idea generated by the sign asks us to do so.

We can quickly detect the paradox here, a paradox that will recall Saussure's own notion of referentiality.

The sign generates another sign (the interpretant) in our minds. So, if we want to use Saussure's concepts to understand Peirce, a signifier generates yet another signifier in our mind. This process of signs giving rise to other signs in our act of reading or listening is a feature of language (we already have Saussure's idea that words do not refer to reality but to other *words*). We, therefore, have an unending semiosis where the representamen/signifier generates more signs, which we then have to interpret leading to more signs, and so on infinitely.

Signifiers—we will opt for Saussure's signifier as a term since it is more commonly used than representamen—are related to their objects of referents in three modes.

1. *Symbol/Symbolic*: Where there is no relation between the signifier and the object or referent, and the relation has to be learnt. *All* language is symbolic, since there is no real connection between the word 'cat' and the animal. We acquire the relation through use. For example, we understand that a sign of the red cross on a name plate indicates 'medical doctor'. A red light on the traffic signal indicates 'stop'. There is *no* intrinsic connection between a woman or man who practices medicine and the red cross. Similarly there is *no* connection between the act of stopping your vehicle and the red light. These are 'meanings' we have acquired. The symbolic sign is *arbitrary* in the relationship between signifier and signified. It is also clear that the meaning and relation between signifier and the object is known by conventions and a set of rules established by common use.

2. *Icon/Iconic*: The signifier here resembles the object it seeks to represent. It mimics the signified or the concept, takes on some of the object's qualities. Onomatopoeic words are a good example of the iconic sign. Here the signifier 'hssss', for instance, seems to capture the actual sound made by the snake. Similarly, when we say 'he fell with a thump' the 'thump' tries to capture the sound of a body falling down and hitting the floor. The iconic sign is imitative in the relationship between signifier and signified.

3. *Index/Indexical*: The signifier here is directly connected to the signified in some way. A good example of the indexical sign would be the knock on the door. We infer that the signifier (the knock) is produced by, is connected to the presence of somebody outside who wishes to come in. Another example would be the simple fever. Fever is a sign that is directly connected to a pathological cause. The fever is a signifier that suggests something is wrong.

Semiotics suggests that for users of language signs stand in for, or represent, something. Signs are made of signifiers (words/sounds) and signified (objects), and the relation between the two can be arbitrary, imitative or directly connected. The process of interaction between the word (signifier), the object referred to (signified) and the idea or sign generated in our mind upon hearing/reading the word is semiosis.

Semioticians, therefore, believe that reality is understood as a set of signs. Signs *construct* our reality. It will be this particular notion of language and signs that poststructuralism will build upon in the 1960s and later.

Julia Kristeva's early work on 'poetic language' argued that the entrance of the subject into language was motivated by pleasure. Signification included two main components:

(i) *The Semiotic*: This is associated with the mother, the body and the pre-linguistic, or what she calls the *chora*. This is the material, poetic dimension of language (see Chapter 2 for Kristeva's *chora*). It is the foundation of language for Kristeva, and is what she terms the 'genotext'.

(ii) *The Symbolic*: This is the syntax, the grammar, the expressed linguistic acts. It is the language of communication as we know it, and is what Kristeva calls 'phenotext'.

Signification is a combination of these two elements. Kristeva located the maternal (as seen in the theorizing of the semiotic) at the heart of language—a theoretical shift that was at once startling and innovative for it proposed a strong case for returning to the materiality of language and subject formation, the body. Kristeva sees art as a means of articulating the semiotic.

STRUCTURALISM AND NARRATIVE THEORY

Narrative is an extraordinarily complex term in literary and critical theory. It is used interchangeably with story, form, plot and even structure. Let us try and define narrative first before exploring the structuralist analysis of narrative (postmodern and poststructuralist theories of narrative will be dealt with in subsequent chapters).

Paul Cobley provides a succinct definition when he states: 'narrative is a particular form of representation implementing signs' (2001: 3). Thus, a narrative is a system of signs (we know that signs can be verbal, written, aural, gestural, iconic) in a particular sequence or order.

But narrative is not restricted to stories or films. Narrative is also the construction of a nation, history, sports and violence. Paul Wake defines narrative as 'the ways in which we construct notions of history, politics, race, religion, identity and time. All of these things ... might be understood as stories that both explain and construct the ways in which the world is experienced' (2006: 14).

For purposes of literary and cultural analysis, we can define narrative as

- the act of representation using signs in particular sequences so that we construct specific notions of reality, self and the world,
- our construction and interpretation of the world through the use of words, sounds, figures, gestures and relations,
- intrinsically linked to language (since, as we have already noted, sounds, words, gestures are all signs, or language).

In the twentieth century, structuralism generated some of the most rigorous analyses of narrative and its forms. In what follows, we look at a few of the most important theorists of narrative. The study of narrative is called narratology, a term often used interchangeably with 'poetics'.

A term that is often used to describe the language of narrative, and has come to occupy centre stage in almost every theory today is 'discourse'. Discourse traditionally meant *spoken* or *written presentation*. It is what we read or listen to. In the case of structuralism this is the sense in which 'discourse' is used.

Now, after poststructuralism it refers to the language used in *social* practice. That is, discourse now refers to the functional as well social, political and ideological aspects of language—something we shall explore in the chapter on poststructuralism.

RUSSIAN FORMALISM AND THE POETICS OF FICTION

As we have already noted, the Russian Formalists were more interested in the language of poetry. In their later work, however, critics like Vladimir Propp, Viktor Shklovsky and, much later, Tzvetan Todorov explored narrative structure in fiction. More contemporary narratologists like Gérard Genette also build on the structuralism of the Russian Formalists as they refine their study of prose narratives.

The Folktale

Vladimir Propp's analysis of the folktale is a classic example of structuralist criticism at work. Propp argued that every character in a folktale's plot had a specific function. This in itself is hardly new: We know after structuralism that a plot is the consequence of many elements in relation with each other. What was fascinating about Propp's analysis is that he is able to locate a mere seven key performers, who create seven spheres of action. That is, all fairy tales can be reduced to a set of seven characters who generate the entire plot through their various relationships.

Here is Propp's list:

1. hero
2. false hero
3. villain
4. donor or provider
5. helper
6. princess and her father
7. despatcher

Now, Propp also identified 31 functions to be found in every folktale. These are absentation, interdiction, violation, reconnaissance, delivery, trickery, complicity, villainy and lack, mediation, counteraction, departure, first function of donor, hero's reaction, receipt of magic agent, spatial transference, struggle, branding, victory, liquidation, return, pursuit, rescue, unrecognized, unfounded claims, difficult task, solution, recognition, exposure, transfiguration, punishment, wedding (from Chandler 2003: 94–95).

The folktale is thus reducible to this set of functions created by the seven performers. It is important to realize here that the number of spheres of action is finite even when the number of characters is infinite. That is, whatever be the number of characters, they all combine in specific ways to generate the plot.

We can discover such a scheme in, say, popular Hindi films. We have the hero, the heroine, the villain. The hero has a task set out for him, through which he has to prove himself. During the course of the task he is helped by some and obstructed by others. He eventually triumphs and the villain is destroyed. The underlying scheme here is of 'good versus evil' where evil is ultimately defeated and good triumphs. After all the permutations and combinations in the plot, this essential scheme does not change: It is the *structuring principle* of the film.

Here is a basic 'formula' (and it is no coincidence that these are called 'formula films'):

> Boy meets girl : they fall in love : tensions in families as a result : boy or girl has to prove himself/herself : plot to ensure the lovers do not have a smooth path to marriage : villain plays dirty tricks : struggle of hero/ine : villain defeated : parents reconciled : marriage

STRUCTURALIST NARRATOLOGY

The study of narrative was greatly facilitated by structuralism. It systematized the study of plot, character, symbol and provided a formula for narratives, as seen in the work of Propp (above).

One of the earliest practitioners of structuralist narratology was A. J. Greimas, whose work in *Semantique Structurale* (1966, *Structural Semantics*) built upon Saussure's idea of binary oppositions to develop what has been called *structural semiotics* (semiotics is the study of signs).

Structural Semiotics

Greimas paid close attention to the way in which oppositions help us organize meaning. He suggested that there are semantic units that work in opposition. He termed these 'semes', and argued that meaning emerges in the contrast between semes. Some common semes would be:

> light–dark
> up–down
> male–female

This binary opposition is the *primary structure of all meaning-production* (meaning-production is technically called *signification*, a term used with perhaps alarming regularity in literary theory today). It is possible that we see the paired opposites or semes as positive and negative, where one element is the negative component of the pair: dark as the negative of light, female as the negative of male. This aspect of a negated component of entity would be discussed extensively by poststructuralism and feminism.

Greimas went on to suggest that these semes work as *actants* to generate narrative. What Greimas was proposing was effectively a Saussurean notion: The semes form the basic *formula, the rules* and *the underlying structure* of language (in Saussure's formulation, this is *langue*, as we have seen). They *express themselves* or are manifest as narratives and plots and stories in contexts (*parole*). The semes in various combinations are *enunciated* in particular contexts to produce stories.

Greimas evolved a set of six actants, that is, a set of 'semes' or binary oppositions that provide the grammar and rules for all narratives as follows:

- Subject/Object
- Sender/Receiver
- Helper/Opponent

These are the actants who perform specific functions in all narratives.

    i. *Desire, search, aim*: The Subject has a certain aim and desire directed at a particular goal or Object (to be achieved).

    ii. *Communication*: The Subject is sent out on his or mission by a Sender who facilitates the mission, and will reward the Subject upon her or his success. The Receiver is the one who rewards.

    iii. *Auxiliary support* or *hindrance*: The Subject is helped in his or her quest and mission by the Helper and obstructed by the Opponent.

In many cases, the categories might merge. For example, the Sender actant might very well be the Receiver. According to Greimas, a formula for the narrative can, therefore, be as follows:

- Contract or prohibition where the Subject is sent out on a quest or mission;
- The Subject might accept the contract or disobey the contract. If the Subject accepts then we have *establishment of contract*. If the Subject declines or disobeys we have *violation of contract*.
- If the Subject accepts we have rewards (from Sender-Receiver), if the Subject violates we have punishments.

The whole process can be read under three main *structures* or *syntagms*, that are common (according to Greimas) to all narrative.

    1. *Contractual Structures*: Where the 'hero' (Subject) is given a task by a Sender, sent on a particular mission, seeks an Object, is offered a contract or prevented from doing something. Contractual structures launch the plot.

2. *Performative Structures*: Here the Subject undertakes the tasks, battles obstacles aided by the Helper or thwarted by the Opponent, is lured into traps, is faced with trials and tribulations, loses heart, finds courage and hope. This is the 'action' in the narrative.

3. *Disjunctive Structures*: These are moments of arrival, departure and movement in the narrative when the Subject leaves the palace or the home, arrives at the Opponent's den or the palace. These are interludes in the narratives where the scene for the next action is set. For example, in Hindi films, the hero swears vengeance and races out to the villain's house/den—here there is a gap between the scene of the swearing and the next one, where the hero wrecks vengeance. This gap is the disjunctive structure that enables a shift between scenes and brings in new actants. From a scene involving a hero-actant, we now have one with the villain-actant too.

Tzvetan Todorov, like Greimas, builds on the notion that there is a definite grammar to all texts. Todorov isolates three specific components of texts

- *semantic*: which would be the form
- *syntactic*: which would be the arrangement of structural units
- *verbal*: words and phrases through which the story is told

Todorov's interest lies mainly in the syntactic arrangement of units within a narrative. He identifies two key structural components of all texts: *propositions* and *sequence*.

Propositions are the basic actions in a narrative. In a novel like R. K. Narayan's *The Guide*, the basic propositions may be listed as following:

Raju meets Rosie
Rosie and Raju fall in love
Raju encourages her in her art
Rosie becomes popular
Raju 'betrays' her trust
Raju goes away
Raju is transformed into a saint by accident
He decides to accept his 'sainthood' and fulfils his vow.

Now, these propositions have to be arranged in a sequence to generate a story. There can be many sequences in a text.

Propositions can be arranged in any of the three sequences:

1. *Temporal*: where there is a sequence in time (this happened and then this happened).
2. *Logical*: where there is a cause–effect sequence (this happened and therefore this happened).
3. *Spatial*: where the plot has many sub-divisions (this happened meanwhile this other thing also happened).

Mikhail Bakhtin and Dialogism

The Russian thinker, Mikhail Bakhtin, whose works appeared in English decades after he wrote them in the 1920s and 1930s, proposed dialogue as the intrinsic feature of language. While Bakhtin himself never used the term *dialogism* it has been associated with his work, and is the most recognizable concept from his oeuvre. In order to understand his work on the novel (i.e., narrative), it is important to look at his notions of dialogue. There are a few key terms in Bakhtinian thought that have to be understood, namely, *dialogue, heteroglossia, chronotope,* and *carnival.*

Dialogue   Dialogue is a differential relation, and dialogue always implies a *relationship*. In any conversation, the speakers are different from each other. But what is interesting is that these differences are *retained* in the conversation—they are held in place in the relation which is the dialogue. Dialogue is imposed upon us; we do not set out to engage in dialogue. Dialogue, therefore, is a concept that gestures at the *mutual difference* at the heart of all conversation, it asks us to pay attention to relations in language. It is, Bakhtin believed, the existence of mutual difference that enabled dialogue. Bakhtin was, therefore, focusing on the self/other aspect of all language where there is always the 'other' within my speech. In fact, my speech anticipates and prepares for the other's response.

Bakhtin's emphasis on dialogue means that his focus was almost entirely on *utterance*. Utterance takes place between speakers, who are located in a *social* context. Speakers have to assume that their values are shared by the others (the audience). Dialogue is the central feature of all speech. What Bakhtin does is to underscore the novel as a form that explicitly foregrounds this dialogic aspect of speech and everyday communication.

Bakhtin begins by assuming that literary texts, especially novels, are utterances in a given context of the text's production. Dialogism has already told us that meaning in any utterance is based on the social context. Indeed the context is what makes us understand the words themselves. For example, when I hear a sentence like 'The ball is in the box', I immediately understand that it refers to *this particular box* and *not* to any box anywhere in the world, even though the sentence itself does not clearly specify which box.

Heteroglossia   Bakhtin proposes that novels are a prime example of what he calls *heteroglossia*. Heteroglossia is the simultaneity of many levels of dialogue and language. The subject, about to make an utterance, can pick one response out of the mass of languages around him/her. It would be impossible to systematize the mass and variety of languages because of the sheer heterogeneity. The other's voice is given as much importance as the self's. In the case of the novel (Bakhtin's example is Dostoevsky), the many voices are given equal importance, thereby showing the novel as a site of struggle, carnival and subversion. Working-class discourses, women's language, the language of ethnic minorities are all represented alongside that of the dominant one. Even if these other voices do not overthrow the dominant one, their very existence suggests that the main voice is not overwhelming or unchallenged.

In the case of a novel, every novel refers to other works, other discourses. The novel is a genre that gives space, very consciously, to other works. This is what is now called *intertextuality*, and is a feature Bakhtin was particularly fond of in the novel. A novel refers to the discourse of history, of literary texts, of social conditions like poverty, of philosophy and theology. This leads Bakhtin to suggest that the novel embodies other voices. In fact, it gives space to the other, the different. For example, in a realist novel like that of Dickens' or Balzac's, the narrator controls the lives of his characters very firmly. Yet, even these authors sometimes slip into phrases like 'I think' or 'I suppose'. What does this mean? It means, simply, the novelist is unsure of the moral stance he or she has taken. The characters and their situations are not as rigidly controlled as one perceived. The main moral stance in the novel is, therefore, undermined by the other voices and opinions that circulate through the text. This is *heteroglossia*. Later, critics like Julia Kristeva built upon this notion of intertextuality.

The novel is constituted by the dialogue between discourses. What is clear, and important, is that the novel's dialogism even breaks down the distinction between literary and non-literary or extra-literary.

Chronotope   Bakhtin further proposed that a novel often renders in an artistic way the interconnectedness of spatial and temporal relationships. Space and time are interconnected in plots and are central to the narrative/plot. This interconnected aspect is what he terms *chronotope*. Chronotopes are recurring, structural features of the narrative (therefore they are like the motifs or actants in structuralism). Using the example of Greek romances, Bakhtin shows how time and space are both *fluid*. Every age has its own notions of space and time, and therefore chronotopes are rooted in their *local* conditions. In the twentieth century, after Einsteinian science and the developments in physics, we have a different sense of space and time. Chronotopes in science fiction today, therefore, suggest multiple worlds whose time zones are also multiple. The simultaneity of worlds and times is also connected with the globalized geopolitical world where radio, telephone, television and now the Internet and call centers functioning in a different time zone (USA and Europe) have altered our concepts of space and time. Rushdie's novels slip between past and present, while also having fantasies woven into them. Ben Okri's fiction, especially texts like *The Famished Road*, does not allow us to know with certainty whether the world depicted is real or in the imagination. 'Magic realism' in postcolonial texts from South Asia, Africa and South America today generates chronotopes that are about multiple times–spaces co-existing next to each other, simultaneously, and is the effect of twentieth century's historical developments of theories in physics and communication–transportation technologies.

Bakhtin, as we can see, is keen on showing how the novel as a form is inherently heteroglossic, giving space to many voices. The novel resists monologic, and situates languages and discourses along side each other.

Carnival   Bakhtin evidently was attempting to find literary examples where power was subverted. In order to do so, he outlined a concept of the *carnival* via a reading of the works of Rabelais. The carnival was laughter, the bodily, parody, the ugly, the grotesque and the so-called 'low'. The laughter is not sanctioned by the government or the institution. It resists such control, and is, therefore, politically subversive. Bodily functions are a part of the carnival because they do not find expression in official cultures. Clowning, again not part of the official culture, is also a key element in the carnival. Clowning and the carnival cannot be theorized about because they resists any academic discussion—they are rooted in the everyday life of the people. The carnival is the ultimate *other*. It is what escapes classification, theorization and control. The carnival is a useful mode of discussing popular or mass culture because Bakhtin is essentially speaking of the need to subvert and interrogate established/institutional authority over meaning. We see instances of the carnival in the writings of Salman Rushdie. Rushdie shows how the serious discourses and political themes of nationalism, patriotism and identity are often taken far too seriously. Rushdie inverts their significance by showing how these notions are accidental, highly personal and often limited. In *Midnight's Children*, for example, Rushdie's Saleem believes that the Indo-Pakistan war of 1965 happened because he *imagined* it. Here Rushdie is reducing a massive event to a single individual's fantasy. There is nothing remarkable in the situation of war—it all exists in the person's mind. This is carnivalesque because it subverts a so-called national event and transforms it into a mundane act of day dreaming and adolescent fantasy. Margaret Atwood creates a heroine, Marian McAlpin, who cannot accept the ideal form of the fiancée that society wants of her in *The Edible Woman* (1969). Her anxiety over the changes she is expected to make results in an eating disorder. Her body—the epitome of identity and looks in the consumer society she lives in—is what she takes as the site of the battle for identity when she goes on eating binges or fulfils her culinary cravings. In a later novel, *Lady Oracle* (1976), Atwood creates a bored housewife, once an overweight teen, who abandons her quiet life for a wild one. In both these novels Atwood creates heroines who do not fit the model of the quiet, amenable (and of course slim) fiancée or housewife. She is questioning the ideal of beauty itself: Does slimness alone constitute beauty? Does it matter that it is a *woman* who is fat? Atwood poses these questions when her heroines' fat and grotesque body inverts the traditional stereotype of the 'heroine'. This is another example of the carnival.

Roland Barthes and His Codes

Barthes is an interesting figure in literary theory because he is located at the intersection of structuralism and poststructuralism. His early work is inspired by structuralist ideas and later works on the 'death of the author' gesture at his post-structuralist sympathies.

Barthes in his *The Structural Analysis of Narrative* (1977) and *S/Z* (1970) developed a detailed model of narrative. Like the structuralists, Barthes believed that one can break up a narrative into its constituent elements and discover how they combine with each other. Reading a short story by Balzac, Barthes identified 561 units of meaning, or what he called 'lexias'. Barthes proposed (and here the parallels with Propp and Greimas must be evident to us) that we could organize the lexias into five main groups, all working in combination in a narrative. That is, the five groups, or *codes* as he called them, are the narrative's modes of organizing the units so that meaning is generated. These codes, argued Barthes, are common to all narratives.

1. *Proairetic Code*: This is the most visible aspect of a narrative, and refers to the *sequence* in which the events of a story unfold. It is often a temporal sequence: This happened and *then* this happened. This code governs our *expectations* of a narrative: If this happened, then this must certainly happen.

2. *Hermeneutic Code*: This is the code that informs our *interpretation* and the questions we ask of the narrative: What happened? How? Why? By Whom?

3. *Cultural Code*: This is the code that narratives assume we all share. Cultural codes are those elements of common knowledge that we share as a community and therefore do not require a glossary. This can be medical, literary or even symbolic knowledge. An example would be a narrative that uses a sentence like 'during the Raj things were very different'. Most Indians would immediately understand the term *Raj* without any glossary or explanation. It is the cultural code in the narrative.

4. *Semic Code*: This is the code that draws upon, like in the cultural code, a common set of stereotypes that are self-descriptive and self-evident. When, for example, we see a man in white clothes and wearing a Gandhi cap, we know immediately that he is a politician. The stereotype is well in place for all readers and, therefore, does not require explanation. On the other hand, like the cultural code, semic codes require explanations to a person coming from outside the community.

5. *Symbolic Code*: This is very similar to the semic code. It extends beyond the immediate icon or stereotype to refer to something larger. For example, a horror film thrives on the images of darkness. A shot of the moon and treetops (or streets) automatically functions as a code for night (this is the semic code). But, because we are aware of the significance of night in horror films (and here we are drawing upon our previous experience of such films), we expect something dangerous or evil to happen. This shifts the code from the *semic* where we understand it is night from the signs of

moon and empty streets to the *symbolic* where we know that something evil is about to happen. We move beyond the ordinary day/night semic code to a notion of good/bad that is equivalent to or corresponds to day/night in a process of semantic expansion (that is, the meaning of day and night is expanded to mean good and evil respectively). We have invested the day/night pair the symbolic meanings of good/bad.

> Barthes sees every narrative as being composed of lexias that are orga-nized in the form of five main codes: the proairetic (about sequence of a narrative), the hermeneutic (interpretative), cultural (common knowl-edge), semic (stereotypes) and symbolic (semantic and symbolic expansion of semic codes).

Gérard Genette, Narrative Discourse and Paratexts

Genette's work on narrative discourse has spread across many areas. His contributions include studies of narrative voice, levels of narration, and, more interestingly, on what he calls 'paratexts'.

Genette identifies three levels of narrative:

(a) *histoire,* or story, which is the set of real actions events that happened and need to be told
(b) *récit,* or narrative, which is the telling of the story, either in oral or written form
(c) *narrating,* the larger process of recounting that produces the *récit*

Another way of putting these would be:

- *histoire* is the *content*, the story, the *signified* of all storytelling.
- *récit* is the speech or the written act, the *signifier* or *form*, through which the story is told and narrating is the telling *within* the speech or writing.

If we want a scheme that shows the break-up of Genette's organization of narrative it would be:

$$histoire \quad > \quad récit \quad > \quad narrating$$
(signified)   (signifier)

A commentator on Genette, Shlomith Rimmon-Kenan, suggests that these are equivalent to *story, text* and *narration* respectively (1983: 3). Genette's scheme can now be elaborated as follows:

1. Story (*histoire*) is the larger set of narrated events, arranged in chronological fashion, no matter how they are presented in the text. *The story is what we understand and interpret even without particular details from the storytelling.*

2. Text (*récit*) is the organization (or what Genette calls 'narrative discourse') of the events for the purpose of storytelling. It can be in the spoken or written form. *The text is what we read or listen to.*

3. Narration is the act of producing the text, either by the speaker or the author. This can be a fictional narrator inside the text who delivers the story or it can be the 'real' author.

> A more common way of putting Genette's scheme would be: Unless somebody tells or writes (narrates) the events in a particular way (text/récit), the story (histoire) would not be available to us.

Some of Genette's key formulations can be organized under 'narrative voice', narrative levels (this is, a subcategory of narrative voice in Genette, but deserves wider study), and perspective (which is a subcategory of narrative levels).

1. *Narrative Voice:* Genette identifies three elements that make up narrative voice:
   (i) *Narrative Instance*: The actual moment and context of narration. This is the setting of the narration or utterance itself.
   (ii) *Narrative Time*: The verbs and their tenses in the telling indicate the time in the narrative (past, present, future). When we read a sentence like 'they would never see her again', it suggests a future. Here the narrative is in the future.
   (iii) *Narrative Levels*: It refers to the relation of the acts narrated to the act of narration itself and is based on *who* is doing the narrating (first-person or third-person). Mary Shelley's *Frankenstein* opens with Walton's letter to his sister in which he recounts meeting Victor Frankenstein, who, in turn, narrates his story. Thus, the novel's main narrative level is that of Walton's letter. All other narratives are embedded within this level.

2. *Narrative Levels:* Genette discerns four important categories in the analysis of narrative levels. They are:
   (a) *Order*: It is the *sequence of events* in relation to the order of narration. An event may have taken place before the actual narration (*analepsis*, or commonly, flashback). It may not yet have occurred but is anticipated or predicted by the narrative (*prolepsis*). Very often the story's sequence is not the sequence of the plot. For example, in *Frankenstein*, the story is Walton's discovery of Frankenstein. But the plot is the story of the scientist and the monster. Walton's order of events is not necessarily the order in which the plot of Frankenstein-monster moves. This is called *anachrony*. But *Frankenstein* also exhibits another level. It breaks up Frankenstein's story to give us something from Walton. Here the narrative moves between the

two stories or narrative levels. This is *metalepsis*. A scheme would be as follows:

Narrative Level 1, based on who is doing the telling (the main plot): Walton's story, narrated to his sister

Narrative Level 2 (the embedded plot): Frankenstein's story, narrated to Walton

Narrative Level 3: The monster's story, narrated to Frankenstein, who reports it to Walton

The dissonance between 1 and 2 is anachrony. The *shift* between 3 and 1 is metalepsis. The sequence is from 1 to 3. And then, after the monster's story is told, it moves back to 1, where Walton describes how Frankenstein dies and the monster disappears into the icy wastes.

But there is another level that we have ignored: Who is telling us narrative level 1? Who is giving us Walton's story that he narrated to the sister?

(b) *Duration*: This is the rhythm at which the events take place. There are following four speeds of narration:

   (i) *ellipsis* : infinitely rapid, with quick shifts in time, space and plot

   (ii) *summary* : relatively rapid

   (iii) *scene* : relatively slow

   (iv) *descriptive*: no progress in the story. These are the set descriptions of Coke Town in Dickens or Egdon Heath in Hardy, where no plot movement occurs.

(c) *Frequency*: It refers to the extent of repetition in a narrative. This is the question captured in 'frequency': 'How many times has an event happened in the story?'

(d) *Mood*: It is distinguished by Genette into two further categories:

   (i) *Distance*: This is the relationship of the narration to what it narrates. This distance may be *diegetic* (a plain *recounting* of the story), or *mimetic,* or *representing* the story (or character, situation, event).

   (ii) *Perspective*: This is commonly called 'point of view' or focus. Focus determines the *extent* to which the narrator allows us to penetrate into the character or the event. Narrative focus alternates and shifts throughout the narrative and may be of two kinds:

   • *paralipse*: where the narrator withholds information from the reader that the reader *ought to receive* according to the prevailing focus. This is a frequent device in detective stories where the narrator deliberately or unconsciously withholds information. For example, in Agatha Christie's *Sleeping Murder* the story is told by the doctor. Only towards the end do we realize that the narrator is the real murderer.

- *paralepse*: where the narrator presents information to the reader that the reader according to the prevailing focus *ought not to receive*. For example, we have noted a sentence like 'They never saw her again'. Here the narrator is giving away information about the end of the narration—information that the reader does not need to know *at this stage*.

3. *Perspective*: Genette isolates several perspectives. Perspective is based on the role of the narrator and her or his location vis-à-vis the story being told. The narrator, for Genette, has five main functions:

- *Narrative*: to tell the story
- *Directing*: when the narrator interrupts the story telling to describe the process of narration, her/his sources, organization of the story.
- *Testimonial*: where the narrator affirms the truth of the story s/he is about to narrate. It also involves, in many cases, a description of the narrator's responses (emotional, intellectual, political) to the events s/he is narrating.
- *Communicative*: a frequent feature of the eighteenth- and nineteenth-century narrative where the narrator addresses the reader directly with a 'dear reader'.
- *Ideological*: where the narrator uses the story to generalize, speculate, philosophize about universal matters, make moral comments and so on ('such is the fate of women', for example, would be an ideological comment that steps out of the text to describe a general condition).

The kinds of narrators are based upon their position relative to the story they narrate. Genette develops a whole classification of narrators. In order to understand the typology of narrators we need to first look at the levels of narratives.

A. The *first* level of a narrative based on who is doing the telling, is the *main text of the novel*. This is *extradiegetic*, over and above the story to be told, it frames the story to be narrated. So, in *Frankenstein* the extradiegetic level is the novel *Frankenstein* itself. All later stories are *embedded within* this level.

B. The *second* level is Walton's story about his meeting with Frankenstein (who in turn narrates *his* story), embedded as a narrative within the first level. This second level is the *intradiegetic* level and contains the events or story being narrated.

If the narrator is *inside* the story-*level* s/he is narrating it is a *homodiegetic* narrator. This narrator may narrate the events unfolding but *may not be a part of the events*, a kind of silent *witness* or camera who is reporting or recording. This is often called a *first-person narrative*. And, if the narrator is telling her/his own story we have an *autodiegetic* narrator. Narrators in the autobiographies such as *The Story of My Experiments with Truth* are autodiegetic–homodiegetic narrators: They are inside the story and the story is about themselves. Lockwood in *Wuthering Heights* is an intradiegetic narrator because he is narrating a story (though not the main one) in which he is one of the characters.

A narrator who is outside the story s/he is narrating is a *heterodiegetic* narrator. This generates what Genette terms *zero focalization*, which is indeterminate and above everything that happens. It also means that the narrator knows more about all the characters. This is the *third-person* or *omniscient* narrative. Now, sometimes a heterodiegetic can function as an intradiegetic narrator too, and narrate a story about *other characters* but from the inside of the story (that is, narrate a story that is *not* about himself/herself). An example would be Walton's letters to his sister about Frankenstein. As we have seen, the first level of narrative is the text of the novel. The second level is Walton's intradiegetic narrative about Frankenstein. Then a third level would be Walton *reporting* Frankenstein's story in which he is *not* a character. This makes Walton's story about Frankenstein a heterodiegetic–intradiegetic narration. On the other hand Frankenstein narrating his own tragic story would be another intradiegetic narrative, but narrated by a man who is a character in the story he is narrating. This makes the narrator a homodiegetic one.

Let us sketch a map to help us here.

Level	Story Narrated	Narrator (Name)	Type of Narration	Type of Narrator
I	*Frankenstein*, the novel	Implied Author	Extradiegetic	
II	Walton's story about Victor Frankenstein	Walton	Intradiegetic	Heterodiegetic
III	Victor Frankenstein's story about *his* life/ experiments	Frankenstein	Intradiegetic	Homodiegetic (character narrator, inside the story he is narrating)

It is evident that an intradiegetic–homodiegetic narrator can only narrate those aspects of the story with which s/he is familiar. Since s/he is a character in the story, s/he cannot be aware of everything happening to everybody else. To use an example, as a character-narrator, you can tell the story of your classroom. Additionally, you can tell the story only from your *subjective position* as a partici-pant in the story. But you cannot tell the story of all the other classrooms unless you are above them all, watching and recording.

If the narrator is not a character then it is an external or extradiegetic narrator, outside the level of the story. To use the earlier example, the person who is *above* the college watching every class can be an extradiegetic narrator because s/he sees all and is not involved with the events. This is what we commonly call the omniscient or the 'third-person narrator' who stands outside the story.

Narratives and Their Intertexts

Genette is also interested in the forms of narrative that occupy the awkward and the undefinable places in the main narrative. His book, *Paratexts* (1997) is an excellent analysis of such 'odd' narratives and narrative devices. Intertextuality, it must be remembered, is a system of relationships that link texts to other texts or parts of the same text. Genette proposed the term transtextuality as a more wide-ranging one, and isolated five main types of intertextuality:

- *Paratexts* are epigraphs, prefaces, forewords, epilogues, addresses to the reader, acknowledgements, footnotes, drafts, illustrations that are somehow connected to the main narrative.
- *Intertextuality* refers to the allusions, references to other works, echoes, quotes and citations, and even plagiarized sections of a work.
- *Architextuality* is the relationship of a text to other texts in the same genre. For example, the connection between a twentieth-century satirical poem by W. H. Auden has an architextual connection with the satires of Alexander Pope.
- *Metatextuality* is the relationship between a text and the critical commentaries, biographical commentaries and other references on the main text.
- *Hypertextuality* resembles metatextuality in that it refers to texts that come later or after the main or original text.[1] The original text is hypotext and the later text is hypertext. Thus, parodies, spoofs, adaptations are linked to the original text by hypotextuality. The examples of this would be, *Frankenstein According to Spike Milligan,* a hypertext, a spoof on Mary Shelley's hypotext *Frankenstein.* Edward Bond's *Lear* is an adaptation of, and a hypertext to, Shakespeare's play.

Genette's work, as can be imagined by his range and typologies, is enormously useful in identifying features of the narrative.

Julia Kristeva popularized the notion of literary texts as exercises in intertextuality. Kristeva's structuralism emphasized the connections between texts, even as she saw texts not as closed systems but as dynamic processes open to the world. Discourse itself is a practice that involves the linguistic element, but also the unconscious and the social relations in which the linguistic act is enunciated. Literary analysis must not be restricted to the 'text' because the text itself must be seen as located within social relations, ideology, and the unconscious. According to Kristeva, such an analysis means searching for 'the signifying phenomenon for the *crisis* or the *unsettling* process of meaning and subject rather than for the coherence or identity of either *one* or a *multiplicity* of structures' (1984: 125, emphasis in original). What Kristeva is proposing is intertextuality, that is, bringing to the fore the connections between texts, and not to close off a text.

AUTHOR, READER

So far we have looked at the language of a narrative, with little attention to the author or the reader. Narrative theory pays a good deal of attention to the nature of the text, while reader response theory focuses on the reader as the generator of meaning. Our model for reading a narrative is as follows:

Author – Text – Reader

However, it is not really so simple. Where does the narrator fit into this scheme of things? Did the author have a specific reader in mind when s/he wrote her poem or novel?

A more accurate model of the narrative process would be as follows:

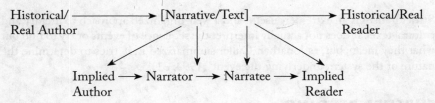

Let us examine this model.

The real or historical author, say, Walter Scott, wrote *Ivanhoe* and other novels. But Scott may have constructed a particular persona while writing the novel. That is, the novelist, the flesh-and-blood Scott is not the same as the model of the writer *constructed* in and by the book. For example, numerous authors have a short prefatory note that provides some biographical details, including some information about how they came to write the book (to go back to our favorite example, Mary Shelley wrote a short account, as a preface, of how she came to write *Frankenstein*). We *assume* that Scott or Mary Shelley is the real author, we merge the historical figure with the person who has composed the book. We *construct* the image of the author from the components of the book. Genette defines the implied author as the 'image of the author in the text' (1988: 41). This is the *implied author*, a term first used by Wayne C. Booth in his classic work, *The Rhetoric of Fiction* (1961).

Then, the person who is telling the story can also be a persona, a *character* adopted by the author. The author may narrate the story through a narrator, a fictitious figure that may have nothing to do with the 'real' author. This is, of course, the *narrator*.

Who does the narrator narrate the story *to*? The text constructs an addressee, to whom the story is told. This is the narratee. The narratee is a figure that is the direct recipient of the story.

But also constructed by the narrative is an imaginary reader with particular qualities. This reader is a model, and not necessarily a true person. The 'dear reader' in the eighteenth- and nineteenth-century novels is not always you, a BA student in Hyderabad or Delhi or London. The 'reader' is a construction, and is implied in the work. This is the *implied reader*.

Finally, the implied reader may not be the same as the real, flesh-and-blood reader browsing through the novel. The historical or real reader is the person who *reads* the text.

Thus, we do not see narrative communication as moving from real author through the narrative/text to the real reader. Instead, we see the real author constructing a persona, an implied author in the text, delivering the narrative via a narrator to the addressee/narratee of the story, to an imagined reader of the book, who may or may not correspond to the real reader.

*

Structuralism is an extremely useful and a well-organized approach to literary and cultural texts. It does not actually interpret the sequence of events or try to find out what they mean, but, as Jonathan Culler summarized it, it 'tries to determine the nature of the system underlying the event' (1994: 31).

FURTHER READING

Rimmon-Kennan, Shlomith. 1983. *Narrative Fiction: Contemporary Poetics*. London: Methuen.

Hawkes, Terence. 1997. *Structuralism and Semiotics*. London: Routledge.

Cobley, Paul. 2001. *Narrative*. London and New York: Routledge.

NOTE

1. Today the term hypertext is used to describe texts generated on the computer screen. It is often used as a synonym for digital texts.

2 Poststructuralism and Deconstruction

Structuralism, as we have seen, developed a model of reading texts and cultural artifacts. Structuralist narrative theory, for example, generated schemes for reading novels and poetry, unpacking the elements that constituted the text's meaning. While it was a rigorous and thorough textual analysis that paid close attention to language and form, it was also rather formulaic. The attempt in structuralism was to seek an order, a structure, to novels, menus, poetry, music and visual texts. It sought grids and patterns, schemes and plots, always assuming that the text would yield its meaning once we unravel its 'core' elements.

In the 1960s, literary critics and philosophers began to rebel against what they saw as a restrictive and limited critical practice of viewing the world. Emerging in the context of civilian unrest (all the major French philosophers and thinkers of the latter half of the twentieth century were associated, in some form or the other, with the 1968 student rebellions in Paris) and geopolitical disasters like the Vietnam war, poststructuralism was the expression of a sense of disillusionment—with the nation-state, with philosophies of emancipation and with critical thinking itself. It emerged as a rupture, a shift away from what the prominent thinkers saw as the formulaic, ordered work of structuralism.

Roland Barthes' later work moved away from his structuralist phase, and he was one of the first to start speaking of the 'openness' of texts, the text's connections with other texts and the reader's role in the production of meaning. The writings of Jacques Derrida in the mid-1960s appeared in English in the form of conference papers, with his first complete book, *Of Grammatology*, appearing in 1976 (translated by Gayatri Chakravorty Spivak). From the early-1970s through the 1980s and 1990s, the work of Derrida, the historian of ideas, Michel Foucault, the philosophers Jean-François Lyotard, Gilles Deleuze and Félix Guattari, the Marxist literary critic Frederic Jameson, the semiotician-psychoanalyst Julia Kristeva, Spivak's own work, that of postmodernists, Slavoj Žižek, Jean Baudrillard and feminists like Judith Butler created a movement in literary criticism, media studies and philosophy. Poststructuralism thus has close contiguities—both thematic and contextual—with postmodernism. Poststructuralism has been one of the most influential movements in philosophy and critical theory in the twentieth century, and helped the rise of new forms of thinking in the social sciences seen in the work of James Clifford, Clifford Geertz, Michael Taussig (anthropology), James Der Derian (political theory), Bruno Latour (social studies of science) and New Historicists (literary criticism).

OPENING MOVES

THE DISCURSIVE TURN: MICHEL FOUCAULT

Michel Foucault, Professor of the History of the Systems of Thought, developed what he called the 'archaeology of the human sciences' in which he studied the rise of the forms of knowledge, the classificatory mechanisms of knowledge and the rules by which knowledge was collected, archived and disseminated. Foucault's interest lay in unpacking the underlying structures of thinking in the various fields of knowledge because, he argued, these structures conditioned and constructed

- the process of inquiry (knowledge-gathering),
- the very nature of the object (about which knowledge is being gathered), and
- the possibilities of using and distributing this knowledge.

In other words, Foucault saw scientific inquiry as an exercise in power where the physician, the scientist and the psychiatrist constructed a particular condition as diseased, an object to be investigated, and knowledge about it to be carefully controlled by certain authorities. Knowledge is constructed, organized, shared and used through particular forms of speech, writing and language—or what is called *discourse*. Discourse is the context of speech, representation, knowledge and understanding. It defines what can be said, studied and the processes of doing so. It is the *context in which meaning itself is produced*. To take a simplistic analogy: In the court of law, emotions and emotional responses to questions cannot be taken as answers. The court insists that the defendant or the accused answer the questions, and not with tears, laughter or anger. The discourse of the law in the court relies upon what it sees as 'evidence', logic and rational argumentation rather than angry outbursts or hysteria. Similarly, in the case of science, it is not adequate to say 'I believe this to be true'. The discourse of science asks for empirical, demonstrable proof that it is true.

Foucault's originality lay in discerning the underlying structures of power that informed 'neutral' scientific inquiries. He argued that some sections of the population were classified as sick, criminal, mad so that they could be placed under surveillance and 'observed' by particular kinds of authorities. This surveillance was coded as a *discourse*, a terrain of thought, a system of knowledge, a particular kind of language that allowed some things to be said and disallowed some others. Thus,

- the priest used the *discourse of religion*, of sin and salvation in order to preach particular norms of behaviour in domains like marriage, sexuality, family and charity,
- the physician used the *discourse of sickness* and health in order to proscribe particular kinds of lifestyles (excessive eating, for example),
- the psychiatrist constructed particular kinds of behaviour as 'deviant' through a *discourse of rationality*.

Foucault's major contribution has been to show how these discourses condition people's lives and inform their thinking. By focusing on power as central to the human condition, Foucault was able to argue that human relations, science, institutions are all caught up in a struggle for power, and discourse is a terrain on which this struggle is carried out. The person/institution that controls discourse also controls the subjects in those discourses.

Foucault underscored the discursive basis of power, social relations and institutions by showing how the so-called 'objective' disciplines like the sciences relied upon underlying assumptions about the object to be investigated, used particular forms of language and thought in order to talk about this object, and eventually constructed an institution around the object for its study and control.

This argument has been best used by the twentieth-century feminisms, which have shown how the *discourses* of patriarchy (with the representation of the pure woman, the seductive woman, the hysterical woman, the vulnerable woman) have been *institutionalized* in the uneven structures of marriage, education, religion, the law, history, literature, science and politics. Foucault's argument helped them show how discourse has material consequences for people, and that discourses construct and legitimize unequal power relations. Every discourse has an object, a language, an authority-figure who uses this language to describe/classify the object and a corrective mechanism that draws upon the description and classification. Here are a few examples of how discourse works in Foucault's kind of analysis:

- The vagrant was the *object* constructed in a *discourse of economics* as a non-productive, itinerant 'body' by the *authority-figure* of the economist/social commentator, and whose 'deviance' (non-employment) was corrected through the *institution* of either forced employment or charity.
- The immoral individual or sinner was the *object* constructed in a *discourse of religion* (with its elements of sin, salvation, virtue, punishment, purgatory and hell) by the *authority-figure* of the priest, and whose 'deviant' morality was *corrected* through penitence, confession and religious rituals (say, fasting) recommended/ordered and sometimes even implemented (for example, branding of witches) by the religious authority, the church.
- The criminal was the *object* constructed in a *discourse of the law* that classified actions as right or wrong, by the *authority-figure* of the court/judge, and whose deviant behaviour was corrected through the institution of the prison.

Foucault's work, adapted in the twentieth-century cultural theory and criticism, has shown how

- the sections of society have been subjugated through particular discourses;
- specific institutional forms of control were created to ensure that these sections remained subjugated;
- popular and other representations (arts, literature) controlled the images of these sections;
- these images in turn naturalized the difference and subjugation of particular sections;
- these discursive processes justified and led to the installation of 'corrective' mechanisms—institutions—to keep the sections controlled;
- the discourse and institutional structures combined to give power to particular classes/authorities.

These discourses are thus a manifestation of the will-to-power where structures of power in society retain their power over the marginal and the subordinates through the creation and control of particular discourses.

Foucault proposed a 'genealogical' or 'archaeological' analysis of discourses—tracing their opening moments and their formations. *Genealogy* is the tracing of those discourses and institutions that have formed our ideas of sexuality, sickness, criminality, morality, madness or improvement. Genealogy does not seek a linear historical account. Rather, it attempts to unravel the contradictory, conflictual forces that have created these abstract ideas and ideals. It can be summarized as a history of ideas that pays attention to social forces, institutional mechanisms and power structures that influence thought, ideas and knowledge-formations.

The clinic, the prison system and the asylum are institutions that began life in particular discourses of sickness, criminality and madness. The prison, in Foucault's now well-known reading in *Discipline and Punish*, for example, is the institutionalization of the *discourse* of discipline. Discipline begins to focus on the body in early modern Europe, and the disciplinary apparatuses shift focus from *public* rituals of punishment (flogging, the guillotine) in the nineteenth century to incarceration where the punished body is *hidden* away from the public gaze. A genealogical reading such as Foucault's traces *not only*

- the institutional structure (the prison) and its evolution in history,

but also

- the way in which concepts of 'criminality' have been defined,
- the kind of discourses that were put in place (for example, the sacredness of property, the body as a site where punishment or rewards can be played out),
- the contradictions and contests over and against these dominant discourses,
- the classes that dominated these discourses and
- the artistic, legal, biomedical representations of these discourses.

THE DECONSTRUCTIVE TURN: BARTHES AND DERRIDA

While Foucault's work involved detailing the structures of power and their discourses, Roland Barthes' later writings began to make the first moves in rebelling against structuralist readings of texts.

Barthes began by suggesting a different view of the text. He argued that texts can be either 'readerly' or 'writerly'. A *readerly text* was one that left the reader with nothing to do—it explained, explicated, described everything. It controlled meaning and the reader was a mere passive recipient of meaning. A *writerly text*, on the other hand, was one where the reader had an active role to play. The text teased, hid, offered clues to the reader to decode. In other words, Barthes was proposing that meaning was not embedded within the *text* but within the *reader* who derived meaning from the textual process. As he puts it in 'The Death of the Author', 'The reader is the space on which all the quotations that make up a writing are inscribed without any of them being lost; a text's unity lies not in its origin but in its destination' (2003 [1968]: 150).

Barthes suggested that a *work* is a physical object that occupies shelf space and is carried in the hand. A *text*, on the other hand, is a process in language. 'Text' here begins to

- mean a series of linguistic processes that are decoded by the reader,
- assume the 'structure' of narrative negotiations between the language (of the text) and the reader.

As Barthes puts it in 'From Work to Text': 'the *text is experienced only as an activity of production*' (1978:156–57, emphasis in original). In addition, Barthes sees the author as the controlling authority that prevents a work from becoming a text. As long as we assume that the author carries and owns the meaning of a poem or novel, it will remain a *work*, and not become a *text*. Barthes writes:

> The explanation of a work is always sought in the man or woman who produced it, as if it were always in the end, through the more or less transparent allegory of the fiction, the voice of a single person, the author "confiding in us". (2003 [1968]: 147)

Thus, a work becomes a text when the reader refuses authorial authority. In Barthes' famous formulation: 'the birth of the reader must be at the cost of the death of the author' (150).

Barthes then proposed that these negotiations are, by definition, endless. This is so because every text is 'open', an endless series of signifiers that refer to other signifiers and other texts rather than point to any definite conclusive meaning. The reader's task—and pleasure—is in playing with the text's endless games of signification. Barthes further proposed that this play is not necessarily controlled by the author. The author-centre as authority, as the controller of meaning, is dead and the meaning of a text lies somewhere in the play between the narrative and the reader. The play and its pleasure arise from the fact that every text is plural in its meaning—it refers to, echoes, parallels, quarrels with, reflects and borrows from other texts. Play is not rational or hierarchic, but random, repeatable differently and endless. For Barthes, therefore,

- the text is plural,
- the text is open to other texts in an endless series of intertextual operations (what Barthes terms 'a tissue of quotations drawn from the innumerable centres of culture', 149),
- the author is 'dead' and is therefore no more the sole authority over a text's meaning,
- the 'pleasures' of a text lie in the process of playing the narrative.

With these moves Barthes has put in place a different view of textuality itself— arguing for an openness and endlessness of meaning-making and narrative process.

Jacques Derrida, often associated with the 'movement' in philosophy known as 'deconstruction', is arguably one of the most elusive, controversial and influential figures in Western intellectual history. His work has spanned philosophy, literature, the law, political theory and social theory. Obsessed with the functioning of language, Derrida's mode of writing is playful, elliptical and sometimes obscure. However, the point is that *the way he makes his arguments is the argument itself*, a degree of self-reflexivity that is not seen in contemporary writing.

Derrida's early work built upon the Saussurean notions of language and signification (discussed in Chapter 1), but took them to radical extremes. Derrida argued that if the relation between signifier and signified is arbitrary and all language is relational then the process of 'reading' is a movement from one signifier to another. We can never come to the 'end' of signification and discover *the* meaning because when we get to the end we are faced not with the signified but with yet another signifier. Every signifier refers to other words/signifiers in an endless postponement—deference—of meaning. We never arrive; we only travel along the path of meaning-making. Thus, in order to explain the word 'cat' we use further terms like 'animal', 'organism', 'whiskers', 'tail'—more signifiers along the chain of signification. There is no 'final' signified because even that signified will consist of more words (signifiers).

Every signifier, argued Derrida, is made up of an *absence*. Building on Saussure's assumption that meaning is the result of difference (cat is different from bat, hat, fat…), Derrida suggests that every word carries within it the words that we are aware of as being different. Every signifier is a series of differences from other signifiers, all of those are the *absences* that constitute this one for us. 'Cat' is 'produced' because fat, hat and bat are absent, but these absences are crucial because without them we would not know 'cat'. This means the meaning of 'cat' is the result of absence rather than mere presence of difference. Meaning, ironically, depends as much on the absence of other words as on the presence of 'cat'.

> Derrida's chief contribution has been to show how language is fundamentally slippery, based on self-contradictory, unfinalizable conditions of difference and deference. His arguments have focused on the need to pay closer attention to the way in which meanings are produced temporarily rather than with any finality, through contradictions and ambivalence, and have consistently rebelled against any 'authoritative' or authoritarian meaning.

What Derrida achieved with these twin moves—of meaning as based on *difference* and absent presences, and as perpetually *deferred*—was a radical rethinking of the very process of language use. Writing and language, he announced, was *différance*: a term that combines *difference* and *deference* (postponement). We shall return to the significance of this term later. All writing is this *différance*, and a study of this *différance* is what Derrida famously termed 'grammatology'.

Derrida's deconstructive turn must be read alongside that of Barthes'. What these two thinkers did was to provide a very significant shift in the way we think of language. Both suggested

- the endless play in language and literary texts,
- the unreliability of any meaning,
- the openness of texts,
- the instability of language,
- the unfinalizability of any meaning or text,
- the relationships between words, meanings and texts as intrinsic to meaning rather than the words themselves.

Deconstructive criticism would build on these themes of unfinalizability, deference, relationality to show how a text can subvert its own stated philosophical or literary assumptions because it refers to and is open to

(i) a different reading,
(ii) another text that rather than reinforce its argument might subvert it,
(iii) revisions even as it states its meanings in unambiguous terms.

Deconstruction, if we seek a simple methodology in its practice, is thus interested in how texts

- break down,
- defeat their stated aims and purposes,
- rely on false or unsustainable oppositions,
- make use of figurative (i.e., literary or metaphoric) language even when trying to be empirical,
- reverse their own arguments,
- depend on other texts/signs,
- conceal arguments that are the very opposite of what they ostensibly show.

If structuralism was interested in how meaning is produced and texts work, deconstruction is interested in the contradictions that resist meaning, in how texts do not work but deconstruct themselves.

TEXT, TEXTUALITY AND WRITING

Deconstruction's attention to the language of texts has often led to accusations of it being another version of New Criticism. Its playfulness and puns have sometimes been seen as frivolous. Both these charges, however, miss the point: No critical analysis of texts and literary language has been as rigorous as deconstruction in

Jacques Derrida, Paul de Man, Geoffrey Hartman and Harold Bloom (for Bloom's work see Chapter 3).

Nicholas Royle (2000) proposes that one way of approaching deconstruction is to see how it treats speech acts and language. A constative is an assertion, and can be either true or false. A performative is a speech act that performs an act in the very act of saying (thus 'I swear' or 'I confess' is a performative because the words 'I swear' or 'I confess' perform the acts of swearing—one does not need to do anything except *say* it). Deconstruction shows how every constative—every assertion—also includes a performative within it. Thus, there are no 'pure' constatives, each being contaminated with the other. Deconstruction's chief strategy has been this: to discover impurities, contamination, border-crossing that upset purity, structure, linearity and origins. In every statement, deconstruction argues, one can see trace elements of other sounds, statements and truisms. In every statement you can see the remainders of something else, and detect what else remains to be said.

PHONOCENTRISM, LOGOCENTRISM AND THE 'METAPHYSICS OF PRESENCE'

Deconstructive thinking in Derrida begins by worrying about the distinction posed in linguistics and culture between speech and writing (Derrida is reading Saussure and Claude Lévi-Strauss here). Speech is privileged because it is seen as more authentic, since it happens only with a speaking person. Writing is treated as artificial, and as suggesting death, loss and unreliability since writing can exist independent of—after the life of—the writer. Thus, speech is taken to mean presence (of the speaker) and writing to mean absence. Writing is, therefore, about absences and thus less privileged in this scheme.

Derrida termed this privileging of speech over writing, *phonocentrism*. Speech is privileged because it seems to have an 'essence': the speaker. Listeners assume the speaker embodies the truth of what is being said because the speaker is *present*. In fact, Derrida proposes, notions of truth are dependent upon this idea of a centre ('logos'), core and essence. This is what he terms *logocentrism*, or the 'metaphysics

*P*honocentrism is a term Derrida uses to describe the privileging of speech over writing in Western thought, a privileging based on the assumption that because speech implies a speaking presence, it is more authentic. *Logocentrism* is the term he uses to describe the assumption and quest for a core, an essence, truth and centre. 'Logos', or the final meaning is believed to vest in God, whom Derrida terms a transcendental signified—a signified that explains and culminates the very process of signification.

of presence', where the core or the presence is seen as being 'truth'. Derrida sees the entire canon of Western philosophy as rooted in this metaphysics, in its search for a core meaning, in its privileging of presence and rejection of absence and difference. God functions, he argues, as a sort of core truth, a 'transcendental signified'. This is where, Western philosophy assumes, all truth originates. Derridean deconstruction's first move is, therefore, to reject this emphasis on centres, origins and essences.

Derrida proposed that absence is the *always present* condition of inevitable death. The sign (or writing) is iterable, repeatable in the absence not only of the writer-speaker but also in the absence of the listener-reader. Iteration is the possibility of *citation*—to quote, repeat, re-write—of texts. Derrida writes: 'It [written communication] must be repeatable—iterable—in the absolute absence of the addressee or the empirically determinable entirety of addresses' (1982: 315). What Derrida is arguing here is that what applies to the addresser-speaker (absence) also applies equally to the addressee-listener.

Writing is seen as an extra, an *addition* to speech, something that is used as a *sign* when the presence of the speaker is not possible. This locates writing as extra, an addendum, and, therefore, subordinate to speech in the hierarchy speech/writing. Derrida terms this the logic of the *supplement*.

THE SUPPLEMENT AND DIFFÉRANCE

The supplement is *différance*. Derrida proposes, following Saussure, that signs cannot ever refer to the things themselves (there is no connection between the thing and the word used to describe the thing. The relation established is arbitrary and through convention). Signs are, therefore, incomplete, and require something else to complete its sense. Supplement is this necessary completion. It is signifier that is *extra*. But Derrida argues that the signifier is also what completes. It is extra (and therefore unnecessary) but also necessary for completion. It is *both* necessity and excess. It can substitute (in the example given above, a sign is a *substitute* for the actual living presence of the speaker) or supplant. The signifier is needed because it tells us that there is a presence (assumed to be the signified) that is *not* here now. In other words, a sign is indicative of an *absent presence* because it *shows* (stands in for) *something that is not here, but makes us alert to the fact that something is not here*. This makes the sign invaluable because it alerts us to signification itself. Derrida typically plays with this double meaning of excess and necessity to show how 'supplement' is unstable and undecidable. The supplement is the *signifier*.

Derrida's deconstructive move is to show how we seek to go from the supplement to the 'core', the main meaning. We wish, in other words, to move *from* the signifier *to* the signified. Without a signifier there would not be a signified. Hence, the signifier is integral to the signified, and the signifier indicates that a signified is at hand, though deferred. The signifier gestures at this absent presence of the signified, and without the signifier we would not know there is ever a signified. Derrida ponders over the consequence of the pursuit beyond the supplement:

'One wishes to go back from the supplement to the source: one must recognize that there is supplement at the source' (2002[1976]: 304). This simply means we start a process that will not end.

The repeatability of the sign, Derrida proposes, is in fact *common* to both speech and writing. If signs are by definition iterable (citable, repeatable), then there is no end to repetition. In other word signs—written or spoken—can be repeated anywhere anytime. When I use the term 'Derrida' here, or in my class, I am not really concerned with where it was first used. I only know that one can use the term in various contexts and people will still understand that I am speaking of a French philosopher. Both writing and speaking depend on the function of the sign's iterability—we can use the same words in different contexts to suit our need of the moment and not worry about where the word comes from or what it has meant before. All forms of language, Derrida shows, are based on this fact of iterability, whether in speech or in writing. Hence, the privileging of speech over writing is false. Derrida uses the term 'writing' to therefore include both spoken and written forms, in order to emphasize that *speech is a form of writing*.

This argument illustrates a basic feature of deconstructive 'method': to analyse a hierarchy, to reverse it and to show how the elements of the hierarchy are constitutive of each other. Thus, speech and writing are not opposing terms or binaries but rather, each contains the other.

In literary and cultural theory, Derrida's arguments about texts have been particularly influential, and to these we shall now turn.

'THERE IS NO OUTSIDE-TEXT'

'Text' requires a clearer explication in Derrida.

   i. 'Text' is not restricted by a book's margins or binding.
   ii. A text overruns, spills over its borders. The end of the 'book' is not the end of 'writing'.
   iii. Every text carries 'traces' of other texts (recall here the notion of intertextuality).
   iv. Every text is, therefore, a network of other texts, from which it differs.

The world, constructed through and in language takes on a *textualized* form, based on difference, deference and multiplicity. There is no reality outside the game of language, of language as difference and open.

Since language is inherently unstable (due to its arbitrariness, traces, absences and deferment) we cannot come to a definite meaning about reality or identity. All we have as reality is a system of shifting signifiers, difference and openness, full of ambiguity, absences, traces of other texts. This notion of reality being located within writing—or text—leads Derrida to declare: '*there is no outside-text.*'[1] Derrida is proposing that everything takes on a *textualized* form (of difference and deference), but also that texts are *politicized*. Derrida's translator and commentator,

Geoffrey Bennington, writes: '"Text" is not quite an extension of a familiar concept, but a displacement or reinscription of it. Text in general is any system of marks, traces, referrals...' (2001 [1989]: 217). Derrida's definitions of texts are worth citing in some detail:

> All those boundaries that form the running border of what used to be called a text, of what we once thought this word would identify, i.e., the supposed end and beginning of a work, the unity of a corpus, the title, the margins, the signatures, the referential realm outside the frame, and so forth. What has happened ... is a sort of overrun that spoils all these boundaries and divisions and forces us to extend the accredited concept, the dominant notion of a "text" ... *that is no longer a finished corpus of writing, some content enclosed in a book or its margins, but a differential network, a fabric of traces referring endlessly to something other than itself, to other differential traces.* (1979: 81–4, emphasis added)

Derrida elaborated what he meant some years later:

> "There is no outside-the-text" signifies that one never accedes to a text without some relation to its contextual opening that a context is not made up only of what is so trivially called a text, that is, the words of a book or the more or less biodegradable paper document in a library. If one does not understand this initial transformations of the concepts of text ... [and] context, one understands nothing about nothing of ... deconstruction. (1989: 841)

Derrida here proposes that history, politics, economics, reality itself is based on difference. And difference, as he had argued, is the basis of writing. What Derrida suggests is that all these domains take the form of writing, of texts. Bennington writes:

> Deconstruction does not have a place for language over here, and a world over there to which it refers ... There is no essential difference between language and the world, the one as subject, the other as object. There are traces. (2001 [1989]: 218)

Texts are undecidables. Later critics have theorized about textuality as being different from 'text'. Textuality is what constitutes the text in particular ways. This involves interpretive acts, contexts and the knowledge produced through the text. Textuality is the process of reading the text. To put it differently: A text is the *object* that is read, and textuality is the *act* of reading/interpretation (Edward Said, the postcolonial critic, called textuality a 'practice', 1978b: 703). This reading reveals the slippages of language. Derrida writes:

> [T]he reading must always aim at a certain relationship, unperceived by the writer, between what he commands and what he does not command of the patterns of the language that he uses. This relationship is not a certain quantitative distribution of shadow and light, of weakness or of force, but a signifying structure that critical should produce. (2002: 158)

Textuality—the process of reading—is what *constitutes* the text (the parallels with Barthes' 'work' and 'text' are to be noted here). But this process of reading is undecidable, infinite and open because we always bring other textualities into our reading. And this means, because textualities are open and undecidable, texts are also rendered open and infinite.

PAUL DE MAN AND RHETORIC

Writing on literature, Paul de Man, possibly the most influential deconstructive literary critic of his generation, argued for 'rhetorical reading'. De Man argued that there was no referential language because all signifiers referred not to a reality 'out there' but to other signifiers. All language is, in one sense, *figurative* because it refers to more and more words rather than reality. The linguistic sign is a site of conflict, ambivalence and instability. Looking at the literary texts and their language, de Man argued that the literal meaning of a text is often deconstructed and contradicted by its figural meaning. De Man took this line of thinking further, showing how even the so-called non-literary language (law, economics) used tropes and figurative language, just like literature. What he was demonstrating was that when a text seeks to be persuasive and objective is when it relies on fictional tropes and figures. The text is thus self-deconstructive where the literal level is subverted by the figural. This makes all texts undecidable in their meaning.

Rhetorical reading pays attention to the limits of interpretation in de Man. Even before we set out to interpret a text we have decided what interpretation is. In this sense we are a part of a process already in place even before we embark upon it. When de Man 'reads' he suggests that critical practice, however rigorous, takes recourse to the very tropes and figures it hopes to unravel. Thus, when we assume a binary-like form and content in a literary work, we assume that form and content constitute meaning, and the task of the interpreter is to either look at form (if one is a structuralist, for example) or content. We cannot think *beyond* form and content as basis for interpretation. De Man's example serves well here to understand this *aporia* of criticism. Reading Proust, de Man argues that his (de Man's reading) is facilitated by what the text *itself* provides. De Man writes:

> The reading is not 'our' reading, since it uses only the linguistic elements provided by the text itself; the distinction between the author and the reader is one of the false distinctions that the reading makes evident. The deconstruction is not something we have added to the text but it constituted it in the first place. A literary text simultaneously asserts and denies the authority of its own rhetorical mode, and by reading the text as we did we were only trying to come closer to being as rigorous a reader as the author had to be in order to write the sentence in the first place. (1982: 17)

What one can write about a particular piece of writing or text is made possible by the conditions of that text or writing itself.

J. HILLIS MILLER'S DECONSTRUCTION

A colleague of Hartman at Yale, and one of the central figures in American deconstruction, Hillis Miller's readings of Victorian fiction and poetry have been exemplary.

Miller's first major deconstructive essay, 'The Critic as Host' (a response to M. H. Abrams' 'The Deconstructive Angel', in which Abrams attacked the deconstructive strategy of leaving a text undecidable) remains his best, and best-known, writing on the subject. In this essay Miller begins what would become a standard deconstructive move: a problem of words and their meaning. If a citation C from a text B occurs within a text A, is that citation parasitic upon the 'main' text A? Or is it that the 'main' text A limits and determines the citation? Miller argues that citation C and text A constitute each other. When Abrams and other detractors treat deconstruction as parasitic on the main text, they ignore the fact that the text deconstructs itself: Deconstruction is a part of every text. For this purpose he turns to the figure and etymology of 'parasite', and shows how the 'para' of the term means 'besides the grain' and 'site' comes from 'sitos', or food. Thus, a parasite, Miller notes, 'was originally something positive' (2003: 257). It is one who shares your food, as your fellow-guest. Host, often taken as the opposite of guest, is the one on whom the parasite preys: The host is the food who gets eaten, the one who (biologically, medically) is the host to the parasite. But the word 'host' etymologically means both 'guest' and 'stranger'. It is also connected to 'hostis', meaning enemy or stranger. Thus, the one to offer hospitality (host) is also a stranger and the one you see as an unwanted guest (parasite) is also a fellow guest.

With this etymological game Miller is able to demonstrate how meanings of words are sometimes antithetical and, therefore, unstable. As he puts it: '[T]he uncanny antithetical relation exists not only between pairs of words in this system, host and parasite, host and guest, but within each word itself' (258). We cannot rely on this or that meaning of a word. What deconstruction does is to point to these crises of meaning within the heart of any word: Where the heart itself is made of many. Thus, to argue that deconstruction is parasitic on the main text is to ignore the condition that the host text (what Miller terms 'narrative') is itself a stranger, an enemy: It is the deconstructive 'figure' that hosts the narrative.

Miller's work has relied on such close readings of Tennyson, Hardy, Dickens in order to reveal how every text's internal logic collapses upon examination because language is forever slippery.

BINARIES, REVERSALS AND DECONSTRUCTIVE READING

Deconstruction is interested in the hierarchic binaries set up within texts. These could be: man/woman, speech/writing, white/black, inside/outside, full/empty, identity/difference, light/dark, presence/absence, similarity/difference. In each of these binaries, one term is privileged over the other. A deconstructive reading would show how, even when a text appears to privilege one term over the other (say, inside over outside), the text's logic of rhetoric reveals that there can be no inside without the outside. In other words, deconstruction shows how the less privileged term is central to the dominant term. By showing this centrality deconstruction reverses the hierarchy, for if the inside can exist only if there is an outside it means that the outside is the dominant element. In its next stage, deconstruction destabilizes this reversed hierarchy too. It questions the *new* hierarchy and thus leaves even the displaced one unstable. Thus, the text remains unresolvable where neither term is privileged, and where both terms are privileged—a situation termed 'aporia'. Let us take as an example, a painting as a text and deconstruct it.

(i) The painting is the figure in the centre of the canvas.

(ii) It is bounded by a frame.

(iii) When we talk about/look at a painting we only observe the figure in the centre. We do not talk about the *frame*.

(iv) Thus, the painting privileges the figure *over* the frame. In the binary figure/frame, the first is the privileged term.

(v) But then, the figure is made possible because the frame limits it. Without the frame the figure would escape borders, endlessly proliferating. The frame also distinguishes it from the surroundings. It marks the painting itself as separate from the wall on which it hangs. Thus, the painting and the figure exist as unique pieces of art on the wall precisely *because* the frame isolates it as such.

(vi) This means the frame is central to the figure. It is privileged over the figure because there cannot be a figure without the frame. With this the hierarchic binary of figure over frame has been reversed.

(vii) Once we establish that the frame is important, we can then see how the frame participates *in* the figure. It is included within the painting as a boundary, the figure assumes that the border exists and contains it. The frame limits our vision when we trace the painting with our eyes, the signature of the artist is placed in a particular position vis-à-vis both the figure and the frame, and so on. Without the figure the frame would be without any value, just an empty square. It is the figure that bestows a quality *to* the frame, as something that contains a special feature (the figure). In other words, the frame comes into the painting even as the figure extends toward the frame and we cannot treat the frame as privileged over that of the figure because the figure is what marks the frame as the frame *of* something.

(viii) With this move deconstruction shows how neither frame nor figure and both frame and figure are constitutive of each other. That neither can be privileged. This is undecidability of the painting.

Let's summarize. In a typical deconstructive reading of texts what we see is a three-part movement in the analysis:

(i) A text proposes a literal meaning and a hierarchy.

(ii) The deconstructive reading reveals a figural meaning and reverses the hierarchy.

(ii) It then displaces even the reversed hierarchy, leaving the text open, neither here nor there.[2]

POSTSTRUCTURALISM, SIMULATION AND THE POSTMODERN

In the writings of Baudrillard, Deleuze-Guattari and Lyotard we see a strong poststructuralist stance: a distrust of finalizable meaning, a resistance to authoritarian discourses, an emphasis on play, possibilities and contingency (the 'here and now' rather than 'forever') and a focus on the tension between the real and the imitation. Mostly associated with postmodern cultural theory and practices, these thinkers have, however, extended the concerns of poststructuralism about signs, meaning and contexts of meaning-production. Terry Eagleton provides a succinct definition of postmodernity and postmodernism as an intellectual 'movement'. He calls postmodernity, 'a style of thought which is suspicious of classical notions of truth, reason, identity and objectivity, of the idea of universal progress or emancipation, of single frameworks, grand narratives or ultimate grounds of explanation', and goes on to list the features of postmodernist art and culture, which according to him are characteristically '[d]epthless, decentred, ungrounded, self-reflexive, playful, derivative, eclectic, pluralistic … which blurs the difference between 'high' and 'popular' culture, as well as between art and everyday experience' (1996: vii).

Postmodernism is a philosophical and cultural theory that rejects totalizing narratives in favour of partial, fragmented and incomplete ones, and questions the idea that there is any 'real' beyond representations. It argues that images and signs constitute our only reality because signs now refer not to reality but to other signs in the age of the hyperreal. It also rejects elite culture, and its practitioners in art and literature seek to mix high culture with the low. Postmodernism is suspicious of 'truth' and focuses on the production of truth in language and narrative.

JEAN BAUDRILLARD, THE HYPERREAL AND SIMULATION

Baudrillard's notion of 'simulacra' is linked to the idea of 'hyper-reality'. Baudrillard's interest lies in structures like Disney World, television and photography where, he suggests, we are so caught up in the image and its copies that we have no access to any reality beyond the image itself. The representation, i.e., the image, 'bears no relation to any reality whatever: it is its own pure simulacrum' (Baudrillard 2003: 405). What we see in Disney is a glossy, glamourized visual representation of something whose original we will never know. The use of Raja Ravi Verma's paintings in calendars, of Picasso and other artists in mass/popular cultural forms popularizes these 'great' works of art. However, our only access to these great works is through the copy or imitation where we will never see the original. In other words, for us the copy is, serves as, becomes the original. Copies and further reproductions of the great works are made from these copies. What we thus have are *copies of copies,* like Che Guevara T-shirts, or Nike's swoosh on locally manufactured products, each of which is 'cloned' or copied from an earlier copy. Postmodernity is characterized by the endless circulation of the copies.

Signs are not exchanged for objects or even meaning (which is the traditional function of signs; they stood in for objects, were symbols for the objects), 'never again exchanging for what is real, but exchanging in itself, in an uninterrupted circuit without reference or circumference' (2003: 404).

Thus, the image, the copy and the photograph constitute our knowledge of reality because we cannot know anything other than the image. This is simulation, where the process of image-making and the copies and the reflection are more important than the 'real' because there is no real. Baudrillard writes: 'There is an escalation of the true, of the lived experience; a resurrection of the figurative where the object and substance have disappeared' (2003: 405).

We cannot distinguish between the real and the copy any more. Thus, the reality of a war for us is the image, the visual that appears on our screen. The image-making of the war itself is so realistic—with the superior technology, the embedded journalists—that it takes on the appearance of cinema. When the WTC towers fell, one of the comments recorded was: 'It is like *Independence Day*'. The comment suggests that the only way we can apprehend and approach the horrific event is by comparing it to cinematic scenarios of disaster. The very language of horror is cinematic, and our access to the reality of WTC is via a movie image. The only way we can make sense of Mumbai 26/11 is through televised images that seem to echo/double/parallel commando action films. Our 'knowledge' of commando action on 26/11 is based on a simulation of it that we have seen in films.

Simulation is the norm of postmodernity, according to Baudrillard. We live in an age saturated with images, maps, models and signs that have become ends in themselves, and for which we have never known originals. Thus, we only have signs without an external reality, copies without originals. We cannot distinguish between real and artifice any longer because there is no 'real' we can recognize: We only know the image of the real.

What Baudrillard is painstakingly developing here is a theory of representation. He suggests that nothing exists outside representation. The *hyperreal* is this world of simulations and excessive 'signs', and is the only real world we will ever know. We do not consume objects but the signs of that object. This is what he terms 'implosion', the collapse of meaning in the age of empty signs, or signs without referents for us to connect to. Every sign merely refers us to other *signs*.

Baudrillard attributes this simulation culture to the excessive influence of the media, especially television and screen cultures. We see the world only through this media, our appraisal and interpretation of reality is influenced by films, media representations and images of such a reality (embodied in the comment that WTC was like *Independence Day*: There is no way of grasping reality except through the media images circulating about it. Responses to Mumbai 26/11 recorded opinions like 'we have only seen people dressed up as commandos on film screens, and we now see real commandos do real work.') He also links it to urban capitalism, where capitalist strategies involve concealing the inequalities of society behind images of production, prosperity and efficiency. Consumer capitalism takes this a step further where we can only know the finished product, but will never know where the product comes from, the processes of production or distribution. Thus, we consume a mango drink, even though, it is more than likely that we in urban India may never see a mango plantation or even a mango tree. Our 'knowledge' of the mango is only through the sign or representations of the mango on the bottle. This is our only reality because, in consumer capitalism with differentiated production, outsourcing and scattered markets, products are not local, and we do not attach a history, culture or specific practice (of say, growing mangoes, the smell in the marketplace) to that product.

GILLES DELEUZE AND SIMULACRA

Deleuze in *Difference and Repetition* (1994) extends Baudrillard's notion of simulacra but also contests it. Baudrillard, we have seen, proposes that there is no possibility of distinguishing between the real and the virtual, the original and the copy. Deleuze argues that this is a false dichotomy because, very simply, the *original is itself a copy*. The actual or real building is based on the *idea* of a building, an *image* in the builder's eye or mind. For us to recognize the building we need to have a *prior image* of a building. Thus, Deleuze sees the actual as actual-virtual, where everything 'real' has the potential to become virtual, to produce its own images.

Deleuze is here responding to Plato's argument that there exists a true model (the ideal) of which we see copies. Further, Plato distinguishes between good and bad copies. The good copy is what Plato termed 'eikon' and the bad copy was 'phantasma', or simulacrum. 'Eikon', or a 'good' copy, is one that possesses an 'inner' resemblance to the original model, whereas in a phantasm/simulacrum there is only a superficial resemblance to the ideal. Deleuze argues that Plato finds simulacra frightening because they have no fixed identity. Their identity is slippery, ephemeral and illusory. They resemble the original, but that resemblance is itself illusory and minimal. In other words, simulacra refers to a condition where the illusion is all there is, lacking depth or 'inner' essence that recalls the original.

Deleuze's shift was in treating the actual or real as possessing the ability to become virtual. He argued that we cannot discern the virtual *potential* in any building or anything real, *until it has become an image*. That is, the potential of the real to become 'virtual' is *not* visible to us when we see the building. We can realize this only when we see the *image* (photograph, cinematic image). This process of actual-virtual, of the inherent potential for all real to become virtual is what Deleuze calls simulation. Simulacrum is the power of anything (actual) to become something else, to become an image, to be other than the actual. In other words, simulacrum is the *power of the actual to become virtual*.

LYOTARD AND THE POSTMODERN

One of the most influential theories that arose in the latter half of the twentieth century was developed by Jean-François Lyotard. Often described as postmodernism, Lyotard's work has influenced numerous thinkers in social sciences, philosophy and literary criticism.

Lyotard begins with a simple enough idea. In the age of computers and multinational corporations, new modes of knowledge emerge, over which the state or any dominant ideology may have little or no control. Knowledge becomes a commodity whose acquisition leads to power. The status of knowledge changes because the nature of acquiring it, storing it and disseminating it changes. This is 'postmodernity'. Lyotard argued that identity and the sense of self of a culture is based on the knowledge generated and codified about this culture—either by itself or by others. We exist within language and representations: as names, as affiliations and as descriptive categories. As Lyotard puts it in a move that anticipates the work of poststructuralists, 'the human child is already positioned as the referent of a story recounted by those around him, in relation to which he will inevitably chart his course' (2004: 15). This 'positioning' is the location of the child, his identity and self within a body of knowledge. Lyotard then proposes that this body of knowledge is, in fact, an organization of narratives. Every body is located within narrative because narrative is the 'quintessential form of customary knowledge' (19). It is therefore important to see what *kinds* of narratives any culture produces about itself. A country's history, for example, that showcases the achievements of its 'great' men and women, or the narrative of progress in any culture constitute such an organization of the nation through narratives. In India, for instance, a history book that maps India's progress from various dynasties to a republic would be the production of a body of knowledge in a particular kind of narrative. The cliché 'unity in diversity' is a narrative where we suggest that India is a pluralistic, multicultural society. These narratives and clichés are not neutral bodies of knowledge—they are politically significant because they create and disseminate ways of thinking and identities.

Lyotard argues in his classic work, *The Postmodern Condition*, that no philosophy or political theory—or narrative—can be totalizing. Thus, Marxism's idea of class conflict and emancipation, Hegel's 'spirit' of History, Freud's repressive psychosis are totalizing perspectives, and give very little space for alternative views of the world. These could be speculative narratives (about the march of history, for example) or they could be emancipatory narratives (such as the one about the right of man to pursue happiness—the narrative that inspires the American War of Independence). In postmodernity, argued Lyotard, we can perceive a 'resistance to grand narratives' (what he famously called 'incredulity towards metanarratives', xxiv). There is no credibility left for any such 'grand' narratives because they have revealed themselves to be oppressive and homogenizing, and because we have seen them to be representations rather than absolute truths.

Instead of these grand and totalizing narratives we have small, local, hetero-geneous narratives. Postmodern thinking opts for the fragmented, the anecdotal, the liminal and the marginalized. It celebrates the contingent and the fluid over the fixed stability of totalizing theories.

> Lyotard inaugurated the key theoretical note in postmodernism when he characterized it as a resistance to grand narratives, and focused on the marginal, the liminal and the fragmented, arguing against totalizing systems of thought.

History writing is one of the most important forms of narrative in any culture. Lyotard argues that in an age when grand narratives have collapsed we cannot anymore study a 'universal history' because that would mean ignoring the periph-eries in favour of a unified account. Events such as the Holocaust upset the grand narratives of modernity, argues Lyotard, and thus suggest that universal histories are simply untenable. Events unassimilable to grand narratives are what tell us about the necessarily incomplete nature of all narrative.

By rejecting totalizing narratives, postmodernism resists any homogenized explanations or theorizing. Notions of 'truth' within any such narrative, argues postmodernism, are exercises in power and seek to homogenize differences in order to create a sense of harmonious truth. In actuality, such 'truths' conceal dif-ference, prevent resistance and gloss over the minor and the marginal.

Postmodernism overlaps with poststructuralism in its emphasis on language and the idea that meaning is unfinalizable. Like poststructuralism, it calls for a greater attention to *strategies of representation* rather than the final meaning of such representations. As we have seen in the case of Baudrillard, postmodernism focuses on the modes of meaning-production without seeking the 'truth' or the 'real' behind the production. It argues that we can only know the images and the repre-sentation, and not the reality beneath it, if any. That is, like poststructuralism, postmodernism also believes in the discursive and linguistic construction of reality and truth: *Nothing exists outside language.*

Here Lyotard proposes that scientific knowledge cannot exist outside of nar-rative, even though science has always presented itself as beyond narrative. Thus, knowledge itself demands a narrative form. Lyotard expands the notion of narrative to include history, science, social theory, in addition to the literary narratives. Scientific statements, he argues, are presented in particular kinds of narrative, and every narrative follows the conventions of that discipline. Thus, the narrative of science appropriates the language, or the discourse, of empiricism, proof, methodology (in the 1990s Bruno Latour in a series of innovative works would argue for scientific discourse as including narratives, and science itself as involving 'actors' such as the laboratory, administration and the humans).

In literary and cultural theory, postmodernism's greatest contribution has been to collapse the distinction between high and low (or mass) culture. Postmodernism treats the shopping mall, the advertisement poster, the bumper sticker, graffiti and Shakespeare as equally important, even it they belong to distinct genres. Genre-mixing and collapsing categories are favourite postmodern devices. Postmodern authors like Márquez, Rushdie, Barthelme, Barth often embody postmodern views in that the sense of play (for example, non-linear, circumlocutous narrative styles), the mix of genres, the rich mix of street culture with 'high' culture like Shakespeare are features of their works. In each case the author shows how we cannot take any one form of thought or one genre as distinctive because every genre partakes of the other. Postmodernism is, therefore, characterized by

- a refusal to accept any system of thought or theory as universal;
- a preference for fragmentation over unity, dispersion over linear order, the anecdote over the epic;
- the blurring of boundaries between 'high' and 'low' culture;
- a sense of playfulness, contingency and self-reflexivity;
- an interest in the surface, the image and the copy rather in the depth, the reality and the original;
- a fascination with the strategies of representation rather than the 'truth' of/ behind the representation;
- an emphasis on the discourse, the language and the narrative rather than on the reality these supposedly convey;
- a desire for flows, shifts, multiplicities rather than order, organization and tyrannical coherence.

SUBJECT AND SUBJECTIVITY IN POSTSTRUCTURALISM

Foucault, Derrida and deconstruction have had profound influences on and resonance in cultural theory, psychoanalysis and literary studies. Foucault demonstrated how the subject—the sick, the insane, the child, the criminal—is constituted within discourse. Foucault's work might be seen as the epitome of the poststructuralist theory of the subject. In this poststructuralist view

- the subject is not a coherent self;
- the subject does not contain an essence;
- subjects insert themselves into roles and subject-positions already available to them in discourses;
- therefore, the subject is constructed within discourses—which bestow upon her/him, an identity, a name, a gender—such as biology, medicine, law, history, science and arts;
- the subject is never a stable entity, it is constantly reconstituted within discourses.

What poststructuralism proposes is that the subject is a social construction—there is no 'innate' or natural self that can exist outside of discourses. *Biology as discourse* constructs a material body-subject of nerves, blood vessels, the various organs and disease. The *law as discourse* constructs the human as one who has rights and responsibilities. *History as discourse* constructs the human as one who has followed a particular trajectory in what history terms 'evolution' or 'development'. *Psychology, philosophy* and *psychoanalysis as discourses* construct the human psyche and self as a set of values, behavioural patterns, predispositions and eccentricities. These discourses operate through *language*. According to Chris Weedon, '[T]he meaning of the existing structure of social institutions, as much as the structures themselves and the subject positions which they offer their subjects, is a site of political struggle waged mainly, though not exclusively, in language' (1987: 38).

When the subject speaks s/he is inserted into the discourse (please see Lacan in Chapter 3 Psychoanalytic Criticism and and Althusser in Chapter 5 Marxisms for theories of subject and discourse). Thus, the subject enters into identity when s/he enters into language and discourse.

Building on these assumptions derived from poststructuralism, thinkers like Judith Butler develop theories of the subject within discourse, and demonstrate how subjects accept and resist subject-positions. If Judith Butler turns to a version of poststructuralism (discussed in greater detail in the chapters on feminism and queer theory) in order to develop a particular theory of gender, Julia Kristeva (whose earlier work was located within structuralism), provides a new approach to the subject and subjectivity. Kristeva here is as much influenced by Derrida as by Lacan.

KRISTEVA AND THE *CHORA*

Kristeva rejects the humanist idea of the subject, arguing that this human subject is seen only as male, unified and coherent when the subject can actually also be female, multiple and fragmented. The psychic apparatus, she argues, is contradictory. The unconscious is undeterminable, illimitable and ungovernable—or simply, unknowable. This is disruptive, and any idea of a coherent human can only emerge from a deliberate glossing over of this unconscious.

Subjectivity is, therefore, always divided, contradictory and unfinalizable. The subject, for Kristeva, is always decentred, ex-centric. It rebels against liberal humanism's view of the subject as rational, cogent and logical, by showing how it is unconscious, radically other and incoherent. It is always becoming, in process and interminable. With Lacan and poststructuralism, the subject is formed *after* entry into *language* (what Kristeva calls a 'speaking body'). However, Kristeva suggests that a material body also becomes a meaningful self *before* and beyond symbolic language, through a language of touch, gestures and laughter. Kristeva proposes a pre-mirror stage that she terms the *semiotic*. It is the language of the flesh—tears, blood, milk, faeces. The semiotic is the stage of the body: laughter, sound, touch. These are forms of signification that *precede*—and this is important—what we see (in Lacan) as symbolic. The mother–child interaction is an example of this kind of semiotic, or what Kristeva terms *chora*.

Kristeva writes of the moment of infantile laughter and pre-symbolic interaction: the 'imprint of an archaic moment, the threshold of space, the *chora* as primitive stability ... markers of something in the process of becoming stability' (1980: 283). Kristeva is pointing to a stage where the subject is in the process of becoming, untouched by what we see as language. The *chora* is this stage, a language *before* language. It is unrepresentable, and to even talk about it is to shift it from the semiotic to the symbolic. It is the place of drives, but remains provisional. Now, drives are both creative and destructive, and so the chora is also a site of dynamic tension between drives.

> Kristeva proposed a stage before that of the symbolic (which is about language): the semiotic, where the semiotic is the mother's body and the non-linguistic interaction of flesh, blood, milk, tears, laughter and touch that takes place between the mother and child. This space of the mother's body is what she terms *chora*.

The *chora* is the mother's body, and occurs in the space of interaction of the mother's body and the child. It is pre-linguistic, but still a process of meaning-making. In order to mark its difference from the linguistic signification, Kristeva terms the *chora* the stage of *signifiance*.

However, Kristeva goes beyond this 'primordial' stage of chora and the pre-symbolic subject. Having discussed a form of the subject that is rooted in the flesh and body, she proceeds to unpack the cultural languages, discourses and structures that restrain this primordial subject (and here one can see traces of the Freudian influence, especially from *Civilization and Its Discontents*, that never really disappears from Kristeva). She points to cultural prohibitions and taboos, rituals of purification as marking the normative subject. If the *chora* was about the bodily, the subject of culture is about restraining the bodily, expelling the impure, organizing the experiences of the flesh.[3] Kristeva argues that this is the symbolic stage. *Subjectivity is a constant oscillation and contest between the carnal/bodily-semiotic and the cultural-symbolic.* This kind of unstable subject is what Kristeva terms the *subject-in-process.*

Both Butler and Kristeva posit a subject that is unstable, shifting and conflict-ridden. It seeks meaning, contests a set of norms and can never be pinned down to an 'essence'. Where Butler suggests a repetitive performative as the process of identity-making, Kristeva sees the contest between the semiotic and the symbolic as marking identity. In both cases what we discern is the subject of poststructuralism.

POSTSTRUCTURALISM, FLOWS AND DETERRITORIALIZATION

A concept introduced by Deleuze and Guattari (2004 [1987]) to describe connectivity and endless proliferation of machines, signs and power, *deterritorialization* captures the postmodern–poststructuralist thinking about authority, power and space.

Deleuze and Guattari argue that machines have no centre: Their very being is in proliferation, connections and traversals of space. Deterritorialization is the process through which the machine becomes something other than itself—a series of connections, intersections, assemblages and negotiations. It has no central self, only a series. To put it differently, a machine is an assemblage, it's *self* lies in being open, endless, proliferating, not closed, coherent and limited. Here they distinguish between a *machine* and an *organism*. An organism is limited, self-contained and closed. A machine has its self only when it connects to something else. Its self lies in this connection with an outside, an Other. For example, a hammer comes into being when it is used by a hand to hit a nail. Its very existence *as* hammer depends on this connection with the hand and the process. Otherwise, it is simply a block of wood and a metal head.

Deterritorialization was also used to describe affect and emotions. Deleuze and Guattari argued that affect constitute 'lines of flight', a series of affective responses that does not stay restricted to the *original* body or event. Deterritorialization describes becoming, process and movement rather than finite event or thing. It is also linked to an important concept in Deleuze and Guattari, that of repetition and difference. Capitalism channelizes desire into production and commodity relations. All social relations, which are the product and site of desire, are reduced to commodity relations. This is deterritorialization. But capitalism also re-territorializes desire by focusing every and all desire into the Oedipus complex and the nuclear family.

Deleuze and Guattari argue that to repeat a play of Shakespeare (as a play, film, or adaptation) is to repeat differently. We grasp a whole new experience and meaning, different from the 'original'. Shakespeare's play is its 'untimely' (a term Deleuze and Guattari use with regularity) nature: It intrudes upon the present, breaks our continuity. It affects the present by bringing the past into it.

Clearly Deleuze and Guattari are interested in *flows* and series rather than in closed systems. The 'untimely' is repetition with difference, deterritorialization as lines of flight. In contemporary social, cultural and political theory these ideas have been used to describe capitalism. Capitalism as a series of flows, extends and expands beyond its origins, is disruptive and uncontrollable, and exists because it is connected with the local specificities and events.

These flows are also flows of *desire*. In *Anti-Oedipus* (1983) Deleuze and Guattari reject Freud's theory of desire as *lack*. Instead they argue that desire must be seen as *production* and *productive*. Desire is a desiring-machine that is linked to social forces and structures. The unconscious and sexual drives are the desiring-machines. The desiring-machine produces a line or flow of desire that intersects, merges and conflicts with social forces. Deleuze and Guattari use a machinic model to describe this process: '[T]here are no desiring-machines that exist outside the social machines that they form on a large scale; and no social machines without the desiring machines that inhabit them on a small scale' (2004: 373). They argue that the very notion of family (with its Oedipal struggles, as Freud argued) was an attempt to regulate the flows of desire. Rejecting psychoanalysis' emphasis on the family, they argue that the 'family' must be widened out to include the social. Flows of desire would produce a new reality, where desiring-production would be the central mode of human production.

The self is the site of a *connection* with the regimes of thought in any culture (note the parallels with poststructuralist views of the self as located within discourse). Deleuze and Guattari argue that the subject's sense of self must be seen as being in constant, dynamic relation with the context. The context might seek order, linearity and suppression of desires. But the self equally constantly, pushes the drives. The self is a territory constantly fought over by the social forces and the drives. They posit a Body-without-Organs (BWO), a site of this contest where the drives and the social forces seek the upper hand. The BWO is constructed and reconstructed endlessly. With this the self is constantly shifting, resisting and expressing. Such a subject is a nomad. Deleuze and Guattari propose *nomadology* as an alternative to the tightly organized, repressive and linear social forces of history, the machinic age, biomedicine and law. Thus, in Deleuze and Guattari, the subject is

- a site of directionless, unorganized flow of drives;
- a site of social forces;

- the territory of the battle between the above two;
- a shifting, evolving, changing site;
- linked to others (through desires and flows) in a rhizomatic assemblage;
- both subject *and* resistant to control (maintenance, order, or territorialization).

Deleuze and Guattari's BWO is a classic poststructuralist notion where the subject is a site of forces rather than stability, always changing rather than static, a series of desires rather than a constant identity. Proposing a *rhizomatic* self—a rhizome is a botanical term where grass, for instance, grows randomly, and the actual plant 'self' is only the series of connections (nodes) with no identifiable beginning and end—where individual boundaries are unclear, and every 'self' is a multiplicity of desire and social forces. Deleuze and Guattari define the rhizome in some detail thus:

> Principles of connection and heterogeneity: any point of a rhizome can be connected to anything other, and must be … collective assemblages of enunciation … multiplicity … has neither subject nor object, only determinations, magnitudes, and dimensions that cannot increase in number without the multiplicity changing in nature … A rhizome may be broken, shattered at a given spot, but it will start up again on one of its old lines, or on new lines … There is a rupture in the rhizome whenever segmentary lines explode into a line of flight, but the line of flight is part of the rhizome. (2004: 7–8, 10)

Deleuze and Guattari are essentially concerned with questions of control, regimentation and limitations. Their ideas of 'lines of flight', desiring and nomadic deterritorializations are moves toward a different way of thinking itself, and shares much with poststructuralism.

POSTSTRUCTURALISM, POSTMODERNISM AND NARRATIVE

Poststructuralism with its notions of contamination, *différance*, textuality and intertextuality destroyed the notion of a single author, meaning or text. By positing multiplicities, lines of flight, openness, rhizomes, reproductions and anti-totality, postmodernism proposed fragmentation, freedom and simulation. Contemporary fiction from the late 1980s has often adopted some of these insights, as exemplified in the work of Umberto Eco, Donald Barthelme, John Barth, Thomas Pynchon, Milan Kundera, Gabriel García Márquez, Don De Lillo, Salman Rushdie, Irvine Welsh, Graham Swift and Martin Amis. These authors destroy our views of what a text is and what the author means. They ask us to distrust their authorial voice and thus take away our certainty in the text (for we assume that meaning rests in the author, and when the author her/himself is uncertain we have no other reliable 'source'). These are the features of the postmodern–poststructuralist narrative form. Thinkers like Brian McHale (1992) and Linda Hutcheon (1995) have explored the numerous narrative consequences of these developments in Theory.

Postmodern narratology and narrative theory examines the nature of these contemporary or/and some older narratives, such as Sterne's *Tristram Shandy* or Joyce's *Ulysses*, the two favoured texts in both postmodernism and poststructuralism, within the frames proposed by these theories. It involves noting the following features:

1. The absence of one consistent point of view (where the narration shifts between narrators, none of whom is privileged over the other), as a result of which we are not sure whose narrative to trust;

2. The merging of 'factual' (i.e., verifiable, documented) history and fiction (for example in Graham Swift's *Waterland*);

3. The merging of fantasy and reality, dreams and reality so that it becomes impossible to rely on any storyline (in Rushdie's *Midnight's Children*, Saleem Sinai's narration of the war suggests his location there, but then he also claims that the war happened because he imagined it into existence);

4. The mix of popular/mass culture and high cultural elements so that no hierarchy of cultural practices is allowed (Rushdie's use of Hindi film songs, but also the opera);

5. The fragmented nature of narrative where there is no linear or cause-and-effect sequence in the plot/narration, even as digressions occur alongside the main story, so that we cannot separate the minor story from the main one (for example, in Alan Sealy's *The Trotter-Nama*, recipes and other stories merge and sometimes conflict with the main story of the Trotter family, even though these recipes are from the Trotter family archives);

6. A sense of play within the narrative, teasing the reader without offering the meaning at once (John Fowles' fiction);

7. The mixing of absurdist, folkloric elements, or the retelling of canonical and well-known tales with a different politics, goal and effect (Barthelme retelling Snow White);

8. The writing drawing attention to the act of writing itself (for example, in the works of Martin Amis or Italo Calvino, where there are struggling authors and the book the reader is currently reading is being written as part of the story s/he is reading);

9. The use of different formats for storytelling: letters, diaries, official documents. In the 1990s the use of the graphic novel medium—associated for a long time with comic books—to talk about traumatic and horrific events like the Holocaust Art Spiegelman (*Maus I* and *II*) or the Bosnian

genocide (Joe Sacco) show a postmodern trend in refusing to privilege only official or 'historical' narrative forms.

POSTSTRUCTURALISM AND THE THEORY OF MINOR LITERATURE

Once again, Deleuze and Guattari have been at the forefront in discussions of subversion and politically significant literature.

Deleuze and Guattari begin their classic work, *Kafka: Towards a Minor Literature* (1975), by arguing that great literature would be minor because its language would be 'foreign', open, unfinalizable, creative and mutating. It would be about process rather than event. In order to understand this idea we need to go back to their earlier work, *A Thousand Plateaus*. Deleuze and Guattari in this work provide a distinction between the majoritarian and the minoritarian cultural practices. Majoritarian is an opposition based on already established terms where the distinction relies on one privileged or dominant term. In the opposition 'man' and 'woman', 'man' is privileged and therefore the opposition itself is majoritarian. There is no norm or standard for 'woman'. Deleuze and Guattari propose that once a term becomes *expressive* rather than creative we can see a majoritarian impulse. Instead we need to think of becoming woman, a possibility rather than a definition. We cannot think of woman as standard because it would then become majoritarian.

Deleuze and Guattari see Kafka as 'minor' because he was a Czech writing in a language not his own, and therefore without 'standards' and definitions. This openness to change, to possibilities and becoming constitutes great literature. Kafka, they propose, wrote without a sense of 'the people' or any fixed identity. Instead he wrote about a world, a people to come, somewhere in the future, a people in the process of defining themselves, rather than a people who 'had' an identity. 'Minor', as we can see, is emphatically *not* a pejorative term, but one that stands as the icon of difference, of process and becoming. 'Minor' stands for freedom from oppressive norms and standards, from fixed definitions. It is the literature that does not conform to role models or of stereotypes. It rejects definitions and is open to difference. It thrives on defiance and subversion and resists totality of any kind.

Language, they argue, is not associated with a body or person, but is collective and dispersed. It is, in other words, deterritorialized. When it becomes associated with a particular person, event or context it is *re-territorialized*. Noise, signs, sounds are pre-human, pre-individual. When we associate humans with inventing language we have re-territorialized it by locating it within the human. Minor literature is the language and literature of groups that seek creativity rather than expression of any identity. Thus, subjugated groups only represent, but subject groups seek identity through writing and language. What we see here is an important distinction. Literature that is searching for an appropriate language, that rejects available language and forms of expression, that invents new languages belongs to subject groups for whom the very act of writing is the search, and the language is the language of this search, of becoming. The subject is formed in the literature. The subjugated groups, in contrast, work with available identities, with ideas of identities already in place.

We can think of Toni Morrison and Alice Walker as writers of 'minor literature'. They refused to accept the identities that were readily available to them: blacks in America. Instead they set about trying to find new forms of expression that would invent new identities—blacks, women, lesbian, marginal. The turn to oral traditions and storytelling formats by Aboriginal writers in Australia and Canada is again a search for a form that can invent new identities rather than simply accept ready-made ones. In all these cases, the significance has been to see 'black', 'aboriginal' or 'woman' not as a fixed identity but as a process, a series of negotiations with other identities (white, male). There is nothing 'proper', no standard identity in these authors. Nothing that is pre-given is acceptable.

If we were to reduce this complex notion of 'minor literature' to its basic assumption, then we can say that any writing that refuses to provide a unified, definitive identity but focuses on escapes, flows, deterritorialization, unfinalizability and becoming would be 'minor literature'. A literature that

- studies differences, deviations, variations and possibilities rather than fixed, stable identities and
- seeks evolution rather than finished products.

would be minor literature. Minor literature adapts other forms, steals from multiple sources, creates disruptive images—Toni Morrison's ghosts, for example—and thus refuses a type. In the late twentieth century some forms of science fiction that refuses easy binaries of man/woman, human/animal would be 'minor literature' (examples would include the white male writer, William Gibson, and the black woman writer Octavia Butler). Minor literature does not have to be *by* and *about* minorities.

FURTHER READING

Norris, Christopher. 2002. *Deconstruction: Theory and Practice*. 1982. London and New York: Routledge.

Smart, Barry. 1995. *Foucault*. London: Routledge.

Bogue, Ronald. 1989. *Deleuze and Guattari*. London: Routledge.

Woods, Tim. 1999. *Beginning Postmodernism*. Manchester: Manchester University Press.

NOTES

1. This sentence has been usually translated as 'there is nothing outside the text', and has been at the centre of controversy, with critics claiming that Derrida was another New Critic underscoring the centrality of texts.

2. For a sample of deconstructive readings, specifically of poetry see Richard Machin and Christopher Norris (eds), *Post-Structuralist Readings of English Poetry* (1987), with essays by some of the best known critics of this persuasion: Catherine Belsey, Geoffrey Hartman, Gayatri Spivak, Harold Bloom, Norris and J. Hillis Miller.

3. In her later work, specifically in *Powers of Horror* (1982), Kristeva would speak of the 'abject'—that which cannot be expelled but must be expelled in order to retain the sense of the self.

3 Psychoanalytic Criticism

We use the term 'Oedipus complex' with a great degree of ease today, and, indeed, it is part of everyday language now. The notion of an Oedipus complex evolved out of an analysis of the situation described by the ancient Greek playwright Sophocles of the Greek king, Oedipus, who killed his father and married his mother, without being aware of the true nature of either of the acts. Critical interpretations of the play yielded a theory of the human (in this case, male) psyche, and proved to be one of the most widely known and controversial intellectual ideas of the twentieth century.

Today, texts are read for the 'desires' they seem to conceal, the kinds of 'drives' in their characters and the 'unconscious' in them. This critical move to explore the nature of the human psyche by exploring the deeper, hidden meanings of texts and their characters is identifiable as a major critical method today, one that we can define as 'psychoanalytic'.

OPENING MOVES

THE PSYCHOANALYTIC TURN: SIGMUND FREUD

Such interpretations of literary texts and figures like Shakespeare's plays and Dostoevsky were not done by academic critics but rather by a man who came from a different profession altogether. Trained as a doctor and a practising therapist for what were considered psychological problems, Sigmund Freud not only invented a whole new discipline and medical mode, psychoanalysis, but also generated concepts and ideas that have had an enormous impact on literary criticism.

Freud emphasized that language concealed, revealed or modified hidden desires, anxieties and fears. His point was that desire does not express itself easily because culture does not allow or facilitate it, and we need to pay attention to language and other forms of symbolic expression—gestures, sounds, facial expression, writing—to discover it. In this, Freud was exploring a link between language and the unconscious—a move that was to become the core of both the psychoanalytic practice (described as the 'talking cure') and criticism. The conscious self projects the kind of image that is culturally and socially acceptable. But the unconscious finds ways and means to express itself too—and this is what literary texts and language allows. This was, in fact, Freud's greatest insight: The mechanisms of the unconscious, of desires and fears also required and acquired a language of their own.

Since sexuality is the drive that is most subject to the social and the cultural norms of control, classical Freudian theory emphasizes the role of the individual's sexuality in making of an unconscious. Thus, psychoanalytic criticism emphasizes the role of sexuality and the sex drive in the making of a person's subjectivity, where many sexual desires are consigned to the unconscious.

> Psychoanalytic criticism, therefore, explores the language of the unconscious, of the repressed and the hidden as embodied in literary or cultural texts such as art or fiction, with particular attention to the repression of sexuality and its desires.

Psychoanalytic criticism uncovers the 'subject' of the author as revealed through the images, the language and the codes of her/his work. It asks questions of the author's attempts to conceal her/his desires and drives, and the cultural codes that force her/him to do so.

Freud's key theoretical moves on the mind and the unconscious in *psychoanalysis* have to be studied in some detail before we look at the use they can be put to in *psychoanalytic literary criticism*.

The Structure of the Human Psyche

Freud distinguished three components of the human psyche:

1. the ego
2. the super ego
3. the id

1. The ego is the conscious mind, which we work with, use and are most aware of. It mediates between the unconscious id and the superego. It is the source of our decision-making and our rational thought.
2. The super ego is what can be called our conscience. It is drawn from social settings and cultural codes and influences the way the conscious works.
3. The id, Freud's favourite territory, is the area of instincts, dreams, desires and all that that does not come to the fore in our consciousness. This is the unconscious.

Freud proposed that the human psyche has an area into which go all those desires and fantasies that cannot be expressed. This area he termed the *unconscious* ('unconscious' because we are unaware of its existence). The process through which certain desires, especially sexual, are pushed into the unconscious so that they do not influence our daily lives and our conscious mind is called *repression*. Freud himself described the concept of repression as the 'cornerstone' of psychoanalytic theory.

Repression is the hiding away of something in our minds; what is hidden away exists in our unconscious. Guilt-inducing desire and traumatic events such as the death of a loved one or abuse are quickly shunted out of the conscious and relegated into the unconscious, to emerge only in particular moments (usually of dreams or stress). The unconscious is the greatest threat to our identity as rational humans.

Thus, forbidden desires that, if expressed, can lead to guilt are shut away in the unconscious through repression.

However, what is repressed does not always stay repressed. The unconscious emerges in particular moments as images, dreams, jokes (famously termed *Freudian slips*, or technically, *parapraxes*) and even art. The psychoanalyst explores these images and uncovers those desires that have been repressed. For literary criticism this is an important insight. Freud was proposing that *art draws upon the unconscious* for its themes and images.

All human life, for Freud, is caught in the tensions generated by two basic principles. The *pleasure principle* is one where all our acts are governed by the need to attain pleasure and avoid 'un-pleasure'. The *reality principle* enables us to understand that our pleasures cannot all be fulfilled the way we want them, and, therefore, inspires us to seek other routes of attaining pleasure.

Sexuality is the primary 'drive' in our subjectivity according to Freud. He termed this the *libido*. The problem is, according to Freud, not all sex drives or desires can be put into operation. Therefore, what gets repressed primarily is the sex drive. An individual's sexual identity is, hence, partly the result of expression of desires and partly the condition caused by a repression of the same. In order to explain this Freud developed the idea of the Oedipus complex.

The Oedipus Complex

Let us take the complex in sequence.

- For Freud the problem with sexual desires begins with the child's dependence on the mother (it must be noted that Freud is here speaking of the *male* child). The love for/of the mother is the dominant theme in the child's psyche in the early years.
- Soon the child begins to see his father as a rival for the mother's love. The father restricts the child's expression of love through a threat—a threat that the child imagines—of castration. The male child imagines that the girl child lacks the penis because she has been castrated for her excessive love of the mother.
- The child, therefore, begins to develop fantasies of killing his father so that he (the child) will have no rivals for his mother's love. This fantasy is what Freud famously (and controversially) called the Oedipus complex.
- Soon the child sees the father as possessing the greater authority (especially because the father can castrate the child for excessive desire) in the relationship (child–mother–father). This marks the shift in affiliation: The child, now seeing the father as the source of all power and desire, shifts his focus to the father.
- The desire for the mother is shut away in the unconscious when the child accepts the law that 'you shall not make love to your mother'. This law becomes the threshold of the conscious–unconscious.

For Freud the Oedipus complex is the source of all repressed desire, the emblem of all that is repressed because even *love is antagonistic* in nature when triangulated between the boy, the mother and the father. The Oedipus complex enabled Freud to argue that all desire, repression and anxiety are based on the condition of prohibition, or what he termed *taboo*. The child never really overcomes the complex, but merely shuts it away.

> The unconscious consists of repressed desires, such as the love for the mother, which has been prohibited by the law of the father where the child imagines he might be castrated by the father for loving the mother, and whose repression produces the Oedipus complex, that, in turn, leads the male child to change affections to the more powerful father, who he now sees as the symbol of authority.

Freud argued, as we have already noted, that the repressed or the unconscious emerges in art, jokes or dreams. Freud analysed each expression of the unconscious in his career, producing cult texts for later critics (the first consists of readings of texts like *Hamlet*, and the novels of Dostoevsky; the second embodied in the essay 'Jokes and their Relation to the Unconscious'; the third in the classic *The Interpretation of Dreams*). Freud proposed, in some of his more controversial essays, that the artist is a kind of neurotic, where art is a means of fulfilling otherwise ungratified desires.

In other cases, when not expressed in some form, the repressed often emerges as neurosis. Hence, the analyst's job is to delve into the unconscious of the neurotic and free the repressed, to find some means of expressing the repressed without prohibitions.

Dreams and the Unconscious

Freud described dreams as the 'royal road' to the unconscious, arguing that dreams provide us with the best understanding of the repressed desires in us. Because the unconscious is precisely that, the *un*conscious, direct access to it and its contents is impossible. However, it emerges when the conscious is shut down, as during sleep.

Freud argued that during sleep there was no danger of the unconscious desires being put into action/articulation. They find a measure of fulfilment when they express themselves as dreams. The dream may not be a direct expression of the repressed desire. In fact, Freud argues that the dream is a state of tension between the power of the impulse or instinctual desire and the power of the repressing force. Dreams are codes, presenting themselves as complex images so that the repressing force is bypassed. They are distorted expressions of desire that have to be decoded by the analyst in order to understand what desires and prohibitions exist in the person's unconscious. Dreams are, therefore, the expression of a repressed desire, they show us the unconscious.

For Freud—and this is the link to psychoanalytic criticism—dreams are a language, the language of the unconscious and of repressed desires. This language is broadly termed 'dream-work' in Freud, and is the mechanism of dreams. The dream work has two central dimensions: latent dream content and manifest dream content.

Latent dream content is the actual content of the unconscious that seeks expression. The expression of the content in the form of images or events in one's dream is the *manifest dream content*.

The problem is that all of the latent dream content is not clearly visible within the manifest one; the latent dream content is concealed inside complex structures and codes. This content can be revealed only through a thorough analysis of the manifest dream. Freud argued that the latent dream content undergoes four processes or stages—the dream-work—before it expresses itself in the manifest dream.

These are as follows:

i. *Condensation*: The manifest dream does not capture the full extent of the latent content. The latent content is condensed in the manifest dream. Several elements are superimposed on each other to produce a complex image in the manifest dream. A situation may be expressed (in the dream) as a symbol. A traumatic situation may be expressed as a face or person. A whole series of events may be expressed only as one particular symbol. The task is to unravel each element so that the full extent of the latent dream is revealed.

ii. *Displacement*: Here the latent dream content works as association, and then is expressed in complex images. Freud gave a great deal of importance to displacement. For example, in Sylvia Plath's poem, 'Daddy', the image of a Nazi soldier/officer occurs. As we proceed through the poem we realize that the Nazi soldier is a version of her father. Displacement works through association, and here an authoritarian father is associated with the authoritarian Nazi officer. One stands in for the other when the power (and cruelty) of one is *displaced* on to another. As we can see, there is a sense of association and contiguity here, and that generates literary metaphors: the Nazi officer as a metaphor for the father.

iii. *Representation and Representability*: The language of the dream often uses complex images that have no apparent basis in reality. Freud argued that the latent dream content took recourse to a strange language or images where there is no rational connection between any of them. Many of these may borrow from cultural contexts, and the dreamer may not even be aware of them. Dreams acquire a language of representation in which contradictory elements may coexist. Phallic symbols in dreams—upright objects like towers, spires or poles—are representations of the male organ, and constitute a language where, even though there is no logical or rational connection between the two, the dream organizes them into one image. Freud's emphasis on such sexual images often led to accusations about excessive focus on the carnal.

iv. *Secondary Revision*: The dreamer himself/herself interprets the dream, but revises it in the process. This process is accompanied by a certain amount of censorship where the dreamer ignores or 'forgets' all the elements of the dream. The conscious mind organizes the elements of the dream into recognizable and acceptable themes or images, and ignores the rest. Thus, in addition to the condensation, the displacement and the representation—all of which disguise the true latent content by providing complex and often unexplainable images in the manifest dream—we also have revision where the dreamer rejects certain uncomfortable aspects of the dream.

At this point it becomes clear that for Freud

- art and dreams are both means of expressing desire,
- art and dreams are mechanisms of avoiding the censorship that prohibits desire or its expression and
- art and dreams bypass consciousness when they express the repressed.

In most cases, dreams and art (and Freud uses Da Vinci's *Mona Lisa* as an example) are expressions of childhood desires and fantasies. These desires have been repressed as taboo, and find expression only in art or dreams.

Psychoanalytic critics, therefore, adapt this model to read literary texts. Such a method embarks on unraveling a text's themes to discover an unconscious buried in it. This unconscious—what Maud Ellmann in her introduction to a volume of essays on psychoanalytic criticism terms the 'textual unconscious' (1994)—consists of repressed desires, anxieties, fears and paranoias. The literary critic's task is, therefore, to locate this unconscious, which often takes the form of locating sexual images, sexual codes and anxieties in texts. Ellmann mentions two such overdone explications of literary texts (Frederick Crews' 1975 reading of Joseph Conrad's *Heart of Darkness* and Marie Bonaparte's 1933 reading of Edgar Allan Poe's 'The Pit and the Pendulum') where the entire analysis unravels sexual themes and ignores everything else in them. There is, therefore, some justification in the charge that for psychoanalytic critics there is only the carnal and the sexual.

Freud on Women

Freud was notoriously uninterested in women's sexuality. His comments on the subject deal indirectly with the matter, focusing instead on women as sex objects for men (in his essays, 'A Special Type of Choice of Object Made by Men', 1910, and 'On the Universal Tendency to Debasement in the Sphere of Love', 1912).

In his work on the Oedipus complex he proposed that as children, the little boy and girl initially share the same sexual history: the desire for the mother. With time, they recognize the phallus is what distinguishes the father. Here the boy acquires the castration complex—that unless he gives up his love for his phallus-less mother his father might castrate him—and strives to represent the phallus himself. The girl is furious with the mother for lacking the phallus, transfers her love to the father-object, and strives to have the phallus. In a later work he was to declare that 'the castration complex is of the profoundest importance in the formation alike of character and of neurosis' (qtd. in Mitchell 1983: 13). The girl, therefore, goes through life suffering from a penis-envy and organ-inferiority. This argument was to divide the psychoanalytic group into two, for many believed that Freud gave too much importance to the castration complex.

As to how the girl, who sets off to be like her father rather than her mother because the father has a phallus, then begins to acquire femininity is something

Freud never really discussed (he puzzled over this process he had expressed in a 1933 essay, 'Femininity').

Freud believed that men split women symbolically into mothers (or sisters) and prostitutes. The paradox is that the former cannot be sexually desired, though they are supposed to be the kind of women a man should marry; while the latter are socially unacceptable and are sexually desired. As long as a woman represents the mother she remains a forbidden oedipal object-choice. The man goes to a woman who is a prostitute to protect the idea of the mother's sexual purity. According to Nancy Chodorow, this argument of Freud's gives us the psychodynamics of a split in Western culture (Chodorow 1991). Men, argues Freud, deny female sexual constitution completely.

Psychoanalysis, as developed by Freud, believes that a person develops through their sexuality. When it proposes that the unconscious is full of unfulfilled (sexual) desires and that the unconscious always returns, it is, in fact, suggesting that our repressed sexual desires play an important role in our lives.

It is also clear that for Freud and psychoanalysis the male is the centre of all discussion, and the female is only an adjunct (A similar charge can be made against Lacan.). Freud anticipated this charge by arguing that psychoanalysis cannot deal with anything other than phallocentric (the term used to describe theories that centre around the phallus) because its analysis is of a human society that is male-centred. The mother–child relation or the development of sexuality cannot be seen without the figure of the father, and hence the significance of the phallus. Following Freud, psychoanalytic criticism:

- looks for the images of authority that stand in for the father figure;
- seeks the themes of taboo and transgression;
- reads the taboo theme as connected to repression;
- seeks to understand the sexual basis of repression;
- unravels the expressions of the unconscious;
- reads the images of repression in literary and visual images;
- reorients the literary analysis into looking at submerged images;
- locates the images at the intersection of repression and expression.

There are variations among psychoanalytic critics. For instance, feminist and queer critics like Shoshana Felman and Judith Butler, who have adapted psychoanalytic modes, often find problems with Freud's male-centric and heterosexual interpretations.

As we have noted psychoanalytic critics who use Freudian theory generally look for a set of themes. We shall now explore the different varieties of psychoanalytic criticism.

But before that, we need to look at a particular school of criticism that, while not being psychoanalytic, shows overlaps with it in terms of its emphasis on the psychology of reception, of the reader's response.

READER-RESPONSE CRITICISM

Reader-response criticism begins with the assumption that meanings of texts lie in the reader's experience of the text. A competent reader perceives deeper meanings from metaphors, figural language and ambiguities. Every reader approaches a text with certain expectations, which the text might or might not fulfil. Readers import into their reading their personal experiences, their psychic structures and their awareness of literary conventions.

In a model of reading that is explicitly derived from psychoanalysis, Norman Holland, in *The Dynamics of Literary Response* (1968), proposed that readers use literary texts to fulfil their fantasies. To begin with, the 'skilled reader also gives the text meaning by making connections between all the parts of the text' (28). These 'connections' are related to the reader's secret fears and desires: 'It is from such deep and fearful roots of our most personal experience that literature gets its power and drive' (30). Literature becomes an enjoyable experience precisely because the otherwise unacceptable fantasies and desires become sublimated into acceptable and bearable literary images, ideas and themes: 'Literature transforms our primitive wishes and fears into significance and coherence, and this transformation gives us pleasure' (30). Many of these fears and desires, Holland underscores, are unconscious. With this move Holland is able to propose that literature appeals to us in some unconscious way where it caters to those fears and desires that we did not even know existed. Literature draws out our expectations and then 'transforms' them. As Holland puts it in his 1979 essay 'Reading and Identity': expectation is 'putting the literary work in the sequence of a person's wishes in time'. In his subsequent work, *5 Readers Reading* (1975), Holland modified this model proposing, instead, that every reader has a 'core' identity that generates a particular kind of reading when it interacts with the text. Holland writes: 'Readers respond to literature in terms of their own "lifestyle" (or "character" or "personality" or "identity")' (8). Developing this theme Holland writes:

> To analyze the text in formal isolation as so many "words-on-a-page" (in the old formula of the New Criticism) is a highly artificial procedure. A literary text, after all, in an objective sense consists only of a certain configuration of specks of carbon black on dried wood pulp. When these marks become words, when those words become images or metaphors or characters or events, they do so because the reader plays the part of a prince to the sleeping beauty. He gives them life out of his own desires. When he does so, he brings his lifestyle to bear on the work. He mingles his unconscious loves and fears and adaptations with the words and images he synthesizes at a conscious level. (9)

This means every reader develops a different meaning of the text based on her/his 'core', or what Holland terms 'lifestyle'. But Holland was also careful to suggest that individuals may share their approaches with other members of their cultural group because, as he puts it, 'people belong to the same cultural group, not merely because they behave alike, nor because they expect the same things of others, but especially because they construe their experience in the same way' (241). 'What the members share,' writes Holland, 'becomes the consensus of thought or action' (244).

A critic working around the same time as Holland, Wolfgang Iser, argued that every sentence in a literary work sets up particular expectations. He writes: 'The individual sentences not only work together to shade in what is to come; they also form an expectation in this regard' (2003 [1972]: 191–92). However, if all the reader's expectations are fulfilled in the next sentence it leaves very little for her/ him to do: '[W]e can only accept or reject the thesis forced upon us' (192). What happens with literary texts, argues Iser, is that every sentence offers, 'opens up a particular horizon', which is then 'modified, if not completely changed by succeeding sentences'. These modifications also cause us, the readers, to reflect on what has gone before. It thus involves us in the text—what Iser terms a 'creative' process. As he puts it: '[T]he literary text activates our own faculties, enabling us to recreate the world it represents' (192). Iser thus locates meaning in the interaction between text and the reader's imaginative–creative faculties.

However, it is not only the individual reader's mind or psyche that determines the meanings of texts. Meanings are established through a consensus among a group of readers, what Stanley Fish famously called 'interpretive communities' (1980). Fish, for example, does not want to know what the text intends or 'means': he is interested in what the text does when the reader opens and 'consumes' it. Thus, the formal, structural features of a literary work do not exist independent of the reader's use of them. A novel's stylistic features, for example, will work only when the reader is able to play with or interpret them. The text, in other words, cannot be taken to exist independent of the reader. A reader 'projects' her/his assumptions—psychological, personal but also cultural and social —onto the text and thus makes meaning out of it. What the reader thinks or believes as s/he approaches the text is determined by the community or social context. As Fish puts it, the reader's reading practices or strategies are

community property, and insofar as they at once enable and limit the operations of his consciousness, he is too [community property]. . . . Interpretive communities are made up of those who share interpretive strategies not for reading but for writing texts, for constituting their properties. (1980: 14)

Communication itself happens, according to Fish, because

a way of thinking, a form of life, shares us, and implicates us in a world of already-in-place objects, purposes, goals, procedures, values, and so on; and it is to the features of that world that any words we utter will be heard as necessarily referring. (303–4)

Reader-response criticism, especially in the modes deployed by Holland and Iser owes much to psychoanalysis and shifted the focus to the *reception* of literary texts. We now turn to a different appropriation of psychoanalysis in critical theory.

C. G. JUNG, ARCHETYPES AND THE 'COLLECTIVE UNCONSCIOUS'

A philosopher and psychoanalyst, C. G. Jung treated the human self as the totality of all psychic processes. Rejecting Freudian theories of the libido as restricted to the sexual, Jung proposed that the libido was energy that could be channelized into any field. His second key departure from Freud was his idea of archetypes.

Freud, as we have seen, saw the self's dreams and fantasies as proceeding from the unconscious. Jung proposed that, while the unconscious was important, the self was also influenced by social norms and the world around it. The human psyche, postulated Jung, draws upon a set of 'primordial images' that are often cross-cultural, and have been existent for a long time in the *collective imagination* of the human race itself. In other words, Jung was suggesting that the human imagination draws upon images and ideas from myths and legends that occur across cultures and time-spans. These images he termed *archetypes*, and they emerge from a 'collective unconscious' common to all mankind and are not restricted to a particular individual or self. Art, argued Jung, often exhibited universal images— the archetypes—from this collective unconscious. Jung's significance lay in a radical shift

- from the individual's unconscious to the social–collective one and
- from the individual creation of particular dreams/images to a social store-house of common images and themes.

In literary criticism Canadian critic Northrop Frye developed Jungian theories to study literary texts.

Archetypal Criticism

Maud Bodkin's 1934 work *Archetypal Patterns in Poetry* and later the works of Northrop Frye developed Jungian psychoanalysis in literary studies. Bodkin iden-tified heaven and hell, the Oedipal, rebirth, father-figures, the hero as literary archetypes. Frye codified literary symbolism based on what he termed 'mythoi'. Literature, Frye argued, drew upon transcendental genres such as romance (summer), tragedy (autumn), irony/satire (winter) and comedy (spring). These four genres constitute a 'central unifying myth' (as he put it in *Anatomy of Criticism*, 1957: 192). Frye further codified these genres and uncovered their basic archetypal structures. The romance is characterized by a quest theme where the hero descends into subterranean depths and danger and then rises. This descent and ascent, Frye argued, constituted the 'mythopoeic' equivalent of Jung's archetypes. Summer stands for the culmination of the year's seasons, just as romance and marriage culminates a life. Comedy is about fantasy and wish-fulfilment and, therefore, suited to spring, while satire's disillusioned mockery suits the coldness of winter. What archetypal criticism did was to link psychological states with literary symbols identified as 'universal'.

We now turn to a different appropriation of psychoanalysis in critical theory.

FEMINIST PSYCHOANALYSIS

The feminist versions of Freud and Lacan have focused on the issues of identity, sexuality (especially woman's sexuality), the structure of the family and the mother–daughter relationship (this last, in contrast with the classical psychoanalysis where the focus is on the father-son relationship).

MOTHERS, DAUGHTERS

Nancy Chodorow focuses on the mother–daughter relationship in her classic work *Reproduction and Mothering* (1978).

- Chodorow argues that mothers experience their daughters as their 'doubles', as an extension of their own life;
- daughters, therefore, find it difficult to form their own identities because they have a strong tendency to intimacy and care (the woman's child-caring role is perpetuated through this relationship between a mother and her child.);
- hence the 'core' identity of women, which Chodorow identifies (problematically) as narcissism, lack of self-control, weak ego-boundaries, proceeds from their inability to discover autonomy from their mothers;
- and, therefore, the daughter turns to the father who represents the outside world. For Chodorow this phase is when the daughter becomes aware of the social privileges of possessing a phallus.

Shifting focus briefly, Chodorow proposes that for boys, masculine identity is also achieved through a relationship with the mother. It is the mother who recognizes and emphasizes gender differences. The mother encourages the boy to *discover* autonomy from her. This is because the mothers experience their sons as separate from themselves (in sharp contrast to their relationship with their daughters where they do not see the daughter as separate).

Thus, for Chodorow, the Oedipus complex and the relationship with the father work differently for boys and girls. Girls, who stay attached in a narcissistic relationship with the mother, develop emotionally through relationships, nurture and care. Boys discover their masculine gender through independence. Chodorow's argument, as can be seen, was one of the first to stress the woman–woman (here the mother–daughter one) relationship as central to identity formation —something the later feminists would build on.

An influential strand within feminist psychoanalysis has been the study of feminine sexuality in the work of Juliet Mitchell, Jacqueline Rose and others (see the chapter on feminisms).

STRUCTURALIST PSYCHOANALYSIS

In the 1930s the French psychoanalyst Jacques Lacan advocated a 'return to Freud'. Lacan's psychoanalysis combined Freudian theory with the linguistics of Saussure and Émile Benveniste to produce some extraordinarily complex theories of the psyche. Lacan's work in *Écrits* (1977) and *The Four Fundamental Concepts of Psychoanalysis* (1977) proved highly influential for feminists and poststructuralists. It also generated a different psychoanalytic practice in France and elsewhere. As Shoshana Felman points out, Lacanian psychoanalysis is praxis (the practical treatment of a patient), a method (the technique used in the praxis) and a theory (2000: 90).

LACAN, LANGUAGE AND THE UNCONSCIOUS

Lacan begins, like Freud, with childhood. Lacan constructs a model of identity-formation that takes a three-stage process or 'orders', as Lacan calls them.

(i) *The Imaginary*. Here the child makes its first identification—with the reflection in the mirror. It now associates coordinated limbs and movements in the mirror with itself and thus forms a sense of the self. In the 'mirror stage', as Lacan terms it, the child's sense of the self is similar to its conception of the relationship between himself and the mother. Just as the child does not see a distinction between himself and the mother (what Lacan calls 'desire-of-the-mother'), looking into the mirror, he does not see any distinction between himself and the reflection. In the Imaginary the child seeks to erase all difference and otherness by imagining himself as the person in the mirror and seeing himself and his mother as the same. In Lacan's terms the mirror stage is a 'homologue for the Mother/Child symbolic relation'. Lacan then describes the child as the signifier and the mirror image/reflection as the signified: The child looks into the mirror and says: 'that's me', thereby giving himself some meaning. He thinks he can substitute himself with the mirror image. The child works with a *misrecognition*—that the smooth, coordinated and whole image in the mirror is himself. This stage is therefore *metaphoric* (we recall from our discussion of Jakobson that metaphor is *substitution*).

(ii) *The Symbolic*. This is the stage when the child acquires language, and is perhaps the most important formulation in Lacan. It is the moment in which the child enters society and social relations. In language, for example, the child discovers that society has different names for 'father', 'mother' and 'child'. She is 'Mother' in language, and is different from 'I'. The child discovers here an endless chain of signifiers: 'I', 'mother', 'father' and thereby discovers social relations. He moves along a chain of signifiers in a *metonymic displacement* from one to the other. It is the first sign of difference. The child discovers that he is different from others, and that he cannot desire the mother. He discovers the Symbolic Order that is external to himself, what Lacan terms the 'Other'. Thus, the 'desire of the mother' is now prohibited by the order or Name-of-the-father. There is a name (of the father) even when the father is not necessarily present. That is, the child may be threatened with a statement like: 'I will tell your father'. Here the absent father acquires a threatening presence because of the *name*. In the Symbolic, therefore, the absence of the Mother (absence because the child *cannot* have her, he is *not* her, she is *different*, and will always be desired because of her *absence*) is linked to the absence of the father, who is present only as a name. There are thus two absences: in the case of the mother, the desire of the absent mother, and in the case of the father the threat of the father in the very *name* 'father'. Lacan here is working with the *language of the Symbolic order* where 'Mother' stands for the desire of the absent mother and 'Father' stands for the threat of the absent. Both language and absence go together here. What is important to note here is that Lacan sees language as constituting a social bond in the Symbolic—an idea that would influence poststructuralist thinking later. Desire is based on a series of signifiers where the lost object of desire generates a chain of names acting as substitutes for the lost object. And desire, for Lacan, is primary.

(iii) *The Real.* This is the order that both the Imaginary and the Symbolic try to control. This is where the child's illusions (of being one with his reflection or being one with the mother) from the Imaginary is at odds with the sense of otherness from the Symbolic.

> Lacan identifies three stages in the making of the psyche: the Imaginary is the pre-linguistic (i.e., before language) where the child sees himself reflected in the mirror and considers himself whole and complete and one with the mother; the Symbolic is when the child acquires language and begins to understand difference, social relations, that he is not one with the mother or the primary desire of the mother and that the law of the father is supreme; the Real is the stage where the Imaginary and Symbolic both seek power and the psyche is caught between the 'lack' (i.e., the desire for the absent mother discovered during the Symbolic stage and eventually pushed into the unconscious) and the need to fulfil this lack.

Lacan suggests that all desire is linked to a lack: In fact, the lack *is* desire. Here he turns to linguistics and suggests that all signifiers merely gesture at the lack. When we pursue the signifier's meaning (i.e., the signified) to fill the lack what we find are more signifiers. We thus proceed on the chain of signifiers without ever reaching an *end-signified*. Desire thus remains as a lack, and constitutes our *unconscious/ repressed*. What is crucial here is that the loss of the object of desire (Mother) is what gives the child language. Language, therefore, is always connected with the *loss* of the object and the desire. Language itself is about lack, since signifiers do not lead to a final meaning but more signifiers. As Elizabeth Wright summarizes it, 'language imposes a chain of words along which the ego must move while the unconscious remains in search of the object it has lost' (1984: 111).

With this move Lacan links language with desire and the unconscious. In the unconscious desire is structured like language: the name/signifier ('Mother') as opposed to the signified (the object, Mother) that the child will never get. To put it differently:

- 'Mother' is the *name* (signifier) the unconscious gives to the absence and to the desire.
- Mother is the object/body (signified) the child seeks but never acquires.

The unconscious thus develops a language of/for desire: 'Mother'.

This language comes from the *outside* (as we have seen in the section on the Symbolic Order) and is, therefore, the language of the Other. Between the signifier and the signified mediates the language of the Other (the *name* of the father that pushes the desire for the mother into the unconscious). And, therefore, the unconscious with its desire is the discourse of the Other. This complex argument is worth mapping as a step-by-step process.

1. There is desire.
2. There is an object of desire (the Mother).
3. The child discovers that there is a *name* for the Mother.
4. This name is from the language, which comes from outside the child, from the social order, i.e., from the Other.
5. There is *only a name*, the Mother cannot be attained.
6. The missing object of desire is *replaced* by a name.
7. The name or speech of/from the Other drives desire *inside* by replacing the object of desire with the name.
8. Desire is thus repressed and enters the unconscious.
9. Desire is always, therefore, about *lack/ absence* of the *object* of desire, which has been replaced by a name.
10. In the unconscious desire is always linked to names, where the names lead to more names but never to the object of desire.
11. The unconscious is about a perpetual lack/desire.
12. The unconscious is also based on a structure of difference (between names that become codes for relations: 'mother', 'father', 'child', and the chain of

signifiers), just as language is based on a structure of difference and endless chains of signification (As we have seen, the child proceeds along a chain of names seeking a signified that he will never reach, just as in Saussure's notion of language, we move along a chain of signifiers and every signifier leads us to more signifiers rather than a signified.).

13. The unconscious is *produced* as the repository of desire, through the *effect* of speech/names from the outside/Other, which drives desire inwards, substituting the signifier of Mother instead for the object-Mother.

14. Therefore, the unconscious is constituted by desire and the effect of language of the Other.

This sequence leads to Lacan's more famous formulations: '[T]he unconscious is the discourse of the Other' (2003[1977]: 190) and '[T]he unconscious is structured like a language' (1981[1977]: 20). What Lacan is proposing is that the unconscious is available to us only through language—whether of desire or of psychoanalysis.

Lacan and Feminine Sexuality

Lacan adapted the theories of language from Saussure and Benveniste to outline a theory of feminine sexuality. Lacan suggests that the symbolic plays a significant role in the development of feminine sexuality.

Woman's sexuality is inseparable from representations (that is language, the Symbolic) of the same. The images and the symbols for 'woman', in fact, begin to define the woman. Thus, symbols that identify men and women differently in terms of their bodies (genitals), as in signs over toilet doors (Lacan's own example), imply that *anatomical difference is sexual difference*. The sexual difference is based on the *language of difference*. The circulation of the phallus as a signifier constructs the signifieds of the sexual difference.

Further, Lacan located women in the social sphere where she is constructed as an object of exchange and as the object in language (i.e., woman as a category in language). In anticipation of later writers like Luce Irigaray, Lacan proposed that women are constituted in language as an *exception*, as what she *lacks* and what she is *not*. She is defined against the man (woman is *not* man). It is not that she is outside language but that she is constituted within language only in particular ways as a *negative*.

Lacan's theories of the unconscious and the three 'orders' proved controversial and influential. Jacqueline Rose, Elizabeth Grosz, Shoshana Felman, Juliet Mitchell worked through both Freud and Lacan with a feminist agenda.

POSTSTRUCTURALIST PSYCHOANALYSIS

With the influence of Jacques Derrida and poststructuralism psychoanalytic criticism entered a new phase in the 1970s and after. One of the key thinkers who combined insights from deconstruction with the kabbala (Jewish mystical writings and teachings about the world, the creator and the nature of human beings) and Freudian theory was Harold Bloom. Bloom's work has particular interest for literary critics because he focuses mainly on literary texts and authors (Lacan writes on painting, Derrida writes on painting, architecture, law and literature).

FREUDIAN REVISIONISM: HAROLD BLOOM

In *Agon* (1983), *A Map of Misreading* (1975) and *The Anxiety of Influence* (1984) Bloom developed a full-fledged reading of 'influence'. Bloom begins with the assumption that all poets start their career with an anxiety. This anxiety is a father-threat: that older, earlier poets, who come to symbolize the father, have already done all there is to be done. The newcomer or the latecomer poet cannot escape the unconscious threat of the father-poet. The younger poet fears castration. Hence, the younger poet embarks on a process of re-reading (what Bloom terms 'misreading') the earlier poets in order to survive. He must deal with the (Oedipal) threat of the father so that he can write.

Misreading is thus a *psychic defence* against the father. It takes the form of a series of tropes that slowly allows the younger poet to incorporate the older poet into his work. This results in the making of the new poet into what Bloom terms a 'strong poet'. According to Bloom, it is through the six *revisionary* modes given below that the anxiety of the father-poet is subsumed and negotiated.

Primordial Forces	Rhetorical Figures	Psychological
(1) Clinamen	Irony	Reaction-formation
(2) Tessera	Synecdoche	Reversal
(3) Kenosis	Metonymy	Regression
(4) Daemonisation	Hyperbole	Repression
(5) Askesis	Metaphor	Introjection
(6) Apophrades	Transumption	Projection

Clinamen is the mode through which the new/younger poet uses irony to show how the precursor poet was accurate up to a point, but then went wrong. The poem ought to have taken a different route, such as the one the new poet has written. It is a 'correction' of the earlier poem.

Tessera is actually completion. Here the younger poet extends the precursor poem, under the assumption that the older poet did not go far enough.

Kenosis is a break. The younger poet acknowledges influence and the significance of the precursor, but decides that he cannot repeat (the repetition-compulsion of psychoanalysis) the precursor. He, therefore, has to break away from the older poet.

Daemonization is a countermove where the younger poet suggests that the precursor poem has a hidden power that ought not to belong there—it belongs to him, the younger poet. He, therefore, accepts the hidden power of the precursor poem and reduces the intensity or greatness of the earlier one.

Askesis is where the younger poet curtails his poem's power and that of the precursor's.

Apophrades is literally the return of the dead. The younger poet revisits and rewrites the older poem in such an effective way in his revisionary poem that when we now read the older poem we imagine it to be written by the younger poet and not the precursor.

SCHIZOANALYSIS: DELEUZE AND GUATTARI

Feminist critics like Hélène Cixous and Luce Irigaray were greatly influenced by both Lacanian psychoanalysis and poststructuralism. Their work proved to be extremely complex theorizations about the body, sexuality and identity. Iragaray and Cixous will be discussed in the chapter on feminisms.

In the 1980s and '90s Gilles Deleuze and Félix Guattari produced a series of works where they combined psychoanalysis with poststructuralism. Studying the operations of power, capitalism and the psyche, Deleuze and Guattari developed what they called 'schizoanalysis'.

Deleuze and Guattari in *Anti-Oedipus* (1983) begin by looking at the structure of desire. They argue that the attempt to create an ego in the schizoid leads to sickness. The attempt to foster an Oedipus complex or interpretation for the schizoid's images—in Freud, Melanie Klein—means that the unconscious in the schizoid is forced to enter the chain of signifiers. Building on the life of the unconscious, they suggest that the unconscious in the schizoid is *productive: there is no lack because it is full of images, presences.* This argument, as we can see, is opposed to the one Lacan made where the unconscious is always about a *lack*, is structured around a lack. For Deleuze and Guattari desire is a productive force, it is energy. Desire extends and includes everything, it knows no borders, it is nomadic, it is 'desiring-production'.

Lack, they propose, is created and planned through social *production*. It is a function of the market economy (to suggest a parallel from everyday life: We are always warned to acquire something 'while stocks last', and are requested to 'hurry' so that we do not face a situation where we suffer a lack). It organizes wants and needs and then instills the fear that our wants may not be fulfilled.

Further, the schizoid transforms (the term they use is 'decode') the discourse of the analysis (i.e., the analytic practice in the clinic) into something else. Deleuze and Guattari suggest a series of terms to explain this 'decoded' state of the schizoid: atheists, nomads, orphans. These, in fact, are people who refuse to be structured around signifiers, to be restricted to them. Decoding, according to Deleuze and

Guattari, 'means destroying the code as such, assigning it an archaic, folkloric, or residual function' (1983: 245).

This decoded state is what Deleuze and Guattari associate with capitalism. Capital can fit into any cultural and social configuration. It enters the system and breaks down all and every code. It reaches the limits of the system, deterritorializes it and then has to recode (or re-territorialize) the structures. These renewed structures are as monolithic and oppressive as the older regime they supplanted. The capitalist machines are afraid that the flow of capital might escape them. Capitalism, therefore, fixes limits, relations and signifiers among men. Everything has to have an equivalence: Bodies, knowledge, fantasies are all commodities that can be translated into other commodities. Capitalism has to impose a unified organization. But, within this new system the schizoid is nomadic, refusing to be confined or coded or commodified. This is the limit condition imposed on capitalism. As they put it: 'Schizophrenia is the exterior limit of capitalism itself or the conclusion of its deepest tendency, but that capitalism only functions on condition that it inhibit this tendency, or that it push back or displace this limit...' (1983: 246). Capitalism's flows exhibits the schizophrenic's desire to form random associations.

Deleuze and Guattari depart from Freud and Lacan's conceptions of the unconscious. In their later work, *A Thousand Plateaus* (1987), they see psychoanalysis as having a 'dictatorial conception of the unconscious' with hierarchical graphs, a central organ (the phallus), trees and such organized structures. Schizoanalysis on the other hand treats the unconscious as 'acentred' and rhizomatic (19). Deleuze and Guattari build a different version of the unconscious. Their rhizome—elaborated in detail in the opening chapter of *A Thousand Plateaus*—is not linear or sequential, it can be broken at any point and any point connected to any other.

FURTHER READING

Wright, Elizabeth. 1984. *Psychoanalytic Criticism: Theory in Practice*. London and New York: Methuen.

Ellmann, Maud (ed.). 1994. *Psychoanalytic Literary Criticism*. London: Longman.

Wollheim, Richard. 1991. *Freud*. 1971. London: Fontana.

Freund, Elizabeth. 1987. *The Return of the Reader: Reader-Response Criticism*. London: Routledge.

4 Feminisms

Feminism is both a political stance and a theory that focuses on gender as a subject of analysis when reading cultural practices and as a platform to demand equality, rights and justice. Feminism's key assumption is that gender roles are pre-determined and the woman is trained to fit into those roles. This means that roles like 'daughter' or 'mother' are not natural but *social* because the woman has to be trained to think, talk, act in particular ways that suit the role.

Feminist literary and cultural theory draws a link between

- the representation of women in art and
- the real, material conditions in which they live.

If we are to distinguish feminism from feminist *theory* then we would have something like this:

- Feminism is a stance, a political position.
- Feminist theory is the philosophical and analytical approach that employs this political position to read cultural practices like art or literature.

Feminist theory argues that the representation of women as weak, docile, innocent, seductive or irrational–sentimental is rooted in and influences actual social conditions, where she does not have power, is treated as a sex-object or a procreating machine, has fewer political and financial rights and is abused. Feminism, therefore, is a world view that refuses to delink art from existing social conditions and practices. Feminism explores the cultural dimensions of the woman's material life. Feminist literary–cultural critics assume that cultural texts such as cinema, TV soap opera, music, painting *parallel* and *duplicate* real-life power struggles between genders. Cultural texts naturalize the oppression of women through their stereotypical representation of women as weak/vulnerable, seductress, obstacle, sexual object or a procreating device. The task of criticism, therefore, is to reveal the underlying ideologies within these texts because these ideologies are instrumental in continuing women's oppression.

Feminism's key political and theoretical stance is this: The inequalities that exist between men and women are not natural but social, not pre-ordained but created by men so that they retain power. Religion, the family, education, the arts, knowledge systems are all social and cultural 'structures' that enable the perpetual reinforcement of this inequality. These structures are effective means of reinforcing male domination because they do not *appear* oppressive. They retain power because, with their ability to persuade, the structures convince the woman that she is

Feminist cultural theory analyses prevalent gender roles as they are represented in cultural forms like literature, cinema, advertisements; an approach that focuses on how such representations of women reflect, and are connected to *actual* life and social conditions.

destined to be subordinated. Cultural structures are, therefore, ideological: providing a system of beliefs that seek and attain the woman's consent to be subordinated. Feminist theory works to unpack these ideologies of dominance.

It analyses gender relations: how gender relations are constructed and experienced (by both men and women). Toril Moi is emphatic that feminist criticism is a political project: 'Feminist criticism ... is a specific kind of political discourse, a critical and theoretical practice committed to the struggle against patriarchy and sexism' (1987: 204).

Since the 1990s even this stance of the feminists has been questioned, mainly by the 'Third World' (i.e., non-white) women thinkers. The postcolonial feminists suggest that the category 'women' is itself a dominating ideology because it sees only white women and their lives as standards. The postcolonial critics have argued that women are not homogeneous and that the experiences of a woman in interior Rajasthan or Kenya cannot be compared with that of a white woman banker on Wall Street. As we shall see, the 'Third World' or postcolonial feminism has refined feminist theory to account for race as a crucial category in analysing gender.

A timeline for the twentieth-century feminist thought would be as follows:

1830–1920: First wave—suffragette movement, civil rights movement
1960s: Second wave—networking of women's groups, deeper engagement with political debates
1980s: Post-feminism—cyberfeminism, ecofeminism and the emergence of a postcolonial slant to feminist theory

'Women's studies' as a discipline began in the USA in the late 1960s and was established in other First World nations in the 1970s. Women's studies has focused on, and built upon, three key areas in feminist theory:

- Feminist critiques of knowledge (where knowledge is seen as generated and controlled by men and which excludes women's knowledge),
- The recovery of women's texts, modes of knowing and experiences, and the reevaluation of existing epistemological, pedagogic and cultural practices and
- The shift from liberal feminist views to more socialist and radical views of gender roles and culture.

While these three domains are more characteristic of women's studies in the West (as argued by Mary Maynard, 1998), women's studies in postcolonial nations have further refined and added to them. In India, with the work of journals like *Manushi*, the *Indian Journal of Gender Studies* and later *Samyukta*, interdisciplinary work in gender studies was encouraged.

Postcolonial women's studies in Asia and Africa have foregrounded issues like women's health, legal rights, domestic abuse, wage legislation, the rights of the tribal and the Dalit women. In the case of India, for example, feminist critiques, as seen in the works of Susie Tharu, Tejaswini Niranjana and others, call attention to the other crucial factors in gender identities, namely, caste and class. The Dalit woman as a subaltern figure, as opposed to the upper-caste, upper-class professional woman, constitutes, correctly, new 'subjects' in gender studies (and a critical approach now called 'Dalit feminism').

With more sophisticated theorizing about gender (the work of R. W. Connell, for example), a related development has been masculinity studies (with a full journal devoted to the subject). Sexuality studies now includes lesbian, gay and bisexual studies (under the aegis of LGBT, or Lesbian, Gay, Bisexual Theory) and explores the domain of transsexuality and transgender cultures.

OPENING MOVES

THE GENDER TURN: MARY WOLLSTONECRAFT AND THE RIGHTS OF WOMEN

The changing levels of literacy and cheaper publishing with the arrival of printing in early modern Europe meant that more women read about others' lives, and wrote about their own. However, European feminism as *theory* might be traced back to the eighteenth-century writings of Mary Wollstonecraft.

In an age where the labour of men (whether in the field or in literature) was privileged over that of women, Wollstonecraft provided the first major theoretical exploration of gender inequality.

In her *A Vindication of the Rights of Women* (1792) Wollstonecraft rejected the established view that women are naturally weaker or inferior to men. The unequal nature of gender relations, she proposed, was because the lack of education kept the women in a secondary position. Wollstonecraft proposed that women must be treated as equals because they play a crucial role in society, namely, bringing up children. Women themselves should strive to become 'companions' rather than mere wives to their husbands. For this change in status and role, women should acquire an education. Here Wollstonecraft attacks male thinkers like Rousseau who had argued that women did not need an education. Wollstonecraft astutely unpacked the stereotype of the woman as a creature of sentiment when she argued that the woman prone to excessive emotions abandoned rationality. It was this tendency, Wollstonecraft argued, that kept the women subordinated. Influenced by the ideas of the European Enlightenment, Wollstonecraft suggested that rationality and reason must be given importance over sensibility and feeling.

Wollstonecraft noted the significant contribution of the socializing process in the subordination of women. She was one of the first thinkers to propose that gender roles are not natural but social. Thus, the love of finery (jewellery and fashion), romance or beauty in women was not natural. The woman has been socialized and trained to believe that these are what make her truly feminine. That is, the characteristics one associates with the feminine in women are socially given values, and the woman assimilates these values so that she fits into the category of the feminine. This shift—from femininity as natural to femininity as social—is Wollstonecraft's major contribution. Wollstonecraft was thus one of the pioneers who moved away from a biological view of gender to a social one, where she saw social norms, values, laws and cultural practices as demanding, imposing and recommending particular forms of behaviour from women. The woman had little choice, in Wollstonecraft's critique, but to adopt these forms and norms; if she didn't she would be treated as a freak, a monster or a witch. Thus, the woman consented to feminine roles and to her own subordination.

While Wollstonecraft was radical in seeking education as a means of 'improving' the women's position in society, she was hesitant to upset the gender hierarchies. Wollstonecraft, for instance, believed that men did have superior virtues. 'Education', as Wollstonecraft saw it, was about 'improvement'. But she did not see it as a means of overturning hierarchies of power. Thus, she believed that education should instill a love for the domestic life. In effect, then, Wollstonecraft was proposing a clear distinction between genders.

MARGARET FULLER, WOMEN'S EDUCATION AND REFORM

In the USA Margaret Fuller's activism and writings, especially her *Woman in the Nineteenth Century* (1845), can be seen as a parallel origin for Western feminism (along with Wollstonecraft's). Like Wollstonecraft, Fuller believed that education was the means of emancipation for women. Education, employment and political rights were Fuller's key planks, and she championed these throughout her life. Unlike Wollstonecraft, Fuller, however, did not support specific gender-roles. She believed that women need not be confined to the domestic duties, and there are no 'feminine' roles (she was herself a distinguished editor and journalist).

Fuller was also a radical thinker in that she questioned the categories of gender. There cannot be a completely 'masculine' male, just as there is no truly 'feminine' female; each contains a bit of the other, argued Fuller. In the late twentieth-century criticism the concept of androgyny and the transcendence of gender would become a major theoretical move, but it was Fuller who first propounded it (influenced, no doubt, by mysticism, but no less powerful for that).

Fuller extended her concerns with gender roles and unequal power relations to classes (and here she differs from Wollstonecraft). She supported prison reform (and was particularly keen on ensuring proper conditions for women prisoners) and was one of the first to seek a solidarity between African Americans and women, seeing both as the victims of a racist–sexist social structure. She suggested that anyone who supported the cause of the Blacks would support the woman's cause.

VIRGINIA WOOLF, AUTHORSHIP, ANDROGYNY

In the twentieth century the novelist Virginia Woolf provided the first critiques that we can recognize as marking feminism as we know it today. In works like *A*

Room of One's Own (1929) and *Three Guineas* (1938), Woolf explored gender relations. One of the first writers to develop a woman-centric notion of reading and
education, Woolf argued that the patriarchal education systems and reading practices prevent women readers from reading *as* women. They are constantly trained
to read from the men's point of view. Aesthetics, values, literary merits and tradition are adopted by *male* literary authors and critics within the patriarchal
institutions (such as the university or publishing). These aesthetics, values and
merits are then touted and promoted as universal even though they are clearly
male-centered. The women are also trained to adopt these aesthetics, values and
merits as universal. The effect is that the woman's experience does not ever inform
the reading. Women's texts, when available, are rejected by the male critics as
minor or domestic without any virtue. Women readers, following in and trained
within the male-defined forms of reading, agree with this assessment. As a result,
Woolf notes, women's texts do not survive except as the poor cousins of the male
authored texts.

Woolf also argued that authorship itself is gendered. The language available to
the woman is patriarchal and inherently sexist. But the woman author, having no
other language at her command, is forced to use this sexist language, a language
that does not capture the woman's experience. Diction, realism, linearity, order—
the literary modes that have been promoted as 'true' aesthetics, are all
male-generated. Works by women that do not possess these qualities are rejected.
Thus, for a woman author to be accepted, she must per force use these same qualities in her writing.

Woolf was, however, careful to ensure that she was not privileging the female
way of thinking. Her idea of the androgynous creative mind (first elaborated in *A
Room of One's Own*), and perhaps one of her most controversial ideas, was an
attempt to go beyond the male/female binary. Woolf argued, building on the psychological theories of Carl Jung, that

> in each of us two powers preside, one male, one female; and in the man's brain the
> man predominates over the woman, and in the woman's brain the woman predomi-
> nates over the man. The normal and comfortable state of being is that when the two
> live in harmony together, spiritually co-operating ... (2006:102)

The best artists, believed Woolf, were always a combination of the man and the
woman, or 'man-womanly', and 'woman-manly', as she termed it (103). In her
novel, *Orlando* (1928), Woolf would explore this androgynous state where man
and woman as *mind* switch places in the same body. Later French feminists such
as Hélène Cixous and Luce Irigaray (see below) would also build on this notion of
androgyny.

After Woolf and the rise of the Women's Movement in the 1960s we have
what is now termed Second Wave of feminism. Before we explore the arguments
and approaches within second-wave feminism we need to study how gender and
sexuality have been analysed within contemporary cultural theory. Contemporary

social constructivist views of gender owe much to critiques of patriarchy in the works of Simone de Beauvoir.

SIMONE DE BEAUVOIR AND EXISTENTIAL FEMINISM

De Beauvoir's status as a feminist has always been open to debate. The reason lies not in her own work but in the contexts in which the work circulated. De Beauvoir was writing in the late 1940s, and her views were then truly radical. But by the time she began to be popular in the English-speaking world, many of the ideas in her work were common currency and hence did not attract attention as radical at all.

De Beauvoir argued in her most famous work, *The Second Sex* (published in French in 1949; English translation, 1984), that men are able to mystify women. This mystification and stereotyping, she argued, was instrumental in creating patriarchy. She argued that women, in turn, accepted this stereotype, and were thus instruments of their own oppression. She further argued that women were always the negative of the men, where man was the ideal, the norm and the woman the deviant or the Other, who sought perfection by trying to be as much like the man as possible. Women are measured by the standard of men and found 'inferior'. This is the process of Othering where women will always be seen, not as independent or unique but as a variation and flawed version of the Male. Men and Women are, therefore, constantly engaged in this Subject–Other relation where the Man is the Subject and the Woman the Other. It is based on this myth of the woman as inferior Other that gender inequalities are perpetuated in society.

De Beauvoir's major insight was that there is no 'essence' of a woman, a woman is *constructed* as such by men and society. As she puts it: 'One is not born a woman but becomes one' (1984: 267). De Beauvoir's main thesis is that biological sex and social gender are not accidental: Patriarchy makes use of sexual difference so as to maintain an inequality between men and women. It (patriarchy) argues that, biologically speaking, women are unequal to men—an argument that naturalizes inequality as a pre-ordained condition of biology itself. De Beauvoir argues that while sexual difference is real and unalterable, it cannot be the grounds for injustice and inequality.

De Beauvoir proposed that women must take charge of their own choice. Instead of being the negative, inferior Other, they must become Subjects in their own right. They need not be restricted by or to the roles and identities fostered or imposed on them by patriarchy. As a true existentialist de Beauvoir was arguing a case for women being responsible for themselves— a process that might require some socialization among women.

De Beauvoir thus offers feminism two key ideas: (i) the social construction of gender where women accept their men-ordained roles *as* women and (ii) the necessity for women to take responsibility and choose for themselves. When women choose for themselves they choose for the entire society. Thus, the woman's choice is about social transformation. Her influence on the American feminists like Betty Freidan helped launch second-wave feminism. De Beauvoir's major contribution was to shift the focus from a biological substrate to the man/woman debate to a *social* one. She located gender as a social category rather than a merely biological one, arguing that women are socially conditioned, trained and pre-scribed so as to assume the *role* of 'women'. In this de Beauvoir was one of the first feminists to turn to a social constructionist argument of gender where social con-ditioning, contexts and structures create specific roles based on the biological difference, but roles that are then seen as 'natural' and timeless.

SEX AND GENDER

Sex and gender do not mean the same thing within feminist studies. The first moves in making this distinction were made in second-wave feminist thinking. These moves also marked a shift from the biology-based arguments about male and female to a more social-centered one.

THE SOCIAL CONSTRUCTION OF GENDER

Feminist cultural theory calls for distinguishing between sex and gender. As we have seen in the previous section, the French feminist philosopher Simone de Beauvoir was an early proponent of the social constructionist view of sex and gender.

Sex is biological, and includes anatomy and physiology. The reproductive systems of men and women are biological, but they are invested with particular meanings through a social process. Take a simple biological fact: Women are bio-logically capable of bearing children. This is not a disputable statement. Now take the values associated with the biological act of child-bearing:

- Motherhood becomes a symbol of the true 'female',
- It becomes the central role for women to perform (no woman is complete unless she bears children),
- Nurturing a child is the woman's 'natural' job.

Feminists argue that none of these three is biological: They are *social values attrib-uted to biological acts*. This means that the woman's biology and biological functions

> Sex is biological, but the values and meanings associated with the female and male body are socially ascribed. Gender is this system of values and meanings. If sex and biology is nature, then gender is about the social and, therefore, culture. 'Female' and 'male' refer to the bio-logical (anatomical and physiological) characteristics, while 'feminine' and 'masculine' refer to the social values assigned to these.

are evaluated, determined and governed not merely as biology but from the social values attributed to them. This attribution of values is what constitutes gender.

Thus, *sex is biological, gender is social*. In Gayle Rubin's words: 'Sex is sex, but what counts as sex is ... culturally determined and obtained' (cited in Glover and Kaplan, 2000: xxv). The key phrases here and in de Beauvoir are 'counts' and 'becomes' respectively, and refer to the evaluation and assigned to particular sexes and the civilizing/socializing processes that make the female a woman. Gender is a system of roles and values assigned to the biological traits and functions. In other words, gender is a social construction, a process whereby meanings are allotted to the acts like birth, sex (as in sexual intercourse), homosexuality and nurture. Feminist theory argues that gender is an ideology because

- it naturalizes what is a social performance (the woman's role),
- it naturalizes inequality between the sexes by proposing that the biological differences are the determining factors rather than economic, social or educational ones, and
- it proposes and reinforces the difference in social performances (men's roles, women's roles) as natural, pre-ordained and unalterable.

The woman is made to accept the idea that she is *made* or *born* to be a mother, a device for procreation and nurture. The lower wages of the woman are justified by suggesting that the woman is weaker and less efficient. Woman's writing is rejected on the grounds that it deals only with the less important issues like the home. What we see in each of these cases is that the social differences are masked in favour of the biological difference. The economic and political inequalities in the society are ignored because the biological categories and differences are invoked.

The feminist attempt has been to try and end this biological determinism in favour of a more social constructionist (by which we mean an emphasis on how categories are constructed socially) view of gender. This also means a refusal of biological essentialisms such as 'men cannot know or speak about a woman's problems because they are not women'. In other words, the biological fact of being female cannot be treated as the source of authenticity. The presence of particular biological features is not a guarantor or source of authority over 'women's questions'. As K. K. Ruthven puts it in a caustic tone: 'The sense of 'being a woman' cannot be treated as if it were a pre-constructed given – and therefore a source of incontestable authority to be appealed to when the going gets rough in arguments with men' (1986: 8).

However, one major problem with this notion of gender as a social attribute and category is that it sees gender almost entirely as an imposition. It does not offer the individual a choice in the matter of gender because society assigns it to her/him. This is a deterministic and inflexible view of gender, according to the latter-day feminists.

POSTMODERNISM, GENDER AND PERFORMATIVITY

In the late 1980s and 1990s feminist philosophers and theories began rethinking this view of gender. The third-wave feminism of the 1990s argued that 'men' and 'women' are social categories that can only be defined in relation to each other. Influenced by deconstructive thought, the writings of Judith Butler embody a postmodern view of gender.

Butler (1990) argued that far from being a set of fixed and stable values and roles assigned/imposed by society, gender was a *performance* or *role* enacted by individuals. This performance of gender is, of course, social in the sense it is enacted, validated and accepted by the society. But what is important is that the role is also open to negotiation and alteration, to conflict and contest. By arguing that gender is a performance, the theorists were able to suggest that gender is not a fixed category: Its meaning depends on the location, time, cultural frameworks within which it is performed. In other words, gender is a continuous performance whose meaning can never be fixed for all time or as universal. This 'performance' is the repeated *citation*—iteration—of the role in particular contexts. With each citation the signifier/role acquires a meaning depending on the context in which the citation occurs. Thus, gender and its meaning is constructed through *repeated* performances (behaving 'as a woman', or 'as a man'). As Judith Butler put it: 'Identity is performatively constituted by the very "expressions" that are said to be its results' (1990: 24–25).

These 'expressions' are discourses and representations. Bodies functioning (behaving) in particular ways send out a message: This is the way this particular body behaves, and, therefore, it is a woman's body. Clothing, mannerisms, speech and language are all signs that bodies use to declare their gender to the world. To put it differently: Men and women use language and clothing as signs of their being men and women. This is 'performance', where wearing a particular kind of clothing (saris rather than trousers, adornment rather than functional devices) is the use of a language (where objects constitute a kind of language) to declare one's gender.

What is important here is that this language must be something society and that culture recognize as *belonging to* or *characteristic of* a woman. That is, clothing or speech by men and women must fit in with what is accepted and recognized as 'men's style' or 'women's manners'. In this, gender is like the meanings of signs: For

Postmodern theories of gender argue that gender is not a fixed or stable category across the world. Gender, like a text, is a performance, the playing out of roles, that has to be repeated ('cited') and validated within specific social and cultural contexts, but which is also open to contest and negotiations.

a sign to retain meaning it must be repeated in different contexts and be recognized as being the same (a sign like 'cat' will mean the same when it is used and understood despite variations in the contexts of its articulations, its typesetting, font or size). A woman becomes a woman, or 'possesses' a woman's *identity* because she plays the role of a woman repeatedly.

Gender is, in other words, the *repeated citation of a sign, the repeated enactment of a language*. This is the reason why cross-dressing or transvestitism becomes a mode of confusion: because it does not conform to standard practices of 'men's' or 'women's clothing'.

Poststructuralism has argued that a text is a system of signs. This text is open-ended because it is never finalizable in terms of its meaning: The signs must be repeated endlessly and meaning emerges in the context of the reading *at that point*. That is, a text's meaning is made available in the process of interaction between reader (context) and the text (signs). The text is 'performed', engaged with, negotiated in the act of reading. Unless there is reading, there is no text. Gender is, therefore, like a text because

- it has to be performed,
- the performance is context-specific,
- it has to be repeated in order to be recognized (as in the case of texts where the word 'cat' must be identifiable every time it is written, no matter what the font, type, size),
- it has no stable meaning because it is performed endlessly.

This is a postmodern and poststructuralist view of gender because it refuses a fixity of categories. Instead, it sees gender as provisional, shifting, contingent and performed. The 'meaning' of being female or male, in this view, is dependent upon a local citation of signs that are then accepted and validated. Postmodern views of gender thus reject essentialisms and stable identities or meanings. Instead, they project gender as an unstable category that has to be repeatedly reinvented.

The postmodern views of gender are also anti-essentialist. Critics like Butler do not believe that there is (or can be) an 'essential' woman or man because 'woman' and 'man' are meanings that emerge in performances relative to each other. What it means to be a woman is different if the 'performance' is in tribal India or a BPO office in Gurgaon.

The postmodern theories of gender also reject notions of authenticity, authority, universality and objectivity. With postmodernism's characteristic fear of totalizing explanations postmodern feminism believes that

- gender and its meaning depends on location,
- it cannot be universal because meanings are local,
- it cannot be fixed because it demands and depends on repeated performances and in relation to other performances,
- one cannot step outside the performance (as 'male') to be objective.

MATERIALIST VIEWS OF GENDER

One of the problems with postmodern views such as Butler's is that they empha-size discourses rather than the material conditions, the representational over the lived. Since the 1990s, materialist feminist critics have turned away from the post-modern flexible, shifting, discursive view of gender by focusing on the social conditions, the economy and the politics.

Materialist feminism adds one more category in its study of gender oppres-sion and inequality: that of *class*. The addition of class as an analytical category helps feminists to see how the material conditions of work and wage alter gender power and relations. The Marxist-socialist influence in the feminist theorizing here and materialist feminism is often known, therefore, as socialist feminism. In their introduction to *Women, Class and the Feminist Imagination* (1990), the repre-sentative anthology of materialist feminism, the editors Karen Hansen and Ilene Philipson argued that women's oppression can be attributed to both patriarchy and capitalism (19). It implies that gender inequalities are also determined by the class affiliations in a male-dominated social structure.

The materialist views of gender focus on issues of social structure and political economy as informed by capitalism and patriarchy and the kinds of gender roles these demand. Thus, the materialist feminists look for the link between gender roles and issues of household economy, labour and wages. For example, a material-ist criticism of gender would ask a question such as: Is the woman professor of English in a metropolitan university performing the same kind of gender role at a faculty meeting as the tribal woman seeking the right to health in rural India? Can we speak of a common denominator of gender-based suffering when class matters, financial power and social prestige overlay gender roles in these contexts (arguably the woman professor of English with a five-digit salary and enormous social pres-tige has managed to overcome at least some of the disadvantages of her gender, whereas the tribal woman is triply disadvantaged by virtue of being, poor, tribal and a woman).

> Materialist feminism adds class as an analytical category to its study of gender, arguing that women's oppression stems from a combina-tion of patriarchy (based on unequal gender relations) and capitalism (based on unequal class and economic power).

These are arguments that clearly foreground the material conditions of gender roles. If capitalism depends on the exploitation of labour then, feminists argue, we need to explore the role of the women's labour. The people in power in capitalism have historically been men. But what interests materialist feminism is not the realm of industrial labour alone. Their focus is on domestic labour—a form of labour performed almost entirely by women but almost always unpaid and even unacknowledged. Materialist feminists argue that domestic labour contributes to the household economy, but is rarely seen as 'productive'. In other words, the work done by men in fields and factories is treated as productive labour, while the work done by women inside houses is rendered 'invisible'. This distinction and division of labour, argue the feminists, is a part of the gender wars within capitalism. The sexual division of labour replicates the unequal power relations of patriarchy and capitalism: Men and men's labour remains the keystone for capitalism, while the woman toils on.

FEMINISM AND THE LITERARY CANON

Perhaps the most significant contribution of feminist thought in cultural theory has been its critique of the 'Eng. Lit.' canon. Marxist criticism (see Chapter 5) argues that cultural practices and structures (arts, music, film, sport, religion, the family, education) reflect the material conditions in society. In other words, unequal economic and political relations between groups, individuals and genders are reflected in films and literature. This means, the unequal power relations between men and women might find expression in literary texts.

The task of feminist criticism is to pay attention to how patriarchal structures operate within male-authored texts or are assimilated as value systems by women authors. In Annette Kolodny's terms, feminist literary criticism is marked by an 'attentiveness to the ways in which primarily male structures of power are inscribed (or encoded) within our literary inheritance: the consequences of that encoding for women – as characters, as readers, and as writers' (1989: 162).

WRITING WOMEN

Literary texts, argue feminists, constitute an important mechanism by which the unequal power relations in society are naturalized. By taking recourse to stereotypes of the virtuous woman, the seductress and the sacrificing mother, literary texts ensure that these roles become acceptable and even desirable for the girl children to acquire when they grow up. Literary cultures, therefore, play an important role in the socialization of girls and the naturalization of the power structures because women consent to accept these roles. Literature, in other words, is ideological.

The literary canon has invariably been constituted of male writers. The canons bestow prestige and visibility to the authors. The authors in the canon are studied, circulated and discussed. Since literature, as noted in the preceding paragraph, serves an important ideological function, it is significant that the male authors are taken as the commentators on the woman's condition. There is a need for a canon of women's writing for precisely this reason: A woman's text will suggest an alternative picture of the conditions, desires, psychology of the woman.

The woman's experience is not articulated by women authors—if it is, these texts are often dismissed as possessing little or no literary value. The feminist project has been to reclaim a woman's tradition of writing where alternative world views and values are depicted, different aesthetics are deployed, where the woman's experience is not reduced to the way men think it should be and, in some cases, offering new possibilities for society itself. Dale Spender's *Mothers of the Novel: 100 Good Writers before Jane Austen* (1986) sketched out such an alternative canon. Spender was reacting to male critics like F. R. Leavis who could only think of George Eliot and Jane Austen as women authors worth reading. Spender wrote:

> For the more women novelists I found, and the more women's novels I read, the more I was convinced of the desirability, and the necessity of reclaiming this lost tradition, and of challenging the received wisdom of the literary establishment – that for women novelists it all started with Jane Austen.(2)

In her *A Literature of their Own* (1977), Elaine Showalter demonstrates how the nineteenth-century England ensured a secondary position for the women authors even though women authors had been publishing since the 1750s. The woman writer, Showalter shows, was caught in a double bind. In the first place she was limited to certain themes in her writings by the prevalent male critical opinion. These themes included domestic problems, children, clothing fashions and food. What this meant in literary practice was that these were the only themes a woman writer could use if she were to be even published and read. Yet, this same male establishment attacked the woman novelist's work as inconsequential or limited *because* she wrote only of home, fashion and food! Feminist criticism seeks to unravel the politics behind the establishment of such values of literary judgement. Can there be, feminist critics ask, different standards of judging women authors?

Feminist critics have argued that women authors have been excluded from the literary canon, a canon that circulates stereotypes of women that then naturalize their gender roles. Showalter argued that a canon of women authors does exist. She classifies the authors into three main types, corresponding to three main stages in the development of women's writing itself.

Showalter argued that a canon of women authors does exist. She classifies the authors into three main types, corresponding to three main stages in the development of women's writing itself.

In the *Feminine* phase, 1840–1880, women writers mostly imitated the male writer's modes. This meant, further, an adoption of the patriarchal aesthetic, social values and even masculine names (George Eliot is the best example of this). Some even advertised their marital status to show they were respectable (examples would be Mrs Gaskell and Mrs Oliphant). These authors explored the daily lives of women within the family and community, but often tried to 'reveal' the inner woman to the world.

The *Feminist* phase begins in the 1880s and '90s and extends to around the 1920s. Showalter sees this as a protest phase, where women authors rebelled against prevalent patriarchal attitudes. The authors began to explore the woman's position in terms of work, class and the family. This phase is marked by the demand for autonomy on the part of women.

The *Female* phase is writing from the latter half of the twentieth century. It is marked by the woman writer's search for her own voice and identity as opposed to the identity imposed by patriarchy. This writing often perceived sexuality as the possible source of creativity. It did not shy away from explicating the woman's sexual desires, body and unconscious—quite the contrary.

Sandra Gilbert and Susan Gubar re-read several women authors to see how they had responded to patriarchy. In their now-cult work, *The Madwoman in the Attic* (1979), Gilbert and Gubar argued that all women's texts are *palimpsests*: They mask secret subtexts of desire, politics and meanings. While their 'surface' meanings might be those that were acceptable during their time, the palimpsest reveals something else altogether. An example of such a palimpsest would be Gilbert and Gubar's reading of the madwoman theme. Women authors, they argue, had to negotiate with the male fantasies of the female, which were either of two stereotypes: the submissive female-as-angel or the dangerous female-as-monster. These fantasies served as literary models for women authors. Gilbert and Gubar argue that the madwoman image in most fiction by the woman author represented her (the author's) double, the 'schizophrenia of authorship', and the anxiety/rage of creation. Beneath the surface of the conformist woman's text, Gilbert and Gubar detect a more authentic woman's story. Gilbert and Gubar were proposing that women's writing was subversive even when it appeared to be conformist. But in order to discover this strand within literary writing, we need a new critical approach itself.

As we shall see later in the chapter, women writers in the 1980s and '90s would find new ways of writing about the body, desires and sexuality.

Women Writing Criticism

Gynocriticism was a term coined by Elaine Showalter (1979) to describe critical responses that accounted for the woman author as a producer of texts and meanings. She defined gynocritcism as a concern with

> Women as writers … the history, styles, themes, genres, and structures of writing by women; the psychodynamics of female creativity; the trajectory of the individual or collective female career; and the evolution and laws of a female literary tradition. (2003 [1981]: 311)

This kind of criticism is necessary because, as Showalter puts it, "'male critical theory" is a concept of creativity, literary history, or literary interpretation based entirely on male experience and put forward as universal' (310).

Showalter, like Ellen Moers in her justly celebrated *Literary Women* (1977), argued that women authors, from the perspective of gynocritics, were not deviations from the patriarchal norm. On the contrary, they constituted a very strong subculture *within* patriarchy. Gilbert and Gubar's work bears a strong sense of such a gynocriticism when they explore the subtexts of women's writing. Extending this work Gilbert and Gubar's *No Man's Land* (3 volumes, 1988) suggested that the twentieth-century literary history is marked essentially by gender and sexual conflicts. They documented instances of rape, domestic abuse, sexual tensions and sexual imagery to demonstrate modernity's (and modernism's) continuing obsession with sex and sexuality.

> Gynocriticism has sought to uncover particular modes of women's writing by positing the woman's experience as being at the centre of both writing and criticism.

Later day gynocritics were unhappy with the approach outlined by Showalter, Gilbert–Gubar and the early feminist critics. Influenced by deconstruction, critics like Mary Jacobus, Bonnie Zimmerman and Chandra Talpade Mohanty began to critique the early feminists saying that they indulged in supplanting one tradition (male-dominated) with another (female). Such a critical approach, argued the post-1980s feminists, homogenized all women into one category as though their experiences were the same and interchangeable. Such a homogenization denied a diversity of women's experiences and, therefore, of women's writing—something women critics had accused the men critics of doing! The black woman was as marginal to white women's writing and criticism as women were to men's writing. That is, even within the 'new' canon of women authors, there were no lesbians, women of colour or 'postcolonials'.

Thus, race, ethnicity, class and geography came to be included as analytical categories within feminism, and produced new forms of feminist cultural theory: black, lesbian, 'Third World' or postcolonial and, more recently, cyberfeminism.

WOMEN, LANGUAGE, WRITING

If, as Virginia Woolf proposed, women authors are forced to use male language because they have none of their own, then the attempt among feminist philosophers and writers has been to explore alternative forms of language that would be feminine and female. That is, feminists ponder over the possibility of a *female language*.

WOMEN, LANGUAGE, DISCOURSE

In the 1970s and early '80s linguists explored the idea of a gendered language. Robin Lakoff (1975) and Dale Spender (1980) argued that woman's language was deferential, passive and apologetic, while men's language was aggressive, imperative and declarative. Women's language was also characterized by indirectness, tentativeness and diffidence. This difference in men and women when it comes to the use of language was attributed to the unequal positions they occupied in society. However, as Sara Mills has pointed out, the results of experiments in gendered language has almost always been contradictory (Mills 1995, 2003).

ÉCRITURE FEMININE

With the arrival of poststructuralism on the critical scene, philosophers and critics such as Hélène Cixous, Julia Kristeva and Luce Irigaray developed a notion of 'women's writing'. Focusing on the language of women's writing they postulated (and practised) a fluid, non-linear, elliptical, part-mythic, mystic writing. The fiction of Jeanette Winterson, A. L. Kennedy, Fay Weldon, Kathy Acker and Angela Carter embodies what came to be termed the *Écriture feminine*. *Écriture feminine* works predominantly to upset the notions of language, form, narrative 'order', organization. The new language of women's writing is fluid, non-linear, elliptical, part-mythic and part-realistic, mystic and slippery. It is part autobiographical and part fictional. It thrives on sexualized imagery, and seeks to capture the fluidity of women's bodies. It identifies mother figures and refuses to privilege the male. In addition, it experiments with typography itself—visual and graphic alterations to fonts, blanks, parentheses, breaks, hyphenated words and altered punctuation. Maggie Humm (1998) proposes the term *gynographic* writing to describe such experimental modes. Gynographic writing uses the body as a source of language and metaphor. Puns, etymologies and word games that work with the body are used extensively. Thus, Irigaray makes a point about women always touching themselves as 'collaborators' because etymologically the word comes from 'labia': Women's lips always touch each other in 'collaboration'. Mary Daly speaks of 'crone-logical' time and Cixous uses blood and menstruation as sources of a woman's language. Angela Carter's shifts between myth and reality, fable and the real world in her fiction is another instance. Humm's argument is that such writing breaks down the borders between genres, disciplines, private and public and, finally, the body and the text.

Écriture feminine is exemplified by Cixous' critical work and Irigaray's philosophical writings. Now, traditionally, criticism has sought to be pedantic, logical and 'objective'. The work of these feminists, in sharp contrast, uses poetry, slippery metaphors, circumlocution and extensive body-images in order to develop a whole new critical language. A celebratory and ecstatic tone is visible in this writing. The style shifts between the poetic and the theoretical. Cixous, in particular, ensures that her academic discourse merges with poetry and autobiography. In her attempt to dismantle the binary opposition between academic/autobiography, theory/poetry, argument, sentiment Cixous creates a slippery prose of excesses, flows and shifts.

THE BODY, IDENTITY AND THE SUBJECT

The woman's body, argue feminists, has been represented as mother, seductive, material, sexual and procreative. Patriarchal society attributes particular values to the woman's body, and the woman assimilates these values. Thus, feminists have noted and objected to several kinds of objectification of the woman's body as following:

- Women as self-sacrificing mothers or faithful wives become stereotypes.
- Beauty contests commodify the woman's body for the men's gaze.
- Cosmetic surgery and body adornment become 'feminine' modes.
- Thinness associated with feminine beauty (seen in advertisements, films, fashion) drives young girls to drastic measures to lose weight.
- The country is itself imaged as a woman's body ('motherland') that demands protection by men.

In none of these cases, argue feminists, does the woman have a say, even though it is her body. The woman's body, therefore, is only the object of study, control, discipline and gaze. The woman is never her own subject. Her sexuality, desires or identity is determined by the social norms that have themselves been produced by men.

THE POLITICS OF WOMEN'S BIOLOGY

Some of the most trenchant feminist criticism has been directed at the biology of bodies, specifically reproductive biology. Feminists argue that the woman is reduced to the womb, almost as though her only function is procreation. Further, when Freud famously theorized that all women suffer from a 'penis envy' he offered a biological explanation for women's psychology—one that determined social constructions of women as the 'second sex' suffering from a 'lack' (on psychoanalysis and feminine sexuality see Chapter 3). As Juliet Mitchell puts it: '[T]he lack that is psychologically attributed to women became treated as an actual lack ... The psychological mode of oppression was taken as the cause of oppression' (cited in Chow 2003: 99).

Shulamith Firestone in *The Dialectic of Sex* (1970) had argued that women could be truly free only if she and her body were freed of reproduction. Ruth Hubbard's pioneering work in the area of reproductive biology (1992) noted that women initially had control over the domain of childbirth because they gave birth within the home. When the event was relocated to the hospital the woman and the process came under the control of the male physician. Indeed techniques in childbirth (such as episiotomy) were developed not only to help in the birth but the woman's husband who would derive pleasure from the tightening of the vagina (Hubbard: 150). As Hubbard puts it: 'We [must ask] to what extent different ways of giving birth empower women or, alternatively, decrease our power to structure childbearing around our own needs and those of the people with whom we live' (162).

Further, reproductive technologies themselves are patriarchal mainly because motherhood is projected as the climactic moment of the woman's life—and those who are not mothers are believed to/represented as lacking something. Indeed, as Valerie Hartouni (1991) has demonstrated, new technologies such as in vitro fertilization (IVF), are offered and promoted as blessings for women, to help women fulfil their maternal natures and their lives (49). IVF has given rise to a more technologized form of older biases about women's bodies. Women's bodies have become, in Sarah Franklin's argument (1997), conduits for technological miracles. Nature itself, and biology, become both knowable and controllable through technology. In other words, it is not about the technology per se but about the social relations between genders and the gender roles that is important. IVF is a social technology because it aims to 'normalize' families and gender relations ('families' must have children in them, a couple constitutes a 'complete' unit with children).

The labouring body of the woman becomes the subject of reproductive technologies and medicalization techniques (ultrasound scans). Pregnant women are under surveillance to prevent drug abuse. The maternal rights of the woman are set against the rights of the foetus (Balsamo 1998 [1995]).

THE SUBJECT AND SUBJECTIVITY IN FEMINISM

Feminists have consistently argued that the male becomes the standard model for all things human. The woman is never seen as anything other than an object, a secondary figure to the primacy of the male. The feminist debates about 'subjectivity' have revolved around issues like:

- Does subjectivity occur in the body, the psyche or the socially conditioned/determined experience?
- Is subjectivity individual or social?

The most common and sustained notion of the subject has come from within the liberal humanist tradition. The subject here is seen as the rational, coherent individual who can act according to her free will. In other words, liberal humanists privilege the individual over the social or collective. The individual is the seat of free will and has the power to alter the course of her life—a power that in critical theory is commonly termed 'agency'. Latter-day feminists have had serious problems with this notion of the subject. They argue that

- the individual is not simply about rationality alone, but includes things like emotions.
- men have traditionally been projected as rational, and women as 'irrational' or emotional.

From these it follows that if subjectivity is seen to arise only from rationality then it automatically excludes the woman as a subject with agency.

Further, the individual in many societies is located within communities and groups who also contribute to her sense of self ('I belong'). Thus, subjectivity is not always located in the individual alone, but is socially validated, determined and constructed. Roles pre-ordained for women—such as mother, wife or daughter—are subject-positions into which the women need to fit themselves (what later Marxism would term, in Althusser, the process of 'interpellation'). This means, while the man might be able to choose his subject-position, the woman's is predetermined.

Feminist theory, especially of the socialist-Marxist variety, therefore, sees subjectivity as at least partly socio-cultural.

Feminist theory tries to locate the basis for the woman as subject of her own self, desires and identity rather than as object for the male. Subjectivity has been variously located by feminists in the body, collectivity and the social.

Radical feminism shifted as far away from the liberal humanist notion of the subject as possible. Radical feminism treats women as a class, or a *collective subject*. They see all women as linked by a common structure: patriarchal oppression. 'Sisterhood', therefore, became the code for this shared oppression. It must be noted that within this discourse of radical feminism, the woman's body was central—because it was the body that suffered (in terms of sexuality, labour, procreation). Later, the radical feminists also proposed that once women gained control over their minds and bodies they would develop their true subjectivities. This woman-subject would perhaps be a lesbian.

In other cases, such as ecofeminism (see Chapter 10), critics like Mary Daly (1979) linked the oppression of women to that of nature—treating both as victims of the patriarchal-capitalist modernity. Woman's subjectivity was aligned with other dimensions such as compassion, emotion and care—all of which, ecofeminists argued, were features of *nature* too.

Judith Butler and the later feminists under the influence of poststructuralism treated subjectivity and identity as embodied 'performance' (see above for postmodernism and the performance of gender). Here subjectivity is the consequence of discourse, is fragmented, contingent and shifting. In other words, it is impossible to claim a subject-position because the subject is always relational and temporary. A key moment in this rethinking of the nature of the subject is post-structuralism-inspired French feminism.

Luce Irigaray's work *Speculum of the Other Woman* (translated 1985), and *This Sex Which Is Not One* (1987) proposes that the woman always lacks a subjectivity in Western discourses because she is constructed always as the Other of the man, never as a free subject with her own identity. The female is always nothing more than a *deviation* from the norm which is the male. As Irigaray puts it, in the 'logic of sameness' there is 'man' and 'not-man', A and *not*-A (or A-minus). This means that instead of two separate autonomous entities A and B, we have one positive (A) and its negative. The second term/identity is only what the first is not. All difference between the sexes is eradicated through this 'logic'.

Cixous pleads for a return to the pre-Oedipal stage as a means of undoing the male/female binary. This would mean a return to the early stage of *bisexuality*. Bisexuality, for Cixous, is the means to collapse the unitary sexual identity. Cixous rejects any sexual essentialism arguing that each gender includes the Other. There is no inside/outside, male/female: Each is constitutive/consists of the Other.

Irigaray, like most French feminists, locates subjectivity within discourse and treats it as something shifting, contingent and fragmented. But other critics have been unhappy with the transient, contingent and slippery notion of the subject that poststructuralism proposes. The notion of a contingent and ever-postponed subject means that for coloured, tribal, Dalit or disabled women there will never be the chance to develop their own subject-positions. This argument is an important one, for its political consequences are very significant.

- Politics is based on embodiment: Voting rights, welfare, employment and citizenship are based on identifiable bodies.
- Thus, the nature, colour and 'type' of body are important.
- Many 'bodies' have historically been excluded from the public-political sphere: blacks, women, the differently-abled, the queer.
- These bodies have always been only objects—of oppression, welfare, history, control—but never subjects of their own lifestyle choices, future or identity. They have been granted identity but not allowed to develop one for themselves.
- Political claims and rights have been generated in the late twentieth century because those who have been denied these rights have fought with and for their bodies: claiming rights *as* queer or *as* differently abled bodies.
- If subjectivity and identity are contingent and shifting then people of particular bodies (queer, black, coloured) do not get to claim anything based on their bodies.

- Therefore, just when minority bodies begin to develop arguments about rights and politics based on their embodied subjectivities, poststructuralist notions of the subject destroy the subject.
- This leaves minority or 'different' bodies with nothing on which they can claim rights or citizenship, while people who have always been subjects with agency and rights (white, males, heterosexuals) have nothing to worry about.

Nancy Hartsock summarizes this politically explosive shift towards poststructuralist ideas of subjectivity well:

> Why is it that just at the moment when so many of us who have been silenced begin to demand the right to name ourselves, to act as subjects rather than objects of history, that just then the concept of subjecthood becomes problematic? (1990: 164)

SEXUALITY AND DESIRE

Contemporary feminist theory has consistently argued that female sexuality has been marginalized as insignificant, mysterious or monstrous and that such representations of the woman's body/desire/sexuality have been made by men. Adapting psychoanalytic theories, Euro-American feminists have developed new models of female sexuality that, they believe, empowers the woman.

Feminists like Juliet Mitchell suggest that Freud's work, contrary to common beliefs, is a critique of contemporary patriarchal society. Mitchell links the psyche with cultural contexts of identity where the woman's identity is already determined by the structures she inhabits. She was one of the first feminists to explore a theory of female psychic processes.

Mitchell's adaptation of social contexts with that of psychoanalysis resulted in a productive mix. She argues that the laws of society and life are built into the unconscious, or rather that 'the unconscious mind is the way we acquire these laws' (1974: xvi). Mitchell marks a shift from the psyche to social order (for example the *ideology* of femininity, beauty or family), and argues that psychoanalysis is necessary to uncover this unconscious where the laws have taken root.

Mitchell argues that women are 'objects' in social transactions and exchanges. Further, in this process, the woman is always defined as a lack (as lacking the penis). She is always, therefore, anxious about her lack. While the male is only threatened with castration, the woman believes she has already been castrated. Thus, the woman's identity is born in a state of anxiety and absence. While the man is self-determining and autonomous, the woman is never so. She becomes the Other of the man, an Other with a lack.

With the Oedipus complex the boy soon realizes that the law of the father is what prevails, and he is the heir to this law. Hence, the Oedipus complex is in reality a 'patriarchal myth' as Mitchell puts it (403). The woman also desires the father's place (and Mitchell notes that Freud did discuss a parallel, the Electra complex), but only the boy will be allowed to do so. Femininity is born out of this repression—that she will never be the heir to the father.

Gender differences are, therefore, constructed in contexts of the family and society as difference in genitals: one possessing, one lacking. This, for Mitchell, is a social and cultural *fantasy* where the woman is, right from girlhood, made to believe the male is complete and she is not. As she put it in another essay, the feminine, the intuitive, the religious, the mystical, the playful—seen as components of feminine identity—are assigned to women by the patriarchal society (2003 [1984]). Mitchell thus proposed that femininity is 'held in the heart and the head as well as in the home' (1974: 362), a statement that provoked cries of essentialism from later feminists because it was proposing an absence of resistance to the imposed feminine identity. If the woman assimilates such an identity, then what possible chances exist for feminist thinking? As Elizabeth Wilson put it, if women do 'internalize "femininity", psychoanalysis ... does not give us much idea how we might escape' (1991: 220). A mode of such an 'escape' was proposed by later feminist psychoanalytic thinkers.

Jacqueline Rose suggests a way out of the imposed feminine identity. She takes the identity argument a step further when she proposes that the Freudian unconscious is actually an example of how imposed identities like 'feminine' or 'woman' fail. Rose, therefore, suggests that psychoanalysis reveals the failure of social processes (identified with the ego in Freud and the Symbolic Order in Lacan) to impose identity. The unconscious is the site of a *resistance* to identity. Rose argued that women, because of their unconscious, are always resistant to their psychically acquired feminine identity. This argument was one of the first moves towards the notion of a *decentered* subject—a common theme in poststructuralism. What Rose was suggesting was a feminine subjectivity and identity that was not coherent or whole, but fractured and internally divided.

In her later work (1986), Rose linked the sexual with the visual. Noting that postmodernism was obsessed with the image and simulation, Rose ponders over the implications of this for feminine sexuality and representation. Rose suggests that since feminism is concerned with social norms and structures it has to pay attention to representations of cultural stereotypes. We, therefore, need to look at the visual space in which feminine sexuality is represented and played out to unravel the cultural ideologies behind these representations. That is, there is a close link between sexuality and the image (of woman, of man, of sexual relations). Images locate and describe women as fantasies, as 'looking good' so that men find them acceptable despite their 'lack'. Rose argues that the position of woman as fantasy or as a sex-object or as an object of desire depends on what she calls a 'particular economy of vision' (232). Later feminist interpretations of art and cinema utilized this notion of sexualized vision—a process through which a body is sexualized as a woman—to read ideologies of (patriarchal) representation.

NATIONALISM

The woman has always been represented as a territory to be conquered and dominated. Equating the nation with the mother (as motherland) is an old trope in cultural practices across the world. This equation has been a source of contention among feminists because, as they see it, it enables the male to control the woman and the country, even as this control masquerades as protection. The Chicano writer Cherríe Moraga made this point forcefully:

> Chicanos are an occupied nation within a nation, and women and women's sexuality are occupied within the Chicano nation. If women's bodies and those of men and women who transgress their gender roles have been historically regarded as territories to be conquered, they are also territories to be liberated. Feminism has taught us this. The nationalism I seek is one that decolonizes the brown and female body as it decolonizes the brown and female earth. (1993: 150)

Anti-colonial movements appropriated the woman as the boundary figure to be protected against the colonial male. If the nation is gendered then nationalism is patriarchal nationalism, as Partha Chatterjee has influentially argued (1993). Chatterjee notes that Indian nationalism equated the woman with the home: the spiritual and private space that is untainted by colonialism. Thus, the anti-colonial struggle was to ensure that this space remains sacrosanct. Women in the national struggle endorsed this view, and thereby reinforced patriarchy and the nation. Thus, the cultural politics of the anti-colonial nationalism was gendered. In Chatterjee's words:

> Women from the new middle class in nineteenth-century India thus became active agents in the nationalist project – complicit in the framing of its hegemonic strategies as much as they were resistant to them because of their subordination under the new forms of patriarchy. (1993: 148)

Feminist critiques of nationalism and the nation-state, therefore, explore the following:

- The gendered nature of the very idea of nation (often termed as 'fraternity');
- The rights to citizenship;
- The civil society within a nation-state and its treatment of women;
- The rights of women within their communities and religious systems *and* the nation-state;
- The cultural rights of women within the nation-state.

FEMINIST CRITIQUES OF THE NATION

Postcolonial nation-states, having inherited the gendered anti-colonial struggle and the stereotypical triad of woman–home–nation, have appropriated the woman in different ways. The woman is the guardian of virtue and tradition, as an object to be controlled, as mother, and so on. Noted postcolonial critic Elleke Boehmer has argued convincingly that male roles in the national 'family drama' may be seen as *metonymic*, where the male is part of the national community. But the figure of the woman serves as a *metaphor*, in the representative maternal form, *standing for* the national territory and values (2005b: 229). The nation is seen as a fraternity (brotherhood), a male-centered construct. Women's movements all over the world have been advocating and campaigning for citizenship rights and reform within nations. Such movements also have to negotiate the tensions between women's civil rights and national struggles. In other words, the 'woman question' is often merged with the nation question. Cherríe Moraga's statement cited above captures this dilemma:

- How can women's activism support the national cause when the nation itself oppresses the woman?
- Is it possible for a woman to be a feminist, situated within a global continuum of oppression, and a nationalist committed to a nation that is an instrument of patriarchy?

Cynthia Enloe (1990, cited in West 1997: xix–xx) has argued that nationalism is a masculine construction. Women rarely acquire power within the state structure and are, more often than not, victims of unfair legislation (demonstrated in India by the law of inheritance or property) promulgated by the state. In other cases, if traditional communities exist within, a weak nation-state ensures that the state does not implement modernizing legislation in favour of women (as has been argued in the case of Afghanistan by Valentine Noghadam, 1997).

Nira Yuval-Davis in her *Gender and Nation* (1997) has presented one of the most sustained feminist critiques of nationhood and the nation. Yuval-Davis begins by proposing that the struggle for reproductive rights has been at the centre of feminist struggles. In the West, Malthusian discourses about population and eugenics have effectively placed this right beyond the woman. Women function as symbolic border guards and as embodiments of a collectivity and, therefore, its cultural reproducers. Thus, not only is the woman the biological reproducer of the nation (by helping the national population), she is also the cultural reproducer. This last is the reason why women's dress codes, behavior and rights are so closely monitored and regulated by fundamentalists (Hindu, Christian or Muslim). Yuval-Davis notes that state citizenship is the most inclusive (i.e., anybody can join) mode of membership in the national collective. However, women have not always been treated as equal citizens by the state. Unfair legislation, rights (such as the right to education or property) and refugee laws have treated men and women citizens differently. Further, Yuval-Davis notes, women might be included in the general citizenry, but there are also rules and policies specific to them. Finally, wars have always been gendered. Military movements and wars affect women adversely: rape being one of the most horrific weapons used against civilian populations by invading armies (as I write, for instance, comes independent and other media news of rape camps in Darfur, Sudan[1]). Yuval-Davis proposes a 'transversal politics' as an alternative to the universal/relativism binary within feminism (feminism as a universal project versus local and culture-specific feminism). In such a politics, each woman participant in the dialogue 'brings with her the rooting in her own membership and identity, but at the same time tries to shift in order to put herself in a situation of exchange with women who have different membership and identity' (130). It is important that this 'shifting' does not mean a sacrifice of one's position or identity. What it demands is an empathy and respect for others' positions. It is also important not to homogenize the other. Yuval-Davis' 'transversal politics' asks women to move beyond the identity politics prevalent so far (where women speak only of their specific locations), and develop solidarities with others through dialogue and understanding. There has to be a mutual respect for others' cultural positions. It is an attempt to retain difference while simultaneously seeking points of commonality. As she concludes: 'the struggle against oppression and discrimination might ... have a specific categorical focus but is never confined just to that category' (131). Thus, women from Muslim, Hindu and Sikh communities can come together based on a common platform of 'rights for women' where their specific cultural standpoints are respected but do not constitute an obstacle for dialogue. A good example of such a transversal politics rooted in feminism, and which problematizes the idea of nation is Women Against Fundamentalism (WAF). The organization seeks to fight fundamentalism in all religions. While it respects cultural differences, as a women's organization, it underscores the gender dimension to debates about integration (of immigrants), multiculturalism and communities (*http://waf.gn.apc.org*).

Lois West (1992) has suggested three forms of feminist nationalism: historical and national liberation social movements (which are mostly anti-colonial in nature); movements against neocolonialism (environmental movements led by women against MNCs in numerous Third World countries, including India, would be examples) and; identity-rights movements. This last is women's movements for equal rights, better work conditions or any movement for cultural or economic rights *as* women. West is emphatic that the women's movements must be relativized to their time and place because struggles are local and specific to cultures. West proposes a dialectical model of feminist nationalism where state structures (law) interact with culture (including religion, education, ethnicity). West argues that gender must be worked into every structure, whether it is the law or the education system (1997: xxxi–xxxii). If a feminist perspective is integral to all debates about women's rights, then nationalism and national identity must also be analysed through this perspective keeping the woman's rights in mind. In other words, national identity and the state must be examined through a feminist lens for the ways in which the nation treats its women.

> Feminist nationalism interrogates the gendered nature of the nation state and seeks to find ways of ensuring equal citizenship and other rights for women within the nation-state, while also recognizing cultural differences among the women in this process of claiming rights.

In India, Rajeswari Sunder Rajan's work has explored this dialectic of state and civil society via gender. Writing about the Uniform Civil Code debate, Sunder Rajan (2000) notes a conflict between the exercise of women's citizenship rights and the claims of the religious communities (Hindu, Muslim) they belong to. Sunder Rajan argues that women must be seen as 'national subjects' in relation to, but simultaneously beyond, the state and the religion-based community. Sunder Rajan notes that the Indian constitution promises equality and freedom from discrimination, but this does not work for women. Women continue to be governed by personal laws of their community, and the violence against women continues unabated. In her later work, Sunder Rajan detects the deep-seated contradiction within the state: 'the contradictions between a secular constitution and a state that administers religious laws and is indulgent toward religious communities' demands' (2003: 150).

Nawaad El Saadawi's fiction and other prose works, for instance, explicitly link religious doctrines (or rather male interpretation of religious doctrines) with women's oppression in Egyptian postcolonial society. Pakistani writer Tehmina Durrani in her autobiography, *My Feudal Lord* (1991), and novel, *Blasphemy* (1996), explores the lives of women in patriarchal families where religious doctrines are used to circumscribe, exploit and oppress them. In Islamic societies the 1990s has seen the rise of Islamic feminism, where the nation-state, patriarchy and religion have all been subject to a feminist scrutiny. Islamic feminism has mainly sought legal reform of the Islamic nation-state, and seek a better deal for Muslim women within the ambit of Islam. Thinkers such as Hashemi and Hoodfar argue that there is scope for a more gender-sensitive interpretation of Islamic laws (see Mojab 2001). African writer Mariama Bâ states: 'We no longer accept the nostalgic praise to the African Mother, who, in his anxiety, man confuses with Mother Africa. Within African literature, room must be made for women' (cited in Schipper 1984: 46–7).

In each of these cases we see feminists find the nation-state as well as civil society (and religion) a problem.

RACE AND ETHNICITY

Race had not been a critical category within feminist thought till about the 1980s. One of the major problems for Third World thinkers in the humanities and social sciences was that feminism seemed addressed to and theorized by First World, white women. As early as the 1850s activist Sojourner Truth in a landmark speech, 'A'int I a Woman?', had proposed that ideas of womanhood in America seemed to see the white woman as standard, and the black woman's experience had escaped the attention of the feminists because they were all white. As Cherríe Moraga put it: 'The deepest political tragedy I have experienced is how with such grace, such blind faith, this commitment to women in the feminist movement grew to be exclusive and reactionary' (cited in Kanneh 1998: 87–8). In 1983, the anthology *This Bridge Called My Back* drew attention to the schisms within the feminist movement and showcased the differences within the 'woman's' experience by collecting the writings of women of colour.

There was an increasing dissatisfaction within the feminist movement itself, especially from black, Aboriginal, minority and other non-white women from Asia, Africa, South America and those with multiple cultural roots (Asian-American). Women and feminists from these regions felt that 'woman' as a category could not include the multiple and different experiences of Asian or African women. Their ethnic roots, cultural origins and geopolitical locations demanded that feminism become more 'refined', and account for diversity within the woman's movement. This meant a paradigmatic shift within feminism itself, as race and ethnicity was added to gender for cultural theory. In the mid-1980s Kum-Kum Bhavnani and Meg Coulson (1986) argued forcefully that the political alliance of women must address the charge of racism and exclusion leveled against feminism if it were to be globally effective and participatory for *all* women. One significant movement that emerged as a result was black feminism.

BLACK FEMINISM

Black feminism emerged because of a convincing argument: The black woman's oppression was the result of a double bind—of being woman *and* being black. Black feminism was oppositional to both patriarchy as well as white feminism. bell hooks writes that 'black feminists found that sisterhood for most white women did not mean surrendering allegiance to race, class, and sexual preference ... we witnessed the appropriation of feminist ideology by elitist, racist white women' (188–89).

Thinkers like bell hooks noted that even within the black arts movements and the massive civil rights movements, the problem of black women was rarely addressed. The women also argued that Black Power movement was inherently patriarchal. As Michelle Wallace put it:

> The black man ... particularly since the Black Movement has been in a position to define the black woman. He is the one who tells her whether or not she is a woman and what it is to be a woman...(cited in Simmonds, 1990: 314).

In short black feminism emerges with a two-pronged agenda, to

- question the *masculinist-patriarchal* ideologies of the black movement and
- question the *racism* in the feminist movement.

In the 1950s African American women conformed to white ideals of femininity, as bell hooks notes, and 'many black women believed black liberation could only be achieved by the formation of a strong black patriarchy' (1981: 178, 182). After the civil rights movement, argues hooks,

> black women do not find it necessary to place their willingness to assume a sexist-defined role in the context of black liberation; so it is much more obvious that their support of patriarchy was not engendered solely by their concern for the black race but by the fact that they live in a culture in which the majority of women support and accept patriarchy. (185)

In 1990s, writings by Patricia Hill Collins, Hortense Spillers and Hazel Carby, it could be argued, mark the beginnings of black feminist thought. The aim of these writings was to create forms of knowledge built upon the experiences of black women. This entailed the creation of an archive, a tradition of black women's writing. When Alice Walker retrieved the work of Zora Neale Hurston it was part of such a project of building the canon of black writing. More recently, it has expanded to include archives of oral traditions in black cultures, the compilation of folk lore, myths and other forms of cultural practices (as a result the researches threw up and showcased Ma Rainey, Bessie Smith, Billie Holiday and Blues). It also meant a reappraisal and critical scrutiny of early forms of black writings (Hazel Carby's critical work on nineteenth-century black women novelists, *Reconstructing Womanhood: The Emergence of the Afro-American Woman Novelist*, 1987, for instance).

Black feminism underscores the need to include race and cultural difference within feminist arguments. It suggests that feminism has traditionally been 'white', ignoring the lived experience of blacks and women of colour because it propounded the idea of a universal 'woman's question'. Or else it homogenized all black experience into one ignoring marginal and minority experiences within black cultures. Black feminism seeks the empowerment and emancipation of women not just in relation to whites but also in relation to black men.

The idea was not, however, to plead a case for separatism. As novelist Alice Walker argued about 'womanism' (1984) it is about *all* people of colour.

Black feminism, in a turn away from the 'high theory' of the age, self-consciously paid attention to questions of political economy and material life. It, therefore, looked at issues of black woman's labour and the structure of family oppression. In its critical approach it unravelled stereotypes of mammies and matriarchs, arguing that these stereotypes constructed the black woman as the Other. The black woman is either the mammy (the faithful family servant) or the sexual object. However, as Hazel Carby pointed out, notions of family, patriarchy and reproduction critiqued by white feminism mean very *different* things for the *black* women: Black men have not always held the same positions of power within the black family, black women have headed households, and they have often laboured within both black and white households. Carby argues that such concepts need to be carefully teased apart to understand their contexts for black women:

> What needs to be understood is, first, precisely how the black woman's role in a rural, industrial or domestic labour force affects the construction of ideologies of black female sexuality which are different from, and often constructed in opposition to, white female sexuality; and second, how this role relates to the black woman's struggle for control over her own sexuality. (2000: 392)

Carby here imbricates race, class, gender and sexuality in her analysis of the concepts of labour, family, patriarchy and reproduction.

Black feminist criticism did not spare black writings or pedagogic practices of American universities. When, for example, Hurston's *Their Eyes Were Watching God* attained cult status, Hazel Carby pointed out that this was perhaps because the work 'acts as a mode of assurance that, really the black folk are happy and healthy' (391).

Black feminism paid attention to

- issues of class and labour, i.e., the *material lives* of black women;
- the patriarchal nature of black society and traditions;
- the possibilities of communities—*sisterhood*—of black women;
- the differences *among* black women in terms of class or sexual preferences;
- process of minoritization (especially in the case of lesbians or the differently abled) within blacks.

Black feminist writing also focused on the formation of communities of black women. Informal friendships and family interactions; black churches and black women's organizations constitute (as Patricia Hill Collins argued) 'safe spaces' where black women could meet and form 'sisterhoods'. In this domain, older and peripheral forms of association such as networks of *bloodmothers* and *othermothers* (those who assist bloodmothers by sharing mothering responsibilities) play crucial roles in building communities. Evangelical work and travel by black women (Nancy Prince as early as the 1850s, Amanda Smith who traveled to India as a missionary in the 1890s) mark the territorial connections forged by black women. Far from the domestic or slave system that controlled and circumscribed women such work of evangelical black women marks new forms of mobility and agency (Nayar 2009a).

Black women's writings—and Toni Morrison is the best example of this—explore the possibilities of communities. This stands clearly opposed to the individualism that marks white fictions. Black feminist theory thus takes as the starting point not the individual as subject and agent but the community as a whole. Most importantly, of course, is the fact that it is the black woman who forges this community linkage in a place.

Finally, it involves breaking the stranglehold of heterosexual thinking on women. Black lesbian activism that emerged in the 1990s has played a major role in foregrounding the sexuality of the black woman, her sexual preferences and of course, the aesthetics of the black body.

Within legal studies and Critical Race Theory (CRT) the 1990s has seen the emergence of Critical Race Feminism (CRF). CRF focuses on the legal issues faced by women of color within the USA, and includes African Americans, Chicano/a, Asian and Native Americans. It rejects essentializing minorities and is closely involved with grassroots praxis such as welfare, employment and education (Wing 2002).

POSTCOLONIAL FEMINISM

Even black feminism did not fully address the question of race and ethnicity. Asian Americans and Chicanos, for instance, were 'people of colour' as opposed to 'blacks' and their lived experiences within the context of Africa, South America and Asia were markedly different from that of African Americans. Women from these contexts, therefore, felt the need for new alliances that would include the black woman's experience but also that of Chicanos, Asian immigrants in First World nations, Asian and African women. The result was the formulation of what came to be known as Third World feminism or postcolonial feminism. While postcolonial feminism draws on black feminism's insights—especially regarding the centrality of race and ethnicity—it extends the latter's concerns.

> Postcolonial feminism extends black feminism's concerns in order to address the experiences and oppression of Chicano, Asian American and women of other cultural, national and geopolitical locations. It considers difference to be of primary importance and rejects mainstream (white) feminist homogenization of a universal woman's questions. It seeks emancipation and empowerment, keeping in mind the cultural differences between women.

Postcolonial feminism emphasizes location and cultural difference among women. It notes how spirituality, language and experiences of age, sexuality or motherhood are context-specific: for the woman in remote Rajasthan embedded in traditional Jat cultures to tribal women in Congo to professional Asian American women in First World cities. It is this cultural relativism of the woman's experiences that postcolonial feminism underscores and retains as a major critical lens. Postcolonial feminism is concerned with

- the homogenization of cultural difference among women into a universal category,
- the erasure of differences in lived experience for Asian, South American and African women in the name of this universal category,
- the assumption that the Western model of the feminine or feminism is the standard one,
- the rejection of alternate modes of life—such as spirituality—within 'modern' Western feminism.

In an essay that inaugurated the field, Chandra Talpade Mohanty (2003 [1984]) argued that the entire feminist discourse about 'Third World Women' homogenized women from Asia, Africa and South America into a single, coherent category. This, argued Mohanty, was the homogenization of the rest of the world's women as 'one' woman that stands in contrast to the white woman. Mohanty uncovered three problematic analytic principles in Western feminist discourses. Mohanty's critique of these principles can be taken as a postcolonial feminist project in itself.

First, the category 'women' implies an 'already constituted, coherent group with identical interests and desires, regardless of class, ethnic, or racial location, or contradictions ... [and] a notion of gender or sexual difference or even patriarchy that can be applied universally and cross-culturally' (21)

Second, the proof of universality and cross-cultural validity where particular women's experiences (and Mohanty looks at the discourse of the Islamic veil or the sexual division of labour in Western feminism) become descriptive generalizations.

Third, as a result of the above two modes, there arises a model of power and struggle and the homogeneous notion of the oppression of women. This produces, argues Mohanty, the 'average Third World woman'. Mohanty went on to note that Western feminism posited a linear progression: from the primitive, vulnerable and ignorant 'Third World' woman to the modern, knowledgeable and empowered Western/white woman.

Elsewhere, Chela Sandoval (1991) has proposed a 'US Third World feminism' where women of colour stand in opposition to the prevalent white feminism. Mainstream white feminism is 'hegemonic feminism', argued Sandoval, and it constructs itself as the standard feminism by ignoring black feminisms and the Asian-African-South American woman.

What postcolonial feminism, like black feminism, emphasizes is difference.

A particular brand of postcolonial feminism finds Western feminism's rejection of spirituality objectionable because, as they argue, the spiritual constitutes an important component of women's lives, and spirituality can be a means of self-empowerment too. An early form of the retrieval of the spiritual and quasi-mystic dimension within feminism is seen in black lesbian feminist poet Audre Lorde. Arguing a case for the erotic as a spiritual mode, Lorde writes of 'inner experiences' as empowerment:

> When we begin to live from within outward, in touch with the power of the erotic within ourselves, and allowing that power to inform and illuminate our actions upon the world around us, then we begin to be responsible to ourselves in the deepest sense ... Our acts against oppression become integral with self, motivated and empowered from within.(1984: 58)

Alice Walker, in similar fashion, also gave primacy of place to the Spirit: '[A womanist] loves the Spirit. Loves love and food and roundness. Loves struggle ... Loves herself. Regardless' (1983: xii). The 'Amman' goddesses from Hinduism, and even Draupadi, adapted by regions in South Africa, can become role models for women, argues Alleyn Diesel (2002). Suniti Namjoshi's fiction contains quasi-mystic and spiritual elements that foreground the role of the mother-spirit, as in *The Mothers of Maya Diip*. The matriarch visits a temple that only has the goddess:

> The goddess was everywhere, depicted among her friends, her lovers, her warriors, her servants, her enemies and her babies. And she was there in all her aspects: grim, giddy, austere, tender and maternal, languid and luxurious, asleep and waking, austere and amorous, warlike and proud ... This was stone made flesh. She [Jyanvi] was overwhelmed.(1989: 56)

Other Third World feminists have argued for the return to spirituality as a source of feminist power. Jaimes Guerrero calls for a return to the 'sacred kinship among ... bioregionally based indigenous people and their respective cultures', what she terms a 'native womanism' (2003: 68). Kristina Groover (1999) has argued that native accounts of spirituality within feminism turns to the community rather than the individual (the latter being the focus of Western feminism). In this, spiritualized feminism has a larger social role because it works with ethnic communities and entire localities. It links the woman's experience with both the community and the natural setting/surrounding. As we have seen in the case of black feminism, the woman remains the cornerstone of community-formation, and spirituality becomes an instrument of this kind of native feminisms.

TECHNOLOGY AND THE FEMINIST RESPONSE

Feminist critiques of science and technology have been built on particular assumptions: that technologies are social and that women's experience of technology are different from that of men. Any technology emerges in a social context, and is mired in contemporary social relations and structures. As feminist studies of technology have demonstrated (Cockburn 1985, Wajcman 1991), technological developments have, historically, been used to limit the woman's sphere. Feminist readings of science have addressed a variety of concerns: birth control, the environment in the age of high tech, psychiatry, health, among others. Science, argues one of its most influential feminist critics, Evelyn Fox Keller, is 'based on a division of emotional and intellectual labour in which objectivity, reason, and "mind" are cast as male and subjectivity, feeling and "nature" are cast as female … celebrating … ultimately, the dominion of mind over nature' (cited in Smith Keller 1992: 14). This emphasis on the 'objectivity' of science also meant that women's knowledges were discounted as knowledge (women who were deemed to possess unusual knowledge were identified as witches and often burnt at the stake). Women's contributions to science and technology have remained hidden from history as a result.

In the twenty-first century the technology that dominates everything else —in mundane matters about domestic life to global economy—is information and communications technology (ICT). How do globalization and ICTs affect women?

Feminist studies of cyberspace explore the *material* (or 'real'), the *symbolic* (representations) and *virtual* (cyberspace) worlds without privileging any one. A series of feminist questions about ICTs would be as follows:

- Do women use computers and cyberspace differently?
- How many women figure as CEOs of software firms?
- How many women take higher degrees in software engineering?
- Does cyberspace offer different opportunities and greater freedom for women?
- Do women in South East Asian sweatshops designing computer chips get the same wages as their American counterparts?

These are questions that deal with all aspects—material, symbolic and the virtual—of cybercultures because, as I have argued elsewhere, cyberculture is recursively linked to and must always return to the real (Nayar 2009b).

CYBORG CULTURES

Cyberfeminism is a form of feminism that not only interrogates the patriarchal nature of the new ICTs but has also developed feminist appropriations of the same. The critique of cybercultures and contemporary technoscience may be traced to—if one is interested in origin stories—the works of Donna Haraway.

Donna Haraway proposed that the machine–human interface, or the cyborg (cybernetic organism, made popular by Arnold Schwarzenegger with *Terminator*), transcends the gender binary. Cyborgs are constructions that do not fit any category. Like women, cyborgs are biologically and symbolically produced and reproduced through social interaction. As Haraway puts it: 'I am making an argument for the cyborg as a fiction mapping our social and bodily reality and as an imaginative resource suggesting some very fruitful couplings' (1991: 150). It is, she continues, 'a creature in a post-gender world; it has no truck with bisexuality, pre-oedipal symbiosis, unalienated labour, or other seductions to organic wholeness through a final appropriation of all the powers of the parts into a higher unity' (150).

Since the woman has traditionally been reduced to the body/matter (and the man is 'mind'), the new cyborg body is a fragmentation of the category of 'woman' itself. The cyborg breaks down the barrier between self (the human) and Other (machine). It is thus beyond gender and identity determinism.

Haraway claims the cyborg for the feminist movement for another reason too. Traditionally the woman has been confined to and attached to the family as 'mother'. The cyborg also escapes the theme of woman as mother and primary care-giver. It thus breaks the 'normal' structure of the heterosexual family itself.

Haraway does not call for a rejection of technoscience. Instead, she argues, women need to respond to technology without recourse to the traditional structure: technology versus nature. In other words, Haraway seeks to reclaim the technological realm for women.

However, critics have noted that Haraway's cyborg culture is similar to the shifting, fragmented identity posited by postmodernism and poststructuralism. And what minorities need is not fragmented or dispersed identities, but *located* ones (Schueller 2005).

Reading cyborg cultures, Sadie Plant has proposed that retrieving the metaphor of the 'weave'. In her 'The Future Looms: Weaving Women and Cybernetics' (1995) she links the weaving of the World Wide Web (www) to the craft of weaving, a profession that has traditionally been the women's. Here the Web is a woven network, with links woven together by the individuals who are themselves woven into the network as a result. The weave of the Web is an act of *agency*, where the women consciously 'connect' as an assertion of selfhood and identity. Instead of cyberspace as a new frontier to be conquered and dominated, 'weaving' suggests an alternate view of thinking about cybercultures: The feminist 'weave' suggests linkage, mutual dependency and community.

Feminists propose that women need to be not only involved in the 'building' of cybercultures but also ensure that the new technologies further human interest rather than reinforce existing power relations, injustice and inequalities (Arizpe 1999). Cybercultures are as unfair and unjust as the real, and, as Rosi Braidotti has warned, 'Hyper-reality does not wipe out class relations: it just intensifies them' (*www.let.uu.nl/womens_studies/rosi/cyberfem.htm*). For example, 'Third World' women and underpaid non-white women labour in order to produce the very technological structures that generate cyberspace: but this cyberspace offers freedom mostly for white women. In other words, even within cyberfeminist versions of cybercultures, we need to account for differences of class and race because cyberspace is *not* used or available in the same way for women of colour.

CYBERFEMINISM

The attempt at appropriating cyberspace for the empowerment of women has taken many forms: the creation of online communities, counselling (cybersolace), information networks for women entrepreneurs, and art works. Here I build on an earlier argument that I have made: that a counter-public sphere might be emerging in cybercultures through its appropriation by women (Nayar 2006).[2]

> Cyberfeminism is the theoretically informed appropriation of cybercultures in the information age. It includes close analysis and attempts to access the material contexts of cybercultures (jobs, education, community) as well as cultural forms of this appropriation (art). Cyberfeminism is the feminist response to and negotiation with the contemporary culture's extensive informatization.

Women in/and Cyberspace

One form of feminist theorizing about cybercultures is to show its linkage with and embeddedness in real, material lives. It is not adequate to treat virtual environments as providing greater freedom to women, but to locate these environments in actual material, social practices within which the women live and work.

Women's networks are a key form of online usage. They constitute a means for women to enter the public sphere. Computer literacy and networking thus provide the women—as traditional education did—a mode of 'leaving' the circumscribed space of the home.

The 'public sphere' has been treated as the site of rational dialogue (Habermas). However, this means perpetuating the old divide between reason and emotion. And since traditionally women have been seen as emotional creatures and men as the rational ones, it excludes the possibility of the woman's participation in the public sphere. Feminist appropriations of cyberspace allow counter-publics based on 'rejected' or rational aspects as sentiment to be formed (Travers 2003). A feminist reclamation of cyberspace as a more open public sphere requires not an escape from but a *return to embodiment*. Greater numbers of women users, online support groups and political activism alters the public sphere as a feminist counter-public sphere. Demands for rights, information about the law, cultural expressions, health advice are all central to such a reclamation.

Women in India, statistics reveal (Internet and Mobile Association of India, February 2006. *www.iamai.in/section.php3?secid=16&press_id= 813&mon=2.*), use the Internet more for personal activity than professional work. This means their use of ICTs depends on their family responsibilities and domestic arrangements. This suggests, unsurprisingly, that the woman's use and work on the Internet is embedded in her material context.

However, the feminist appropriation of the materiality of cyberspace is altering in significant ways. Women-owned and operated e-businesses have grown since the late 1990s (Sassen 2002: 114). India's famous Self-employed Women's Association (SEWA), for instance, has used ICTs to create extensive databases, mailing lists and networks (*www.sewa.org*). Elected women representatives in politics have been enthusiastic about the new technologies as a means of widening their mass base and popularizing their agenda (Gopalan). This is a feminist *material* appropriation of cybercultures.

Cyberfeminist Art and Culture

Informed by theories of cyborgs and feminism, and determined to utilize cyberspace for their own ends, cyberfeminist writers, artists and groups have begun to develop a different relationship with virtual worlds. Building on the work of Donna Haraway, Sadie Plant, Katherine Hayles and other thinkers on cyberculture, cyberpunk fiction by feminists (Marge Piercy, Pat Cadigan) and cyberfeminist art work (such as the VNS Matrix) proposes a new 'form' of the virtual.

Cyberculture for feminist cyberpunk is the product of an unequal system of finance, technology, labour and cultural stereotyping where

- the woman's contribution is ignored or undervalued,
- the emphasis on reason and scientificity ignores emotional responses to and relations with technology,
- the female body is still sexualized for male consumption, and
- the woman's relationship with technology is never seen as primary.

Feminist cyberpunk sees technology as rooted in a specific social and cultural context. ICTs emerge in the age of globalization, transnational labour and financial flows. The 'wired' world is predominantly 'First World'.

Feminist cyberpunk shows magic, spirituality, emotions as equally important responses to and modes of appropriation of the ICTs. Pat Cadigan, for instance, renders cyberspace and its attendant features as a shamanic, quasi-mystical space in her novels. Writers like Cadigan, Piercy and Scott find the theme of the transcendence of the body—so central to male cyberpunk—an illusion. For the white *or* coloured woman the body remains central to structures of exploitation and freedom/justice/empowerment. The transcendence of the body once again privileges the mind over matter—a stereotype that, since the early modern period, has been gendered, where the male is mind and woman, matter. Hence, the escape from the body is a male fantasy, the search for a realm of 'pure' consciousness, whereas for the woman the body is at the centre of the search for identity and

emancipation. Hence feminist cyberpunk sees computers, ICTs, body modifica-
tion technologies and cyberspace not as a means of escaping embodiment as much
as an augmentation and re-grounding of the body. Emancipation must proceed
from the body, must account *for* the body. To reject the body in favour of the mind
is to willfully ignore that material lives are lived through the body, especially in the
case of coloured or queer women. For the coloured women, therefore, cyberspace
foregrounds the black body's subjectivity in technology.

Cyber-art influenced by feminist theory—especially Luce Irigaray and Hélène
Cixous—first became manifest online as the *VNS Matrix*. The *VNS Matrix* was a
group of four Australia-based artists—Josephine Starrs, Francesca de Rimini,
Julianne Pierce and Virginia Barratt. This was the VNS Matrix's agenda, politics
and slogan:

> We are the modern cunt
> positive anti reason
> unbounded unleashed unforgiving
> we see art with our cunt we make art with our cunt
> we believe in jouissance madness holiness and poetry
> we are the virus of the new world disorder
> rupturing the symbolic from within
> saboteurs of big daddy mainframe
> the clitoris is a direct line to the matrix
> VNS MATRIX
> terminators of the moral codes
> mercenaries of slime
> go down on the altar of abjection
> probing the visceral temple we speak in tongues
> infiltrating disrupting disseminating
> corrupting the discourse
> we are the future cunt.
> (*'The Cyberfeminist Manifesto for the 21st Century'*, 1991. *Archived at* www.sysx.org/
> gashgirl/VNS/TEXT/PINKMANI.HTM. *Accessed 25 October 2007*)

The idea was to shock, even as their feminist appropriation of technology received
the enthusiastic support from theorists like Sadie Plant. Sexual difference, identity
and the question of women's 'weaves' and networks were assimilated into techno-
art forms here by the *VNS Matrix*, and thus marked what a departure from the
masculinist-capitalist technology.

More feminist subcultural forms within cyberculture emerged in the 1990s.
Ambitious Bitch, a CD-ROM art piece created by Marita Liulia (1996), for
instance, deployed the image of the bitch as the centerpiece (Donna Haraway's
more recent *Companion Species Manifesto*, 2003, replaces the cyborg with the dog).
In 1994 *VNS Matrix* was back with its CD-ROM *All New Gen*. Combining the
video game with SF, this once more focused on the slut (by now called 'cyber-
sluts'), with a play on 'Gen' (taken to mean both generation and genders), the
parody used extensive vaginal imageries. The idea was to replace, or at least offer

an alternative to, computer games that were exclusively male-centered, with soldiers ripping up spaces, male explorers, city-builders, images of masculine conquest and penetration—actions in which predominantly male players participate.

Rather than be reduced to a sexual object defined and described by the male techno-user, cyberfeminists transformed cyberspace into the realm of the decidedly, irreducibly female. Where pejorative terms like 'sluts' used by men as categories of disparagement and marginalization, cyberfeminists reclaimed and turned them into *positive* identity categories to describe cyborg/wired women: The 'bitch' or the 'slut' becomes a term of *self-definition* (see, for example, 'Bitch From Hell', *http://www.yoni.com/bitch.shtml*).

FURTHER READING

Ruthven, K. K. 1984. *Feminist Literary Studies: An Introduction*. Cambridge: Cambridge University Press.

Collins, Patricia Hill. 1991. *Black Feminist Thought: Knowledge, Consciousness and the Politics of Empowerment*. New York: Routledge.

Jacobus, Mary. 1986. *Reading Women: Essays in Feminist Criticism*. London: Methuen.

Wajcman, Judy. 1993. *Feminism Confronts Technology*. Cambridge: Polity.

NOTES

1. 'Darfur's Rape Camps', 16 July 2008, http://antwerpen.indymedia.org/news/2008/07/15903.php (Accessed 13 September 2008). Also see earlier reports of rape as a mode of war in Sudan, Craig Timberg, 'For Darfur Women, Survival Means Leaving Camp, Risking Rape', *Washington Post*, 16 September 2006, http://www.washingtonpost.com/wp-dyn/content/article/2006/09/15/AR2006091501157.html (Accessed 13 September 2008).

2. Other forms of appropriation of cyberspace by minorities and the marginalized have been noted elsewhere. For example, I have argued that the Sarai project's 'Cybermohalla' is a new public space facilitated by digital technologies (Nayar 2008a).

5 Marxisms

Writing in the nineteenth century Karl Marx and Friedrich Engels located all forms of 'culture'—music, painting and literature—within a social context. Attempting to provide a theory of the industrialized society Marx and Engels also treated art as an important component of human life. However, their main contribution

Marxist cultural theory locates all forms of art within existing social conditions of economics and politics, even as it approaches the art-object as an important 'element' within social relations through which particular meanings are standardized and held up as 'good taste' in order to marginalize and ignore other meanings. Marxism sees this battle over meaning as reflecting a battle between dominant and oppressed sections of society. As a result, Marxist theory pays attention to the modes through which literature and art actively help maintain power relations at the cost of the weak.

was to locate the so-called 'aesthetic' realms such as art within the contexts of politics, economics and history. The 'Marxist' approach to questions of aesthetics often, therefore, links them with questions of class, economic conditions and power.

Marxist thinking has been influential in cultural theory, anthropology, history and literary criticism. It is one of the most political forms of cultural theory because (i) it links art with actual conditions within a particular culture and (ii) it sees forms of art not as some special realm but intimately linked to the existing power relations within a particular culture. Marxist criticism, therefore, explores power relations embedded and concealed in cultural texts.

OPENING MOVES

THE CLASS TURN: MARX AND ENGELS

By the nineteenth century, nations such as England had become industrialized societies. Marx and Engels undertook detailed studies of the condition of culture, paying particular attention to questions of political power and economic conditions. Noting that in industrialized societies, political power rested with individuals or groups of individuals who controlled the factory or the industry, Marx and Engels noted that 'class' was the key element in such societies. Developing this theme, they argued that such societies exhibit a battle of the classes where the upper classes (feudal landlords, factory owners, capitalists) sought to keep the working classes (serfs, factory workers, proletariat) under their control. This process of domination—or *hegemony*—within the society becomes the central feature of Marxist thought.

Class, in simple terms, refers to a division within a particular society. In Marxist thought class refers to the *economic* groups within the society:

(i) A class of people controls the factory and the industry (called 'means of production') and

(ii) A class of people works in the factory.

In the case of a feudal society we have the land-owning class and the peasants.

Thus, we have two main classes here: the owner or the capitalist class and the working or the labour class. These two classes are always in conflict because the upper classes, or what Marx and Engels called the *bourgeoisie*, owned the means of production and the working classes owned nothing except their labouring bodies. Marxist thought terms this conflictual relation between classes as the 'social relations of production'. These social relations are conflictual because they are exploitative: The dominant classes seek to control the working classes because their profits depend on an efficient management of the working class. Marxism argues that this relation between classes is the one that structures a society itself. What is clear is that, for Marxism, the economic realm (the means of production, the classes, the ownership of the means of the production) is the most important realm in any society, and class is the basic unit of a society.

Class was, therefore, a matter of hierarchy within society, power and economic privilege. Being a member of the upper classes confers certain privileges upon a person. Every class develops particular forms of culture and forms of behaviour—what is often described as 'working-class culture', 'mass culture' or 'middle-class values'. Notice that in each case we are speaking of things that are not strictly about economic conditions. This was the radical contribution of Marxist thinking: It associated religious beliefs, art forms, behaviour, moral codes, and other such non-economic—or cultural—aspects of life with an individual or group's class affiliation. Culture, therefore, is not about truth, beauty, taste or aesthetics. Rather, culture is a system where particular ideas about truth, beauty and aesthetics are developed in relation to particular classes. Let us take an example.

'Taste' becomes a marker of upper-class identity in the nineteenth century when aspects of the working-class 'culture'—the street play, the football match, the comedy, boots and dirt—become classified as filthy, crass, crude, tasteless and ugly. In sharp contrast to these forms of culture visible in working-class sections, there emerged 'high culture': the opera, the art gallery, the novel of ideas. To bring the debate closer home, the films of Satyajit Ray or Shyam Benegal are treated as 'intellectual' or 'artistic' even though the crowds do not go to watch them, while the films of David Dhawan, which draw bigger crowds, are treated with disdain by film critics (this trend begins to change with popular culture studies in the 1970s). If the audience numbers is any indication then we can see that Dhawan's films appeal to more people, just as a street play attracted more spectators than the opera. However, this mass appeal is not the criterion used to classify films. Rather, categories of 'taste' and art are invoked to privilege Ray over Dhawan. To use another example, in the famous posters for *The Devil Wears Prada* we see a pair of red high heel shoes. The shoes represent, as the film does, aesthetic sense and high fashion. Why isn't a pair of working boots used? The answer is: Working class boots do not qualify as 'fashion', even though so many use/wear them. Fashion is intrinsically associated with the footwear of particular classes and professions: those who do not work in factories but in offices, those who not work in muddy areas but in carpeted surroundings.

Popular forms of culture, therefore, do not receive the same kind of acclaim, attention or privilege as particular forms such as an 'art film' or the art gallery. This distinction of treatment is not always about the quality of the art-object, but with the class to which the art-object appeals or is deemed to be connected. Working-class art, it is argued, does not possess the 'qualities' necessary to make it 'art'. For the Marxist, the very use of concepts of 'quality' suggests a power relation where the upper classes are the ones who define what quality means. The dominant classes do not see working-class art forms as possessing any quality worth praising. What we can conclude from the Marxist argument is that

- social aspects are intimately connected to *economic* ones and
- class is more than an economic category, it refers to matters of evaluation, ideas about taste and *social* power.

To build on this sense of class as a social group/feature, we need to shift focus slightly. Class, as we have noted, is related to matters of taste, manners and aesthetics. It is about status and power. The power that proceeds from being a member of the upper class does mean simply economic power. The upper classes marginalize the experiences and aesthetics of the working classes because it is the upper (or dominant) class that does the classifying of art as 'good' or 'bad'. In other words, the dominant classes also possess considerable *social* and *cultural power*. The social here is dependent upon the economic. If we were to refine what we understand as 'class' we would, therefore, describe it as a 'social formation'.

Forms of culture such as the novel, the opera, painting all reflect, in Marxist thinking, the deeper economic conditions in a society. This is the most important insight within Marxism.

MARXISM AND CULTURE

Marxism provides a sociological context and interpretation of cultural forms, whether it is a film or a novel. It locates, as noted already, all cultural forms within social and economic conditions existing in a particular society. Thus, it believes that cultural forms *reflect* social conditions, and the novel or film often reveals the truth about classes, class conflict and power relations within a society.

Marxist criticism, following from the above view of culture, seeks to explore the links between a literary or cultural artifact and the social and economic conditions in which the artifact is formed and exists. Thus, Narayan's novels depict middle-class life in a small, south Indian town, while Rushdie's fiction after *Midnight's Children* deals almost exclusively with upper middle classes in metropolitan Bombay/Mumbai. The films of Amitabh Bachchan in the 1980s depicted an individual's fight against social evils in an age when corruption was still (comparatively speaking) a shocking social problem that could be solved. A Marxist approach would suggest that

- the cultural form (the novel or film) *exhibit* or *represent* the worlds Narayan and Rushdie have observed or experienced.
- the form and themes offers particular visions and *plans* for that society: Rebellion in Amitabh Bachchan's films suggests that society can be changed through the (heroic) effort of individuals.
- such cultural forms and their themes *influence* the readers/viewers because these appear to be convincing, realistic and therefore *appeal* to them.

This 'language' or 'form' appeals to viewers because it captures a social experience, even as it offers suggestions to change that experience. Terry Eagleton refers to the

> The 'language' or 'form' of a work of art (which would include films and novels) captures, therefore, a *social experience*.

social–cultural and economic aspects of society in traditional Marxist terms. The economic dimension is the 'general mode of production' while literature and art correspond to the 'literary mode of production' (1985 [1975], Chapter Two). Eagleton suggests, in classical Marxist terms, what we have proposed so far: 'The forces of production of the LMP [Literary Mode of Production] are naturally provided by the GMP [General Mode of Production] itself, of which the LMP is a particular substructure' (1985: 49).

What a Marxist view of culture does, therefore, is to seek a 'social referent' (a term favoured by John Hall in his work on the sociology of literature, 1979). A 'social referent' describes the themes and representations within a work of art that somehow refers to the actual existing social conditions, contexts, conflicts. Thus, when the leading Marxist historian of his age, E. P. Thompson in his works on the English working class (*The Making of the English Working Class*, 1963; *Customs in Common*, 1991) analysed Thomas Hardy's *The Mayor of Casterbridge*, he suggested that the wife-selling scene actually referred to particular form of divorce within plebian communities.

Any work of imagination, in other words, also offers us a view of the tensions, problems, exploitation, within a society. A work of art—the product of the imagination—helps us understand our 'real' world. As we shall see, this Marxist insight has enormous significance.

It is also important to note that Marxism's 'contextual' reading of art—that is, locating art (its author, production, reception) within its social contexts—has parallels with other forms of critical thinking in the late twentieth century. New Historicism and Cultural Materialism also focus on the social contexts of art. Stephen Greenblatt's early essays (notably 'The Circulation of Social Energy' and others in *Shakespearean Negotiations*, 1988) seek to unravel, for instance, the processes of monetary exchange, the issue of authority and power and the dynamics of institutions. When Greenblatt proclaims that 'this institutional improvisation frames the local improvisation of individual playwrights' (2003: 506), he is locating an individual author/text within contexts of production (for a detailed exposition of New Historicism and Cultural Materialism see Chapter 8).

A Marxist approach to culture focuses on both the production and consumption of the cultural artifact. That is, it focuses on the artist—author as well as audience—reader. By focusing on the elements and processes of production, Marxism seeks a material basis for abstract things like aesthetics or truth. It suggests that concepts and representations of beauty or ideals in literature and art are in some ways connected to (either directly and accurately, or indirectly and altering) material realities of economics, class relations, power and suffering. Marxism thus asks us to locate a *material* basis for culture.

> Marxism is often termed 'materialist criticism' because it seeks to establish a link between actual, material conditions—the economy, salary, factory conditions, profits, forms of living, population—and cultural forms (art) and abstract representations in cultural forms.

The Marxist approach does not accept the theories of 'artist-as-genius' or 'artist-as-solitary-thinker'. Such a notion of the artist disconnects him/her from the milieu in which s/he undergoes certain experiences and, therefore, creates particular kinds of artifacts. In other words, Marxism asks us to focus on the social position of a writer. Thus, in order to understand why particular forms and themes appeared in the first kind of English poetry we study—the early modern poetry of Chaucer, Spenser, the Cavaliers—we need to locate these authors in their contexts.

Printing made books cheaper in the fifteenth century. On the other hand, patronage continued to be a key system of poetic survival because the poets did not usually have another means of livelihood. This means poets like Chaucer or Spenser wrote particular kinds of work because of the patronage system, while, independently, books for the masses were being produced through printing. To extend this argument to William Shakespeare, we need to see the themes and forms of Shakespeare's plays not simply as aesthetically polished but as determined by what the 'market' was like for such works. This implies that the plays took those forms and themes that people would pay to watch. Shakespeare had to entertain the masses, not the aristocrats alone. Thus, he had to ensure that his plays were 'popular', that they contained things that people would pay and view. In effect, therefore, Shakespeare wrote for the general public, and the market demand for particular kinds of works determined what he wrote. Yet he could not afford to annoy the royalty by making his plays so 'populist' or works of simply 'mass appeal' (which would be seen as crass and 'tasteless' by the upper classes). In short, what we like to think of as 'Shakespeare's genius' was the genius of a marketer, a businessman: He was able to sell his product to both the royalty and the masses. To use a more contemporary example, films and even computer games coming out from the USA have regularly portrayed other cultures as evil and the Americans as saviours. The hugely successful popular films like *Air Force One*, *Independence Day*, *Armageddon* or *Die Hard* showed Americans saving the world, almost as though no other race or nation wanted this responsibility. In the post–Cold War era when only one superpower remained, American films depicted Americans as the all-powerful people and America a country every nation turned to in moments of crisis.

This, in very simplistic terms, constitutes the *sociology of cultural production*. Yet we need to also understand that cultural products such as a film or a novel cannot be reduced to social contexts alone. Thus, Hollywood that routinely produces war films full of the 'American vision' about terrorists and attacks, also produces 'different' visions of terrorism and America in films like the lesser-known *Syriana* (starring George Clooney).

A Marxist approach asks us to pay attention to the profits—financial as well as cultural—made by artists and writers that determine the kind of work they produced. When writing became a profession in eighteenth-century England, writing itself changed. Writers were, like all other 'artisans', 'producing' works that would *sell*. The eighteenth century is, therefore, the age of the professionalization of the artist. To take a more recent example, that of Harry Potter, we need to locate Rowling within contemporary cultures of production. Brand managing, diffuse audiences (that is, Rowling's audiences are scattered across the world), and an excellent publicity machine (Warner Bros) have helped create 'brand Potter'. The 'genius' of Rowling, such as it is, must be seen at least partly as the effect of some of the most brilliant marketing and media strategies in recent times. We are speaking here of a multi-billion dollar industry that has grown up around Harry Potter, helped by strategically placed stories about her single motherhood and poverty days, the careful referencing to an earlier fantasy (J. R. R. Tolkien's) to mark a continuity of tradition, the law suits that ensure that she remains in control of all Potter 'texts', among others.

While this helps us understand how a work of art is formed, it does not quite explain how we, the readers/viewers, make meaning from texts. A Marxist approach locates not only the text and author within a social context, but also the reader. Readers make particular kinds of meaning from texts because of their social position such as class/caste/race/gender affiliations. Literacy changed with the cheaper books available as a result of printing in early modern England. As a result the nature of readership changed; now more middle-class people could afford to read. This meant that books had to cater to this new kind of readership. As a result writers like Thomas Deloney were hugely successful when they catered to the middle classes rather than the aristocracy. Deloney's works, full of bawdy humour, problems of the working classes and simple prose appealed to the new literates.

Hindi films of the late 1990s rarely show large families. In fact, films like *Dhoom* show families that consist entirely of the two partners— no parents, no children. These appeal to a metropolitan audience where such families are increasingly common. Individuals find the *individualism* of such films, and their blatant consumerism, resonating with their own lives. There are no references to caste in these films, even though caste is a key element in the life of individuals in most parts of India even today. Such films that decontextualize (that is, erase) markers of identity such as caste or class—everybody lives in fancy apartments, and possesses a certain amount of wealth, vocabulary and social circle—appeal to a generation of viewers from metropolitan backgrounds. This means, an urbanite of a particular class responds better to the lifestyle depicted in *Metro* or *Dhoom* than to, say, rural India.

The appeal of Chinua Achebe's *Things Fall Apart* (1958) to readers from Asia, South America and Africa had to do with the fact that here was a novelist describing the racialized aspects of colonialism as no white author had done. Achebe's fiction generated a readership because these readers could relate, from their own experience and a memory of colonialism, to what happens to Okonkwo and the African protagonists.

Thus, a Marxist approach to culture also asks us to pay attention to the social contexts of cultural consumption, i.e., the contexts of readers, film-goers, theatre fans and TV viewers.

> The sociology of culture in Marxism focuses on the social contexts of the author and reader, the production and consumption of cultural artifacts. It thus examines the author's contexts—social, economic, cultural, technological, including media, publicity, funding, class/race/gender—as well as the reader's to see how culture produces certain kinds of texts and particular meanings of those texts.

Marxist literary and cultural theory has certain key modes of analysing cultural texts. In the rest of this chapter we shall examine these modes.

CULTURE, IDEOLOGY AND HEGEMONY

Cultural 'products' like films, the afternoon soap opera or comic books are created and consumed in particular contexts, as we have seen. Such products explain the world to us. With their 'social referents', they help us make sense of the world, even as the world we live in helps us generate the meanings from a text. This means, works of art function as codes for experiences and realities. We 'decode' a work of art depending on the contexts we occupy (what we have identified above as the 'sociology of consumption').

Marxist criticism suggests that all cultural forms seek to ensure that the dominant classes in a society remain dominant. In order to do so, it must convince the working classes and the oppressed not to rebel or revolt. The dominant classes usually achieve this by suggesting to the working classes that the present social condition is 'natural', benevolent and ultimately beneficial to them. One needs only to think of the factory owners in Dickens' fiction and the way a character like Stephen Blackpool (*Hard Times*) is convinced (at least partly) of the 'naturalness' of the industrial system. In order to achieve this convincing argument about the 'just' and 'natural' order of things, the dominant classes need to control the kinds of art and cultural products that circulate. Since books, music, films, theatre are consumed by the working classes as well these become important means of conveying the argument. To put it another way, cultural forms carry a message that the dominant classes want to pass on to the working classes, a message that suggest that things are quite all right, that the capitalist is a benevolent man and that the workers are not really oppressed.

In other words, cultural artifacts *represent* the world to us (what I have termed, rather crudely, message) in certain ways so that we obtain particular meanings from them. Marxist criticism is attentive to the ways in which art or a cultural artifact does this 'representation'. Does a novel like Arundhati Roy's *The God of Small Things* accurately reveal the exploitative nature of gender relations and caste conflicts in small town India? Do Ekta Kapoor's serials present particular kinds of women, and offer us particular roles of women (as mother, wife, girlfriend) as 'good'? Does the superhero comic book suggest that individuals with extraordinary powers are better 'human' beings only because they serve the humans?

These questions focus on the *nature* of representations in works of art/culture. These are questions that we need to ask if we are to understand the full implications of what we see/read/consume. These implications are—and this is important—not simply aesthetic or artistic but social. The way a novel or film portrays women or the working classes can influence the audience's perceptions of them. Further, the novel or film can 'twist' reality to represent—as Hollywood films do in the case of 'terrorists'—it in certain ways. It convinces us, to some degree, that *this* is the way the world is.

> Cultural forms are modes of representation. The task of Marxist criticism is to see how such representations reflect or refract existing economic conditions so that the dominant classes retain their power in any society.

This aspect of masking, altering and customizing reality in art is the central concern of Marxist criticism. If art and culture are social aspects of real economic conditions then it follows that representations in art and culture either reveal or conceal the real conditions on which it (art and culture) is based. If a work of art explains things with a 'twist', then the task of Marxist criticism is to unravel that twist, to expose the work of art as an exercise in manipulation of public opinion.

Cultural forms are modes of representation of reality. We have already noted how, by invoking criteria of 'taste' or aesthetics, the art of working classes can be rejected by the dominant classes. This means, only the dominant classes' representation of that society is treated as valid or correct. When the working classes are shown films or plays created from the upper-class point of view, they naturally believe that 'this is how things are'. Thus, the Victorian novel depicted (represented) the working class as dirty, immoral and dishonest. Since there were few working-class authors who produced any counter to such a representation, the ones produced by the dominant classes reigned supreme. It is, therefore, necessary to see if such representations twisted reality.

This 'twist' of reality—the real economic conditions in any society—is what Marxist criticism calls *ideology*, and is the first key concept in Marxist theory.

Marx and Engels argued that the capitalist mode of production justified and naturalized itself through certain patterns of thought or ideas (what I have termed 'representation'). With social structures such as education, culture and religion the oppressed classes believed that the order of inequality in society is 'natural' or 'pre-ordained', and do not recognize that they are oppressed. This system of thought or representation that helps naturalize economic inequality and oppression is termed *ideology*.

Ideology is the writings, speeches, beliefs and opinions—cultural practices—that assert the 'naturalness' and necessity of economic practices. The ideology is, therefore, an instrument of power because it helps prop up the dominant classes by naturalizing an exploitative relationship and convincing the working classes that this is how things are. Ideology prevents the recognition of oppression by the oppressed. Thus, it is a blind, a veil that prevents the oppressed from proper under-standing. Hence, Marx termed it *false consciousness*.

> 'False consciousness' or ideology is a mode of misrecognizing the true nature of our material lives and social roles when we consume a cultural artifact. It is a system of ideas, values, beliefs that we live by, through which we perceive the world.

Ideology is about power because it legitimizes the power of the dominant classes or sections of a society. From the examples above we have seen how the capitalist class tries to naturalize conditions of exploitation. Ideology is what enables the capitalist class to naturalize these conditions because ideology provides a system of beliefs and ideas that the working classes absorb. In John Thompson's definition 'to study ideology is to study the ways in which meaning (or signification) serves to sustain relations of domination' (1984: 4). The task of Marxist criticism is to locate the ideologies implicit in any cultural text.

The domination and reinforcement of power relations is termed *hegemony*, a term popularized by the Italian thinker Antonio Gramsci. Hegemony is akin to ideology, but is more than that. It includes ideology because, as we shall see, hegemony works most effectively when the dominated accept their domination.

Hegemony refers to the processes—including ideology—through which the dominant classes maintain power through the consent of the people.

> Hegemony is the domination of particular sections of society by the powerful classes not necessarily through threats of violence or the law but by winning their consent to be governed and dominated. Hegemony, like ideology, works less through coercion than through consent.

Thus, First World nations often seek privileged trading arrangements for their products. They can achieve this domination of Third World markets by threatening the Third World with economic sanctions, or war. However, the more effective tactic is often to persuade the Third World nation that such a trade agreement is mutually beneficial. The Third World is made to believe that 'free trade' would benefit them too, when actually free trade turns out to expand First World trading territory and profits. The Third World nation usually accepts this 'mutual benefit' as a given and approves of the agreement. This is hegemony not through coercion but through consent.

As can be seen, hegemony involves questions of ideology because it seeks to 'naturalize' and legitimize an unequal power relation by suggesting, i.e., representing the trade agreement as a mutually beneficial one. Hegemony is achieved through the circulation of ideology.

Antonio Gramsci argued that 'revolutions' are not always at the level of the economic structure but at the level of ideologies. Gramsci's notion of ideology converts it into something more than just 'false consciousness'. Ideology can circulate in popular culture, folk songs, legends and local myths and constitute the very structure of people's lives. Thus, ideology manifests itself as a *material* force.

It is important for hegemony that ideology is made available to the working classes not as a visible *instrument* of power and hegemony but more subtly, as a commonplace, invisible, unconscious *suggestion*. For this suggestion, ideology requires a commonly accepted cultural form.

> Ideology enables the dominant classes to reinforce their power over the oppressed and marginalized classes because ideology serves as a system of beliefs that naturalizes the unequal power relations, and leads the oppressed to accept it as natural, a given and as self-evident and therefore beyond questioning.

Ideology is sustained, reinforced and reproduced through cultural forms such as art. As we have already seen, films depicting the American as the world's saviour suggest that Americans alone are good and capable of saving the world. This is *ideology* because it *masks* the exploitative relation America has with other (specifically Third World) nations, the wars it has itself started and the economic terrorism it propagates through forced 'Free Trade' agreements, embargos and sanctions.

However, we need to also understand layer of complexity to the theme of ideology. A film-maker or an artist need not be deliberately setting out to portray the Muslim as a terrorist or the American as a saviour. Ideology works at an *unconscious* level. Consumer culture proposes that consumers are free to 'choose' their product. However, the task of advertising and branding is to convince us to choose particular products. In this we are not really free. For example, using a doctor to sell a toothpaste uses several kinds of consumer ideology.

- It appeals to us because we traditionally *trust* doctors.
- Doctors are not commonly associated with commerce, and hence it seems to be *medical–professional advice* on our screen rather than any commercial.
- We believe that a when doctor recommends a toothpaste, s/he does so based on 'expert' opinion and *not* on marketing and profit concerns.

Notice that the sale of a toothpaste cashes in on several areas of 'belief': trust in doctors, the reliance on medical–professional advice, the refusal to see the man on screen as driven by commercial concerns. Ideology here is this set of beliefs the advertisement relies on to sell its product. It converts a capitalist and profiteering project into a health concern, a medical 'situation' and a social value. This is the 'mechanics' of ideology.

Such a mechanics of ideology that serves hegemonic purposes are summarized by Terry Eagleton. Ideology works, according to Terry Eagleton (1991a: 5–6), through six different strategies:

(i) By promoting beliefs and values congenial to it;
(ii) Naturalizing these beliefs to render them self-evident;
(iii) Universalizing these beliefs;
(iv) Devaluing ideas that might challenge it;
(v) Rejecting alternative or rival forms of thought;
(vi) Obscuring social reality.

For hegemony to be effective it has to become invisible, and this is where ideology comes in. The 'civil society' with its structure of courts, the bureaucracy, religious and educational systems spread ideology through the law, textbooks, religious rituals and norms so that the people imbibe them unaware of the ideology.

Ideology provides the justification for any action. In order to locate ideology we need to examine the discourses within which it operates. Thus, to return to the example used above, the ideology of consumption works within several discourses: health (good teeth = healthy living), safety (healthy teeth = good life), expertise (trust the doctor, he knows best). Yet, these discourses are all located within a larger discourse that we often miss when we see the advertisements: the discourse of consumer culture. The discourse of consumer culture—'you can choose', this is the 'lowest price'—masks the ideological basis for all the other discourses. The invisible-but-present ideological basis is this: selling the product as though it is not about sales and profits for the manufacturer but about the consumer's correct choices in matters of healthy teeth. The ideology working at the level of discourses, therefore, suggests rather than tells something, it obscures the profit motif in favour of the health-and-choice one.

This also means that ideology requires a language, a form of representation, for expression whereby the hegemony is rendered invisible. Since we do not like to be dominated and treated as subjects without choice or power, the domination must be achieved through consent, and our acceptance of it as a natural, inevitable and 'good' state of affairs. Hegemony is almost never about threats of violence but more about ideology.

> Ideology is dependent upon language and signs because it has to present reality in particular ways by obscuring other, harsher aspects of this reality. Ideology is conveyed through particular forms of representation.

The ideology, from what we have said above, is about conveying the belief system regarding health and good teeth and concealing the profit theme. This means the language of the advertisement must not offer clues about the profit theme at all. Instead, it must throughout emphasize the health aspect. This is a strategy in language, signs and representation because it is about what meanings are produced.

We have thus far argued that ideology is a conscious effort on the part of the capitalist, the marketer, the politically dominant classes to increase profits and maintain power. This suggests that dominant classes generate particular forms of representation in cultural forms deliberately. But this argument needs to be modified slightly because, if by definition ideology works at the level of illusion and suggestion, then it follows that even the artist (film-maker, novelist) might have imbibed the ideology *unconsciously*. An artist may therefore unconsciously replicate the dominant ideology in his /her works and thus disseminates it among the readers.

Traditionally Marxist criticism treats *all art as ideological*. It believes that all forms of culture are basically exercises in ideological dissemination. If ideology is the set of beliefs and representations that 'sell' the world to us (readers, viewers) so that we are convinced that the representations are true, then it follows that all art seeks to ensure a status quo in society. Art's ideology is a device in the hands of the dominant to ensure that no rebellion occurs. It does so by convincing—to repeat the argument made above—the oppressed that things are fine.

Yet we also know that literary and cultural texts—I mentioned *Syriana* above—often go against the prevalent ideology. Mulk Raj Anand's *Untouchable*, for example, for all its flaws, challenged the prevalent thinking about caste in 1930s India. The novel was ideological, but one whose ideology was *in sharp opposition to the prevalent one*. Thus, it cannot be accepted that all art is ideological and geared to the interests of the dominant classes. Resistance literature in every culture—working-class poetry, anti-colonial writings or women's narratives—has provided ideologies different from the acceptable ones.

In order to remedy this traditional Marxist view that all art is ideological, the French thinker Louis Althusser proposed a new scheme. Althusser suggested that art has a particular relationship with ideology. If ideology is imaginary (beliefs, values, abstract ideals are 'imaginary') and art is also about imaginary things, then there is a more complicated relationship that exists between the two.[1] Althusser argued that art does exist within ideology but often *distances* itself from it.

More importantly, Althusser argued that ideology is circulated through particular structures in society. These he termed 'ideological state apparatuses' (ISAs). Althusser proposed that the state imposes an ideology through the threat of sanctioned violence (the police, the law, the army). This means, ideology is imposed by offering a threat of violence: This is coercion of the people to accept a particular ideology. The acceptance of cultural norms and habits because of the fear of state reprisals is the coercive mechanism of ideology. Thus, when the Taliban insisted on Islamic dress for women and when the US government put in place the Patriot Act post-9/11, the ideology of 'Islamic culture' and 'patriotism' were imposed through the threat of legal action and violence.

However, as states have found, it is more effective to impose ideology by smuggling it in and getting the population to accept it. This is the 'consent' mode (as opposed to the coercive mode) of ideology dissemination. Ideological state apparatuses that include institutions and structures such as the family, religion, the media, the education system convince people of the 'correctness' of ideology by presenting it as a desirable object or idea. Thus, the privileging of the family in Ekta Kapoor serials or a standard Hindi film suggests that the best arrangement of sexual relations is a family that consists of a man, a woman and children. This is the ideology of heterosexuality as normal that is suggested to us. It rejects the possibility of a homosexual family *as a family*. In this case, by circulating images of the happy heterosexual family these media representations suggest that only a heterosexual family is a real family.

In this sense, ideology is material because it is embedded in and works through material institutions such as the family or the schooling system. Ideology constructs the individual as a *subject* because it makes the individual accept reality, understand it, and live within it. Ideology is the context in which we lead our lives, and is hence a material reality. But what does it mean to say that ideology constructs the subject?

Let us go back to the family as an example. The ideology of the heterosexual family provides particular roles for individuals, roles that are gendered: the male as head of the family, the female as primary care giver and the children as dependents (though these are not fixed in all households). Indeed the heterosexual family *begins* with the assumption that males and females will live together for the purposes of raising children and, therefore, 'building' a family. By proposing that this heterosexual family is 'normal' and could be happy, ideology suggests that within such a family, we can all play our roles and thus make it happy. That is, by representing the family and family roles as ideal, the ideology of the heterosexual family constructs us as individuals who play these roles because we *believe* in them. We believe that if males and females within a family play their 'proper' roles then the family would be happy. It is important to see here that at no point are we aware of the fact that we are playing a *role*: We assume it is 'natural' to be 'father' or 'mother'. At no point are we alert to the fact that perhaps these are only roles that the social order has invented so that the woman will do most of the housework and caring! When we accept the role as natural we have become 'subjects' within ideology. The problem, of course, is that we see ourselves as having voluntarily chosen the role, that we are free and that it is natural. This is precisely how ideology works: by naturalizing our constructed roles. This construction of subjects through ideology is what Althusser termed 'interpellation'.

> Interpellation is the process of consenting to ideology, accepting it and not being aware of it. It makes the subject believe that s/he is an independent being and not a subject at all controlled by outside forces. In other words, ideology interpellates the individual as a subject but makes her/him believe s/he is a free agent.

Interpellation consists of two stages:

- Ideology precedes the individual and an individual is inserted into the ideological scheme.
- There is a pre-determined set of roles out of which the individual 'automatically' chooses a few, all the while assuming that s/he has freely chosen them.

Thus, the woman is 'interpellated' as 'girl-child', daughter, mother, wife but made to believe that these are her 'natural' roles. In fact, she is carefully nurtured into these roles—a process of 'culturation'—by being made to adopt certain postures, perform certain kinds of function and behave in certain ways. Her subject-position as woman is created in advance of her, and she is simply inserted into the ideology of patriarchy even though she never realizes this.

The most significant feature of ideology is that it is invisible. This means we are not aware of ideology because it pervades our lives. It is, in other words, so real that we do not notice it exists. Just as we are often blind to everyday and routine features—the number of steps to my office, for instance—ideology is lived reality where the features have become so familiar as to be invisible. It is not, therefore, a question of consciousness as orthodox Marxism proposed. It is a solid, lived reality. This twisted reality masks, as we have repeated several times now, unequal social relations.

Unequal social relations take us to the question of power, as noted earlier. In the toothpaste episode the ideology of capitalism masks the ideology of capitalism. The key thing is: The power the capitalist has in selling you the toothpaste and making a profit is invisible because it is sold to you as a consumer choice, a medically approved product and a health choice. The domination of the capitalist system over the consumer is the maintenance of the unequal power relation through ideology. In the case of the factory, the workers are dominated by the capitalist factory owner through the ideology of benevolent paternalism (the factory owner as the kind father figure).

BASE AND SUPERSTRUCTURE

Perhaps the most common concept and set of terms associated with Marxist thought would be 'base and superstructure'. We know that in Marxism the social and cultural aspects of life are believed to be dependent upon the economic ones. This is essentially the base–superstructure model. The economic conditions in a society constitute the 'base' because they determine the nature and character of the social and cultural forms. The cultural aspects constitute the 'superstructure'.

> 'Base and superstructure' in Marxist thought refers to the relationship between the economic and social–cultural aspects of society where the economic base (which includes factors and relations of productions) determines, influences and forms the cultural superstructure (which includes arts, religion, the law, media, lifestyles).

'Base' refers to the factors and relations of production. This could be the industry, the labour, the markets and the commodities. 'Superstructure' refers to the law, literature, the arts, religion and lifestyles.

What this means is that the nature of the base will be crucial in determining what kinds of cultural forms emerge in any society. This means, cultural forms have a *material* basis. Films and art forms will be connected to the kind of economy that exists in a particular society. American films reflect the capitalist nature of production where individuals are 'alienated' from their work as well as each other. Hence their films also often show a sense of fragmented society with a high degree of individualism. India's experiment with socialism till the early 1990s meant that the community was an important aspect of Indian social life. Hence the Bachchan films of the 1980s often showed the hero as a crusader for the working classes and actively championing social justice by battling landlords, capitalists and the moneyed classes. The ideology of the cultural forms—social justice, rebellion—reflects the economic conditions here (as studied in detail by Madhava Prasad, 1998).

Class conflict, exploitative capitalism, the domination of the bourgeois class will manifest as political power. Once capitalists (who are part of the 'base' because they constitute the factors of production) acquire political power then they seek to introduce measures (as in economic or legal policy) that will help them reinforce and expand their power. In other words, the base, which provides a superstructure, will in turn be strengthened by the superstructure.

Thus, for example, if one reads the Paul Krugman column in newspapers one can easily see this model at work in the USA. Big business corporations make their money from capitalist and ruthless business practices (including low wages). Then, when they have made their profits, they sponsor or contribute to political parties during elections (commonly referred to as 'donations'). Once 'their' candidates are elected these candidates push particular policies through the Congress. These policies, which are a part of the 'superstructure', include things like tax cuts for big businesses. Thus, the 'base' has been strengthened.

In order to understand the fiction of Joseph Conrad or Rudyard Kipling we need to see how they are located within their economic contexts of Britain's colonial empire in the nineteenth and early twentieth century (something that has been explored by postcolonial critics). Shakespeare's plays and the work of other Elizabethan and Jacobean writers are obsessed with the nature of kingship because they wrote at a time when Elizabeth I and her successors like James I were trying to impose the absolute power of the monarch over their subjects (as has been studied by critics like Stephen Greenblatt, Jonathan Goldberg and others).

As we can see the base and superstructure model seems to argue for a deterministic view of culture. If all culture is determined and formed by the economic base, then it means that there is little autonomy for, say, the arts. Do all films depend on the nature of production? Can Eliot's *The Waste Land* be adequately explained (if it ever can be!) by connecting it to Eliot's American-English existence or England's between-wars economy? Do the paintings of M. F. Husain reflect the conditions of factory production and the national economy? Is the nature of cricket as sport determined by rising or falling stock markets? Does the change in family structure reflect the changing nature of the Indian economy?

When we ask these kinds of questions we are struck by their incongruity. This is so because every art form or cultural practice cannot always be traced to an economic 'base'. To put it differently, one cannot identify a cultural form as simply an expression of an economic structure. Marxist thought in the latter half of the twentieth century realized that the 'base and superstructure' model was too limited to explain culture.

Louis Althusser and the later Marxists proposed that the cultural realm enjoys a certain degree of autonomy from the economic base. It is indeed determined by the base, but it is determined only in the last instance. That is, the economic base only provides a general framework within which cultural practices and forms appear.

RAYMOND WILLIAMS, CULTURAL MATERIALISM AND 'DETERMINATION'

Raymond Williams, of Welsh origins and a distinguished Professor of English at the University of Cambridge, was perhaps the most influential Marxist critic of the twentieth century and one of the leading figures of the New Left. His work with the journal *New Left Review* and the Birmingham Centre for Contemporary Cultural Studies laid the foundations of what is now known as Cultural Studies and his elaboration of concepts like 'hegemony' and 'ideology' helped later generations of Marxist scholars analyse cultural practices.

In his 'Base and Superstructure in Marxist Cultural Theory' (1982), he argued that Marxism has for too long seen the 'base and superstructure' model as one of exact correspondence. But, in fact, he argued, there is often a 'lag', especially a temporal lag between the two. The important thing is, argued Raymond Williams, to see the processes that determine the cultural forms (superstructure). We need to study, suggests Williams in *Marxism and Literature*, the mechanics of this 'determination' (1986: 83–89). How exactly does the economic base influence something as removed from material conditions of production and the markets as abstract painting? Do objective material conditions that exist *outside* the realm of art influence the form and practice of the art?

Williams argued that 'culture' is ordinary; it is a whole way of life. In his now classic work *Keywords* (rev. ed. 1983), he identified culture as 'one of the two or three most complicated words in the English language' (1983: 87–93). Williams traces the history of the word from its Latin roots (which signified cultivation, tending, caring) to show how the word's changing meanings can be linked to a changing 'new social and intellectual movement'. What Williams shows here is the ideological bases for the meaning of a word.

Arts are a component of a social organization that is affected by changes in the economic conditions and political change. This means, culture is always political—social changes triggered by political processes are always reflected in the cultural practices and artifacts. In keeping with his thesis that cultural artifacts and the arts reflect social change and political processes, Williams' study, *Culture and Society* (1958) traced English social change especially after the Industrial Revolution through the writings of major authors such as Blake, Wordsworth, Edmund Burke and George Orwell. Williams was thus in general agreement with the Marxist model of culture. However, this straightforward linkage between culture and economic base was, for Williams, too easy an equation. Williams' 'cultural materialism' never abandoned the economic and political bases of cultural practices. Williams' definition of cultural materialism indicates that it is 'the analysis of all forms of signification … within the actual means and conditions of their production' (1981: 64–65). Or, as he made more explicit later in this same work: 'Whatever purposes cultural practice may serve, its means of production are always unarguably material' (1981: 87).

Cultural materialism is an analytic practice that seeks to situate and interpret a cultural practice or artifact within the following:

- *institutional* structures (the film industry, state-owned radio or television, the publishing industry)

- *intellectual* contexts (schools of thought, movements such as modernism, postcolonialism or nativism)
- *forms* and their requirements and limits (such as the history of the Western novel as a form, the oral epic traditions in India, the magical realist novel from Latin America)
- *modes of production* (printing, digital printing, mass media)
- *organization* and regulatory mechanisms (legislation on censorship, copyright laws, patents)
- *reproduction* (sales, exhibitions, dissemination through reviews, adaptations)

In keeping with this line of interpreting culture, in a later work on television (*Television: Technology and Cultural Form*, 1974) Williams proposed that, contrary to the established view that television was an agent of democratic change, it was used to further the interests of a few who decided *how* the new technology was to be used. Williams saw apologists for the (then) new medium—his target here is Marshall McLuhan, the Canadian media theorist—as ignoring the politics of technology. Williams wrote:

> It is an apparently sophisticated technological determinism which has the significant effect of indicating a social and cultural determinism: a determinism ... which ratifies the society and culture we now have, and especially its most powerful internal directions. For if the medium – whether print or television – is the cause, all other causes, all that men ordinarily see as history, are at once reduced to effects. Similarly, what are elsewhere seen as effects, and as such subject to social, cultural, psychological and moral questioning, are excluded as irrelevant ... The initial formulation – 'the medium is the message' – was a simple formalism. The subsequent formulation – 'the medium is the massage' – is a direct and functioning ideology. (1974: 127)

Technology too, Williams demonstrated, was a cultural practice with its own ideology and politics.

Williams sees the traditional Marxist notion of base as too rigid. The economic *base* is a process, he argues, and not a static condition or object. The base includes the industry that produces but also human labour that reproduces. Totality is the combination of the base and the superstructure, i.e., the *entire* realm of social practices. Thus, the task of criticism is to study the relationships between elements—economic, political, social and cultural—of the way of life.

Williams proposes that 'determination' is the exertion of pressures on individuals and cultural forms. Determinations are, in Williams' definition, 'experienced individually but ... are always social acts ... social formations' (87). Williams suggests that social factors are not simply 'out there'; these are *internalized* by individuals. Further, it cannot be that only one set of factors determines the cultural practice. There are many social forces that determine the nature and content of a cultural practice. This is 'overdetermination', a term that is used to describe the multiple forces that influence a cultural form. Overdetermination helps us realize that even contradictory forces can influence a cultural practice.

Building on Williams' influential work Terry Eagleton identifies a host of 'ideological determinations' in the fiction of George Eliot: Evangelical Christianity, rural organicism, incipient feminism, petty-bourgeois moralism. In *The Mill on the Floss* Eagleton detects a pastoral as well as a psychological ideology—two 'conflictual modes' (1985: 113).

In similar fashion the Hindi film need not be 'determined' exclusively by the economic situation in India or the Mumbai stock market. It could be 'overdetermined' in the sense that Hollywood films, another art form (say rock music) or a war elsewhere could also be factors. Ideologies that inform any cultural practice might be contradictory. Contemporary Hindi films, therefore, seem to be caught between the individualism of the American variety and the inability to completely abandon the (traditional Indian) notion of the family. Indian literature in English seeks to present an India that is recognizable as India, but within a language that carries a colonial legacy. Thus, Amitav Ghosh's fiction presents extraordinarily sensitive portraits of India, even though the *form* he uses (the novel) is a European one. Ghosh simply uses the form that he finds suitable to his task (some years ago, Vikram Seth retrieved the epic novel form for his *A Suitable Boy*, a feat unusual even in the 'Western', Euro-American tradition in the twentieth century). In this sense his novel is 'overdetermined' by

- the economics of the novel as the most saleable (profit-making) form,
- the tension of writing about India in a European form,
- the contradiction of writing about rural Bengal in English,
- his location in multiple spaces—of Third World India and the First World USA,
- the 'production' and marketing of his fiction by worldwide publishers,
- the apparent contradiction between the prizes and awards given by global bodies and the settings of some of his novels (semi-urban and rural India).

We can see here the analytics of cultural materialism, since we are looking at the institutional, commercial, ideological, formal properties and contexts in which an author writes his literary work.

What we discover here is that the traditional Marxist categories of 'base and superstructure' do not always explain art forms or cultural practices. An art form might reflect an *earlier* economic 'base' and a cultural practice might capture new forms of economic and material conditions that are only *emerging*.

Ideology is often incorporated through educational institutions and the family. A selective tradition is passed off as *the tradition*. From the archives of the past certain meanings and images are chosen for emphasis, and established as the *standard* or *the tradition*.

DOMINANT, RESIDUAL AND EMERGENT CULTURES

From the discussion above we see that cultural practices and art forms might not always reflect or be determined by the material (economic) conditions of a society. What we need is to see a cultural practice as part of a process trying to negotiate with an economic condition. We need to recognize that cultural forms and practices are in a *constant dynamic relation* with the economic 'base' where the base might try to determine the cultural form, even as the form seeks to escape the 'base'.

Cultural practices often make use of the material conditions of the past. Some elements of the earlier age might survive in the present. This is what Raymond Williams terms 'residual culture' (122–23).

> Residual culture is the continued presence in the present, in some form (as fantasy, the exotic, as ideal), of the past.

Thus, the experience of the wars with Pakistan and China continue to be useful themes in Hindi films that want to speak of the nation or propound the ideology of 'national interest' (examples would include *Border*, *LoC*, *Gadar*, among others). Gandhian non-violence and forms of protest constitute the experience and meaning understood better by the senior generation of Indians. Yet this 'element' provides the scope, plot and attraction of the hugely successful *Lage Raho Munnabhai*. Indian novels continue to portray the family as the centrepiece of an individual's existence even though, as social scientists will tell us, divorce and the single life are commonplace. Indian films (in Hindi as well as regional languages) idealize the 'happy' family when documentation of child abuse (Pinki Virani 2000) or domestic violence (Rinki Bhattacharya 2004) within families reveals the problems and oppressions within families.

The past here serves as an ideal (Gandhianism), a point of inspiration (war films and patriotism), nostalgia (the Barjatya films and the Indian family) for contemporary culture. It is not that many of us can actively recall any of these past elements. Yet they seem to continue to haunt us as residues even when our dominant cultural form is radically different. Thus, the Gandhianism of *Lage Raho Munnabhai* merges with the arguably more recognizable (for us, in this generation) consumerism of *Dhoom* or *Kuch Kuch Hota Hai*. Thus, the residual cultural element often works alongside a dominant cultural one. Rural and semi-urban India serves as the locale for Arundhati Roy's novel as well as other fiction (say, of Anita Nair). Consumer India and the metropolis is the *dominant cultural norm* (in fiction, film and non-fiction), even though alternative views of, say, the continuing existence of caste oppression in Dalit memoirs and fiction alter our views of Indian society.

Art forms can also, often, gesture at the arrival of new cultural contexts and norms. New meanings and values constitute what Williams terms 'emergent culture' (123).

> **E**mergent culture refers to the arrival of new meanings, beliefs and values within a particular art form or cultural practice.

Thus, even as the films of the late 1980s were speaking about 'reforming' Indian society (most notably in Bachchan's quasi-socialist works), films about nuclear families, diaspora and consumerism were making waves. It is at the cusp of this transition that a film like *Dilwale Dulhaniya Le Jayenge* appears. This film contains residual cultures (as in its glorification of the Hindu family) as well as emergent ones (diaspora, the Westernized Indian male). This, of course, gave rise to films like *Pardes* that sought to capture the diasporic Indian cultures. *Rang De Basanti*, likewise, generated enormous appeal because it marked an emergent cultural trend: the socially committed youth (whose immediate context we see on a regular basis with software professionals involved in social–national causes like traffic regulation or environmentalism). The *Dhoom* films did away with social commitment (except in vague terms like the law) and promoted a hedonistic lifestyle and therefore represented the dominant culture. Just when economic surveys such as the ACNielsen Consumer Confidence and Opinions Survey 2006 conducted with over 25,000 respondents from 45 countries, including 15 from the Asia-Pacific region informed us that India is at the top of the consumer confidence index for the fourth time in a row, films like *Rang De Basanti* and *Lage Raho Munnabhai* presented an emergent value system (or at least an alternative value system).

What is clear is that cultural forms cannot be tracked down to their immediate economic origins or influences. Cultural and art forms might draw upon a set of values, meanings and signs from an earlier age, or might provide insights into an emerging trend in society. But what Raymond Williams did was to emphasize that cultural forms and language were linked to social and historical processes. Meaning processes in language reflect social forces, ways of living, economic conditions.

THE CULTURE INDUSTRY

From what we have seen thus far we understand that Marxism views culture also as a 'product'. Like material commodities produced in factories, art forms like films or novels, structures like the law or the schooling system are also 'produced'.

The term *culture industry* was coined by Max Horkheimer and Theodor Adorno, two German theorists, in their work *Dialectic of Enlightenment* (1995

[1944]). The term readily captures the Marxist assumption that cultural forms like paintings, soap operas or films are no different from cars, television sets or domestic appliances. It indicated the Marxist belief that 'culture' is not an abstract thing that is created by a solitary individual genius. Rather, 'culture' is a product of social and economic conditions in any society. Thus, art is not a 'pure' aesthetic realm but one which is produced and sold like any other consumer good.

The use of the term *culture industry* also proposes a more political function for culture. Adorno and Horkheimer argue that the culture industry takes up the utility that consumers derive from any commodity (what in Marxist terms is called 'use-value') and makes it a product of the capitalist system. In order to understand this, let us look at a specific example.

In contemporary Hindi films characters wear recognizable brands of clothing and consume or hang out at recognizable malls and spaces. Particular fashions or food products are treated as means of acquiring pleasure and social prestige (internal branding becomes more visible with *Kuch Kuch Hota Hai* and in other Karan Johar films though advertisements and product banners have figured within the scene in films before). The *utility* to be gained (pleasure, privilege, friendship) from the use of particular products is transformed into a *product*. In other words, what is marketed in the film is not the product but a lifestyle: If you use this perfume/clothing line/hair gel you will have friends, win hearts and be the star of the evening scene.

The term *culture industry* is used mainly to describe mass cultural forms. It transforms the individual from a thinking and discerning individual into an unthinking consumer. The 'culture industry' does not want the consumer to think but to merely consume. In Adorno's words from his later essay 'Culture Industry Reconsidered' (2006 [1991]):

> The masses are not primary but secondary, they are an object of calculation; an appendage of the machinery. The customer is not king, as the culture industry would have us believe, not its subject but its object … The masses are not the measure but the ideology of the culture industry. (99)

'Culture industry' refers to mass culture where entertainment and its forms convert individuals into passive consumers. Pleasure and fun are 'standardized' market 'products' and the individuals are obedient subjects who consume them. The 'culture industry', therefore, produces unthinking masses of people who accept commodified sentiments and entertainments as 'natural'. The concept is indebted to Marxist views of the function of ideology.

However, we should not take the term 'industry' literally as 'factory'. 'Industry' here refers to the standardization of the cultural product, its meaning and value. Thus, 'prestige' or social value becomes standardized as 'brands' in consumer culture. In films values and meanings become attached to themes and stereotyped characters: patriotism standardized as 'hating your neighbour', happiness standardized as 'loving your parents and family' and 'corruption' standardized as 'politician'. Notice that these have very little to do with the *artistic* value of individual films or books. If *Vivah* makes the value system of marriage obvious, other films convey the same standard meaning in more subtle ways. The culture industry has converted the value, meaning and pleasure to be obtained from the *use* of the product into the product and its elements.

Adorno and Horkheimer (1995 [1944]) treat even urbanism as a form of the culture industry. They argue, therefore, that housing projects that are supposed to respect the individualism and independence of the individual actually transforms her/him into one more 'unit' like thousands of others. The living units, as they put it, become 'well-organized complexes' (120). What we see here is 'massification'.

Adorno warns that this standardization does not mean that consumers are passive recipients of the meanings dished out by the culture industry. Adorno argues, instead, that the consumer's consciousness is 'split' between the 'prescribed fun' offered by the culture industry and a 'doubt about its blessings' (2006 [1991]: 103). We are both swayed by what the culture industry offers, even as we are uncomfortable with succumbing to the 'role' of passive consumers that the culture industry wants us to don.

ART, WORK AND PRODUCTION

Films, books, artworks are not merely artifacts and works of the imagination. They are also commodities produced, marketed, sold and consumed to make profits for the manufacturer and (we assume) pleasure for the consumer. Thus, art and culture are social activities—produced and consumed like any other form such as a car or a refrigerator. We have already noted Eagleton's phrase, the 'literary mode of production', a phrase that captures the Marxist view of cultural products as commodities akin to any other material commodity.

PIERRE MACHEREY AND LITERARY PRODUCTION

In Pierre Macherey's *A Theory of Literary Production* (1978) we see the most detailed exploration of this view of literature (or art) as a product. Macherey transformed the very idea of the author. He proposed that the author was actually a 'workman'. Macherey argues that Literature (with an upper case L) does not really exist. Instead we need to study literary phenomena within social reality. A literary 'work' may adopt a particular form for its present purpose. However, the form has a history of its own, and need not always function as the elements of the present work alone. What Macherey is arguing for is this: A form like a novel, or a set of aesthetic elements within the novel, cannot be reduced to that particular instance (*George Eliot's* novel). The form of the novel has a certain history and therefore has a social life beyond the Eliot novel. In short, every aesthetic element belongs to the work at hand but is also located in a certain history. Macherey's argument rejects the idea of a work of art as an instance of singular genius or unique form. But locating itself as historical, Macherey demolishes the uniqueness of a work of art. He makes the artifact a social one by seeing aesthetics itself as a social product. As he put it:

> The work of literature cannot therefore be studied as if it were a self sufficient totality … The literary work only exists with at least a part of the history of literary production which hands down to it the essential elements for its work. (67–68)

Macherey proposes that questions of literary form need to basically interrogate the ideologies that these forms replicate and reinforce. In other words, literary texts are things that serve specific functions, especially in their reception. Macherey further argued that a text often contains silences because a text is ideologically prevented from saying certain things. This makes all texts 'incomplete' in a certain way. Thus, an industrial novel that highlights the exploitative nature of capitalism might not, however, highlight the gendered angle. While it might promote equal class relations, it might stay silent on the matter of equal wages for men and women and the problematic question of domestic labour where the women work unpaid within the house.

AESTHETICS, IDEOLOGY AND CULTURAL PRODUCTION

Macherey's argument links aesthetics with ideology, and proposes that aesthetic values in a text are often masks for very real social conditions. 'Aesthetics' in a text offers the images as real and as reflecting a general human condition. Yet what it conceals is a problematic situation where class conflict or unequal power relations exist. Raymond Williams (1973) demonstrated how in seventeenth-century English poetry and in eighteenth-century arts the landscape becomes a dominant aesthetic field. Landscapes with manor houses were treated as ideal, aesthetically appealing and attractive. These landscapes included rolling meadows, gardens, pastures with domesticated animals and, on many occasions, the landowner (one only has to look at the paintings of Thomas Gainsborough here). What is interesting, according to Williams, is that the landscape is rendered as something beautiful and perfect by evacuating it of its key people: the labourers. Labourers, Williams notes, were absent from such paintings and poems, or, if they were, they would only be marked as dots in a distance, thus reducing their 'role' in the aesthetics of the paintings.

Thus, the aesthetics of landscape masked the social fact that the pasture or the garden was the result of active labour. It marked the manor house or the landscape as connected only to the landowner and his family and removed all 'problematic' characters like labourers from it. There is no dirt, sweat or pain (features of hard labour) but only beauty, cleanliness and pleasure (an excellent example would be *Mr and Mrs Andrews* by Thomas Gainsborough).

Aesthetic theories about art have always supported such a depiction by arguing (as John Constable was to say) against the representation of particulars (which would include labour). Art, aestheticians such as Shaftesbury, Addison and Steele, Mark Akenside, Immanuel Kant and of course the English Romantic writers argued, was about beauty not sweaty, tiring labour. Concepts of beauty and aesthetic theories themselves are, therefore, ideological because they support the dominant classes when they argue in favour of representations only of the upper classes. Aesthetics, in this sense, is an ideological device that *naturalizes* the social conditions of production where the landowner is 'naturally' the owner and the fields are 'naturally' beautiful precisely because there are *no* labourers. This is precisely what Terry Eagleton is gesturing at when he speaks of the 'ideology of the aesthetic' (1991b).

> Aesthetics cannot be separated from their ideological function. Concepts of beauty and taste invariably mask questions of power—who decides what is beautiful?—and class where particular forms and styles become established as standards.

In his earlier work Eagleton had elaborated this aesthetic ideology. Aesthetic ideology is only one instance of general ideology, which would be the larger social and economic ideologies of a society (capitalism, patriarchy). It works along with other such regions such as the ethical and the religious to disseminate ideologies that reinforce existing power relations and systems of dominance. Aesthetic ideology includes, for Eagleton, the literary one constituted by multiple 'levels': theories of literature, critical practices, literary traditions, genres, conventions, devices and discourses (1985: 60). The aesthetic serves the same purpose in the realm of art as religion elsewhere.

This kind of Marxist criticism treats art as a product of its time and social conditions (i.e., contexts). Authors and painters appropriate, consciously or unconsciously, the prevalent ideologies. More importantly, they promote certain values as 'natural' and unchanging. In this, we have to be alert to the function of this product (art). We cannot delink the aesthetic appeal of the artifact from its social function—naturalizing a dominant ideology. Just as commodities, manufactured and marketed, mask the conditions of production, art objects also mask their ideologies. 'Values' as assigned to artifacts are, therefore, the result of the reception of these objects within a particular context. What we think of as an aesthetic response is the reception of an ideologically loaded object within our own (ideologically influenced) contexts. In other words, art is a social practice where a product is 'produced' and 'consumed'.

PIERRE BOURDIEU AND CULTURAL PRODUCTION

Pierre Bourdieu in a series of work dealing with French cultural practices sought to locate subjective attitudes and behaviour within social contexts. Bourdieu proposed that all human beings occupy a 'habitus', a practical sense and set of dispositions (modes of perceptions, thinking, behaviour) that generate particular attitudes and behaviours. 'Habitus' is the subjective component of a cultural practice. Further, every individual also occupies a 'field', i.e., social conditions that embody specific social relations. 'Fields' are the objective components of cultural practices. Social formations are organized fields—the family, religion, educational or economic domains. Each field is a structured space with its own laws and norms of functioning. Individuals compete for the control of resources within a field.

Individuals acquire particular habitus, or dispositions, as a result of their encounter with particular social fields. Here Bourdieu rejects the Marxist emphasis on social conditions (the 'objective' approach) as well as the psychological approaches that privileged the individual by showing how individual subjectivity and predispositions were gathered from the social domains. The subjective structures of the individual grow out of the objective ones, and in turn influence how that individual deals with social structures later. A working-class individual, for instance, is trained through his social contexts not to aspire for or desire a large mansion or recognition from the government. He aspires only to a modest apartment and a minimal standard of living. Now this aspiration—his disposition—is not his creation alone: it emerges from his social conditions. Once these dispositions have been instilled, the individual deals with life and social conditions according to these dispositions. Bourdieu saw all cultural production and practice as the result of the interaction between the habitus and the field, between the subjective and the objective components.

Bourdieu suggests that the competition is not always for material benefits or resources. Much of the competition is directed towards acquiring

- symbolic capital—the accumulated prestige, honour and recognition based on an individual's acquisition of knowledge or expertise and
- cultural capital—the forms of cultural knowledge and competence that enables and empowers an individual to appreciate or evaluate cultural practices (for example, the expertise that allows one to understand art).

Bourdieu proposed that cultural capital is often the result of pedagogy, family or institutions. More significantly, cultural capital can be exchanged for economic capital or gains. Thus, 'taste', which supposedly sets the upper classes above the lower, is related less to the object's value than the social position of the perceiver. Styles of walking, eating, clothes and talking—'taste'—are instilled by families into their children. These become markers of social rank. Thus, responses to cultural practices proceed from such trained values of 'taste'.

Symbolic capital also generates violence, by those who possess it more against those who possess less. Thus, disapproval or contempt of the upper classes towards working-class behaviour or practices such as sporting events becomes a symbolic violence.

Any material or cultural artifact acquires some value. This value is often the result of the work of 'cultural intermediaries'—the advertising industry, the marketing units, the publicists, the institutions of mass media, etc. Individuals who seek to gain from a particular material or cultural object/artifact also acquire a set of skills through which they can gauge that object's symbolic and cultural value. In other words, cultural productions are the consequence of the interaction between material factors and symbolic-cultural factors.

FREDRIC JAMESON AND POSTMODERNITY

Jameson's writings on postmodern architecture and genres such as cyberpunk provided a Marxist approach to culture in the postindustrial era. In his earlier work (*The Political Unconscious*) Jameson argued that narrative is central to our understanding of reality. All narratives must be read for their connection with the concrete material realities 'outside' (a process Jameson termed 'dialectical criticism'). This requires situating a cultural object/practice within its specific historical conditions. Further, we need to possess a *totalizing* thinking where we are able to locate culture within social and political structures. Narratives are invariably techniques of containment where the contradictions of history are masked or silenced. For Jameson, history (or rather the narratives of history) plays a crucial role in repressing the contradictions and realities of society. Every text thus possesses its own 'repressed'. Narratives are, therefore, political; they help repress contradictions and thus prevent revolution. There is a 'political unconscious' that can be discerned in cultural texts.

Cultural texts code/conceal or thematize the repressed so that they can be 'managed'. Social and political anxieties are transformed into themes in films or narratives so that, on one hand, they find some 'expression', but on the other they remain at the level of narrative. What Jameson is proposing here is that narratives such as films or literature help transform the threat of a social or political anxiety (which might lead to revolution) into a mere literary representation or theme.

In his later work, Jameson turned to what he termed the *cultural logics* of various social–economic conditions. Linking capitalism with particular cultural forms, Jameson proposed that every 'moment' in capitalism has its expression or literary–cultural equivalent (cultural logic) in particular modes of writing/representation or aesthetic approach:

- market capitalism had realism
- imperialism had modernism
- multinational capitalism has postmodernism

In other words, realism, modernism and postmodernism are the cultural expressions and methods and aesthetic styles of a deeper socio-economic form of capitalism.

Jameson's analysis of postmodernism began with two key assumptions as follows:

(i) Popular and mass culture was a means of evaluating and assimilating political conditions and

(ii) Postmodernity was a consequence of late capitalism (the age of diffused production, multinational capital, speculative finance and electronic linkages).

Proceeding from these two assumptions, Jameson argued that postmodern cultural trends and practices were cultural expressions of the deeper economic structures of new forms of capitalism. As Jameson put it: 'This whole global, yet American, postmodern culture is the internal and superstructural expression of a whole new wave of American military and economic domination throughout the world' (1991: 5). Mass culture in the postmodern age assimilates even what was once radical (and Jameson is looking at Andy Warhol's work here) into commonplace work. In other words, postmodernity converts all art forms into *commodities*. Art is another consumer product with little intrinsic value *as* art.

Such a commodification of art implies, for Jameson, the culture of surface appearance rather than depth value. Postmodern culture, he suggests, is the culture of the signifier rather than the signified. Art becomes another product with no deeper narrative or meaning. The absence of depth also leads to a culture where surface meaning and appearance is everything. The 'subject' lacks any uniqueness and fragments. This fragmentation and depthlessness is what Jameson identifies as the culture of *pastiche*. Pastiche in postmodernism is the repetition of former (modernist) styles. In fact, repetition without any uniqueness to itself—mimicry, parody—constitutes postmodern style. What Jameson is proposing is that the repetition of older styles becomes a style in itself. There is no 'original' artist or object that the viewer/reader can identify. The viewer has to be content with the imitation and pastiche, which constitutes the original for her/him. To put it differently, in postmodern culture, the copy is all we have. There is no prototype or original we can compare it with. A good example of pastiche as a style would be the remix phenomenon. While older generation of music lovers and cinemagoers might be able to identify the 'original' version of 'Ek ladki bheegi bhaagi si' or 'Pardesiya', for the new generation the remix version is all there is. This pastiche of an original is an end in itself, a copy without a 'true' original text.

STUART HALL AND THE RISE OF CULTURAL STUDIES

As noted earlier Raymond Williams helped establish a tradition of Marxist cultural analysis. The work of Stuart Hall and Richard Hoggart with the Birmingham Centre, later expanded through the writings of David Morley, Tony Bennett and others, established Cultural Studies as a discipline. The focus of this Centre and the practitioners of Cultural Studies has been mass/popular culture, questions of identity and power, all informed by a Marxist commitment to emancipation and social justice. Their work in mass culture has involved looking at culture as a site of struggle where different social groups seek to impose their meanings and values upon cultural practices. They see cultural forms such as film and football, TV soap opera and shopping as spaces where power is coded into symbols, meanings and consumption practices.

Stuart Hall, working with Paul du Gay and others (1997), proposed a theory of 'articulation'. In their work on the Sony Walkman, Hall et al. proposed a 'circuit of culture'. Cultural analysis of artifacts requires a study of five key elements:

(i) Representation (what a medium or artifact represents and how it is represented?)

(ii) Identity (what kinds of identity—of gender, nation, class, individual are offered, reinforced or contested in a TV soap opera or a mobile phone?)

(iii) Production (the industry that produces the film or comic book—the industry's organization, capital, policies, profits)

(iv) Regulation (is the industry and production subject to state control?, or is it a capitalist monopoly corporate body?)

(v) Consumption (how is the cultural practice received or interpreted?)

Articulation is the *linkage* between each of these elements to produce the meaning of a cultural artifact or practice. 'Articulation' is also about the power and hegemony that affects and is affected by the temporary linkages between these elements. As Stuart Hall puts it: 'An articulation is ... the form of the connection that can make a unity of two different elements, under certain conditions ... The 'unity' that matters is a linkage between the articulated discourse and the social forces' (Hall 1996: 141).

Stuart Hall (1992) exploring race and identity in 1980s Britain also adapted poststructuralist thought in order to reject any notion of an essentialist identity. Hall suggested that the self was not (as the Enlightenment and Western philosophy had believed) a coherent entity but was made of multiple and constantly shifting identities. Thus, sexuality, race, class, gender, age, ethnicity, religion are also factors that contribute to identity. None of this contributes alone to an individual's identity. In some situations one's ethnic identity or age becomes central, in others it might be religion or gender. These are positions that link up temporarily to produce a subject at that point in time. For example, for purposes of state pension, age is the dominant factor, for affirmative action like reservation, gender or caste might be the dominant factor.

Hall argued that cultural identity is based as much on difference as on similarity, and that *this identity is subject to change*. Thus, blacks in Britain constitute a British identity even though, traditionally, British identity has been associated *only* with white culture. Hall argued that it was possible to possess multiple elements of an identity—one could be black as well as British. He further argued that blacks in Britain could draw connections with black cultures in the Caribbean (Hall himself is of Jamaican origins), in Africa and in Britain. What Hall was saying, in other words, was that there is no way of speaking of a fixed or essential 'British' identity because this identity was evolving, shifting and composite.

With the work of Hall and later Left-oriented thinkers, Cultural Studies evolved into a major discipline in the UK and the USA and has now found its feet in Europe and elsewhere. Cultural Studies adapts various theories from poststructuralism, postcolonial and race studies as well as the more radical critiques from feminism and Marxism in order to study mass culture. Cultural Studies is interested in how cultural artifacts (film, music, novels) and practices (sports, national events) generate meaning. It assumes that some meanings are privileged while some are marginalized because meaning-generation is about power. Privileged groups seek to impose their meanings on cultural practices. This struggle for power is fought out in everyday life and common (mass) practices—and this is the site for Cultural Studies work. Cultural Studies

- examines the languages, discourses and rhetorical modes through which meaning is made in mass cultural forms,
- examines how these meanings reflect the existing struggle for power and domination in that society,
- examines how the privileging of some meanings is at the cost of others.

Thus, the privileging of national identity over the regional in all countries is a struggle for establishing a particular meaning (nation) while marginalizing another (region). Cultural Studies would see questions of identity as essentially being about power.

*

Marxist literary and cultural theory refuses, therefore, to privilege individual genius or taste above social conditions. It links cultural practices to social, economic and political structures existent in that epoch and shows how aesthetics, literary works and cultural artifacts participate in the struggle for power between the classes.

FURTHER READING

Day, Gary. 2001. *Class*. London: Methuen.

Eagleton, Terry. 2002. *Marxism and Literary Criticism*. 1976. London and New York: Routledge.

Eagleton, Terry. 1985. *Criticism and Ideology: A Study in Marxist Literary Theory*. 1975. London: Verso.

Williams, Raymond. 1986. *Marxism and Literature*. 1977. Oxford: Oxford University Press.

NOTES

1. In fact Pierre Macherey used the term *illusion* to describe ideology, and thus underscores the primacy of imagination.

6 Postcolonial Theory

European modernity, dating back to the fifteenth and sixteenth centuries, was characterized by organization of time (through clocks), professions, space (through mapping) and labour (through the specialization of disciplines and crafts). Modernity emphasized rational and optimal use of resources in order to achieve maximum profits. This was directly linked to the economic system of capitalism where profits and efficiency were seen as intimately linked. The other side of this modernity was that as it expanded, more countries in Europe sought greater profits, resources and labour outside Europe. That is, modernization and industrialization (after the seventeenth century) needed sources of labour and raw materials and markets for their products. European markets and factories could not generate profits from within European sales alone. This meant that European countries began to look at Asia, South America and Africa as sites providing them the much-required resources. In this way, modernity directly led to voyages of discovery (for trade routes) and conquest (for control over resources in other parts of the world). Colonialism emerged out of this process of industrial modernity and its capitalist modes of production.

For various nations in Africa, Asia and South America modernity has historically been characterized by the rule and dominance of native cultures by non-native, usually European ones. Modernity has thus been *colonial modernity* for many regions of the non-white world. Colonialism can be described as the process of settlement by Europeans in Asian, African and South American territories. Colonization found its climactic moments in the eighteenth and nineteenth centuries. It was an exploitative mechanism—economic exploitation of resources, the use of native peoples, the conquest of territory and markets—based on the difference in race, culture, forms of knowledge, technological advancement and political systems between the Europeans and the natives.

Structures of colonial domination were, of course, racialized in the sense that they were created and administered by acknowledging and reinforcing the racial difference between the natives and the colonial masters. The European master possessed the power to govern, and the natives were *subjects* to the systems created by the master. These structures were sustained not merely by the use of military and economic powers—though these were, expectedly, central to it—but through a complex dynamic of *representation* and *discourse*. Colonial presence produced images and representations of natives—by which I take to mean, essentially, non-white races and ethnic groups in Africa, Asia and South America—that were consumed by both colonial races back in Europe as well as the natives themselves. This latter phenomenon, where the native assimilated and believed his/her prejudiced, skewed and often downright false representation of him/herself by the European was made possible through the education system, religion and the law. The history of nations like India and countries in Africa is, therefore, very often, a history written (documented) *by* the Europeans. Colonial modernity is thus a conjugation of acts of representation and acts of political and economic power.

Twentieth-century commentators from Africa and Asia—Mahatma Gandhi, Aimé Césaire, Leopold Senghor, Albert Memmi—during the anti-colonial struggles pointed to the racial dimension of colonial rule, the inequalities of power and the slow but steady erosion of native values and cultures (especially languages) by colonial rulers. They interpreted colonialism as something more than mere military–political power, viewing it as a process of *cultural* domination through representation, discourse and documentation. This critique of colonial racialized

Postcolonial theory is a method of interpreting, reading and critiquing the cultural practices of colonialism, where it proposes that the exercise of colonial power is also the exercise of racially determined powers of representation.

acts of representation in law, history writing, literature, religion and educational practices provides the opening moves of what has come to be known as postcolonial theory.

Postcolonial theory focuses on question of race within colonialism, and shows how the optic of race enables colonial powers to represent, reflect, refract and make visible native cultures in particular ways. It begins with the assumption that colonial writing, arts, legal systems, science and other socio-cultural practices are always racialized and unequal where the colonial does the representation and the native is represented.

OPENING MOVES

THE IMPERIAL TURN: GANDHI, ANTI-COLONIAL STRUGGLE AND THE EARLY POSTCOLONIAL

Postcolonial theory draws upon key ideas and concepts developed in the anti-colonial struggle. It would not be accurate to say that postcolonial theory originated with Edward Said—though he certainly generated the modes of 'postcolonial reading' that we now see everywhere—because much of the ideas of resistance, cultural nationalism, nativism emerged in the contexts of anti-colonial struggle in Asia, Africa and South America.

The anti-colonial struggle in India was of a very different nature from that in the other colonized nations. Gandhi's *satyagraha* system of protest was a local and indigenous form of struggle that was based on a larger idea of non-violence. Passive resistance and personal discipline became the key modes of struggle. In addition, his vegetarianism, support for local languages and culture, and the anti-industrial stance all constituted key early elements in what postcolonial theory after Fanon would consolidate, namely, *cultural nationalism* and *cultural affirmation*.

Gandhi's major contribution to postcolonial thought can be best identified as a *moral* one—which is perhaps why he does not sit quite well with Marxist postcolonial theory—because his notion of *Swaraj* (self-rule) was, as Robert Young notes (2000: 320), directed at both the nation and the individual. Asserting moral superiority, of both the individual and the culture, against the colonial ruler (for example, by not hitting back when beaten) was Gandhi's masterstroke. Fasting, passive resistance and non-violence all contributed to the moral stance. His rejection of an armed struggle against the British and the foregrounding of the moral offered a sense of power to the anti-colonial as nothing else did. Gandhi's genius was to embody subaltern agency and resistance not in violence but in passivity, not in revolution but in moral positions. It is this that characterizes one of the most radical developments in postcolonial thought.

Gandhi was astute enough to see how colonialism was linked to capitalist modernity in the West. His anti-industrial stance—which to many did, and continues to appear, rather naïve—was born out of the belief that capitalism is inherently exploitative. His early moves in the experiments in the anti-colonial struggle were, therefore, really class struggles: peasant and working-class resistance in Kheda and Bardoli (eventually he distanced himself from unionism, and even pleaded for some kind of benevolent capitalism where the capitalist would be a 'trustee' who would care for the labour).

Ashis Nandy in his study of Gandhi (1983) has persuasively argued that Gandhi developed a response to the ultra-masculine colonial. Gandhi did not offer a counter-masculinity. Instead, what he did was to propose a masculinity that also took into account a certain feminization. This nearly androgynous, childlike femininity in Gandhi was also aligned with his support of notions of *shakti* ('power', but also feminized *shakti* in Hinduism) as non-violence. Thus, Gandhi countered the machismo cult of colonialism with a feminized one. This gendered resistance—not without its problems, though—would later reappear in the feminist dimensions of postcolonial theory.

The turn to moral resistance in Gandhi was also, again problematically, linked to religion. His effective deployment of the moral drew upon Hinduism and may well have contributed to the schism within the Indian National Congress between the Hindus and the Muslims. The use of Hinduism as a means of forging a cultural and national identity alienated large sections of leaders and the population and, cleverly exploited by political leaders, resulted in the disaster that was Partition. This instrumental use of religion and cultural practices (and here Gandhi must be located alongside figures like Bal Gangadhar Tilak) was, indisputably, effective in the anti-colonial struggle. It produced a strong sense of national and cultural identity, but also ran the risk of either homogenizing different cultural practices (in this case the so-called Hindu practices becoming a code for 'Indian' practices when it was simply a majority practice) or alienating minority and other practices (Muslim, Sikh, native Christian). Anti-colonial cultural nationalism, as later thinkers like Frantz Fanon and others discovered, very easily swerved into intolerant xenophobia, nativism and 'tribalisms'. Gandhi's Hinduized cultural nationalism and anti-colonial thought has, for this reason, not suited postcolonial theory very well because the latter seeks a more secular version (Chakrabarty 2000).

What is often overlooked in Gandhi is his syncretism, the mix-and-match method of his ideas. More recent work (Nandy 1983, Parekh 1997, Young 2000) has argued for a 'hybridity' in Gandhi where, they propose, he adapted and adopted Western thinkers (his fondness for Ruskin and Thoreau, for example) along with Hinduism (but a Hinduism without the scriptural tradition). Gandhi spoke of the assimilation of cultures. In *Hind Swaraj* he famously declared: 'The introduction of foreigners does not necessarily destroy the nation, they merge in it' (Gandhi 1909,

under 'The Condition of India'). It is this syncretism, hybridity and cosmopolitanism that later postcolonial theorists such as Homi Bhabha, Ashis Nandy and
others would appropriate in different and startling ways.

FRANTZ FANON AND THE PSYCHOPATHOLOGY OF COLONIALISM

Writing in the 1960s in the context of Algeria and its French colonial occupation,
Frantz Fanon has been an influential figure in postcolonial theory. His *The Wretched
of the Earth* (1963) and later *Black Skins, White Masks* (1967) rank with some of the
most influential texts in the twentieth century.

Fanon was fascinated by the psychological effects of colonialism on both the
colonizer and the colonized. He argued that, for the repressed and suffering native,
colonialism destroyed the very soul. The colonial master's constant representation
of the native as a non-human, animalized 'thing' annihilates the identity of the
native.

Fanon's insight into the psychology of colonialism was simply this: When the
colonial paints the native as evil, pagan and primitive, over a period of time the
native begins to accept this prejudiced and racialized view as true. As a result, the
native comes to see himself as evil, pagan and primitive. The black man loses his
sense of self and identity because he can only see himself through the eyes of the
white man. Fanon argues that for the native the term *man* itself begins to mean
white man because he does not see himself as a man at all. In terms of culture, the
native extends this accepted notion to believe that the only values that matter are
those of the white man.

For the white man, the native is always the negative, primitive Other: the very
opposite of what he and his culture stand for. Fanon here develops a psychoanalytic theory of colonialism where he suggests that the European self develops in its
relation and encounter with the Other (the native). Thus, colonialism engages the
white and the native in an encounter/relation where one develops only in its contrast with the Other.

> Colonialism is a violent conjugation where the sense of self develops
> through a negotiation rather than a separation, a relation rather
> than a disjunction, with the Other.

For the native the only way of dealing with this psychological inadequacy is by
trying to be as 'white' as possible. The native takes on western values, religion, the
language and practices of the white colonial and rejects his own traditions. He
puts on, in Fanon's phrase, 'white masks'. However, this 'mask' over the black skin

is not a perfect solution or fit. Fanon argues that the native experiences a schizo-phrenic condition as a result of this duality.

The build-up of this sense of inadequacy and inferiority in the colonized's psyche, argues Fanon, results in violence. Violence, writes Fanon, is a form of self-assertion. When the native discovers that he cannot hope to become truly 'white', or even expel the whites, his violence erupts against his own people. Thus, tribal wars, for Fanon, are an instance of this the violence generated through the colonial system where the 'wretched' turn upon each other, haunted by a failure to turn against the colonial master.

Fanon recognized the significance of cultural nationalism when he pro-pounded the idea of a national literature and national culture (in his essay of the same title in *Wretched of the Earth*) leading to a national consciousness. His deploy-ment of the term *national culture* was an attempt to plead for a greater, pan-African cause (and not just narrow, sectarian–tribal ones). The blacks had to create their own history, write their own stories and it is through this control over representa-tion that the native can break free of the colonial shackles.

Such a national culture, believed Fanon, must take recourse to, or return to, the African myths and cultural practices. It is within this mythic, cultural and even mystic traditions that black identity can be resurrected. A national culture is framed in three stages. In the first, the native intellectual is under the influence of the colonizer's culture, and seeks to emulate and assimilate it by abandoning his own. The native thus tries to be as white as possible. In the second stage, the native discovers that he can never become truly white, or white enough for the colonial master to treat him as an equal. The native intellectual now returns to study his own culture, and might even romanticize his traditions and past. Here Fanon sug-gests that there is no critical engagement with native cultures, just a celebratory tone. In the third stage, the native intellectual is truly anti-colonial. He joins the ranks of his people and battles colonial domination. This is accompanied by a careful analysis of his own culture. Such an analysis hopes to abandon those ele-ments of native culture that seem dated or even oppressive so that a new future (after colonialism) is made possible.

However, Fanon was also prophetic enough to argue that the idea of a 'national literature' and 'national culture' might result in xenophobia and intolerance. He proposed that national culture had a limited value: It could help define native culture against the overwhelming assault of the colonial. However, the return to a pre-colonial past through the espousal of a pre-colonial national culture did not guarantee that the working classes and the oppressed would benefit. For such a national culture to be effective, it has to account for and remedy the economic conditions of the working classes. With this, Fanon was moving away from a purely representational and cultural view of national identity towards a more materialist–economic one. Fanon was one of the first theorists to realize that the anti-colonial struggle must be fought at the level of both culture and economics, just as postcolonial states would have to frame their identities within the cultural and economic domains.

Fanon astutely noted that culture must be dynamic and open to change. When he spoke of the third stage of the development of a national culture he was proposing not an ossified or stable culture/tradition but one that must be critically evaluated so as to bring in suitable changes. In other words, Fanon was keen on traditions and cultural practices as responsive to changed historical circumstances rather than staying fixed in its older forms.

Fanon also drew unfavourable parallels between the colonial masters and the elite of the postcolonial nations. He argued that the power struggles between the colonial master and the native subject ends with political independence. However, ironically, this soon re-emerges in a different form: the battle for power between the elites and the rest in the postcolonial state. Native elites occupy the spaces of power once occupied by the white masters, and the corruption, oppression and exploitation of the working classes continue—this time at the hands of fellow natives (a theme seen in novels such as Ayi Kwei Armah's *The Beautyful Ones are Not Yet Born*, and a reality we have to acknowledge marks most postcolonial societies in the latter decades of the twentieth century). This, in effect, is neo-colonialism. The middle classes and intellectual classes that were educated in the colonial system now acquire power and duplicate the unjust and exploitative colonial system even after political independence.

AIMÉ CÉSAIRE, LEOPOLD SENGHOR AND NEGRITUDE

Aimé Césaire is best known for his term *negritude*. Negritude was the cultural response of the native to the onslaught by colonialism's culture.

Césaire argued that colonialism's evangelical and reformist mission was essentially a farce. Colonialism was never a benevolent enterprise because it was spearheaded by the pirate, the opportunist, the adventurer and the merchant. There is nothing other than profit as a motive behind the colonial project.

Césaire argued that community-centred, anti-capitalist native cultures were destroyed by the colonial's capitalist one. The sustained presence of the colonial meant that the native was in despair about ever finding his own identity. Native cultures are rejected by the colonial, and negritude evolves as a means of battling this rejection. Negritude is the black colonized people's salvaging of their own identity and consciousness. Influenced by the Harlem Renaissance of African Americans and the Black Arts movements in the USA, Césaire's negritude was characterised by a cultural separatism and the rejection of assimilation (of the colonial's culture by Africans).

Césaire's fellow intellectual in the negritude movement was Leopold Senghor (later, President of Senegal). Senghor's notion of Africanite has remarkable parallels with negritude. And, like Césaire, Senghor was influenced by Marxism and his idea of negritude exhibits clear socialist sympathies. Senghor's socialism was, however, not the type endorsed by the USSR and the communist world. Senghor, like Césaire, believed that African cultures were inherently communitarian and socialist. In fact, both believed that colonialism had destroyed native socialism and installed capitalism in its stead.

Senghor pleaded for an African unity, but also believed that African nations would continue to stay within the European 'commonwealth'. Thus, Senghor was not in favour of a complete break from the colonial legacy.

EDWARD SAID, *ORIENTALISM* AND THE POSTCOLONIAL MOMENT

One of the most influential books of the modern era, on par with Darwin's *On the Origin of Species*, Marx's *Das Capital* and Freud's *The Interpretation of Dreams,* the Palestinian immigrant Edward Said's *Orientalism* (1978) may be said, quite accurately, to have inaugurated the postcolonial field. Written with breathtaking erudition and an engaging style (for an academic, that is), *Orientalism* was a book whose time had come. Appearing around the same time as the works of Derrida, Foucault, Althusser and the French feminists, it set in motion an intellectual turbulence that altered the shape and canon of Western and Eastern academia. What we see today in the work of the postcolonial writers in American, European and South Asian university departments of English, Comparative Literature and Area Studies is the abiding influence of this one text.

Edward Said saw colonialism as a project that was, undeniably, military–political. However, colonialism also had a *discursive* component. That is, the primitive or pagan East was the literary–discursive creation of the European imagination that then begins to be accepted as true. What Said is interested in here is the literary–documentary and ideological construction of the non-European cultures in European texts and thought. By discursive construction, Said means the apparatuses of representation, such as, archaeology, literary, history, music, ethnography, political theory and social commentary, used by the European colonial powers to talk about the East in a certain way. Said argued that this representation of the East was integral to the conquest of the East: the epistemological domination of the East through documented knowledge and archivization enabled Europe to obtain and retain power. To word it differently, discourses that constructed the Orient in certain ways contributed to the political and military power of the European over the native.

Said's major contribution was to see colonialism as rooted in an epistemological inquiry and project: constructing the Orient. 'Orientalism' is this European construction of the East as primitive, savage, pagan, undeveloped and criminal. Such a construction then enabled the European to justify his presence: The poor, weak native needed to be governed and 'developed', and it was the task of the European to do so. Oriental 'reality' is interpreted in particular ways, ways that are usable by the Europeans. Thus, Hindu and Islamic religious texts and beliefs are constructed within this discourse as pagan, primitive and requiring reform. Now it is important to see the stages in which this so-called truth is produced:

(i) The European has particular ideas about the Hindu/Islamic systems within his consciousness (Said's 'latent Orientalism').

(ii) The European collects notes about the native 'systems'.

(iii) The European interprets these notes from the standpoint of his already existing (mis)conceptions and ideas.

(iv) Native opinions on native reality are ignored in favour of 'authoritative' European readings/interpretations (Said's 'manifest Orientalism').

(v) European interpretations become the standard readings that then reinforce the 'latent' ideas about the Hindu/Islamic systems.

(vi) These readings are actively linked to and reflect the political demands and acts of the colonial administration.

As we can see, Orientalist discourse moves from imaginative (what Said calls 'fantasies') representations of the East to actual administrative manifestations: It moves from *discourse to event*.

Said also argued that European identity in the eighteenth and nineteenth century evolved through a confrontation and engagement with such non-European cultures. 'Europe' and 'the Orient' were discursively represented in literature and history as *binary opposites*. Europe was all that the Orient was *not*: developed, Christian, civilized. Europe saw the Orient as different, and treated this difference as *negative*. As Said puts it, the Orient is Europe's 'contrasting image, idea, personality, experience' (1978a: 2). In what is a classic deconstructive move, one can see the argument in Said very clearly: European identity was established only because it had the East to contrast itself with. Or: The Orient was integral to the very formation of a European identity. Gayatri Spivak, therefore, opens her essay 'Three Women's Texts and a Critique of Imperialism' (1999 [1985]) with a very Saidian statement that illustrates this theoretical move within postcolonial studies:

It should not be possible to read nineteenth-century British literature without remembering that imperialism, understood as England's social mission, was a crucial part of the cultural representation of England to itself. The role of literature in the production of cultural representation should not be ignored. (1999: 269)

The discourse of the 'Orient'—the production of ideas, knowledge and opinions—that constructed it as primitive and pagan also froze the East into an unchanging, fossilized state. Europe could not deny that places like India or the Arab world had been civilized for centuries. But what Europe did in its representations was a simple manoeuver. It accepted that the Orient had had its great civilizations, but these had remained at the level of their early achievements. That is, the Orient was a place frozen in time with no progress or change. With this 'freezing' of the Orient, Europe was able to develop another theme: Progress and development are features of European/white cultures while Oriental cultures remain static. Positing an unchanging Orient also enabled the European colonial master to deal better with the colonies because there was no threat of change: They could draft laws, prepare educational policy or governance structures without worrying that the native cultures would evolve.

> 'Orientalism' is a style of thinking, a form of representation that created opinions, ideas and images of the non-European culture in racialized ways so that (i) the East was always contrasted negatively with Europe and (ii) it justified the colonial presence in the East.

In effect, Said's work showed how discourse and rhetoric, language and writing were essential to the colonial project because writing and rhetoric are *ideological*. The ideology of empire required certain forms of discourse to support and justify it, and Orientalism was this discourse. Educational syllabi, literary texts, anthropological studies were all discourses that treated the Orient and native cultures as subjects to be studied, disciplined and governed.

In the early stages (1750–1850), Orientalism was the discourse of 'discovery', when the Europeans 'discovered' the East. The Orient was mysterious and demanded exploration and study, and texts from the period showcase the adventurous European on the voyage of discovery. Later scholars (Jyotsna Singh 1996 ; Barbour 2003; Nayar 2008a) have shown how this discourse of discovery goes right back to the sixteenth and seventeenth centuries and extends to even the Americas (Greenblatt 1991). The discourse of discovery within Orientalism spoke of the mystery that had to be unraveled by the European. By the nineteenth century, the discoveries were validated and proved as negative, evil and primitive. The arguments about the discoveries are now made and the Orient is located 'outside' Europe, as its dark Other.

Discourse, in Said's reading of the imperial archive, had very serious material effects: It justified and reinforced the empire. Texts such as Kipling's *Kim* (which Said analysed in his *Culture and Imperialism*) are thus 'worldly' in that they demonstrate the ways of the world around them. Said inaugurated the postcolonial field with this move when he argued that colonial literary and anthropological texts may be 'imaginative' or 'factual', but they invariably code political ideologies of their age (and are, therefore, never 'innocent'). Postcolonial studies would build on this notion by reading practically all of English and European literature for their colonial ideologies.

These ideologies became integral to the colonial enterprise in varied ways. They informed policy decisions and the system of administration. More insidiously, these ideologies circulating as literary and other texts worked their influence on the natives too. Structures and institutions of learning, universities, professional societies, exploration and geographical organizations, publishing industry, helped disseminate the Orientalist ideology. Translations and interpretations of the Orient by scholars like H. H. Wilson and William Jones appropriated and presented the Orient in certain ways to the West, in the process becoming 'authorities' and 'authors' over various Indian and native subjects like Hindu law, Sanskrit literature and tropical diseases. When English education was introduced, when native texts were translated into English, or when Europeans framed laws for the natives, they used the stereotypes already in existence: primitive, pagan, childlike natives. This European hypothesis about the nature of the natives was then demonstrated to be true by seeking 'expert' opinion. The 'expert' opinion also came from Europe. This was a brilliant move, argues Said, for both hypothesis and proof came from the same ideological–political formation: colonialism. When such irrefutable 'proof' was provided to the native, s/he accepted it as true. The consequences are fascinating: The native began to look at him/herself through the eyes of the European because s/he, the native, had accepted truth of all the representations made by the European. Effectively, this meant that Orientalism achieved the acquiescence of the natives because it convinced the natives that all the stereotypes about their cultures were true, and that they needed the Europeans. Said's work demonstrates, after this extraordinary insight, a fairly simple truth: The empire may have been won by the sword and the gun, but it was kept through the active acquiescence and obedience of the native who, by accepting the truth of Orientalist discourses, sought, demanded and reinforced European colonial presence. Said was arguing in the tradition of Althusserian Marxism where the native subject is interpellated into colonial structures and roles through ideology. The identity of the native is what the colonial discourse generates and the native assimilates. It is this process that helps colonialism attain and retain its control. The empire, Said thus demonstrates, was kept not through coercion but through consent, and consent is achieved through discourse.

Orientalism demonstrated the political nature of culture, of the ideological basis of acts of imagination (literature) and the material effects of particular kinds of representation. Said located 'culture' as central to the empire, and thus demonstrated the materiality of discourse and rhetoric. He asked us to read literary and other texts 'contrapuntally', against the grain in order to detect the racialized, imperialist discourse within it and to resist it. Postcolonialism is possible through such a resistant reading, where we identify the ideological grids of the so-called literary texts, when we begin to develop a different historical narrative other than the one handed down to us by the colonial discourse.

Edward Said's epoch-making work does present some problems. For example, Said does not account for the differences *between* colonialisms (the French occupation of Algeria, the settler colonialism in Australia and the British colonization of India)—a problem addressed in Lisa Lowe's work (1991)—treating all colonialisms as one homogenous structure. He ignores the gendered and sexualized nature of colonial discourses: the representation of the veiled Algeria woman, the 'innocent' Indian widow who needs European (male) help, and the homophobic ideology of colonialism. He does not address the theme of native complicity and the class dimension (a criticism Aijaz Ahmed launched in his important *In Theory*). Despite these problems—some of which Said corrected in his *Culture and Imperialism*—the overall argument is compelling and undeniable. The emphasis on discourse as possessing material consequences and as constitutive of a political project is a useful mode of reading, and one that has enormous scope for literary and cultural theory.

Contemporary literary criticism and cultural theory adopted Edward Said, Fanon and the early critics in order to read diverse cultural practices: films, literature, anthropology and ethnography, law, translation and medicine. 'Postcolonial studies' is a holdall kind of term to describe postcolonial theory (especially in the field of literary studies), cultural studies (in film and museum studies) and diaspora studies. In the next section we shall map the terrain of postcolonial studies in terms of its major topographical features.

COLONIAL DISCOURSES AND ENGLISH STUDIES

Colonial discourse, in simple terms, is the narrative construction of the non-European by Europeans in literature, arts, law, social science inquiries, archaeology, political thought, museology and other fields.

THE LITERATURE OF EMPIRE

The task of postcolonial literary criticism has been (primarily in English studies), to locate modes of representation—narratives—where Europeans constructed the natives in politically significant ways. Colonial discourse is racialized, of course, and because racial discourses feed directly into the imperial–colonial system (colonialism being the conquest and domination of one race by another), the task of postcolonial literary studies has been to unpack those literary figures, themes and representations that have enforced imperialist ideology, colonial dominance and continuing Western hegemony. Adapting Said's argument that discourses shape and determine colonial experiences for both colonizers and colonized, postcolonial studies locate a political role for literary representations.

Within colonial discourse studies, postcolonial literary criticism has focused on the role of 'Eng. Lit.', English language and cultural representations, demonstrating how canonical Eng. Lit. texts are imbricated in colonial structures of dominance and oppression.

A now-classic method in postcolonial literary studies is to, therefore, uncover the 'subtexts' of Eng. Lit. texts, to probe beneath the obvious and apparently universal/

humanist/aesthetic themes in order to reveal their racial, gendered, imperial assumptions. One of the principal critical texts in this postcolonial approach is Gauri Viswanathan's *Masks of Conquest* (1989). Viswanathan demonstrates how English literature as a discipline was introduced in India by

(i) rejecting native literary traditions in Sanskrit, Persian and Arabic,
(ii) installing English texts in their stead,
(iii) using these texts as modes of creating a class of Indians who would be trained to serve the colonial administration.

English literary texts are neither universal nor simply about human values. They encode prejudices that are racial, attitudes that serve the empire and carry stereotypes that are false but powerful in their consequences. The task is one of *re-interpretation*, to examine the values of literary texts for what they conceal.

Re-interpretation in postcolonial literary studies involves paying attention to the contexts in which English literary texts were produced, and to work colonial ideologies through these texts. Thus, Chinua Achebe's famous reading (1975) of Joseph Conrad's cult novel, *Heart of Darkness*, argued that Conrad had absolutely no interest in Africans, and reduced them, in his novel, to animal and dehumanized images. Edward Said (1993) reading Jane Austen's *Mansfield Park* argues that the Caribbean plantation in Antigua is linked inextricably to the family's fortunes and life in England and thereby showing how the colony is inseparable from the European country. Sara Suleri (1992) reading Kipling's *Kim*, Homi Bhabha (2007b [1994]) reading Forster's *A Passage to India*, Peter Hulme (1986) reading Defoe's *Robinson Crusoe* and Nigel Leask's work (1993) on the English Romantic poets are some of the key texts that illustrate this process of postcolonial readings of colonial literary texts. More recent works have not dealt directly with literary representations but have paid attention to literary cultures—the publishing industry, libraries, the circulation and consumption of texts. Thus, Priya Joshi's *In Another Country* (2002) carefully teases out the impact of English novels in the literary cultures of nineteenth-century India. Others have expanded the study to look at how postcolonial works also exhibit significant overlaps with colonial ideologies, and refract postcoloniality itself in ideologies of commerce (Caroline Davis' excellent work on the Oxford University Press in postcolonial Africa is an instance).

Postcolonial *cultural* studies have included re-interpretations of other kinds of colonial writings. Thus, Mrinalini Sinha (1995), Inderpal Grewal (1996), Antoinette Burton (2003), Betty Joseph (2004) and Anindita Mukhopadhyay (2006) have worked at the interface of literary studies and history to unpack colonial ideologies in a wide variety of administrative, legal and ethnographic texts. Colonial medicine has been examined for its racialized vision of the tropics, and for the construction of particular kinds of 'diseased' native bodies (David Arnold, Mark Harrison, Alan Bewell). Material cultures of the colonial period (Swati Chattopadhyay 2002), the role of family ideologies within the empire (Elizabeth Buettner), the disciplines of geography and cartography (Matthew Edney), law

(Radhika Singha) have also been studied for their complicity in the empire's political and social projects. Linda Colley (1992), M. L. Pratt (1995), Tim Youngs (1994) have argued persuasively that England 'forged' itself as a nation through the conscious utilization of distant cultures/places encountered through travel. Sanjay Srivastava's innovative work (2007) demonstrates how sexual discourses combined with colonial ideas of health/hygiene/eugenics and later, in independent India, with notions of Hindu tradition.

Another strand within postcolonial studies has been the exploration of how native presences in England and Europe may have contributed to imperialism (or its subversion). Michael Fisher's pathbreaking work, *Counterflows to Colonialism* (2004), the work of Rozina Visram (1984, 1989), C. L. Innes (2002) and Catherine Hall (2002) have pointed to imperial cultures in London as actively engaged with natives at home rather than in the colonies. Thus, imperialism itself may have taken particular forms by accommodating and engaging with these 'foreign' bodies within Europe itself.

If reinterpretation involves unpacking colonial ideologies in English literary texts, then the obverse of this critical inquiry has involved detecting modes of *resistance, subversion* and *dissent* in English texts as well as native ones. This process of reinterpretation is the search for a colonial discourse that could be called *anamorphic*. The texts that Homi Bhabha studies, for instance, in his essays in *The Location of Culture* (2007 [1994]), suggest that beneath the overt colonial ideologies, the author might be subverting colonial discourses. Bhabha's emphasis on 'ambivalence' suggests that colonial authority was often subverted from the inside, by the colonial (on some occasion) and by the natives.

According to this reading anamorphic literary texts from the colonial period did not, for obvious reasons, resist the empire, or critique imperialism. However, works such as Forster's *A Passage to India*, the conclusion of Jonathan Swift's classic *Gulliver's Travels* do exhibit signs that their authors were not entirely convinced of the 'rightness' of the empire. In fact, Bhabha's often virtuoso readings reveal that colonial discourse was fractured and flawed. Kumari Jayawardene (1995), Indrani Sen (2002) and Indira Ghose (1998) have also, in a similar vein, demonstrated the incomplete nature of colonial discourse in their readings of literary texts.

Here postcolonial reinterpretations work at something else: They seek not the Saidian kind of colonial discourse that dominates and controls the native, but rather the gaps and fissures within this discourse that

- actually provide the native with the means of resistance and
- the dissenting colonial with the modes of articulating opposition.

The significance of such postcolonial re-interpretations cannot be overemphasized. They show

- how not all English writing is necessarily racist or imperialist,

- how, by seeking colonial ideologies in all English texts, postcolonial readings perform the same act of homogenizing all Western literature that we once accused the West of doing to native writings and
- that resistance is always possible even within the so-called overtly imperialist texts.

In such postcolonial readings, Edward Said's sweeping judgments of European writings get overturned.

LANGUAGE AND IMPERIALISM

Moving from literature to the language, postcolonial studies proceed to locate European languages as instruments of colonial power. Walter Mignolo (2003) in his grand study of the European Renaissance meticulously teases out the imperialist-colonial politics of Spanish grammar books and their role in the conquest of South America. This magisterial study shows how grammar, syntax and dictionary projects are never *only* about language, but rather serve very devious imperial purposes and often determine interpretations in other disciplines such as education, history and the law. Bernard Cohn has shown how English became the 'language of command' and helped the English colonial ruler to 'order' India in particular ways through the use of classificatory regimes and the catalogue. The language of aesthetics—derived from English and European theories—has also been used, as studies have shown (Leask 2002, Nayar 2008a) to homogenize, catalogue, organize and discipline native landscapes, peoples and cultural practices.

The destruction of aboriginal and vernacular languages, as numerous writers from Asia, Africa, North and South America, and Australia have argued, can be readily traced to the imposition of European languages with colonial rule. Even translation from the vernacular-native into European languages, as several postcolonial translations scholars (Harish Trivedi, Tejaswini Niranjana, Susan Bassnett) have shown, is a political act.

The acceptance of English by natives in the colonial period created a politics of representation because the language was racialized and gendered. English became the means of acquiring power for the native elites. With political independence English continues to be the language of power (in administration, finance, law and, increasingly, global commerce), and the metropolitan sites and English-speaking minority are able to dominate postcolonial societies.

This has resulted in a sharp divide between languages and literatures. Writings in native languages are (i) not easily published by the bigger publishing houses, (ii) not circulated, reviewed or accepted easily by audiences, (iii) never acquire the prestige accorded to writing in English. *Nativist criticism*—Balachandra Nemade and others in the representative Makarand Paranjape volume (1997)—has fought this battle, but with little signs of success. Writers like Raja Rao (1963) famously argued that the colonial master's language cannot capture or convey the emotional content or 'core' of the native. Those like Ngũgĩ wa Thiong'o, for this reason, have turned away from English to their native language. Others who seek a more hybrid nature for language identity—Derek Walcott (1986 [1962]), Salman Rushdie (1991)—have argued that English gets *nativized*, that it no longer belongs only to the English people, and that the use of English does not detract from the force of expression by the formerly colonized. As Walcott put it in his poem 'A Far Cry from Africa':

> Divided to the vein
> How choose
> Between this Africa and the English tongue I love?
> (1986 [1962]: 17–18)

The problem of language, especially for literary writing, is exacerbated by the contexts, as noted above, of literary production (including translation and pedagogy). Significant postcolonial criticism—which implies that which is published and accepted in Western academia/publishing—is invariably in English. Even—or perhaps, especially—those who espouse the cause of native languages teach English for a living.

SUBJECT AND SUBALTERNITY

Literature, as studies of colonial discourse originating in Edward Said's work have demonstrated, 'interpellates' natives into the colonial order. A key element in postcolonial studies is the examination of the processes through which the native is rendered a marginalized subject, with little agency or identity.

A key figure in the postcolonial analysis of the interpellation of the native subject is Homi Bhabha. Bhabha's work reveals how the colonial discourse that sought to impose a unidirectional flow of power (colonizer to colonized) and a monolithic structure, often failed. Bhabha's work on mimicry, ambivalence and hybridity radically interrogates the effectiveness in/of colonial discourse, all the while pointing to its fractures.

Bhabha begins his reading by noting how identities in the colonial encounter are never stable or fixed. Colonial encounters are transactions: between the colonizer and the colonized. The European in the colony constructs his identity only through a relationality based on difference. Building on Lacanian psychoanalysis and poststructuralism, Bhabha proposes that identities, even in the colonial context, are based on differential relations: The colonizer establishes his identity by positioning himself against and in opposition to the native. This means, effectively, the colonizer can never posses a self-identical identity, because it requires the colonized to validate it. (We recall here poststructuralism's argument that all identity/meaning is based on the difference of one letter/sound/signifier from another, suggesting that both are linked together in the formation of identities.) Identity, therefore, is constantly shifting, liminal and displaced. With this move, Bhabha suggests that we cannot see colonial identity as fixed or monolithic; it is unstable, shifting and relational.

Bhabha proposes that colonial discourse is actually conflictual and ambivalent. The colonial master, far from being the strong, unflinching and certain Englishman, is actually informed by two contradictory psychic states, what Bhabha terms, fetish and phobia. These two contradictory states result in stereotypes of the native subject. Bhabha argues that the festish/phobia structure of colonial relations results in a condition where the white man seeks and desires the Other, while at the same time wishes to erase the difference. This results in stereotypes such as that of

- the inscrutable native—suggesting an unknowable, radically different Other and
- the vulnerable, innocent or childlike native—suggesting a knowable, controllable subject of colonial power.

Bhabha thus proposes a divided colonial discourse, and a native subject whose subject-position is never stable or automatic (just as the colonial master's position is never stable or automatic). The repetition of stereotypes (such as the ones mentioned above) is not, for Bhabha, a sign of the power of colonial discourse. Rather, he treats this repetition as a sign of its inherent instability. Stereotypes are invoked and repeated not because they are stable but because, unless repeated, they lose their power and validity *as* signs.

> Bhabha's work reveals colonial discourse as unstable and fractured, ambivalent and open to subversion—each time colonialism seeks to impose its authority through a repetition of the sign (the emblem, the English book), the native's repetition of the sign dismantles it by adding or subtracting any intended or original (colonial) meaning depending on his [native's] need.

As an example of this structure of repetition Bhabha cites, in his key essay, 'Signs Taken for Wonders', the 'English book'. The 'English book' is the Bible. Bhabha argues that the Bible functioned as a sign of colonial power/authority: the authority to disseminate the book throughout the colony. However, Bhabha notes, the *sign* (or book) is riddled with ambivalence in the very act of disseminating it. Bhabha suggests that the book is 'translated' by natives into their own contexts, a process that often involves subversion and sometimes resistance. Bhabha here speaks of 'repetition with a difference' (an idea seen in deconstructive criticism, as for example, in Hillis Miller's studies of the English novel in *Fiction and Repetition*). When the native repeats the English book, s/he does so with variations. The book might lose its nuances, and add meanings not originally present. Thus, the books acquires a wholly different form, and, by extension loses its authority as a colonial sign. It is now a sign that has been rewritten by the native. This is the inherent instability of colonial discourse, and the potential for resistance. Bhabha uses the term *ambivalence* to describe this rupture between the hoped-for original authority of the English book/sign and the effect of repetition and difference.

Extending this argument about the potential resistance by the native subject, Bhabha proposes the idea of 'mimicry' (in 'Of Mimicry and Man'). Mimicry is the disciplined imitation of the white man by the native. The native has been taught, consistently, that he needs to try and ape the white man and his culture. Mimicry is sought through Western education, religion and structures where the native is trained to think/behave like the white man. However, Bhabha sees this as a site where colonial authority, rather than being reinforced, actually breaks down. What happens in the colonial encounter is that the native becomes Anglicized but is never fully or truly white. He is a mimic who can now insinuate himself into the colonial structure, respond in English and adopt the structure of logic and reasoning in argument which Western education has taught him. When Raja Rammohun Roy argues in favour of English education (in his letter to Lord Amherst), he appropriates a rational argument rather than a sentimental one: He appeals to the English in the language of logic, reason, administrative convenience and expediency that they would recognize (rather than sentimental pleas, which would have been rejected for being truly 'native'). The mimic man here appears to 'follow' the white man's authority—to show the power of colonial discourse—but in effect fractures and disrupts it. Mimicry here reveals the breaks in the colonial discourse: The native represents him/herself rather than be represented. As Bhabha puts it, 'The menace of mimicry is its double vision which in disclosing the ambivalence of colonial discourse also disrupts its authority' (2007a [1994]: 126).

This mimicry also fails because the colonial master, on the one hand, wants the native as similar to himself as possible and, on the other, wishes to keep the difference between himself and the native. That is, the colonial wishes to both erase and reinforce difference (the ambivalence noted of colonial discourse before). Even as the colonial master works this ambivalent state, the native begins to repeat/mime the master, but with subtle variations and nuances (what we have seen above as repetition and difference). The mimicry of the native often encodes (i) a facile obedience and obsequiousness and (ii) a deeper disobedience and mockery (what Bhabha in his essay of the same title calls 'sly civility'). This dual state of mimicry by the native—one that is the direct result of the fractured nature of colonial discourse—is what Bhabha terms 'hybridity'.

According to Bhabha, this hybridized native who refuses to return the colonial gaze, and who refuses to acknowledge the colonizer's position and authority, is placed in a position of *in-betweenness*: between 'adopted' Englishness and 'original' Indiannness. Mimicry that results in this *dualism of deference and disobedience* is what Bhabha sees as resistance. This hybridity creates a 'third space', a space of relations (between colonizer and colonized). This is a site where

- colonial identity and native identity meet and often contest,
- colonial discourse is both/at once asserted *and* subverted,
- there is deference *and* difference,
- there is a split and a negotiation (within colonial discourse),
- mimicry *and* mockery occur.

The 'third space' is the space where the subject begins to articulate resistance. The 'subject', for Bhabha, is thus the split, decentered, unstable and resistant one.

This reading of the colonial subject by Bhabha can be counterposed with the one by Gayatri Spivak—another theorist whose work with poststructuralism, feminism and Marxism has resulted in now-cult texts in the postcolonial canon.

Spivak's most-quoted essay is surely her 'Can the Subaltern Speak?' (1985). Spivak adapts the notion of the subaltern, meaning the oppressed class, from Antonio Gramsci in order to theorize the condition of the native within colonialism and the woman in postcolonial state. She argues, via a reading of a woman's suicide in early twentieth-century India, that the structure of colonialism prevents any speaking. This structure is doubly strengthened in the case of the native woman, who is silenced through both patriarchy and colonialism (i.e., for both, her gender and her race). Hence, reduced to silence by these structures, the woman writes her body. Spivak argues that the subaltern wrote her body, because there was no other way of speaking.

Spivak's move is to argue, via poststructuralism, that subjects are constituted *through* discourse. Discourse is, of course, a regime of representation that is controlled by power. This means, an individual cannot develop an identity without being the subject of a discourse over which s/he may have little or no control. The subaltern is one who has no position or sovereignty outside the discourse that constructs her as subject. Spivak rejects the idea that one can access a 'pure' subaltern consciousness because, as she argues, the subaltern cannot speak, and is hence spoken *for*. The subaltern woman, in particular, has no position of enunciation: She remains within the discourse of patriarchy and colonialism as the object of somebody else's discourse.

Spivak's influential notion of the subaltern notes the power of both patriarchy and colonialism where the native woman, because of her location within these two structures, cannot enunciate and instead is always spoken for by intellectuals—a process Spivak is critical of because, as she argues, it is better to let the woman remain on the margins of the discourse (thus disturbing it) rather than speaking on her behalf and thus consigning her deeper into the silence.

Spivak is also critical of any attempt to retrieve the voice of subaltern by intellectuals because such an attempt assumes that the intellectual is a transparent medium, or passage, through which the subaltern's voice emerges. Spivak's move is to argue that all notions and representations of 'subaltern' consciousness or 'Third World' women, is a construction of Western discourses. These discourses construct the subaltern and give it a voice.

This interpretation of course produced a body of work that has sought to, alternately, agree with and disparage Spivak. Harish Trivedi (1996), for instance, argues that Spivak seems to ignore the myriad ways in which the subaltern-native woman has spoken. The point is, suggests Trivedi, the subaltern speaks in the vernacular and this speech is, therefore, not seen as speaking at all. Spivak responds to this (1996) by suggesting that 'speak' in the sense she was using it was not a reference to a speech act but rather to the process of meaning-making and interpretation that ensues in any such *transaction* (Spivak's term to suggest the relation of the speaker and listener). Spivak argues that the native woman's speech is understood and interpreted within structures that will only afford particular meanings. The woman's voice cannot attain more purchase because she has been relegated to a category already. This means, Spivak argues, there is an urgent need to create an ethical response to the voice of the subaltern. Spivak proposes that the subaltern can figure only in an ethical relation where there is the deliberate creation of a room, a space for the voice of the radical Other.

Noting how quickly the 'subaltern' has been appropriated by theorists and thinkers, Spivak addresses the theme of institutions. Spivak is acerbic in her critique of institutionalization—and thereby romanticization—of the subaltern. She argues that this appropriation, where the ethnic minority angle is perpetually stressed, ensures that their marginality is retained. It is only through the West's acknowledgement and validation of the margin that the margin finds an identity. Here the discipline of postcolonial studies itself becomes suspect because, for Spivak, it presents the West's longing for its Other.

GENDER, SEXUALITY AND THE EMPIRE

The empire, argue feminist critics, has always been seen primarily as a 'raced' project. This has resulted in the effacement of the woman in studies of colonialism. Feminist readings have foregrounded both the racial as well as the gendered contexts and problems of both European and native women in the colonial context. Others have addressed the sexuality theme by analysing the homoerotic, sexually ambivalent relations, role-playing and power struggles within colonial contexts. The contemporary postcolonial theory focuses on gender and race, and has been instrumental in the rise of black feminist theory and critiques of Western feminisms (see Chapter 4).

In an early work Kirsten Holst Petersen and Anna Rutherford (1986) proposed that women in colonialism experience a 'double colonization'. By this they were gesturing at the extraordinarily oppressive and circumscribed contexts of women's lives in colonialism, trapped by/within both patriarchy and colonialism. This is a useful point to begin the exploration of the gendered and the sexualized nature of colonialism.

The empire was always, primarily, a *masculine adventure*. Discovery, exploration, conquest and rule were acts and symbols of the European male's dominance of the world. This dominance extended to both landscape and women (both their own as well as native). Signs of such dominance are scattered throughout European literature in themes of exploration, hazardous travel, encounters with the strange and the new, the conquest of native lands, among others. In most cases, such themes included clearly the sexualized ones, the exploration of the Arab harem, the 'protection' of the native woman by the ultra-macho European male, the instrumental use of the European women by the European male in the imperial project. As Meyda Yegenoglu and others have noted, central to the imperial project was the attempt

- to penetrate feminine spaces;
- legislate on the colonial personnel's sexuality;
- seek 'reforms' in the domain of gender;
- stereotype the native male as both ultra-libidinous and effeminate.

However, when European women set out into the outposts of empire the relation with the natives, or the 'acts', were not so reductively imperial. Women experienced the East/colony differently from their men. Thus, European women in colonies had multiple modes of dealing with the colony. They

- fought their gendered battle, seeing the colony as a space where their rights and identities could be gained;
- rejected masculinist appropriations and engagements with native cultures;
- were complicit with imperial projects of reform (especially in the nineteenth century);
- built connections with native women, often excluding men (both native and European) from this 'sisterhood';
- even encouraged native women in the anti-colonial struggle.

Thus, European women had interesting and often problematic relations with the imperial project. Many fought, resisted or subverted their own culture's patriarchal oppression, and saw the colony as a site of possible emancipation. For the women evangelicals in the nineteenth century, the 'mission' gave them an identity otherwise denied them (Burton 1996, Murray 2000, Johnston 2003).

When Gayatri Spivak (1999 [1985]) reads canonical English women's texts such as Charlotte Brontë's *Jane Eyre* (1847), she shows how an 'imperialist axiomatics' determines the heroine Jane's move from a 'counter-family' to a legal family. Spivak's criticism of the novel locates the development of Jane's individualism as

aligned with imperialism. Thus, the woman-consciousness and attempted independence in the novel, which the feminist critics have seen as a major achievement,
cannot be studied in isolation from the colonial–imperial context that allows the
white woman to be individualist but consigns women like Bertha Mason (a
Jamaican Creole) to the background as 'mad'. Spivak notes how Mason is portrayed as an animal, in sharp contrast to Jane. In this portrayal of Mason, Spivak
detects the imperialist 'axiomatics': the rational–human white and the animal–Jamaican Other.

Like Spivak, Anne McClintock turns to Victorian ideas of the family and
domesticity, viewing these as sites where ideologies of race, gender and sexuality
are played out. The 'cult of domesticity', as she terms it (1995: 5) appropriated
racial and gendered ideology, alongside that of class, in order to develop a sense of
modernity. McClintock, like many postcolonial theorists, sees imperialism—in
her case a gendered and 'classed' imperialism—as central to the development of an
English identity.

The empire, as Kenneth Ballhatchet (1980), Ronald Hyam (1990) and other
critics have demonstrated, was intensely concerned about the sexuality and sexual
health of its personnel. It made numerous attempts to ensure that English soldiers
visited only those prostitutes who had been 'cleared' by the English medical exam-
iner. Liaisons with native women and the Eurasian ('half-caste') progeny were
seen (the latter especially in the latter days of the Raj) as something to be ashamed
of. The fear of miscegenation—mixed race liaisons—and the resultant hybridity
(as Robert Young's early and influential study, 1995, showed) that informed much
colonial policy was linked to theories of the 'purity' of race and eugenics movement of the nineteenth century. The fear of the rape of white women by hypersexual
native men—a fear that is the subtext of many literary and other works, especially
in the wake of the Indian 'mutiny' of 1857—as well as the fear that the white
woman might take to the native/black man was the accompaniment to the theme
of miscegenation (Alison Blunt 2000a, 2000b, Antoinette Burton 2003, and
others).

Later feminist postcolonial theorists have shifted focus from colonial texts to
the nationalist anti-colonial movements. National movements frequently resorted
to the figure of the woman as a metaphor ('Motherland') and as a 'boundary-
marker' (McClintock's term), the keeper of the tradition (in India Bankimchandra
Chatterjee, *Anandamath* (1882) and Rabindranath Tagore, *The Home and the World*
(1919), and of course the persistent trope of 'Mother India'). The essentializing of
the woman is central to the freedom struggle. Nationalism is always a gendered
project.

During anti-colonial struggles the woman plays a *political–public* supportive
role but once independence is achived, she must revert to her *domestic* one (see
Andrew Parker et al. 1992). Elleke Boehmer (2005) has argued persuasively that
the conflation of nation with family is a metonymic configuration, and the woman
functions as a metaphor for the maternal role. This maternal role is one authorized

for the woman by her sons, where she stands for national values and tradition. Postcolonial feminists have increasingly addressed the gender issue in post-independence nations. In a well-known argument, Partha Chatterjee proposed that colonial/postcolonial modernity and tradition seek power over the familial and domestic space (1986). In a particularly astute theorization Mary John and Janaki Nair (1998) have introduced caste and class configurations along with that of gender and the nation. Looking at India, they write:

> The middle class, upper caste woman has been the ground on which questions of modernity are framed. She embodies the boundaries of licit and illicit forms of sexuality, she is the guardian of the nation's morality. (1998: 8)

The woman has to remain fixed and unchanging, even as postcolonial nation-states themselves undergo changes. The Indian writer C. S. Lakshmi notes:

> The 'notion' of an unbroken tradition is constant and attempts are made to write this notion of tradition on the body of the woman to dictate its movement, needs, aspirations and spheres of existence even while the body is moving along time, space and history. (1999: 55)

Numerous postcolonial writers have called into question the problematic linkage of national identity and gender roles. Michelle Cliff, Keri Hulme, Jamaica Kincaid, Anita Desai, among others, have enabled extensive postcolonial theorizations besides their works of fiction.

Imperialism also had a problematic relationship with other forms of sexuality. The Fielding–Aziz relationship in Forster's *A Passage to India* has overtones of a homoerotic relationship. In Paul Scott's Raj Quartet (set in the last days of the Raj) Ronald Merrick, the homosexual English officer, abuses the Indian Hari Kumar. Homosexuality was, of course, unacceptable but, as these novels show, was very much present as a subterranean sexuality. Specific notions and views of masculinity and femininity informed colonial interaction with natives. When the British, for example, depicted the 'effeminate' Bengali in India, they were positing the imperialist as a masculine Other in contrast. Sanjay Srivastava's recent work (2007), which I have cited before, points out that imperial reform of sexuality and sexual health—often the context for translations of Indian classics such as the *Kamasutra*—were taken up by native commentators too. Iconic figures like Richard Burton and T. E. Lawrence have been revealed as homosexuals whose roles in imperial dominance were interesting negotiations between a masculine dynamic (imperialism, as noted earlier, was a masculine event) and their own 'Other' sexualities.

NATIONS AND NATIONALISM

The anti-colonial movement, in most cases, posited the idea of a nation with a continuous and common tradition. In India, for example, even the uneven 'rebellion' of 1857 invoked the idea of a pre-British 'Hindustan'.

In postcolonial studies the nation figures prominently in several ways:

(i) It has been argued, under the influence of Benedict Anderson (1983), that the nation is 'imagined'. People from corners of the geographical territory who will never meet or know the rest continue to see the other parts of this territory and their cultures as a component of 'our' nation.

(ii) The 'nation' is a collective that exists primarily in acts of imagination and thinking, a 'unity' that might be more fantasy than reality, but is powerful nevertheless.

(iii) This sense of collective unity is generated and sustained by symbolic forms, such as, songs, films, cultural practices like stories, traditions, history writing. Every nation, according to Timothy Brennan (1990), demands a narrative form where continuity, contiguity and commonality are invented, packaged and sold to the people. The national flag, the performance of Diwali, the pride in Sachin Tendulkar, the anxiety over Pakistan, the Hindi film, the slogan 'unity in diversity' are all symbolic forms that suggest to us that 'India is our nation'.

Thus, the nation is a myth that has a very real hold over the people. A national identity is the consequence of such an enabling myth: It unites people under one umbrella, provides them with a sustaining form/story and asks them to function together in the name of the nation. What should be remembered here is that the national identity is freely accepted and assimilated by the people. In Nuruddin Farah's *Maps* (1999) he describes this process of assimilating a 'national' identity:

> Most people they met along the way had their bodies tattooed with their identities: that is, name, nationality and address. Some had engraved on their skins the reason why they had become who they were when living and others had printed on their foreheads or backs their national flags or insignia. (1999: 43)

Nationalism is the ideology and political project that emerges once this myth has been put in place. The African 'negritude' is an instance of such an effect: Once the idea of an 'African identity' was established and disseminated it provided the source for imagining a shared tradition (even if this 'sharing' itself was a fantasy). This shared tradition was then used as a counter to the foreign colonial power, an us versus them argument in which all of Africa was 'native', 'true' and 'pure' and in opposition to the foreign, the intrusion and the false. Nationalism had two components in literature and the arts:

(i) It helped writers seek a pre-colonial past that would help them define the nation and

(ii) It projected a destiny, a future shared by and common to all people within the space of that nation.

Salman Rushdie articulates this 'imagination' of the very idea of a nation:

After all, in all the thousands of years of Indian history, there never was such a creature as a united India. Nobody ever managed to rule the whole place, not the
Mughals, not the British. And then, that midnight, the thing that had never existed
was suddenly "free." But what on earth was it? On what common ground (if any) did
it, does it, stand? (1991: 27)

Yet, such a national identity and its forms have been interrogated in recent
postcolonial studies by historians, political theorists and literary critics.

Partha Chatterjee notes that the very idea of a nation is Western (1986).
Anti-colonial/nationalist movements adopt the idea of progress or modernity
from the West and launch the idea of a nation. Chatterjee argues that natives
transform the Western idea of a nation in three stages. In the first stage, the natives
accept modern Western ideas of progress and modernity. In the second, the elite
in the colony turn to folk and popular cultural forms in order to generate both
mass support as well as a new form of identity based on local cultures. Finally, in
the third stage, the Western and folk cultural forms are projected as a native
nationalism by the elite. The anti-colonial movement is based on the projection of
the Western model mixed with the folk elements as a truly 'national' idea.
Chatterjee terms nationalism a 'derivative discourse' for this reason: that anti-colonial nationalism is built on the conceptual framework and ideas of progress and
history given by the West.

Gyanendra Pandey (1999) proposes that too often is 'national identity' constructed by the majority, while the minorities remain on the fringes of the nation
as 'outsiders' even when they are on the inside. For example, Muslims are rarely
projected as a part of the nation, even though they pre-date the English and are
assimilated into the national fabric. Reminiscent of Pandey's argument is that of
Kancha Ilaiah (1999) who has argued that 'India' has invariably been an upper-
caste Hindu India that did not include the experiences of the Dalits in its grand
narratives. Feminist critiques of the national ideal (see the chapter on feminisms)
have noted how the nation is defined in terms of a masculine space. Such a national
identity ensures that the woman is confined to the home while the public sphere
remains that of the man, but nevertheless asks that the woman be the carrier of a
tradition. In postcolonial nations, certain categories of people, cultures and practices are validated and promoted as national, at the expense of others. This process
of 'postcolonial subalternization' (Nayar 2008b) suggests a postcolonial anxiety.
Women, 'lower' castes and classes, ethnic minorities became the 'Others' *within*
the postcolonial nation-state. The new elite is as oppressive and exclusive as the
colonial master. Human rights claims in postcolonial nations, for example, offer a
different version of these new nation-states where people have been denied their
cultures and even lives supposedly in the larger cause of the nation.

Numerous examples from postcolonial nations indicate that the energizing
myth of the nation does not always retain its hold. The genocide in Rwanda (1994),
secessionist movements in India, Sri Lanka and other places suggest that ethnic

minorities and tribes have been consistently marginalized within the nation and, as a result, now seek recognition and independence. A recent volume *People Unlike Us* (2001) documents peoples marginalized within the postcolonial nation-state: Kashmir, the Northeast India, the Dalits and the tribal people. Siddharth Deb writes of the Northeast:

> The modern, secular nation-state adopted as a political model for India demands a certain flattening out of differences and the imposition of a structure that does not consider small or anomalous groups of people or nomadic movements … If nations have to be imagined into being, the people of the north-east may represent the most remarkable failure of that imagination in regard to India. (2001: 88)

But he could well be speaking of Muslims, Dalits and Adivasis.

Postcolonial theory's reading of the nation thus treats it as an invention that marginalizes some sections of the people in favour of a majority, where the majority and its culture is then projected as a 'national' culture. Postcolonial theory is increasingly uncomfortable with the idea(l) of nationalism or national identity because, as the above critics show, it is exclusionary rather than inclusive, homogenizing in the name of a common identity when real differences (cultural, economic) between people continue to exist.

The question of the nation has also become significant in the light of globalization, and postcolonial studies in the late 1990s has turned to the new forms of nation that emerged in a globalized, networked and neocolonial world.

GLOBALIZATION, DIASPORA AND THE POSTNATIONAL

Globalization involves the movement of people, capital and commodities across national borders. This means that the nation-state borders are made porous in order to facilitate this movement. The movement of people, capital and commodities has a strong cultural component. Globalization can be seen as a mechanism that also results in the merging of cultural practices, the assimilation of the foreign into the native and the encounter between different cultures. Thus, the popularity of Indian food in the UK, McDonald's presence all over the world, the iconic status of global celebrities like David Beckham or 'Brangelina' (Brad Pitt and Angelina Jolie) are instances of the global flow of cultural products and practices. Metropolises across the world have become cosmopolitan, multicultural and hybridized with globalization. Transnational solidarities and political alliances— between anti-globalization groups, ironically—are forged across national borders. Immigrants transform the nature of cities with their cultural practices and politics.

Globalization has also generated a new form of colonial domination, often termed *neocolonialism*. It does not take the form of violent conquest but is a more diffused, insidious and persistent form that makes as much use of culture as it does of political strategies. Global consumer culture, with the proliferation of the McDonald's golden arch or Levi's jeans, are agents of this neocolonialism when they enter and eventually take over the local markets. In an incisive reading of the new forms of colonialism, Michael Hardt and Antonio Negri have called it 'Empire' (in their book of the same title, 2000). Hardt and Negri argue that for the new age colonialisms, older forms of analyses are not adequate. Empire is a whole new form of rule. It is *decentered* (has no 'capital' such as London used to be for British India) and *deterritorialized* (not restricted to specific territories or domains). It erodes the sovereignty of nation-states and incorporates the nation into a global realm. There are no identifiable or recognizable structures of power here because financial, military and political centres are all multi-layered and diffused. It is in this context of globalized cultural regimes, of new forms of domination and exploitation, of multiple displacements and cultural alignments that new approaches to culture and literature and new forms of writing and cultural practices emerge.

DIASPORA

Elleke Boehmer describes the immigrant and diasporic people/authors thus: 'ex-colonial by birth, "Third World" in cultural interest, cosmopolitan in almost every other way', these writers work 'within the precincts of the Western metropolis while at the same time retaining thematic and/or political connections with a national background' (1995: 233). Postcolonial theory studies immigrant and diasporic identities as celebrations of migrancy (most notably in authors like Rushdie). Authors and thinkers like Derek Walcott have argued that the migrant often possesses a double consciousness, a leftover native one and a First World one. One way of locating the immigrant's intellectual–cultural position is Abdul JanMohammed's. JanMohammed makes a mention of the 'specular border intellectual': standing at the border of two cultures, looking critically at both, neither assimilating nor combining either of them (JanMohammed 1992). Hybridity is an extension of this condition of looking toward both, being both here and there.

A concept elaborated by Homi Bhabha, *hybridity* is the rejection of a single or unified identity, and a preference for multiple cultural locations and identities. Hybridity can take the form of revival of a pre-colonial past, such as folk or tribal cultural forms and conventions within nativist or even reactionary movements, or adapts the contemporary artistic and social productions to present-day conditions of globalization, multiculturalism and transnationalism. Hybridity, as seen in postcolonial theory, is the answer to the dangers of cultural binarism (us/them) and the fundamentalist urge to seek 'pure' cultural forms.

Hybridity in postcolonial studies has been influenced by the work of political theorists such as Will Kymlicka (1995) who posits a 'multicultural citizenship' in a globalized world. People in one diasporic community draw upon the resources of another. This is not to abandon historical experience or memory, but to move beyond them, forging solidarities against continuing oppressions of race. Black and Asian immigrants in England are neither entirely black nor British, but a mixture of both. Cultural theorists such as Stuart Hall (1996 [1989]) have argued for 'new ethnicities' that deny ideas of 'essential' black or white identity. Hall, therefore, proposes a 'real heterogeneity of interests and identities' (1996: 444).

Diaspora theorists such as Avtar Brah (1997) and Robin Cohen (2001) propose that the idea of 'home' is a mythic one, a place of desire and longing that sits oddly with the present, chosen location of the immigrant. Brah writes, '"Home" is a mythic place of desire in the diasporic imagination. In this sense it is a place of no-return, even if it is possible to visit the geographical territory that is seen as the place of "origin"' (1997: 192).

The immigrant occupies multiple places and identities. Meena Alexander puts it well: 'That's all I am, a woman cracked by multiple migrations' (1993: 3). Migrant and displacement narratives invariably demonstrate this nostalgia and longing for the mythic and distant homeland.

With much postcolonial theory (Bhabha in particular) and literature (Rushdie, Hanif Kureishi), such a condition of looking back and looking forward, of possessing multiple identities has been valorized as a valuable state to be in. Rushdie endorses the weightless, nomadic, placeless state of being embodied in the figure of the migrant. Bhabha believes that the in-between, hybrid nature of identity is preferable to that of fixed, stereotypical one. In both cases, however, one could argue that such a nomadic, 'in-between' identity does not always work for say, working-class immigrants (Bhabha is a professor at Harvard, and Rushdie a celebrity novelist). The experience of nomadicity is different for migrant labour and the African woman. In these latter cases, they cannot escape their racial or ethnic identity because their gender and class mark them as different—a difference that cannot be overcome just because they have reached the First World. Both Bhabha and Rushdie are silent on the theme of gender, for example, and have nothing to say as to how the African or Asian woman experiences the First World—as an empowered migrant? or as a dependent, racially marked, minority?

COSMOPOLITANISMS

Keeping hybridity and multiple identities at its centre, as well as the possibility of transnational solidarities, recent postcolonial theory has explored, and pushed backward in time, cultural practices and political thought that cut across national borders. In her *Affective Communities*, Leela Gandhi demonstrates how vegetarianism, spirituality and friendship were discourses that linked Englishmen and Indians even in colonial India—an excellent reading of a *postnational* configuration in the heyday of colonialism.[1] Ashis Nandy in two essays, 'Towards a Third World Utopia' (2004 [1987]) and 'A New Cosmopolitanism: Toward a Dialogue of Asian Civilizations' (1998) has offered a new vision of cosmopolitanism and globalization where the 'Third World' plays a major role. Nandy writes:

The only way the Third World can transcend the sloganeering of its well-wishers is, first, by becoming a collective representation of the victims of man-made suffering everywhere in the world and in all past times, second, by internalizing or owning up the outside forces of oppression and, then, coping with them as inner vectors and third by recognizing the oppressed or marginalized selves of the First and Second Worlds as civilizational allies in the battle against institutionalized suffering. (2004 [1987]: 441)

Nandy argues that Third World nations can align themselves with the 'repressed' and oppressed within First World nations. This means, cosmopolitanism can be built on a common ethics of recognition: where we acknowledge the suffering of the Other and work to fight the institutional forms of suffering everywhere. I have argued that this argument in Nandy is a Utopic vision based on *affect*, a recognition of and response to the suffering of Others. This locates Nandy within what I have termed 'affective cosmopolitanism' (Nayar 2008c).

In a more recent work, Ania Loomba et al. point to the historical trajectories of postcolonial studies itself. They point out that 'postcolonial studies has been at various times intertwined not just with multiculturalism and ethnic studies but also with an array of area studies, each with a differing sense of its place' (2005: 5). Postcolonial studies is integral, now, to critical globalization studies because it is a theoretical approach that grounds cultural practices in geopolitics. Thus, postcolonial studies would be able to locate the cultural practice of films within globalization (see discussion of the circulation of the Hindi film across the world, in the collection edited by Raminder Kaur and Ajay Sinha, *Bollyworld*, 2005).

Yet, such a view of globalized cultures and cosmopolitanism does not quite account for discrepancies within it. What about the local resistances to global cultures (embodied, for instance, the battle against Wal-Mart in India)? Pnina Werbner has proposed a 'vernacular cosmopolitanism' in opposition to the hybridityelitist cosmopolitan paradigm as seen in Salman Rushdie and others. Vernacular cosmopolitanism explores whether 'the local, parochial, rooted, culturally specific and demotic may co-exist with the translocal, transnational, transcendent, elitist, enlightened, universalist and modernist'. It has strong parallels with what James Clifford termed 'discrepant cosmopolitanism' (1999) to describe the insidious, subversive and often violently rebellious cultural interaction. It resists elite or homogeneous cosmopolitanism—with the superimposed cultural artifacts or frames such as McDonald's GM foods, IMF policies, Wal-Mart among others. Postcolonial theory, it could be argued, must account for such a 'vernacular cosmopolitanism' as a counter-idea to global cultures.

THE POSTNATIONAL

Social theorists such as Arjun Appadurai (1993, 1996), Jürgen Habermas (2001), Donald Pease (1997) and informational culture theorists such as Manuel Castells (1996) have begun to see the emergence of postnational conditions where the nation-state is rendered obsolete in the age of networked cultures. The nation-state is no longer territorially restricted in the age of transnational business. The nation-state also has a reduced role to play in this age because policies—economic, military, even political—are determined and decided by transnational bodies. Diasporic cultures are linked beyond territory. Cyberculture networks provide a 'home' in cyberspace that is not governed by actual/material geographical location (as M. I. Franklin has shown).

However, as Ali Behdad points out, in the wake of 9/11 national identities have become important, border controls strengthened and difference (racial, ethnic, national) underscored (2005: 71). The idea of the postnational is also a difficult one to accept because the 'flows' that mark globalization (Castells) are uneven: the inequalities of the world continue (and in some cases exacerbated). The domain of cyberspace is itself raced (Nakamura 2000, 2002) and material practices that enable electronic linkages for the world, such as call centres, constitute a new, raced geographical mapping of the world and through offshore business, financial investment are also racially marked between First and Third Worlds.

Rob Nixon in a green turn to the postcolonialism–globalization studies debate proposes that environmentalism could become an addition to the critique. Following Lawrence Buell, Nixon suggests a study, within postcolonial studies, of 'toxic discourse', the land claims, colonial degradation, pre-colonial practices and rewriting of nature in postcolonial literatures (he links together Arundhati Roy, aboriginal writing, as well as American environmental writing) in what he terms the 'postcolonial pastoral' 2005: 233–51). In a different way, and for different purposes, Simon During (2000) has proposed that postcolonial studies must turn to globalization studies because colonialism (postcolonial studies' focus thus far) has always been a form of uneven, exploitative globalization.

FURTHER READING

Loomba, Ania. 1998. *Colonialism/Postcolonialism*. London: Routledge.
McLeod, John. 2007. *Beginning Postcolonialism*. Manchester: Manchester University Press.
Gandhi, Leela. 1998. *Postcolonial Theory: A Critical Introduction*. Delhi: Oxford University Press.
Young, Robert J. C. 2001. *Postcolonialism: An Historical Introduction*. Oxford: Blackwell.

NOTES

1. Gandhi's work here extends her arguments from her *Postcolonial Theory: A Critical Introduction* (1998) in which she argued for a postnational ethic. Gandhi calls for a recognition of the fact that oppressors are the victims of their own forms of oppression. Former political antagonists can be cross-identified with each other without taking away the actual sufferings of the 'original' victim (the colonized native). Since victims have been collaborators within the oppressive system and oppressors have been subversive within the same, the time to forge new identities is here.

7 Queer Theory

Queer theory emerged as gay and lesbian studies, which in turn was the academic wing of the gay rights movement. Literary and cultural studies that focused on sexuality as a key category/was an offshoot of a wide ranging social and activist movement through the 1960s and early 1970s. The Stonewall Riots of 1969—provoked when police raided New York's Stonewall Tavern, a popular meeting place for gays—may be described as the origin of the gay liberation movement. Organizations like Gay Liberation Movement (GLF), Gay Activists Alliance (GAA), AIDS Coalition to Unleash Power (ACT UP) sought legal, medical, social freedom and rights for gays and lesbians. Queer theory drew upon the experiences of these movements while adding philosophical and critical insights into the nature of the body, the geography of sexuality and the question of sexual identity.

This was the age when homosexual artists (Jasper Johns, Robert Rauschenberg, Andy Warhol) and Hollywood stars (Rock Hudson) began to make public their sexual preferences. A revolution in thinking the sexual was on. Academic interest began to show itself in the form of critical essays and collections and *College English* brought out a special issue on gay writing and politics in 1974.

Queer theory today has political affiliations with women's studies, African American cultural criticism and theory and postcolonial studies. The common commitment to centring the marginalized, emancipation for the oppressed and social justice is what brings them together on one platform.

> Queer theory looks at the history of cultural representations of the gay/lesbian as deviant, sick or criminal, while foregrounding sexuality as an important category of critical analysis when dealing with cultural texts. Queer theory moves between literary analysis and activism because it shows how cultural representations contribute to very real material oppression of homosexuals.

Queer theory is thus more useful in the discipline of cultural studies than in old-fashioned literary studies because its interests lie in the connections between the politics of cultural representation and institutional–state constructions of sexuality. It is interested in the power relations, social evaluation and institutional biases that underlie representations of the heterosexual or homosexual. Mapping the agenda and potential of queer sexuality studies, Suparna Bhaskaran writes: 'queer sexuality embodies stories of development and under-development, modernity and tradition, economic (re)production and nonmaterial degeneration' (2004: 148). Queer sexuality, she emphasizes, is linked to AIDS activism, caste, the law and imperialism. Thus, queer theory is about the cultural contexts of queer sexualities.

Queer Cultural Studies may be defined as 'an attempt to redefine identities and carve out a cultural/political space within the dominant heterosexual paradigm, to simply stop being invisible or the "perverted" or "sick" "other" of heterosexuality' (Nayar 2007: 118). Queer theory is, therefore, resolutely *political* in nature because of its concern with structures of power.

Queer theory looks at

- the general construction of sexuality in discourses of medicine, law or religion,
- popular representations of the gay or the lesbian,
- the public understanding of alternate sexualities,
- the institutional (religion, family, medicine, law) structures that undergird popular representations of homosexuality,
- the 'hidden history' of homosexual writing and representation,
- the link between sexuality-based oppression and other discriminatory forms such as patriarchy and racism,
- the geography of sexuality, with specific reference to ghettoization of gays and homosexuals.

It seeks to

- destabilize essentializing identities,

- resist heterosexual cultures through the carnival, transgression and parody,
- be anti-assimilationist,
- be co-sexual: men and women are on equal footing. The term queer is now used to mean both gays and lesbians,
- promote the demand and fight for sexual justice *as part of* social justice,
- use the AIDS crisis to reflect on practices of homosexuality and battle AIDS-driven homophobia.

Queer *theory*, it must be noted, is relatively recent (1990s and after). The turn to 'queer' serves particular purposes. 'Queering' is the process of reversing heterosexuality-as-norm.

'Queer' now refers to not only gay/lesbian issues but also includes other practices, identities and communities—all of which have been marginalized in history—such as bisexuality, sado-masochism, the transgendered and the transsexual. Transgendering, transvestitism, drag and camp, and other sexual identities present the multiple nature of identities that cannot be reduced to one category.

OPENING MOVES

THE SEXUAL TURN

Criticism uses one or more categories to examine texts. These are usually, gender, race, class and nationality. Sexuality, strangely, has been seen as a category that exists only in the form of the man–woman relationship. People looking at relationships in the novel or the short story focused only on this kind of sexual relation. Passing references or biographical information about authors who seemed to have had extremely close ties with men (such as Tennyson and Arthur Hallam) were ignored or seen as marginal to the main theme and relationship.

This marginalization of the non-heterosexual theme or character in literature was an index of the homosexual relationship in society all over the world. Heterosexuality was the norm and homosexuality was the deviation/perversion that deserved medical treatment and imprisonment (Oscar Wilde's trial and indictment at the turn of the nineteenth century was the best known example of this).

MICHEL FOUCAULT AND THE DISCOURSES OF SEXUALITY

A significant moment in lesbian and gay studies was the work of Michel Foucault, especially in the *History of Sexuality* volumes (three volumes, English translations 1977–1986). Foucault theorized sexuality as located within structures and discourses of power. He was thus able to provide, for the first time, a concrete approach to the so-called natural marginalization of queer sexuality by arguing that certain forms of sexuality were constructed as unnatural and evil and its practitioners placed under surveillance. What Foucault was doing in his study of sexuality was to focus on the sexualized and sexual body as a locus of power play, where different forces like law or medicine mapped and categorized the body in particular ways before 'acting' upon it. Foucault thus shifted sexuality from the domain of pure body to discourses and culture.

The recognition that gays and lesbians have been marginalized and demonized in history enabled critics to seek texts that (i) carried gay/lesbian themes and (ii) foregrounded homosexuality as a legitimate lifestyle for social and political purposes. Critics began to detect gay and lesbian themes masked as heterosexuality in the works of canonical English and American authors like E. M. Forster and W. H. Auden. They also detected an alternate tradition (alternate to the heterosexual canon) that explored homosexuality.

Foucault's work also provided the impetus to several sociologists and historians to theorize homosexuality. As we have seen in the chapter on poststructuralism, Foucault showed how discourses of institutions like the hospital and the prison were built on the principle of exclusion. Classification of particular people as sick, criminal or insane enabled the discourse to construct the Other as the deviant opposite of the norm (see chapter on poststructuralism, especially the section on Foucault). Knowledge—medical, psychological, legal, philosophical—about these 'deviants' led to definite material practices of incarceration, punishment and medical treatment. Homosexuality treated as deviant was, therefore, treated as a counter to the standard or norm. It was caught in a relationship of power where a heterosexual society labeled and then punished deviance.

The seventeenth century was a period of sexual frankness. Rules and codes governing obscenity and indecency were lax. The later seventeenth century is the age of sexual repression. It cultivated an atmosphere of silence on the subject of sex except in particular areas that were deemed legitimate to inquire into sexuality. Scientific and medical treatises on sex proliferated as a result. Social control of sex took the form of a religious prescription of compulsory confession and penance. Sex was now *administered*. At the turn of the eighteenth century sex became a police matter, thus moving beyond the religious one of the seventeenth century. The government became interested in birth rates, fertility levels and frequency of sexual relations because it was now assumed that the wealth and prosperity of the nation depended upon these. Bedtime in schools and sleeping arrangements was closely monitored. Medical reports, clinical cases and reform methods became a part of the school system.

Finally, the sexuality of children, criminals, lunatics and homosexuals came under scrutiny. Foucault detects four principle operations of power:

- The sexuality of children was subordinated to that of adults, who were to monitor any 'perversions' like masturbation.
- A list of 'perversions' began to be formulated. The homosexual was now a symbol of disorder.

- A 'medicalization' of sexuality was on as doctors and scientists sought to provide a pathological basis for perversions.
- A compartmentalization of sexualities began to be visible. Sex was restricted to certain ages, relationships, times, and spaces. Age (adults), practice (heterosexuality, monogamy), relationships (conjugal) and space (the bedroom). Sexuality outside these norms was identified as perversion and illness.

Four strategic unities and four sexual subjects emerged due to the development of specific mechanisms of power and knowledge centred on sexuality:

Strategic Unities	Sexual Objects
1. Hysterization of women's bodies	Hysterical Women
2. Pedagogization of children's sex	Masturbating Child
3. Socialization of procreation	Malthusian Couple
4. Psychiatrization of perverse pleasure	Perverse Adult

In (1) the female body was analysed as saturated with sexuality. It must, therefore, be studied medically. To ensure 'normalcy' it must be then placed in the contexts of the family.

In (2) children were defined as 'preliminary' sexual beings. Hence, adults—parents, teachers, families, and doctors—had to take charge of this potentially dangerous sexuality.

In (3) social and economic measures were brought to bear on the fertility of couples. This was the 'responsibilization' of the couple with regard to the social body: their duties as parents, couples capable of reproduction and their contribution, therefore to society.

In (4) psychiatrization of perverse pleasure, sexual instinct was isolated as a separate biological and psychical instinct.

Foucault's work located sexuality within the discourses of medicine, religion and the law. He demonstrated how definitions of 'normal' sexuality, that is heterosexuality, emerged through a demonization of homosexual relations.

THE SOCIAL CONSTRUCTION OF SEXUALITY

An early attempt at exploring the social construction of sexuality can be found in Mary Mackintosh famous essay, 'The Homosexual Role' (1968). Mackintosh argues that society constructed itself as pure and safe by labelling some persons as 'deviant' and criminal. The label was thus a form of *social control* that assumed some people were naturally deviant.

Further, such a labelling provided a distinction between permissible and impermissible behaviour. Anyone indulging in the latter would naturally be prosecuted. Homosexuality and criminality attracted the same punishment from society.

Mackintosh argues that the typology of people as homosexual, black, criminals helped polarize these groups. The homosexual must be seen as playing a social *role* rather than as having a condition. The homosexual has to then be predominantly homosexual in his behaviour, attitudes and feelings. People expect him to be effeminate. Thus, these social expectations will affect even the self-conception of the homosexual individual. As we can see Mary Mackintosh was already moving towards both social constructionism and a theory of performativity (the latter being Judith Butler's key theory from the 1990s).

Contemporary sociologists and theorists in Cultural Studies see sexuality as a social construct. Contemporary thinking on identity is that identity is never immanent in an object, it is constructed out of discourses. That is, a person's identity is the effect of the discourses of naming, family, religion, location, law, medicine, psychology, and others. There is no one identity. Identities are located along several axes: religion, race, class, gender, caste and sexuality. Urbanization, with its proliferation of clubhouses and meeting places, was an important factor in the formation of the 'modern homosexual', even though it meant they were hidden (or 'closet') homosexuals.

Changing family norms, notions of childhood and the role of parents construct the individual homosexual in particular ways. The emphasis on reproductive sex, the insistence on marriage and the laws against sodomy also influence and socially construct the gay.

Social constructionists see the following discourses of sexuality as central:

- sexual difference as pre-ordained, and, therefore, unchangeable
- sexual activity that is procreative (and not for pleasure) alone is 'proper'
- neither man nor woman owns his/her body

Jeffrey Weeks has argued that sex, as an act, attains meaning in social relations. We make choices about sexuality by understanding its social and political contexts. Weeks asks us to move away from a moralistic approach to sex (treating it as good or bad) to look at the power relations that situate these acts, to see how coercive forces in society limit the possibilities of choice, autonomy and pleasure (Weeks 1997: 81–82).

These discourses around sexuality, argue social constructionists, eventually became social sanctions or injunctions, and sexuality outside any of these three discourses was immediately ruled deviant. Every culture decides, based on its own such discourses, what is appropriate and what is not. Weeks (1997, 2000) suggests that there cannot be a universal history of homosexuality for the physical acts of homosexuality may be similar, but their *social implications are different in different societies*. Thus, the 'perverted homosexual' is not a feature of some people. Rather it is a *perception* created through various discourses and representations based on these discourses that label some acts as perverted or unnatural. The homosexual is, therefore, a socially created identity or label that leads to specific legal, cultural, medical consequences for the person labelled as such. Queer theory argues that

- heterosexuality bestows certain privileges, and
- a hierarchy of sexual values is constructed through discourses.

This constructionist view of sexuality suggests that sexual identity is always socially determined. It is never static and is constantly in need of reiteration.

GENDER IDENTITY AND PERFORMATIVITY

Judith Butler develops a poststructuralist analysis of gender (discussed in greater detail in the chapter on feminisms) when she proposes that gender cannot be treated as an essence, but must be taken as a 'performative construct'. Butler writes in her best-known work, *Gender Trouble*: 'there is no gender identity behind the expressions of gender; that identity is performatively constituted by the very "expressions" that are said to be its results' (25). And later 'the gendered body is performative suggests that it has no ontological status apart from the various acts which constitute its reality' (136). This theory of identity as performance has had an impact on postcolonial and feminist theorizations as well.

Butler's basic assumption is that identities tend to be seen as solid and unchanging. Identity and the 'subject', she suggests are *performative constructs*. One arrives at an identity, say, male, through the performative act of *behaving like a male*.

It must be mentioned right away that performance and performativity are not the same (though Butler herself seems to mix up the two in later sections of her classic *Gender Trouble*).

Performance presupposes a subject: It is the subject who performs.

Performativity is a complex notion that argues that it is in the act of performing that the performer is born/constructed. To understand this we need to go back to speech act theory and the performative speech act. Performative speech acts are those where *the action is performed in the very act of speaking*. An example would be a sentence like 'I hereby promise'. There is nothing else one needs to do here: *articulating the sentence is the action of promising*. That is, the act of promising is in the performative *enunciation*: 'I promise'. We shall return to this sense of performativity soon.

Butler argues in a reading of Simone de Beauvoir's famous claim that 'one is not born, but rather becomes a woman' that woman is a process, a becoming, rather than a fixed identity. This ongoing process is constituted by discourse. Gender is a series of acts within specific discourses of law, medicine, religion, family, sexuality that a body performs, which in turn identifies her as a woman. One cannot, Butler suggests, act or acquire an identity outside this system of discourses.

What Butler proposes, in line with poststructuralism, is that one 'does' an identity, a sequence of acts that is inevitable and repetitive. Using Foucault, Butler proposes that critique must focus on the way power structures 'produce' women, or what she calls 'a feminist genealogy of the category of women' (32). Identities are, she writes, the 'effects of institutions, practices, discourses, with multiple and diffused points of origin (viii–ix). Like Foucault, she proposes that gender is not a fact or natural, but the effect of discourses that are controlled by power structures. Central to this discourse and performative construction is language. Butler argues that there is no gender identity prior to or outside of language because identity is the effect of discourse.

> **B**utler's theory of gender and the subject treats the subject as a process, a performative act where gender 'occurs' only through the repetition of particular acts—and argument that suggests the subject is never a stable, cogent entity.

In order to understand this complex theorization of identity, let us take an example. Students are commonly issued ID cards by their universities or colleges. The university's descriptions and conditions constitute the *discourse* in which the student lives and acquires an identity. Her identity as a student is always constituted only through the recognition in the form of the ID. She *enacts the part of a student only when the ID allows her to*. Without this discourse of ID given by the university she is *not* a student. Once the ID card has been issued there is no option other than being a student because the ID states so. You become a student through this process of identification. You identify yourself as the student described with a photo, a number, an affiliation. The university is the matrix, the codified system in which you perform the identity of being a student. Your identity as a student is thus *produced and is not natural*.

Butler works on this same assumption. Gender is discursively constructed within a cultural discourse. Categories of 'man', 'woman' are those that define one's identity. Butler's argument is that sexuality, likewise, is something constructed out of *heterosexuality*. It is produced in a discourse of heterosexuality.

Butler proposes, via a reading of Freud, that the taboo against heterosexual incest is *preceded* by another taboo—against homosexuality. Gender identity, she states, is built on this prohibition against homosexuality. It is the *loss* of the same-sex object of desire that creates a *melancholic heterosexual identity*. Butler thus argues that feminine and masculine dispositions are the result of an internalization of assimilation of loss. This loss and prohibited desire is inscribed (Butler's term is 'incorporated') on the body, which results in the efforts to be *ultra masculine* or *feminine*. The prohibition continues in cultural and legal taboos against homosexuality. One goes through life enacting this loss, and striving to stay heterosexual. As Butler puts it, 'Gender is the repeated stylization of the body, a set of repeated acts within a highly rigid regulatory framework that congeal over time to produce the appearance of substance, of a natural sort of being' (1990: 33). This paragraph from *Gender Trouble* effectively outlines Butler's theories of performativity. Butler argues:

- 'Masculine man' or 'feminine woman' are *signifiers* and speech acts that, in the *very act of naming, construct these identities.*
- Gender (*masculine* man or *feminine* woman) is this *act* of *naming* that constructs what it names (see above example for the phrase 'I promise'). With the act of naming it identifies some body as a masculine one.
- There is no gender identity that precedes language.
- Gender is thus a *performativity* that constitutes identity.

However, what is clear from the passage quoted is that one cannot pick any gender to perform. The 'highly rigid regulatory framework' is the set of cultural codes that circumscribe what roles you can perform. Thus, when a child is born the medical discourse identifies/declares/enunciates it as 'male' or 'female'.[1] This *names* the child, but also identifies the role s/he will have to play. It constructs the child in the very act of saying 'it's a girl' or 'it's a boy'.

From here, all subsequent discourses are repetitions of this first enunciation. The role of 'male' or 'female' that the child has to play out later is already, therefore, determined.

This stress on role-playing enables Butler to proceed to subversion as role-playing. Taking the example of cross-dressing and drag, Butler argues that these deliberate acts reveal that gender is itself an act. Drag—men in women's clothes and vice versa—shows how another gender is being *mimicked* and *performed*. There is a gap or dissonance between the body (male) and the performed gender, calling into question both categories.

Butler's arguments are evidently a major critique about gender and identity. Let us take the performativity-identity process in steps.

- Bio-medical discourse first identifies, declares and *enunciates* a body as 'male'.
- Later discourses of family, fashion ensure that this body dresses, behaves in *fulfilment* of this first identity given to it.
- The body enacts various *roles* that suit the first identity.
- The cumulative *effect* of the many discourse-regulated roles is the Male Body.
- This Male Body is now deemed to be 'natural': it has *always* been male.
- Thus, a constructed identity—one given by the many discourses—is deemed to be naturally male.

As we can see from the above discussion, Butler's work refuses any unitary or natural identity, seeing all identity as the effect of discourse. This line of thought reveals Butler's indebtedness to poststructuralism and deconstruction, which also refuses a monolithic, unified identity.

GAY PASTS, GAY FUTURES

Gay and lesbian writing now constitutes a substantial body of work. Extensive critical writings on the area and institutional presence have made queer studies a massive multi-disciplinary field, aligned with and drawing from sociology, literary studies, cultural studies, psychology and history.

PAST TEXTS AND FUTURE POLITICS

Central to the project of queer theory is the retrieval of gay and lesbian pasts in the form of histories, autobiographies and memoirs and fiction. Queer theorists argue, as we have seen, that mainstream literary cultures have effectively erased gay–lesbian presence from the canon. Margaret Cruikshank writes:

> We feel a special urgency about the work of lesbian studies because so much of our past has been lost. Sometimes editors and biographers hid the truth, and sometimes families destroyed evidence of lesbian relationships. Several of the most interesting documents in the Lesbian Herstory Archives were actually rescued from trash cans on New York City sidewalks. (1982: xi)

K. J. Dover's 1978 work *Greek Homosexuality* traced homosexuality to the ancient period. Martin Duberman et al.'s *Hidden from History: Reclaiming the Gay and Lesbian Past* (1989) is another example of such a retrieval-history project. One of the achievements of these kinds of histories is the evidence they draw of sexual dissidence and social oppressive practices that ensured that homosexuality was always 'closeted'. The disappearance of the homosexual, for these historians, can, therefore, be located in social discourses and practices, and part of their project is to see how exactly the discourses of exclusion worked (the parallels here with feminist attempts to retrieve women's writing should be clear).

The retrieval of the past, for queer theorists, is an occasion to rethink our present. To this end, they suggest critical approaches and reading practices that alert us to discourses of marginalization and exclusion, social constructions of homosexuality as deviance and sexual dissidence. They link alternate histories with new modes of pedagogic instruction, research and activism.

Arlene Stein and Ken Plummer (1996) offer three possible areas wherein queer theory may be assimilated into cultural and literary studies and sociology.

(a) *Reconsidering the Issues*: To analyse social stratification paying particular attention to ideologies of heterosexism and homophobia, and erotic hierarchies. They also argue that we need to see sexuality as linked to other factors such as age, race, mobility and class. Queering cultural and literary studies requires re-situation of sexuality within these other domains.

(b) *Rereading the Classics*: What is needed is a revision of traditional sociological texts (Popper, Giddens, Habermas) to address queer concerns. This is a queering of theory itself.

(c) *Rethinking Pedagogy*: A queer pedagogy is necessary to break the hold of heterosexist thinking.

In keeping with the last point, the Margaret Cruikshank edited *Lesbian Studies* anthology, therefore, devotes a separate section to 'In the Classroom', where critics and teachers like Jane Gurko address questions of 'sexual energy in the classroom' (1982: 25–31).

> Retrieving gay–lesbian texts is central to Queer Studies because it provides a history to not only queer pasts but also to the modes of exclusion that have ensured the marginalization of the queer.

Why read lesbian or gay fiction? What is so crucial about the genre? Bonnie Zimmerman, perhaps the best lesbian critic of the 1990s gives several reasons why: 'The purpose of lesbian fiction is to "map out the boundaries of female worlds" – of Lesbian Nation – and in this way assist women in coming out, provide models for behaviour, and encourage us to feel good about ourselves' (1990: 21). Zimmerman isolates a central strategy in lesbian fiction that achieve these goals: 'Lesbian mythmaking (like the creation of new words and spellings) is a political project aimed at overturning the patriarchal domination of culture and language' (1990: 21).

What is important is to note that Zimmerman sees literary texts and their interpretation as political. Like feminist writing and criticism, the task extends far beyond the textual into social and political realms. Theor Sandfort, likewise, sees queer theory and literary–cultural studies as having a social function. Queer studies seeks to

(i) support people in their expressions of homosexual desires and in building gay and lesbian lifestyles,

(ii) counteract homophobic identities,

(iii) promote the emancipation of homosexuality.

(Sandfort 2000: 15)

This political agenda is central to all queer studies today.

QUEER SUBCULTURES

Along with the political reading of queer texts or queer readings of apparently heterosexist texts, a key element in queer studies today is an exploration of queer subcultures.

Cultural histories of Europe from the early modern period have pointed out that dominant classes often took control of the spaces of 'high culture', such as, the opera houses, museums and galleries. These were thus closed to the general public, and the events within were tightly regulated. Standards of taste were set up and 'low' or mass culture excluded from these spaces. However, the marginalized groups were never completely erased—they survived as subcultures on the fringes, occasionally intruding in.

Queer theory suggests that gay–lesbian culture can be seen as subculture to the heterosexual mainstream one. Camp, drag, transvestitism and cross-dressing are modes of subcultures. Cross-dressing deglamourizes the ultra-feminine stars and masquerade (as we have seen in the section on performativity) draws attention to the role-playing and constructed masculinity of the body. Such subcultures appropriate the icons, signs and 'aura' of the mainstream culture to

(a) show their constructedness,
(b) subvert them as icons of carnival,
(c) highlight the gay or lesbian angle to masquerade.

Cross-dressing is subversive because, as Marjorie Garber argues (1993), we tend to treat the transvestite as a man or woman in another clothing: rarely do we see the transvestite as a third category in and of itself. In a sense it upsets our ideas about men and women, even before we see a third identity (if we do at all). This makes cross-dressing a subcultural form that disturbs our established ideas about gender and biology.

LESBIAN FEMINISM AND RADICALESBIANS

Lesbian feminism emerged from a (sad) recognition of feminism's drawback: classic feminism treated the sexual experience of all women as inevitably hetero-sexual. Thus, there was no scope for female–female relations (sexual or asexual) in this feminism.

Adrienne Rich in a famous essay (1980) argued that 'compulsory heterosexu-ality' ensured a woman's continued subordination by continually privileging a man's needs. The ideology of compulsory heterosexuality forces the girl/daughter to turn to the man, forgetting her *mother and other women*. This turning away of the girl from the mother is not natural but a tacit acceptance of the political envi-ronment of both patriarchy and heterosexuality. An equivalent term suggested by Sarah Hoagland is 'totalitarian heterosexuality' (1981, cited in Cruikshank 1982: xiii).

Rich's insights constituted a major move towards lesbian feminist theory and activism. Lesbian theorists argue that even heterosexual women exhibit a certain fear of lesbianism. Therefore, even feminist thinkers do not want to account for homosexuality in their critiques. Feminism also assumes a heterosexual norm and homosexuality/lesbianism as a deviation.

The New York group Radicalesbians published a manifesto 'The Woman Identified Woman' in 1971 and launched this new phase of feminism. The lesbian, argued this group, is really a natural 'unconscious' feminist because she automatically is inclined to other women rather than men.

Lesbian continuum, coined by Adrienne Rich, is a term that seeks to incorporate a whole range of woman–woman relations. This is more than a sexual phrase or category, and is taken to include: mutual help networks, camaraderie, woman's institutions, female friendships that are not necessarily sexual in nature.

Radicalesbians argue that

(i) even mainstream feminist thought and activism, seeking freedom from patriarchy and the bind of gender, is built on an *ideology of 'sameness'*. All women, feminists argue are heterosexual; Lesbianism presents the unspeakable, the monstrous;

(ii) gay males at least enjoy a certain cultural position. Lesbian sexuality, on the other hand, is simply invisible, erased from the discussion and the social sphere. The lesbian is the 'unthinkable';

(iii) lesbianism is a derivative figure, a *negative* presence within the system of gendered heterosexuality. The Otherness of the lesbian is never admitted here.

Increasingly, lesbian theorists and activists form affinities with gays than with feminists, thereby revealing the deep divide among feminists themselves. Ruth Vanita for instance notes that women's movements in India have always focused on reforming marriage and its social codes. At no time have these sought to rethink gender and sexuality itself, 'to liberate both men and women into developing different kinds of family or collective living' (1997: 16). What Vanita is proposing is this: reform of marriage laws must be geared into accepting and validating same-sex families and same-sex marriage, and stop thinking of family exclusively in heterosexual terms.

RACE AND SEXUALITY

Is the experience of homosexuality in a homophobic culture the same for whites and blacks? Critics like bell hooks, for example, have argued that sexuality and sexual identity is experienced differently for whites and blacks. Dana Takagi goes so far as to argue that the experiences of Asian America and gay America are separate places (1996: 21–35). Cherrie Moraga (1997) has made the same argument with regard to the Chicano/a and Jigna Desai (2002) and Gayatri Gopinath (1996) focus on the minority gays in the First World.

With queer theory's destabilizing of identity and sexual politics, there has been a sub-categorization of the community of 'gays'. In this section we shall look at non-white experiences of gays and lesbians situated in First World contexts.[2] Gay associations such as Bombay Dost (India), OCCUR (Japan), Ten Percent (Hong Kong), Pink Triangle (Malaysia), Anjaree (lesbian group, Thailand), Sangini (lesbian support group, India) and others now seek to build bridges with Western gay and lesbian groups—a move, one suspects towards an international gay community-building.

The link between race, ethnicity and sexual identities is the subject of raced queer theory. (Interestingly, few of the white queer theorists have addressed the question of race.) Three points about the interlinking of race and sexuality can be made right away:

- Heterosexuality is assumed to be the norm even in marginalized groups like blacks or Asians in the USA.
- Moving out of a particular national/cultural/ethnic group or territory is often coterminous with sexual freedom and the opportunity to practice alternate sexualities.
- Bonds and communities based on sexual preferences overcome racial or ethnic barriers.

That blacks are not more open to homosexuality is evidenced by the fact that leading African American intellectuals rejected gays as marginal to the movement. For instance, Eldridge Cleaver, former Black Panther Minister of Information, dismissed black homosexuality as a perversion and a dilution of 'blackness' (Nagel 122).

The first people to speak of the link between race and queer sexuality were the poet Audre Lorde and the novelist James Baldwin. Lorde was in fact described by Moraga as 'the first ancestor of my own colored lesbian tradition' (1997: 42). Lorde represented herself as black, feminist and lesbian, showing how she was *multiply marginalized* because of her skin, affiliations and preferences. Lorde wrote: 'As a forty-nine-year-old Black lesbian feminist socialist mother of two, including one boy, and a member of an interracial couple, I usually find myself a part of some group defined as other, deviant, inferior, or just plain wrong ...' (1984 [1980]: 114).

Lorde also seeks to build a community of similar women. Using poets like the Black Arts figure Dudley Randall and the African Chi-Wara, Lorde shows in her poetry (especially the Black Unicorn poems, in the 'Journeystones I–XI', 1997: 313–15) how patriarchy and racism combine with heterosexism to effectively marginalize her and others like her. As a solution she suggests a community. Race and gender make the black woman the ultimate outsider, being lesbian adds to the outsiderness, and Audre Lorde is iconic of this state. Paul Gunn Allen, novelist and critic, wrote: 'The lesbian is to the American Indian what the Indian is to the American – invisible' (1991 [1986]: 245).

This means one cannot generalize queer experience. Gloria Anzaldúa's location of the queer alongside the 'mongrel, the mulatto, the half-breed, the half dead' (1999: 25) generates the informing assumption of queer theory: *there is no one queer experience*. Homophobia and homosexuality are *experienced differently by whites and blacks*. As Evelyn Hammonds put it, we need to understand the 'way in which black lesbians are "outsiders" within the black community' (Hammonds 1994: 136–37).

Critics like Ian Barnard (2004) have argued that whiteness is always delineated in terms of something else (gayness) or against something else (blackness). This in a sense means that gay substitutes for white, but never for black (there are arguably more representations of white gays than black gays), thus making a discourse of *coloured queerness* an impossibility. Gayness, therefore, *enables* racism (30–33).

Raced queer theory seeks to fight this racism within homosexual communities and thinking. A central mode of doing this is to build *global queer communities*, where people of diverse ethnic, regional, linguistic origins and affiliations come together on the basis of sexual preferences. Queer theorists interested in race theory now posit a *global queer diaspora*. This is perhaps the most significant development in queer theory today and is worth exploring in some detail. It must be mentioned here that such a notion of a global queer disapora is linked to both globalization studies and postcolonial theory.

> Queer theory increasingly turns to race theory and studies to explore how racial differences mark the experience and identity of queers. This is based on the assumption that to be black or brown and gay/lesbian is to be multiply one's marginalization, because even within minority communities there exists a heterosexual norm.

QUEER DIASPORA

In terms of popular culture and mass media culture, the queer is already all over the world. Movies like *Philadelphia* and *Fire* now have global audiences (and controversies). Is there a global queer linkage that makes such films popular? And if so, how or why is it important in terms of a new politics of sexuality and race?

In many cases, as illustrated by Hanif Kureishi, Shyam Selvadurai, Suniti Namjoshi and Leela Gandhi, migration enables the Asian or black queer to escape the claustrophobia (and homophobia) of their original home/nation.

However, this is not always the case. Queer Third World writers who migrate to First World cities do not often find it easy to be gay in the First World. Gayatri Gopinath has argued that queer Asians cannot take their citizenship for granted, unlike white Americans (1996: 120–21). Thus, even diasporic communities assume that all its members are automatically heterosexual. They, therefore, reject a gay diasporic man or woman despite their common racial or ethnic identity.

Chela Sandoval proposes that global queer communities and their networks constitute a 'dissident globalization' (2002: 21). Lesbians and gays overcome their racial and geographical barriers to link across the world. Feminist and gay groups in Ireland are now turning to the European Union, appealing outside the Irish national boundary for rights within Ireland. Gay and lesbian groups have appealed to the European Convention on Human Rights seeking decriminalization of homosexuality.

Queer theory now accounts for transnational identities and linkages. Grewal and Kaplan (2001) argue that the efforts of contemporary (Western) sexuality studies ignore the histories of diverse political economies and forms of governmentality. We need to look at the forms of gender and sexual differences in medieval China and Islam in order to understand the subject positions today. Cultural differences of sexuality today (between Western and Oriental homosexuality, for instance), Grewal and Kaplan point out, are rooted in a specific and local/native *legacy*. This means, studies of contemporary sexuality must account for differences in medical theories, family and kinship structures and scientific discourses in different cultures. Immigration laws and refugee politics, like transnational labour, effects sexual identity politics in the globalized culture. Thus, the family-based categories for immigration into the United States are profoundly anti-queer because they assume models of the family based on Western and hierarchic cultural norms. That is, immigration laws do not see families as anything other than heterosexual, and gay family immigration policies do not yet exist.

One more crucial dimension to a transnational queer identity that builds communities across racial identities exists: global tourism. Men and women from 'First World' nations travel to 'Third World' nations for alternate sexual experiences. Queer identities have become a consumer product in the age of global tourism (Rushbrook 2002). Once again race and sexuality are closely aligned: and, as always, favours the white gay or lesbian over the dark-skinned ones. In Jeffrey Weeks' words:

[L]esbian and gay studies constitutes a part of intellectual and political diaspora. It is not fixed in a single place, or confined to a single disciplinary approach; yet there is a common sense of belonging that transcends differences of country and nation, of gender and of culture ... [it is] a network rather than a fixed positionality...(2000: 9)

Queer diasporas, built on the commonality of sexual preferences rather than racial-ethnic identities, now constitute a global queer culture that has a political agenda and presence. Queer theory sees such a diaspora as both an effect and a counter to globalization.

FURTHER READING

Theo Sandfort, Judith Schuyf, Jan Willem Duyvendak, Jeffrey Weeks (eds). 2000. *Lesbian and Gay Studies: An Introductory, Interdisciplinary Approach*. London: Sage.

Bose, Brinda and Subhabrata Bhattacharya (eds). 2007. *The Phobic and the Erotic: The Politics of Sexualities in Contemporary India*. Kolkata: Seagull.

Fuss, Diana (ed.). 1991. *Inside/Out: Lesbian Theories, Gay Theories*. New York and London: Roultedge.

NOTES

1. In fact, there is a massive debate about what constitutes a biological male body. Gender identification is at best a risky enterprise.

2. I have opted for First World experiences and theorization for several reasons: queer theory developed in the First World to discuss First World experiences of homosexuality. In many African and Asian nations homosexuality is still an offence and a taboo. The first person accounts and, therefore, critical reflection has been understandably thin. For studies and collections of queer writing from India please see Merchant (1999), Vanita (2002), Sukthankar (1999).

8 New Historicism and Cultural Materialism

In the 1970s and early 1980s literary critics, influenced by anthropologists and philosophers of history, began to see contexts and texts as reflecting real, material conditions of social struggle (by social struggle we mean the struggle for power between classes, genders, ethnic groups, communities and nations). Power, they argued, was at the centre of all social relations and this was reflected in the texts of the period. Under the influence of Marxist thinking (see Chapter 5 for Marxist theories) these critics argued that all interpretation was inherently political because it sought to locate social conditions in literary texts. Further, they argued that we need to bring history as the site of social struggle back into the text. We needed what the editors of an anthology on this new form of theory called a 'return to history' (Wilson and Dutton 1992: 1). It is evident that such a reading was a move against the so-called textual obsession of the structuralists and poststructuralists.

This interest in context and history also meant that the new theorists saw all writing as *texts*. Texts, whether in history, poetry or autobiography, the cookbook and the courtesy manual, the war memoirs and the surgical text, are all products of particular social conditions, and share the same prejudices, ideologies, themes and motifs. This means, we need to read a literary text in the *context of several other texts* from the same age in order to locate the social contexts of their production. History and social contexts are to be found only in such a messy configuration of themes and motifs. In other words, literary texts are as much a part of history and political science and anthropology as texts from these disciplines.

This new approach took two main forms: the American 'new historicism' and the British 'cultural materialism'.

New Historicism paid attention to the historical, social, economic contexts of a literary text, while also assuming that literary themes often reflected, refracted, reinforced or subverted historical contexts. In short, New Historicism is a mode of critical analysis that focuses on the text as a site of power relations. It believes that power is everywhere and the task of the critic is to reveal the workings and different forms of power within texts from the past. In the words of Jonathan Dollimore and Alan Sinfield, New Historicism is a critical approach that looks at the 'interaction ... between State power and cultural forms and, more specifically, with those genre and practices where State and culture most visibly merge' (1985: 3).

Cultural Materialists accuse the New Historicists of being pessimist, of seeing no way out of the unequal power relation. They suggest that texts must be read as sites of power relations, but as they *connect with the present*. They, therefore, see critical theory and analysis as social actions for contemporary times.

> New Historicism is a critical approach that locates power relations in society as they are reflected in literary and other texts of the period, suggesting that texts mask social conditions just as social conditions are informed and shaped by textual representations of monarchy, class and race. It proposes that texts and contexts must be read together as sites of power relations and all texts as constituting the social configuration and social exchange, and, therefore, to separate literary texts as purely 'imaginative' is to delink them from other texts that embody the same themes.

OPENING MOVES

THE HISTORICIST TURN

New Historicism, as we have seen, begins with the assumption that all texts are about a particular historical context and the social forms and exchanges of power. But how does one capture the social exchange in a text? How does 'real' history enter a text at all? New Historicism's opening moments drew upon the idea of

a) a textualization of history,
b) culture and cultural forms as linked to social relations of power.

These two may be termed the informing assumptions of the materialist critical practice known as New Historicism and Cultural Materialism.

History and Textuality

Hayden White suggested that all historical 'facts' come to us only in the form of language or narrative. For example, let us take two facts:

   (i) Greased cartridges were given to sepoys in 1857 India.

   (ii) The sepoy mutiny occurred.

We have two facts here. But how do we understand that one led to the other? How can we be certain that one was the cause and the other was an effect?

    The historian links these two facts and provides a narrative where we can see the cause–effect sequence. Therefore, we can know history only in the form of narratives, i.e., texts. White's idea that history required texts was an influential move. The historian arranges the events or facts in a certain order or *hierarchy* so that we pay more attention to some and less attention to others. When, for example, reading about the revolt of 1857 and its causes, do we pay a great deal of attention to the clothes the sepoys wore or to the question of the cartridges? Now, the thick uniforms worn by the sepoys were very uncomfortable, and were part of the army's regulations and customs in which the sepoys' comfort or preference was not given much importance. The same principle applied to cartridges, where the sepoy's feelings were not respected or accounted for. However, when we look at most narratives on 1857 there is almost no mention of clothing. This is not because to the sepoys in 1857 clothing was not a major issue. We do not pay attention because this 'fact' is not given enough importance in the narratives of 1857. This hierarchy in the narrative of history is not dependent on the facts but on the historian's interpretation and evaluation of them as more or less significant. What this means is, our ideas about the past are dependent upon the textual narrative, its hierarchy and ideologies that we are given by the historian.

    New Historicism adapts this notion of history and social contexts: texts are necessary to understand the social context, even though we must be alert to the fact that we only have access to the past through these biased, incomplete and political texts.

    New Historicism, following White's formulations, proposes that history is always written with the historian's present context and its needs in mind. That is, all history writing is about interpreting the past for the sake of the present. New Historicism asks us to be alert to this aspect of history writing: the *location* of the historian.

    It is also important, argue the New Historicists, to see history not simply in terms of 'great' men and women or unifying schemes ('the Enlightenment' or 'Indian modernity') but as made up of conflicting visions and attitudes. They reject any attempt to provide a single interpretation or version of any age, believing that every age has its schisms and tensions: the task of the historian is to locate these conflicting, struggling versions of any society/age. This means paying attention to subversive, anarchic and 'counter' moments and movements in every age. For this purpose New Historicism looks at motifs and themes in texts, or texts themselves where the existing belief systems, values, visions of society and power relations are constructed, popularized or called into question.

The relationship between history and textuality can be summarized as follows:

- History is not a background to texts. Rather, the foreground and the background are interdependent.
- A literary text not only reflects an age's themes and contexts, it *shapes* those contexts by persuading people to accept particular beliefs and opinions.
- We cannot separate literature as an effect of historical or social contexts but have to see literature as contributing to, informing, influencing and participating actively in the *construction* of these contexts.

New Historicism adapts a view of history where all events of the past are available to us only in the form of texts. This textuality of history is implicated in the institutional and social power relations that determine what narratives can get written and what forms the narratives must take. There is no such thing as objective history because narratives are, like language, produced in a context and are governed by social, economic and political interests of the dominant groups/institutions.

Culture and Ideology

New Historicists focus on the very material conditions of power when they adopt the Marxist view of culture. New Historicism accepts Marxism's key assumptions that

- cultural forms and practices are linked to material conditions of social relations, production and profits,
- the culture of a given period seeks to serve the interests of the dominant class, even though many forms of culture also try to subvert these interests,
- culture is about power, where power works through insidious forms—what is called ideology—to inspire people to adopt the interests and beliefs of the dominant classes.

New Historicism, influenced by the work of Raymond Williams (one of the most influential Marxist critics of the twentieth century), tries to explore the complicity of cultural forms with ideologies that support and reinforce the interests of the dominant classes. Thus, a New Historicist reading of Elizabethan drama would be interested in how the genre

- supported the monarchy,
- reinforced the class structure of England,
- constructed specific notions of national identity,
- maintained and 'naturalized' the roles of the gender,
- excluded certain sections of society from the power structure.

New Historicism looks for motifs where existing power relations are called into question and even subverted. They look at modes of exclusion and inclusion whereby literature or cultural forms that reflect the beliefs of the subordinate groups are marginalized by mainstream culture. For example, New Historicism would ask the following questions about the history and canon of women's writing:

- By what modes did women's writing get marginalized as 'romances' or 'domestic fiction' in the eighteenth and nineteenth centuries?
- What were the institutional structures—publishing, reviewing, periodicals, patronage—that relegated women's writing to such a niche?
- Did the logic of publishing and reading reflect real material conditions in which women worked, lived and wrote?
- Was literacy among women encouraged so that they could read 'Literature'? If so, what kinds of books and writing were 'allowed' to women?
- How does a woman writer attempt to get into the canon? Does she subscribe to and popularize the established ideas about women to gain acceptance by male readers?
- How many copies of women's books were printed? How were they circulated? Who read them? Did they get reviewed? Were the reviewers male?
- How do women writers subvert these conventions and practices?
- Are there other texts with which literary texts share the same concerns—women's courtesy books that reinforce patriarchal views, household manuals, travel narratives by women, visual texts? Do these texts represent a set of discourses about women in general?

These questions clearly link a cultural form with social contexts of gender relations, institutions, profits and the market, academia and technology. They address questions of power when they look at factors like the availability of technology, the circulation of books and the very act of publishing.

What is important is that for the New Historicists literature is only one cultural form among many others, one form of representation among several, where each form borrows, adapts and sometimes directly cites other forms. Thus, the

New Historicists, proceeding from the assumption that cultural forms reflect the real/material transactions of power in a society, suggest that the task is to locate cultural forms (history, literature, paintings, memoirs) within institutional practices and social relations of power, to see how these forms support, question, subvert the established beliefs, where all cultural forms are somehow linked, either in support or antagonistically, to the beliefs of the dominant classes in a society.

New Historicists—and here their emphasis is on the intertextual nature of all texts—look for similarities, echoes, and allusions to the law, religion, medicine, biology and the natural sciences, political philosophy in literary texts of an age— together they constitute the cultural matrix of the time. For instance, Louis Montrose demonstrates how the pastoral form of the sixteenth century (a form commonly used by Edmund Spenser, whose *The Faerie Queene* was an allegory about Elizabethan England) contributed to a certain image of Queen Elizabeth I. The pastoral form appealed to the common Englishman because it drew from the humble life of the poorer subjects and yet, Montrose demonstrates, it reinforced the subject–monarch relationship in a different way: it showed the queen as an approachable and friendly soul. Montrose puts it well: '[The pastoral] was a mediation of her greatness and their lowness … The charisma of Queen Elizabeth was not compromised but rather was enhanced by royal pastoral's awesome intimacy' (1994: 110–11).

The point is that institutional/state structures are closely aligned with cultural forms, where the latter participate in circulating specific representations of the monarch for the society to view/read and accept. These cultural forms and representations, therefore, are implicated in the structures of power when they disseminate the ideologies that keep the queen in popularly accepted power: they ensure she is accepted.

CULTURE-AS-TEXT, CULTURAL TEXTS

Culture is now seen as constituted by contested codes and representations. All accounts of culture—literary, historical, anthropological–ethnographic—are *stories* about events and people, marked by the usual structures of language. Culture is a text, a system of difference, arbitrariness and ideology.

The New Historicist emphasis on culture as text—adapted from the work of anthropologist Clifford Geertz—means that there are more objects now that can be 'read'. This is the reason why Greenblatt and others look at marginalized literary *and* nonliterary works. It allows the critic to look at marginal figures and their subjectivities/identities/politics in any cultural formation. As Greenblatt and

Gallagher put it in a passage worth quoting in full because of its politics and insight into New Historicist techniques:

> There has been in effect a social rebellion in the study of culture, so that figures hitherto kept outside the proper circles of interest – a rabble of half-crazed religious visionaries, semiliterate political agitators, coarse-faced peasants in hobnailed boots, dandies whose writings have been discarded as ephemera, imperial bureaucrats, freed slaves, women novelists dismissed as impudent scribblers, learned women excluded from easy access to the materials of scholarship, scandalmongers, provincial politicians, charlatans, and forgotten academics – have now forced their way, or rather have been invited in by our generation of critics. (2000: 9–10)

This means New Historicism *not only* adds more texts to its subject of study *but also* treats various objects *as* texts, as a part of cultural texts.

Thus, icons, monuments, tapestries, jewellery, cookbooks, food, surgery are all texts that constitute a cultural formation in a given era. These constitute, if not complete texts, what Gallagher and Greenblatt term 'textual traces in a culture' (14).

These 'traces' are not merely representations: they are *events* in themselves. As noted above, we cannot see literary or visual texts as merely reflecting social conditions—we have to regard them as actively enabling the construction of those conditions.

But, if we expand the notion of texts to include everything and anything, and assume that every culture has several 'textual traces' the problem that arises is this: how can we identify the more crucial elements (crucial in the sense of their contribution to power structures and social formations). Gallagher and Greenblatt provide the answer: we can only attempt to pursue significant details out of these traces, but we will be certain that these are truly significant in the actual practice of teaching and writing (15).

The point is, we often isolate those elements of 'textual traces' that help us make sense of unequal power relations in that age, and which reflect similar contexts in our own. But this later aspect is more to do with Cultural Materialism as practiced in England than in the New Historicism of the USA (as we shall see below).

Together the notion of textualized history and the (Marxist-inspired) idea that culture is implicated in structures of power enables the New Historicists and Cultural Materialists to seek a more materialist critique/analysis of culture.

MATERIALIST CRITIQUES

We have seen how New Historicists see cultural forms as shaping actual social conditions, contributing to or subverting social relations of power and representing society in particular ways that contribute to or interrogate dominant ideologies. They, therefore, propose that any critique of culture has to take into account

- the material conditions in which a cultural form is produced, and
- the relationship of that form to the social conditions and power relations.

This requires careful attention to, in the case of literature, the

- publication/production of books (including marketing/publicity),
- literacy levels that determine readership,
- kinds of readers the book targets,
- 'aura' of the author,
- circulation of the book in other cultural forms (cinema),
- reviewing,
- academic respectability/acceptance,
- relationship of this book to the genre itself,
- relationship of this book to other books and discourses,
- relationship of the book's themes to contemporary topics/issues.

For example, if we were to look at the Harry Potter books we can see how each of the above has to be carefully explored. We need to pay attention, therefore, to

- the hype and the publicity,
- the 'aura' of Rowling (rags-to-riches story, single-parent status),
- the merchandize (wands, t-shirts, brooms) around Potter,
- the debates about the books' relationship with *The Lord of the Rings*,
- the film version and the Hollywood industry,
- the well-publicized response of authors like A. S. Byatt and Stephen King to the books,
- the conditioning of children as consumers,
- the revival of 'magic' and 'fantasy',
- religious discourses around the books,
- fans and fan responses and the construction of 'Pottermania'.

With these questions we locate the books in a larger context and see how the books themselves contribute to social constructions (for instance, regarding magic, or good versus evil). We see the books as part of a great leisure and profit industry that generates an interest in not only the books but also the merchandize and the personal life of the author, in order to sell the book. Thus, even as we treat the work as a literary text with its own narrative, thematic, structural and aesthetic aspects we locate these in larger contexts of cultural forms and culture industries.

> Materialist critiques focus on the *production* and *reception* of cultural
> artifacts—paintings, music, literature—with the belief that all arti-
> facts are linked to social formations (like patriarchal societies), existing
> ideologies (like the family) and power structures (like capitalism). The task
> of critical analysis is to explore the links of texts with these structures and
> ideologies.

Ivo Kamps sums up the basic 'commitments' in a materialist critical practice:

(a) to a patterned relationship between cultural forms (art) and social relations of production,

(b) to the 'relative autonomy' of the literary text,

(c) a programme of rigorous and concrete historical research,

(d) an ideological critique.

(1995: 1–19)

Having looked at the basic assumptions and concerns of the materialist critique of
culture we can go on to the specific features of New Historicism and Cultural
Materialism.

NEW HISTORICISM

New Historicism locates texts within contexts while showing how literary and
other texts produce contexts. Central to New Historicism, therefore, is a close
reading of *texts* (specific documents, verbal and visual), *discourses* (the speech acts
and images governed by a set of regulations in a particular community) and *material practices* (like institutions, labour, patronage and family).

TEXTS, DISCOURSES, MATERIAL PRACTICES

New Historicism is interested in entire *discourses* that varied texts contribute to.
The assumption is that texts contribute to discourse and discursive constructions
of social conditions (by which they mean that representations of, say, the 'King of
England' contribute to his actual acceptance or rejection by the people) rather
than simply reflect them.

Thus, reading Elizabethan England, New Historicists look at the following
discourses:

- nationalism and 'English' identity,
- the native versus the foreigner (or the Jew, in most cases),
- native country versus foreign lands (the New World),

- cultural nationalism (the 'cottage' as an *English* icon),
- monarchy and kingship,
- aristocracy versus the working class,
- Protestantism and Catholicism,
- the national economy and foreign trade,
- medicine and health,
- morality,
- family,
- vagabonds, unemployed and the gainfully employed,
- gendered divisions of labour and gendered morality.

These are some of the major themes addressed in New Historicist readings of the Elizabethan world. It must be noted that these are not mutually exclusive discourses, and very often one or two merge with each other. For example, Jonathan Gil Harris has shown how discourses of medicine and health often influenced debates about national economy and foreign trade. Harris shows how writers of economic tracts often used images of the 'health of the economy' or 'sick economy' to recommend changes in foreign trade policy (Harris 2004). Harris goes on to show how Shakespeare's plays also took recourse to similar images of healthy and sick economies.

In order to locate these discourses the critic would look at a selection of texts including, plays, courtesy books, health advice books, broadsides and ballads, poetry, maps and local descriptions (called chorographies), exploration and travel narratives, law documents, juridical records, police records, educational documents, religious tracts and news reports. As we can see, the assumption here is that discourses occur across genres and texts.

IMPROVISATION

A key term in Stephen Greenblatt's work (*Renaissance Self-fashioning*, 1980), *improvisation* is the way in which an individual seeks to enter into the power relations. In New Historicism, improvisation underscores specific contexts and strategies:

- all identity is fiction,
- identity is generated through repeated performances and narratives,
- these performances are modes of dealing with historical–social contexts,
- it enables the individual or group to enter the system of power and use it to her/his advantage,
- the system uses it to contain opposition by adapting it, accommodating it so that resistance actually reinforces power structures.

Greenblatt extends his argument about improvisation through two virtuoso readings. In his essay 'Invisible Bullets' (1988) Greenblatt places alongside each other a wide range of texts from Thomas Harriott (who was a resident of the 'New World' colony of Virginia, in America), Shakespeare's Henry IV, Part I, an Italian heretic Mennochio and links it with Elizabethan theatre. Connecting three places, America, London and Italy, Greenblatt shows how power operates by appropriating and negotiating with an Other. The Other is accommodated in such a way that it contributes to the existing power structure rather than subvert it. In his later work, *Marvelous Possessions* (1992) Greenblatt looks at the encounter between Columbus and the natives of the New World in 1492. Reading Columbus' accounts of his 'discovery', Greenblatt looks at the following:

- representations of the native
- the tension between the marvel of the completely Other and the image of the sameness
- the related collapse of the same into the Other
- the role of the native as the 'go-between'
- the use and abuse of language (especially the process of naming) the unequal exchanges (of gifts)
- and the theme of conversion—from commodities to spiritual and vice versa

In both these cases the individual improvises in such a way that he attains the upper hand in the power relation. Greenblatt demonstrates how, in the context of his encounter with the natives of America, Columbus quickly turned the absence of a common language to his advantage. He records how, when he claimed, in the Spanish language (which the natives did not understand, obviously), the land for his monarch, the natives did not disagree. Columbus recorded: 'I was not contradicted.' Greenblatt suggests that this absence of contradiction is taken as a serious *fact* before Columbus makes his legal claim. Greenblatt writes:

> The absence of "contradiction" had a specific force: such a fact would be important in establishing for the Spanish crown a legal claim to the newly discovered islands by the 'voluntary choice' of the original inhabitants. (58)

Columbus thus improvises his speech act into becoming a legal claim for the lands.

Improvisation is a mode of identity-making through which individuals and groups retain their power—appropriating the structures of the relation in order to validate their claims and co-opting resistance in order to manage it, and, thereby, creating their own identity.

CIRCULATION

A term that occurs with astonishing regularity in New Historicist texts is *circulation*. Power circulates through different texts in the form of discourse. Representations, therefore, are never innocent but structures or moments in the circulation of power. Genres are useful to circulate particular kinds of icons and reinforce power relations. We have already noted how the queen's image circulates in pastoral poetry. The queen's image is also circulated in other forms like autobiography, Shakespeare's plays and a travelogue on the Amazon (I am referring to Louis Montrose's essay, 'Shaping Fantasies' here). We need to see this circulation not merely as a literary theme but as actively generating a myth, a fantasy and a persona of a woman at the head of a rigidly patriarchal society. It helped sustain Queen Elizabeth, as Montrose demonstrates.

The problem with this New Historicist version of power relations is that it leaves nothing as agency to the suppressed people. Greenblatt argues that whenever resistance becomes visible in any social formation, the dominant classes co-opt it, they provide a legitimate outlet for resistance and anger so that the essential structures are not disturbed and they retain their power.

Richmond Barbour demonstrates how the notion of an imperial Britain, the discourse of privilege (i.e., class) and a veiled ideology of absolutism circulated through these public spectacles and the 'triumphal arches' (ornate arches set up in the city to welcome royalty) in sixteenth- and seventeenth-century London. Elizabeth's 1558 entry into London highlighted London's *self-sufficiency and local traditions*: 'the queen's highness passed through the city, which without any foreign person, of it self beautified it self' (Barbour 75). She is a very English queen in these representations, and the discourse proudly points to the exclusion of the foreign. Later the discourse changes entirely when James I enters London (1604). The King (it is important to remember that James I of England was James VI of *Scotland*, brought in to rule England) imposes himself upon a city that is proud of its local traditions of government. The city suddenly transforms itself to welcome this outsider as their king. London itself seems to expand to encompass the globe and the foreign. Foreign elements are absorbed into the local and the native via the king.

Another example of how a particular image circulates in order to sustain a power relation is explored in Valerie Traub's work on sexuality in Renaissance drama (1992). Traub argues that feminine subjects and sexuality in Shakespeare served to enforce particular codes of conduct for women, thereby ensuring that women remained carefully circumscribed. She notes following images of the female body, sexuality and sexual relations: female chastity, disgust at sexual relations (seen in the equation between sexuality and disease), fear and fascination for homoerotic desire and the horrors of reproduction.

The circulation of 'sexual energy' results in discourses in following forms:

- Women as objects to be controlled and subjugated,
- Women's sexuality to be curbed because they pose a threat (as temptresses/whores) to the male,
- Women as contaminants and carriers of disease.

All these discourses reinforce the domination of women. The public staging of such plays meant that a large section of the audience or populace in a town assimilated these discourses. The play, therefore, contributes to a material practice—gender inequality—by generating more and more myths that call for greater restraints on women.

> Genres and texts are elements that contribute to the circulation of power and ideologies. They reinforce power relations through the creation and dissemination of myths and fantasies, which are then assimilated by the society of the time.

CULTURAL POETICS

Towards the end of the 1980s Greenblatt and others began using a new term, *cultural poetics* (even though Greenblatt himself had used 'the poetics of culture' before), in place of New Historicism. This shift has not been a change of critical practice as much as a limitation placed on their claims. Earlier, New Historicist readings claimed they were 'doing' history. However, with 'cultural poetics' they soon circumscribed their practice as a more limited project (see Brannigan, 1998, Chapter 3).

Greenblatt defined cultural poetics as 'the study of the collective making of distinct cultural practices and inquiry into the relations among these practices' (1988: 5). This means a study of the following:

1. Cultural practices like literature, music, film, sports
2. The history of the formation of any cultural practice
3. Locating this formation within other social realms (law, religion)
4. Linking one cultural practice with another

Greenblatt suggests we need to see how cultural practices shaped the collective experience and were shaped in turn, how they distinguished themselves from each other while at the same time concealed contiguities.

To take an example, if we were to explore the cultural poetics of the British empire in India we will need to study

- cultural practices like shikar, clubs, dancing, 'nautch',
- trace the history of each practice,

- to see how each of these practices tied in with the imperial structure built on administrative–military power and racial difference,
- to see how shikar and clubs related to each other through common discourses of imperial masculinity, male bonding, leisure and a public culture of imperial spectacle (that is, for natives to see and admire the glory of the Raj).

Together these practices constitute a cultural poetics of the empire. Each is a unique cultural practice with well-defined boundaries (the eroticism of the nautch, the team spirit of polo or club games, the violence and danger of the shikar). At the same time they constitute a contiguity of discourses about the (British) imperial man in India, as noted above.

As a second example, let me move to an entirely different medium and genre. Batman was created by Bob Kane in 1939. Will Brooker's study, *Batman Unmasked: Analyzing a Cultural Icon* (2000), maps the shifts in how Batman was received, appropriated and commodified by and in (i) the comic book industry (ii) the film industry (iii) television industry while also being rooted in *cultural discourses* about violence, the 'seduction of the innocent' (the title of Frank Wertham's 1954 work which attacked superhero and other comic books for corrupting children). Brooker's cultural study constantly emphasizes the links between particular discourses (the 'gay Batman' discourse of the 1960s, or legal discourses of rights and the law), social forms such as fandom, and, of course, the profits of the industry. Brooker's study shows how Batman, a comic-book hero assumes a life of his own, meaning several things to several people, and how the industry constantly modifies the superhero's character (especially in Frank Miller's 1986 path-breaking, and largest-selling Batman comic ever, *Batman: The Dark Knight Returns*) to keep interest and profits alive. The cultural *poetics* of Batman cannot be reduced to the comic books' aesthetic appeal, its mesmerizing superhero, the medium itself or the industry. Each practice is unique, with its own rules and norms, and together they generate a contiguity: the superhero ideology.

CULTURAL MATERIALISM

Jonathan Dollimore and Alan Sinfield (1985) summarize the critical method of the cultural materialists. A Cultural Materialist critical practice is marked by the following:

(a) *Historical context*: Looking at the specific conditions in which certain texts were *produced* and *received*.
(b) *Theoretical method*: The dual emphasis on textual history and the textualization of history involves reading across disciplines under the assumption that discourses cut across texts. In the main, their method is informed by 'socialist and feminist commitment' (1985: vii).

(c) *Political commitment*: All readings must exhibit a political commitment. This means the cultural materialist practice pays attention to questions of power and marginalization of particular groups (gays, women, working classes).

(d) *Textual analysis*: All critiques are derived from close readings of texts.

In terms of critical practice, there is very little difference between the New Historicists and the Cultural Materialists. The Cultural Materialists believe that the New Historicists generate apolitical readings, in which there is no question of agency on the part of the marginalized. There is some justification for this comment. As we have seen how Greenblatt's reading of Renaissance culture suggests that the dominant power structures absorb resistance. This means there is no hope of ever altering the power relations in favour of the marginalized. Their politically oriented criticism, therefore, works in several ways.

THE POLITICS OF INTERPRETATION

All Cultural Materialist interpretation is consciously political. This means they seek readings that not only pay attention to the question of the exploited and the marginalized but also to the possibilities of resistance and subversion in *both* the text and the interpretive act.

1. Cultural Materialists emphasize the need to generate *dissident* readings that seriously tinker with symbolic structures of power. As Dollimore and Sinfield put it: '[Cultural Materialism] registers its commitment to the transformation of a social order which exploits people on grounds of race, gender and class' (1985: viii).
2. This means working present concerns with exploitation and power back into their historical contexts. For example, our present concerns with gender-based exploitation can be extended back to the age of Shakespeare. And, readings of Shakespeare are always connected to the problems in the present. Unlike the New Historicists who keep their readings of Shakespeare at the historical level of Shakespeare's age, the Cultural Materialists opt for seeing Shakespeare in the light of today's concerns and inequalities.
3. They argue that all representation is politically charged, and, therefore, there cannot be a politically 'neutral' interpretation either. All representations are struggles for meaning and power, and literary texts are often sites of such struggles. The task of the critic is to be alert to the values preached within texts—values that seek to reinforce existing power structures and mechanisms of exploitation. To see literary texts as merely embodying 'beauty' or truth' is to refuse the political agenda of the texts.
4. They also locate the potential for subcultural resistance, counter-cultural modes and dissidence even in historical texts. That is, they demonstrate

how Shakespeare's texts can be used to teach resistance to the social order in today's world. They focus on the subversive potential of texts for this purpose.

5. They are interested in the ways in which curricula are designed. They argue that the systematization of interpretation or the 'prescription' of particular texts are done with the intention of inculcating certain kinds of values among the youth/students. Thus, Shakespeare is used to instill a sense of 'English culture' without ever paying attention to
    i. whether the culture is the effect of a forced conformity
    ii. exploitation of particular sections of the people
    iii. Shakespeare's own subversiveness.

Cultural Materialists, therefore, seek to generate what they call 'dissident reading'.

DISSIDENT READING

As we have seen above, the Cultural Materialists are interested in readings that interrogate the hidden political agenda and power structures in texts and simultaneously look for potential subversive aspects in order to relate the text to the present.

A good example would be Alan Sinfield's 1986 book, *Alfred Tennyson*. Reading Tennyson's famous *In Memoriam* Sinfield suggests that Tennyson evokes the foreign lands only in order to reinforce the theme of England-as-true-home. Tennyson sets out to overturn sexual and gender stereotypes and ends up reinforcing them. Sinfield shows, for example, how Tennyson sets out to mourn another man, Arthur Hallam, thereby suggesting a certain relationship between men—a clear subversion of Victorian norms of heterosexuality. But the poem ends with a celebration of a heterosexual marriage. Sinfield argues that despite Tennyson's subversiveness, he ends up treating heterosexual marriage as the only legitimate form of sexual relationships.

However, Sinfield also argues that it is possible to see the resistance to a dominant social order or norm in such works as In Memoriam. The changing of genders of the two lovers in the poem (apparently at Victoria's insistence) can be seen as a mode of rethinking the issue and institution of marriage: it reveals anxieties about homosexuality. What Sinfield does is to show how we can read texts for the anxieties they seek to conceal—these anxieties frequently reflect the instability of a power relation, institution or cultural practice.

Dissident reading is almost always critical of liberal humanist interpretations. A fine example of such a critical text is Catherine Belsey's *The Subject of Tragedy* (1985). Belsey shows how Renaissance tragedy is steeped in the liberal humanist ethos. The texts preach the language of humanism, and the issue of the 'inalienable' rights of liberty, property and rights. However, Belsey's innovative reading locates a paradox in these texts.

- On the one hand they preach the right to freedom and property for *all men*.
- On the other these rights are based on a denial of freedom and property to *women*.

Thus, the term 'man' in the Renaissance served only one section of the population. When Renaissance tragedy is taught as a subject (Belsey's title gestures at both the subject/person in the texts and the *discipline* of literary/Renaissance studies) both students and teachers subscribe to the texts' values of the individual as centre of power and knowledge. They thus validate these humanist values as true and abiding. In a sense we have a circularity of arguments: we read these texts for their relevant liberal humanism, we know these values are relevant because we read them today. Disciplinary formations like literary studies reinforce the unequal power relations through such sanctioned readings that ignore the ideological fissures in a text.

FURTHER READING

Brannigan, John. 1998. *New Historicism and Cultural Materialism*. London: Macmillan.

Veeser, H. Aram (ed.). 1989. *The New Historicism*. London: Routledge.

Sinfield, Alan. 1992. *Faultlines: Cultural Materialism and the Politics of Dissident Reading*. Oxford: Oxford University Press.

9 Critical Race Studies

Since the mid-1980s, race has become a central category in social, political and cultural theory. Critical race theory, includes studies of race in literature and culture, ethnicity studies, studies of minority literatures and specific traditions in literature and philosophy (such as Chicano/a or African American theories). It is a component also of legal theory and explicitly addresses questions of racism and racial discrimination. This latter emerged from and continues to study civil rights discourses and draws upon the work of social theorists such as W. E. B. Du Bois. Race has become a central concern within literary and cultural theory for various reasons.

Race and ethnicity are forms of collective, communitarian identity—one that is *shared* and not necessarily unique to an individual. Thus, the question of racial or ethnic identity has a larger social and political significance. It involves questions of belonging, location, rights, citizenship, empowerment, welfare, affiliation, and could be the locus of discrimination, exclusion and oppression.

Race studies in the latter decades of the twentieth century has thus seen cultural expressions and manifestations of race and ethnicity as both contexts for and consequences of political and social problems. 'Reading' race and ethnicity means, therefore, to read literary and cultural texts for the social roles, prejudices, resistance, collaboration and political significance of a racial or ethnic identity.

Race studies is thus an explicitly political reading/critical practice. It is less a 'theory' than a set of critical practices that examine issues of race and ethnicity. It is more accurate to position race studies as socio-political reading practices within legal studies, historiography, social theory and literary criticism. It has had significant impact within Cultural Studies—especially media studies, Black British studies, Asian American studies—around the world.

It must be pointed out that race studies, especially in literary and cultural theory has, unfortunately, focused mainly on the most visible minority race—black—for many decades now. This emphasis only began to alter in the 1990s with increasing studies of Chicano/a, ethnic literatures and aboriginal writings.

This chapter deals with other literary and cultural domains from around the world in which race and ethnicity are critical categories.

OPENING MOVES

THE RACE TURN

The 'race turn' appears in social and cultural theory in the USA from around the turn of the nineteenth century. The race turn was instrumental not only in developing a social theory about races and racism, but also in the rise of literary–cultural movements such as Black Arts and the Harlem Renaissance.

Du Bois and Social Theory

Sociologist W. E. B. Du Bois, the first African American Ph.D. from Harvard, was a leading civil-rights activist of the early twentieth century. His *The Souls of Black Folk* (1903) is now a classic in race studies.

Du Bois' key focus, besides civil rights for blacks in America, was the scientific racism of his age. Eugenics, Social Darwinism and Nazism combined racial prejudices with scientific theories that 'demonstrated' the inferiority of the black race. This scientific racism was based in biology—a trend critiqued in race studies and feminist theory as 'biological determinism'. It was also visible in aesthetic theories where black bodies and physiognomies were marked as ugly, grotesque and even evil (see Sander Gilman's studies of this in medicine, 1986).

Du Bois disputed the view that the blacks were biologically inferior. He argued that there is no *scientific* basis for such a belief—and that such a belief was more *social* than scientific. In this argument Du Bois was clearly moving toward a social constructionist view of race, where race as a category is not scientifically demonstrable, but in fact emerges within social discourses and practices. Racial *difference* in biology does not, in this social constructionist view, validate racial *inferiority*. Du Bois wrote:

> What is the real distinction between these nations [Europeans, Chinese, Americans]? Certainly we must all acknowledge that physical differences play a great part ... but no mere physical distinctions would really define or explain the deeper differences – the cohesiveness and continuity of these groups. (2000: 82)

Du Bois went on to argue that race groups must develop not as individuals but as races. He also argued against the segregation of races, for it prevented a proper mixing of races and instead inculcates hatred for the other.

Du Bois argued that blacks were always central to the USA because they had contributed to its history in various ways. For example, during Reconstruction, blacks were forging alliances and political platforms with whites. Black Emancipation—often traced to the controversial Emancipation Proclamation by Abraham Lincoln in 1862—was the key element in this Reconstruction, argued Du Bois (though Du Bois was critical of the Lincoln Proclamation), but despite this the USA continued to deny civil rights to blacks.

Du Bois' sociological writings today constitute an excellent example of both social constructionism and race studies. Examining the criminal tendencies of blacks (appearing in his major work *The Philadelphia Negro*, 1899), Du Bois argued that criminality was not an 'essential' feature of the black personality (this argument about black criminality is one that persists to this day). Instead, criminal acts were due to the 'social revolution' as blacks adapted to freedom and changed social circumstances. Crime among blacks, argued Du Bois, would reduce as blacks attained power, wealth and social status on par with the whites. Here Du Bois turned, unforgivingly, to eugenics (the science and genetics that dealt with races and racial groups). Du Bois argued that the best among the blacks—what he called the 'talented tenth'—must lead the black race. With this Du Bois initiated a principle of elitism into black studies, something that has been consistently attacked by later theorists.

One of Du Bois' major insights was the idea of 'double consciousness'. Du Bois argued that the black could never see himself as himself: He saw himself through the eyes of the white. That is, the African American perpetually saw himself as the white man saw him. This 'double consciousness' meant that the black man was always 'two'—a black man and an American.

Du Bois' major contribution to race cultural studies was his active championing of black writers and artists. As editor of the National Association for the Advancement of Colored People's (NAACP) periodical *Crisis*, he published the

Harlem writers Jean Toomer and Langston Hughes. Du Bois was certain that art is propaganda, and that aesthetics could not be divorced from politics. With this shift towards the *politics* of literary and cultural expression, Du Bois marked a major development in race studies.

Hoyt Fuller and Black Aesthetics

Alain Locke's 'The New Negro' (1925) was a defining moment in African American social theory. Locke's essay pleaded for a greater amount of self-awareness and consciousness among the blacks. Building on this view Hoyt Fuller articulated the vision of a 'Black Aesthetics' (1968).

Fuller proposed that because the race worlds of the blacks and whites were so unlike each other and so separated, there could be no compatibility or even conversation between the African American and the white American writer. Black artists and writers would always be conscious of their being black, their history of slavery and their roots in a tradition very different from that of white America.

Fuller argued that black aesthetics would be based in a pride in this difference. The 'black is beautiful' ideology is rooted in this argument of Fuller's. Once the artist has accepted the separateness and uniqueness of black culture it becomes difficult, suggested Fuller, to accept any other writing as universal. Thus, white literature, even of the greatest writers, could never claim to represent black experience. Hence aesthetic theories and literary modes arising out of such white literary cultures could not be an adequate frame of reference for the blacks. Black aesthetics, in other words, would be separatist, distinct and draws upon a very different framework and tradition.

Fuller also argued that black works cannot be judged by white standards of literary merit or quality. While mediocre works by white writers are spared, any work by black writers, argued Fuller, was rigorously examined and attacked as being of low quality. The black writer has to keep writing despite such obviously racist literary evaluation from white critics.

Larry Neal, Myth and Racial Memory

Larry Neal, like Fuller before him, was interested in developing a black aesthetic tradition. Neal locates this tradition in African myth, oral tales and folklore.

Neal retrieves African voodoo, spirit worship, shamanic traditions as sources of a black aesthetic. He turns to figures like the trickster in African mythology as iconic of a black consciousness that resists white interpretation and frameworks (Henry Louis Gates, Jr would also return to the trickster). Neal locates the soothsayer, the griot, the sage as well as the specifically African dance rhythms, styles and music as a black aesthetic.

What Neal was proposing here was a very *political aesthetic*: each of the above was linked to community rather than individual. Every artist, noted Neal, must serve the aspirations of his community and tribe. The use of myth and folklore—which are collective, shared, communitarian and *not* individual—is thus essential to the artist. Neal was arguing that there was no need to invent a black tradition; such a tradition already existed as African American cultural heritage.

Most significantly, Neal's black aesthetic argued that art must be ethical. Therefore, black aesthetic and black arts must represent the truths of the victims (blacks) rather than the consciousness or views of their oppressors, even if this meant being attacked by white critics.

> Black aesthetics emphasized racial identity as a context of reading and writing, and racialized traditions (black, African) as sources for a politically significant/relevant artistic practice that is more communitarian than individual, and whose aesthetics must underscore the race group's experience and must be evaluated through different frameworks rather than universalist, white ones.

RACE AND DIFFERENCE

Michael Banton has pointed out that race as a concept has been used to speak of *differences between populations*, without ever concentrating upon what race is as a *concept* (2000). Banton is accurate in his reading for, historically, racial *difference* has been the basis for discrimination and disempowerment. Colonialism, for example, hinged upon the conquest of one race by another in Asia, South America and Africa. Racial difference has been the cornerstone of violent and brutal campaigns against particular races and groups, especially Aboriginals and First Nation peoples in Canada, Australia and the USA and, of course, the paradigmatic Holocaust. Racial difference has also been marked in terms of economic development, rights and welfare in nation-states. It has informed developments in law, popular culture (with its stereotypes of blacks or tribals) and the market. Racial differences characterize access to education, areas of residence and employment. In culture and literature, the oral and other narratives of blacks, ethnic minorities and migrants have been marginalized and, in several cases (such as Native Americans), often lost from history.

Race, to return to Banton, has been defined and described in biological, scientific, demographic, social and cultural terms. But the meaning of the term has changed over the past one hundred years. In order to understand the implications of what race means (i.e., how it has been defined) Banton's taxonomy (2000: 61) works effectively for us:

- when race meant descent, then it was expected that whites considered alliances with blacks as socially dishonorable;

- when race meant type, whites would have seen sexual union with blacks as producing stock physically inferior to whites and superior to blacks;
- when race meant subspecies, most members of the public would not have comprehended the workings of inheritance and selection.

Cornel West's work has located a genealogy of racism, from Greek antiquity through the early modern period (what he calls the 'first stage') to the 1600–1800 period of emerging botanical, phrenological and other 'scientific' theories (the 'second stage'), the Enlightenment and nineteenth century (the 'third stage'). West locates racism and racial theories as discourses that mix social theories with science, psychological concepts with economic theories in order to show the complex genealogy of the discrimination (West 2002).

> Race has served as a marker of difference, a difference that leads to slavery, exploitation and death. While biological evidence for the superiority of one race or another has not emerged—or has been faulted—the social and political fields remain emplotted within discourses that consistently, if subtly, deploy race as difference. Critical Race Studies examines these discourses and representational strategies of racial marking.

Race, therefore, is a marker of difference. In Henry Louis Gates, Jr's poststructuralist terminology, 'the sense of difference defined in popular usages of the term "race" has both described and inscribed differences of language, belief system, artistic tradition, and gene pool, as well as all sorts of supposedly natural attributes such as rhythm, athletic ability, cerebration, usury, fidelity, and so forth' (1985: 5).

Critical Race Studies (CRS) is an attempt to foreground race and ethnicity as key categories in the analysis of law, history, politics and culture. Our concern here is with its cultural components, even though—and here we might mark its departure from poststructuralism—CRS' cultural theories and studies are never very far from social issues and themes in legal studies or politics.

In the 1990s, emerging from the context of campaigns for minority rights, greater immigration and shifting demographics, came a new domain within race studies: 'white studies'. The discourse of whiteness, notes Giroux (1997), rose as an expression of bitterness on the part of whites when they saw, according to one report 'an identity ravaged by "feminists, multiculturalists, P.C. policepersons, affirmative-action employers, rap artists, Native Americans, Japanese tycoons, Islamic fundamentalists and Third World dictators"' (cited in Giroux 379). Theoretically speaking, it was interesting to see that when scholars like bell hooks, Cornel West and Ruth Frankenberg were examining white identity as a site of privilege and power, there occurred a revival of ideas and discourses about family, traditional values, individualism and nation as a counter to the emergent and emancipatory discourses of democracy and justice and multiracial societies.

AFRICAN AMERICAN AESTHETICS AND THEORY

African American literary and cultural theory in the works of Henry Louis Gates, Jr, Hazel Carby, Hortense Spillers, bell hooks, Patricia Hill Collins (Collins' work is discussed under black feminism in the chapter on feminism) and Stuart Hall, and philosophy in the works of Kwame Anthony Appiah, emerged from the black aesthetic movement and ideas noted above, but was also influenced by developments in poststructuralism and cultural studies. Foregrounding issues of racial and ethnic identity, these theorists have

- generated new readings of canonical Eng. Lit. works,
- provided frameworks for unraveling race and racism as literary themes,
- offered models of reading, writing and critique from within African and African American myth, folklore and traditions, and
- helped conceptualize black or ethnic literatures differently.

HENRY LOUIS GATES, JR AND SIGNIFYIN(G)

Gates' work is a sophisticated appropriation of poststructuralism and African myth for purposes of critical theory. In his *Figures in Black* (1987) and *The Signifying Monkey* (1988) Gates developed a model of African American theory that has remained highly influential.

Gates begins by identifying four key models of African American critical writing (one should note the parallel with Elaine Showalter's model of the tradition of women's writing):

1. *Repetition and Imitation*: The unimaginative borrowing of white, European models of criticism, even when the texts under examination where black.
2. *Black Aesthetics*: This was a separatist move, focusing on black texts as symptomatic and representative of black social conditions and politics. It treated black literary texts as social documents and was heavily influenced by the Marxist model of criticism (where cultural practices were superstructures to the economic base).
3. *Repetition and Difference*: Gates sees this as an innovative use of Euro-American 'high theory' where the theory is 'used' but also critiqued—especially in the writings of Houston Baker (we could add Hazel Carby, Patricia Hill Collins and Hortense Spillers).
4. *Synthesis*: This is the most developed form of African American criticism according to Gates where black traditions meet and synthesize with Euro-American theory.

Gates then retrieves the trickster figure, Esu-Elegbara from African mythology as a trope and concept. Esu-Elegbara is what Gates terms the signifyin(g) monkey. It is a messenger of the gods in Yoruba tradition, and is also the master of the stylus (of course, Gates recognizes that the stylus is also a patriarchal symbol, the phallus) and hence of writing itself.

For Gates the Esu-Elegbara stands for indeterminacy, open-endedness and irony. In order to underline the significance of Esu, Gates contrasts it with Ifa, the 'god of determinate meaning'. Esu, on the other hand, is the

> god of interpretation because he embodies the ambiguity of figurative language …
> [a] metaphor for the uncertainties of explication, for the open-endedness of every
> literary text … the process of disclosure a process that is never-ending … the
> Signifying Monkey exists as the great trope of Afro-American discourse…(1988:
> 21)

Esu, then, is a signifier for magic, disruption, chance and a variety of opposing, indeterminable practices such as closure/disclosure. It combines insult with profundity, and occurs, according to Gates, in numerous African traditions, especially the vernacular and the oral. Gates proposed two models of Esu-Elegbara's signifyin(g): motivated and unmotivated. Unmotivated signifyin(g) is cooperative, respectful and is imitative. Motivated signifyin(g) is oppositional, playful and ironic. This second, motivated form

- adapts canonical texts and rewrites them (Ralph Ellison's rewriting of Wells' *Invisible Man* in order to talk about the invisibility of black peoples would be an example),
- adapts from within the African tradition in an example of African intertextuality and revisionism.

> Signifyin(g) is Gates' term for the conscious reversal and repetition, through the use of African myth and folkloric figures, of Euro-American (white) tropes, figures, languages and forms. It, therefore, becomes a rhetorical strategy through which the black critic or poet assets agency over narrative, language and discourse.

Gates elaborates what he means by signifyin(g) in *Figures in Black*. Signifyin(g) is his term for the revision and reversal of racist tropes. Thus, Tar Baby (Toni Morrison's novel of the same name) or 'monkey' (used as a pejorative to describe the African race) are appropriated as metaphors and tropes by the Africans themselves in an act of linguistic and rhetorical *agency*. Gates writes:

> The ironic reversal of a received racist image in the Western imagination of the black
> as simianlike, the Signifying Monkey – he who dwells at the margins of discourse,
> ever punning, ever troping, ever embodying the ambiguities of language – is our

trope for repetition and revision, indeed our trope of chiasmus itself, repeating and reversing simultaneously as he does in one deft discursive act. (1987: 236)

At this point it is useful to remember that racism has always invented *languages of difference*, of mockery, cruelty and discrimination. Whether it is the 'Babu' in English colonial discourse or the African 'monkey' for Europe, racism has a vocabulary within which it defines, captures and dehumanizes the non-white race. Jacques Derrida—whose work seems to resonate throughout Gates'—in an extended meditation alerts us to the discursive and rhetorical power of racism:

> The word [apartheid] concentrates separation [Derrida is playing with the 'apart' and *heid*—meaning 'essence'—of 'apartheid'] ... at every point, like all racisms, it tends to pass segregation off as natural ... such is the monstrosity of this political idiom. Surely, an idiom should never incline toward racism. It often does, however, and this is not altogether fortuitous: there's no racism without a language. The point is not that acts of racial violence are only words but that they have to have a word. Even though it offers the excuse of blood, color, birth – or, rather, *because* it uses this naturalist and sometimes creationist discourse – racism always betrays the perversion of a man, the 'talking animal'. It institutes, declares, writes, inscribes, prescribes. A system of marks, it outlines space in order to assign forced residence or to close off borders. It does not discern, it discriminates.(1985: 331, emphasis in original)

Derrida is here arguing, in his inimitable elliptical style, that racism has a language, a discourse of its own, and one in which Africans, Asians—non-white races—are Othered, rejected and isolated as monstrosities. Thus, tropes of Othering and of discrimination are markers of material differences, because to consign a black man or woman to the realm of the 'animal' is to deny that human anything like rights or space, for animals do not have human rights (just as, in more recent times, Taliban fighters arrested by the US army were denied Geneva Conventions because they were classified—termed, *linguistically called*—'enemy combatants' and not 'prisoners of war': a shift of *nomenclature* often becomes a shift from life to death, as prisoners in Abu Ghraib and Guantanamo Bay found out). To put it another way, languages of difference have very concrete material consequences in denying cultures, traditions, rights, space and identity to particular groups. Hence the attention to languages of signification in Gates: for to battle the language, the tropes—the Literature—of racism is to battle racism as a political phenomenon.

Later in *The Signifying Monkey* Gates argues that in the black vernacular tradition, to signify is to engage in 'rhetorical games' (1988: 48). Whereas in the English—by which Gates means Euro-American— tradition 'signify' or 'signification' is linked to the relation between signifier and signified (see the account of Saussure in the chapter on Structuralism), in the black vernacular it is the relation between rhetorical figures and the signifier:

$$\text{Signification} = \frac{\text{rhetorical figures}}{\text{signifier}} \quad (1988: 48)$$

Gates then shows how Bloom's theory of revisionism has been adapted within black literature through an intensive use of Yoruba myth and folkloric elements such as naming (which, Gates argues, could be positive or negative in Yoruba).

In short, Gates argues in favour of

- black rhetorical strategies,
- metaphorizations that invert Western, racist tropes, and
- retrieval of African metaphors that enable openness.

While Gates' project does resemble a nativist appropriation of poststructuralism, and a celebration of native tropes as a counter to Western ones, it remains one of the more significant contributions to a race-based critical theory.

FIRST PEOPLES, IN THEORY

Literary criticism, especially with the postcolonial turn, has begun to pay attention to aboriginal and 'First Peoples' cultures. While this arguably becomes a nativist trend, the shift from metropolitan, written and Euro-American (which we can code quite easily as 'English') to oral, vernacular, regional literary cultures is timely and politically significant.

The 'indigenist turn', as this shift may be termed is context-specific. It comes affiliated with social, legal and political movements seeking aboriginal rights, land rights, welfare and recognition. Native Americans have been museumized into 'reservations'—effectively ghettoized. Aboriginal writings, drawing upon oral traditions, native versions of spirituality and a land ethic that emphasizes the interconnectedness of all life, also foreground the domination of white settlers, the exploitation of their lands and the suppression of their way of life. Aboriginal writing has been claimed as 'postcolonial' along with other cultures from Asia, Africa and South America because they have been conquered and oppressed and their cultures marginalized (Nayar 2008b: 89). That is, Aboriginal and First Peoples cultures must be read as one more instance of the *literature of the exploited, the culture of resistance* and the *cultures of revival*. In terms of genre, therefore, we could align these narratives along with much postcolonial literature.

Aboriginal and First Peoples writing is an attempt to not only bring back their traditions but also to ensure that modernity, especially colonial modernity, is revealed as an exploitative mechanism where some cultures have been marginalized or even eliminated. Hence, theoretical frameworks that address questions of emancipation, oppression and cultural survival are needed.

Aboriginal writing provokes a different theoretical frame even within postcolonial thought. First Peoples critical thinking has been marked by two major divisions.

(i) The first strand of critical thinking about First Peoples is embodied in the work of whites and non-aboriginals theorizing aboriginal cultures in what can be termed 'cross-cultural' postcolonial theory. This has resulted in accusations of appropriation and the continued hegemony of urban elite within critical practice.

(ii) The second strand is the nativist one, where Aboriginals and First Peoples develop their own critical strategies—a politically committed stance that involves retrieving Native American intellectual traditions advocated by Craig Womack (1999), Robert Warrior (1992, 1997) among others. This strand results in a narrow, exclusive line of thinking.

Obviously, neither of the two strands are without problems but—and this is a matter of *my* personal credo in literary criticism and theory— the first opens up the field to competent and empathetic readers. Arnold Krupat (1996, 2002) for example, has called for a cosmopolitan critical approach to indigenous writing. Cross-cultural readings are what even postcolonial critics have done when they read Eng. Lit. texts, so why should it be any different for indigenous texts?

> Aboriginal writing gestures at cultures of oppression (settlers) and their binary opposite, 'cultures of survival' (aboriginals) and recent critical theories emerging from within such a writing foregrounds survival, nature, spirituality, home/lands as concerns informing First Peoples cultures.

Jeffrey Sissons provides a point of departure into indigenous studies, and contributes to a theoretical framework for reading Native American, Australian Aboriginal, tribal and other native literatures. Sissons defines indigenous cultures as 'cultures that have been transformed through struggles of colonized peoples to resist and redirect projects of settler nationhood' (2005: 15).

(i) Indigenous cultures are 'cultures of survival' and are defined in terms of their struggles against foreign cultures (Sisson, 2005: 12–13).

(ii) Indigenous cultures are localized, spatially (in terms of territory) circumscribed and rooted in very specific histories.

(iii) Identities in First Peoples writing is collective and communitarian and, therefore, rarely highlight a *Bildungsroman* kind of triumphalist individual narrative.

Helen May Dennis suggests that for Aboriginal and Native American peoples, displacement has been a systematic historical condition. As a result the search for home, or what she terms (after Gaston Bachelard) 'felicitous spaces' (2007), some of which may be imagined or imaginary or even utopian, whether it is home or land. Other critics have argued that 'fringe writing'—a politically loaded term for Aboriginal writing—often exhibits a 'despairing, longing' because 'they speak from a dispossessed reality in which Aboriginality is often an indeterminate yearning' (Knudsen 1991).

The spatialized reading, postcolonial theory and studies of 'fringe writing', among others, combine to open up several key theoretical concerns about First Peoples narratives as listed below.

- Questions of home and questions of homelands are crucial to any interpretation of Aboriginal and First Peoples cultural practices.
- Home is more than a trope in these works. Women authors such as Paul Gunn Allen, for example, interrogate the gendered nature of the very space of home.
- It emphasizes the displacement from and within which First Peoples have produced their cultural practices (Sissons' 'cultures of survival').
- Narrative strategies within these cultures and writings ask us to approach them differently because they are based on a different world vision (of space, time, earth, creation).
- Historical narratives from within these traditions need not necessarily work at 'authenticity', but more often than not (as Helen Dennis argues, 2007: 159–62) focuses on mixed-blood ancestry, cultural hybridity.
- It is not possible to situate these works *only* within the oral traditions. We need to root them, Robert Allen Warrior argues (1992) within particular historical and political contexts because most of these texts exhibit remarkably similar political commitments.
- The emphasis on and privileging of pre-writing, orality and pictographic representation among First Peoples as 'authentic' is also not always tenable because, in many cases of cross-cultural 'texts' from the nineteenth century we can see Aboriginal ideographs inscribed onto European documents, and Aboriginal use of alphabetic characters other than as phonographic script in what a critic has termed 'borderland semiotic transactions' (Toorn 2001). While this takes away the debate around 'authenticity' and 'pure' cultural forms, it also gestures at the double and multiple nature of all representations.

'MIXED RACE' AND MULTIETHNIC CULTURE STUDIES

'Mixed race' studies emerged from three major contexts: poststructuralism and historical research, heightened migration and the formation of multicultural cities and populations, and the rise of black and non-white public intellectuals. The last category, exemplified both by high profile artists–authors like Toni Morrison and Maya Angelou but also university professors like Stuart Hall, Cornel West, Kwame Appiah, bell hooks (all black) Edward Said, Gayatri Spivak, Homi Bhabha (all of Asian origin) and Gloria Anzaldua and Cherríe Moraga (Chicano), were often featured on newspapers, TV and general public culture.

Poststructuralism destroyed the remnants of any notion of a self or identity (Freud had of course demolished a substantial portion of it [the self] a hundred years before this). Thus, ideas about 'pure' identities, 'origins' and coherent selves have been under sustained attack through the 1980s. Historical researches into English, European and American cultures revealed a degree of interracial encounters, alliances and contacts that were surprising and unsettling for theorists of identity. Thus, Dirk Hoerder's grand study, *Cultures in Contact* (2000) demonstrated, with a wealth of evidence, how even the European Renaissance, taken as iconic of high 'European' culture was in fact a messy mixture of several cultures, traditions and practices and that the Renaissance was the effect of this cultural mix. Anthropologists like Clifford Geertz and James Clifford gestured at the 'travelling' of cultures, once again showing how races and cultures can never be unitary or isolated. Literary scholars hunting the archives found instances of non-white lives and narratives dating back to the Renaissance, once again proving that European culture always built itself through a negotiation with other cultures.

In terms of contexts, increased migration after the 1960s, from Asia and Africa into Europe and America marked a major racial upheaval as multiracial cities, families and schools changed the demographics of these countries. Second- and third-generation migrants saw themselves as possessing the traits of both their 'original' cultures/races as well as of their adopted one. From this context emerges mixed race studies, even as postcolonial studies began to grapple with hybridity, migrancy and multiculturalism (see Chapter 6 on postcolonial theory).

The black public intellectuals, as Henry Giroux has argued (2002), were often attacked by white critics for being too narrowly focused on race matters, of appealing only to a small segment of the population and of shoddy research. Responses to such attacks, from very distinguished authors like Toni Morrison, have also emerged, and have rendered black public-intellectual culture a key component of American civic debates.[1]

Having outlined the intellectual and contextual routes mixed race studies has taken, we need to turn to the paradox at the heart of the theoretical and analytical project itself. Jayne Ifekwunigwe in her introduction to *'Mixed Race' Studies: A Reader* (2004) notes that biological, especially genetic, evidence has proved that there are no 'pure' biological races. All races are, therefore, mixed anyway. Hence, all race studies are, in fact, 'mixed race' studies! Ifekwunigwe declares that the intention of her *Reader* is to 'explore why popular and academic interest in the idea of "mixed race" persists ... despite the fact that "biological" explanations for "racial" differences have long been discovered' (4). Ifekwunigwe responds to this paradox by locating the rise, growth and dissemination of 'mixed race' studies within various social and political contexts: colonialism, slavery, race/colour hierarchies and gender hierarchies (7). She also proposes that 'mixed race' studies is intimately linked to the politics of identity in the latter half of the twentieth century. Thus, the US and UK rules go with *biracial* identities that rely only on the black/white racial categories. What about dual-minority 'mixes' that do not include black/

white? What about three or more mixes? Since the late 1990s the perception of 'mixed race' has shifted more toward multiracial paradigms. Danzy Senna (2004 [1998]) speaks of a 'Mulatto Nation' where there could be any number of variations on the 'mulatto' theme, including Jewlatto (Jews *and* Blacks), Gelatto (Italia American *and* African American), Cablinasian (mix of Asian, American Indian, Black and Caucasian), among others (2004: 205–8).

Despite Ifekwunigwe's 'paradox' of racial identity, debates about 'mixed race' and multiraciality will persist because, as Steven Ropp has argued, even if race as a biological determinant has been disproved, 'subtle' forms of thinking linking race with behaviour persist (2004 [1997]: 263). Ropp points to another paradox within multiracial discourses:

> In academic fields like Asian American Studies, race and racial determinism are strongly refuted and yet the construction of multiraciality seems to indicate the continuing centrality of racialized thinking. In academic discourse, multiracial subjects constitute a challenge to that racialized thinking but only to the degree that they can carve out space within the racial logic which, for example, underlies the project of Asian American Studies. (266)

What is obvious is, despite claims and counterclaims, evidence and speculation, race remains a critical category within academic and social theories. Poetics, politics, legal reform, welfare, access to education, health or employment remain embedded in categorization and census-operations that deal in race.

MESTIZA POETICS AND THEORIES

Gloria Anzaldua famously described the Mexican American border as a site 'where the Third World grates against the first and bleeds. And before a scab forms it hemorrhages again, the lifeblood of two worlds merging to form a third country – a border culture (1987: 3).

Artists and theorists like Anzaldua and Moraga have spoken of Chicano/a identity as border-crossing, *mestizaje*. The *mestiza* is the hybrid, the site of cultural encounter, cross-breeding and conflict. Anzaldua makes the borderlands the site of problematic sexual and textual hybridization and mongrelization, the venue of transgression and unacceptable involvements: 'the prohibited and forbidden are its [the borderlands'] inhabitants ... the perverse, the queer ... the mongrel ... the half-breed, the half dead' (3). The subjectivity emerges as a wound, as a bleeding site, and as violence upon the body. It is from this concept that Chicano/a poetics of the 1990s emerges. This linkage of body with land and culture is a key element of Chicano/a theory. Cherríe Moraga writes about Aztlán, the mythic ancient land of the Mexican civilization:

> For immigrants and natives alike, land is ... the factories where we work, the water our children drink, and the housing project where we live. For women, lesbians and gay men, land is that physical mass called our bodies. (1993: 173)

Alfred Arteaga, building on this notion of bodies, borders and border-crossing in his study of Chicano/a poetry, treats Chicano/a subjectivity itself as 'chicanismo', the 'site of cultural interaction' (1997: 9). He emphasizes that Chicano/a poetry and poetics must first address the theme of mixing. For this purpose he invokes a trope *difrasismo*, a term coined by Angel Gabray, which means the coupling of two elements: water and hill, feet and hands, flower and song. The two elements in combination, argues Arteaga, suggests a third (6–7).

Arteaga argues that Chicano/a poetry is located in the racial body because the Chicano/a is racially hybrid—half European and half Indian, a mestizo. As a result of this miscegenated condition of the body and its ancestry there evolves a mestizo consciousness—one of 'subjective ambiguity' (11).

Arteaga is also emphatic that, since the body, the land and the text are linked to issues of production and reproduction (miscegenation), Chicano/a poetics is rooted in an act of sexual violence and interbreeding, what he terms 'colonial sex' (25), referring to the relations between Spanish conquerors and native women. Hybridized, multi-voiced and Chicano/a writings, therefore, for Arteaga, become metaphoric of the interbreeding of bodies and cultures. Arteaga writes in what could very well be the crux of mestizo theory and poetics:

> The mestizo body is made through sexual intercourse, specifically through the biologic interplay of different sexes, through heterosexual reproduction. The Chicano subject comes about through the interplay of different social 'texts,' analogously, through heterotextual reproduction ...
>
> The subject of hybridity plays itself out in heterotextual discourse, conceived from the model of heterosexual intercourse. (1997: 25–27)

This concern with sexuality and textuality, gene mixing and genre mixing in Arteaga is also aligned with questions of language, tropes, gender (he undertakes a reading of Anzaldúa and Moraga to show how they revise the tropes of 'father' and 'reproduction', 34–43) and cultural identity. Arteaga's thesis that Chicano/a identity, body, language and literary expression are always already contaminated, hybridized and hetero is a celebration of plenitude, difference and mixing. Thus, mestizo theories and poetics opt for the following:

- difference
- multiplicity
- unknowable origins
- hybridity and ambiguity
- cultural diversity
- tropes of the body, the land and the text
- mixing of genres, voices, languages and cultures

Arteaga's theorization of Chicano/a 'subjective ambiguity' is complicated by

(i) the emphasis on a border, hybrid identity, and

(ii) the cultural nationalism that seeks a pre-Hispanic culture.

Reviving the ancient culture of the Aztecs the people of the borderlands have proposed Aztlán as their mythic nation and metaphor. It becomes a metaphor for a pre-Hispanic age and space. When the National Chicano Youth Liberation Conference met at Denver in 1969 they produced a document, *El Plan de Aztlán* in which they declared:

> we declare the independence of our mestizo nation. We are a bronze people with a bronze culture. Before all of North America, before all our brothers in the bronze continent, we are a nation, we are a union of free pueblos, we are Aztlán. (*Documents of the Chicano Struggle* 1971: 4)

As I have argued elsewhere (Nayar 2008b: 75), this search for Aztlán marks out the space of a distinct cultural community and identity, but it also reiterates the myth of origins and sources. It also works within the parameters of the nation-state, of the nation as its people (Arteaga 14). Arteaga finds such essentialism of *both* mestizo-as-hispano and mestizo-as-Indian problematic because, as he points out, 'it [hispano subjectivity] restricts the essence of the contemporary subject to a narrow definition that can occupy the present end point of the colonial or even classical trajectory' and 'identity politics that define Chicano as Indian den[ies] the hispano component' (145).

Thus, Chicano/a poetics is driven by these two motifs—of a cultural national-ism that is essentialist and a glorification of a hybrid identity. If the first is territory- and origin-bound, the second is relational and dynamic. Gloria Anzaldúa celebrates the second mode, and consciously uses a rhetoric and form that con-fuses, slips and evades. Her *Borderlands*, for example, uses poetry, the essay, English and Spanish languages and tropes, the autobiography and the descriptive forms—all within the same page. Her bilingualism, mixing of genres and tones are all symbolic of the key aesthetic she espouses: border crossings.[2] In fact, critics have argued that the mixing of modes and registers—like romanticism and realism—are characteristic of the Latin American novel itself (and the Latin American novel is of dual cultural origins—native and European), right from the nineteenth century (Lindstrom 2005: 41).

BEING BLACK, WHILE BEING BRITISH

Paul Gilroy in a justly influential work claimed that there was no black in the Union Jack (1987), referring to the absence of Black cultures in narratives of Englishness. In his later work, Gilroy argued a strong case for treating the Atlantic—and by extension American culture—as an exemplification of black cul-tures in contest, contact and conflict with white ones. The 'black Atlantic', in his work of the same title, becomes the space of diaspora and transnational cultures. Whereas earlier diaspora studies focused on the origin–new home binary, Gilroy argued that hybrid spaces emerge when African cultures meet European ones and vice versa. Adapting Du Bois' notion of 'double consciousness' Gilroy proposed that right from the time of the slave trade Africans moving towards the 'new world' became diasporic, with a consciousness of both European and African cultures. This double consciousness, for Gilroy, is a productive cultural condition. What is interesting about Gilroy's work is that he suggests the black Atlantic and transculturation (a term coined by Marie Louis Pratt in her study of travel writing, 1992) works both ways:

- Africans learning from, adapting to, merging with European cultures and
- Europeans seeing, recognizing an Other culture.

Reading African American authors, Gilroy shows how they all reveal this double consciousness. What Gilroy was proposing that we see displacement, the trans-Atlantic voyage and interaction, the origin–new world binary as encouraging and culturally productive rather than as just displacement. In other words, Gilroy was arguing a case for diaspora as a productive cultural process where every displaced individual adapts and learns from a new space. One cannot, therefore, see African American culture as either rooted in the mythic African 'home' cultures because the trans-Atlantic experience has always been a part of Black consciousness.

Stuart Hall in his series of essays on cultural studies has effectively deployed deconstructive strategies to argue for shifting and multiple identities. For instance, Hall's work consistently probes a problematic area: can one be black and British at the same time? Contemporary cultural studies work has demonstrated the tenuous and often terrorizing intersections of race and national identity. In a particularly poignant passage worth citing in full, Hall offers us an insight into the inextricable blackness of English identity:

> People like me who came to England in the 1950s have been there for centuries; symbolically, we have been there for centuries. I was coming home. I am the sugar at the bottom of the English cup of tea. I am the sweet tooth, the sugar plantations that rotted generations of English children's teeth. There are thousands of others beside me that are, you know, the cup of tea itself … Not a single tea plantation exists within the United Kingdom. This is the symbolization of English identity – I mean what does anybody in the world know about an English person except that they can't get through the day without a cup of tea?
>
> Where does it come from? Ceylon – Sri Lanka, India. That is the outside history that is inside the history of the English. There is no English history without that other history. (2000: 147)

Hall is pointing to the blackness at the heart of all English identity. He elaborates a series of identities for contemporary Britain: 'Third generation young Black men and women know they come from the Caribbean, know that they are Black, know that they are British. They want to speak all three identities.' (2000: 152)

C. L. Innes (2002) has traced Asian and Black writing in Britain, just as Rozina Visram (1984, 2002) and Michael Fisher (2004) have demonstrated how non-white cultures have been, at least since the sixteenth century, 'visible' in English culture. In other words, Englishness was made possible as an identity through a process of differentiation and absorption of non-white cultures within rather than at a distance.

Thus, Ben Carrington in an exemplary reading of black sportsmen in Britain argues that the sportsman has to represent both the nation and the race, and tries to be both Black and British. Carrington suggests that despite the hostile environments of/for these athletes, there *is* Black in the Union Jack' (and thus reverses the title and argument of Paul Gilroy's influential work) in the sense that the challenge is to 'articulate a notion of Black Britishness that allows them to embrace their Blackness' (2000: 152). Youth culture studies (Les Back 2002) of Asian and black British youth have also pointed to the uneasy intersections of race and nation. In some cases (Bhatt 2000) the youth are trained to stay loyal to their 'original' cultures, *even as this identity conflicts with their interracial and internationalized youth cultures*. Bhatt, in fact, sees the rise of cultural and ethnic absolutist movements such as Hindutva among Asian British youth as a challenge to multicultural pluralism because these reactionary movements appropriate the concept of race in the same way as 'traditional' racism did.

Contemporary cultural studies, in particular, has paid attention to youth cultures, subcultures, music and fashion cultures of 'Black Britain' and Asian Britain. This approach to the theme of race focuses on:

- questions of racial identity,
- the processes through which racial/ethnic identity is asserted,
- the intersection of racial–ethnic identity with national identity,
- the displaced and distorted identities of family, origins and 'native' cultures in third-generation immigrants,
- racialized, localized and globalized cultural forms.

NEW THEORIES OF 'DIFFERENCE'

In the last decades of the twentieth century, and especially after 9/11, many First World nations have been concerned with and about the following questions and issues:

- immigration (both legal and illegal)
- minority rights
- human rights
- terrorism
- defence (military, territorial and cultural)
- identity (national, racial, political)

As refugee numbers increase in the context of genocidal wars (in Africa, South America and parts of Europe and Asia), humanitarian crises loom almost every year across the globe. On the one hand is the unification of the globe through telecommunications and the flow of capital, and on the other there are separatist movements that descend into utter brutality. On one side is the battle for national pride and sovereignty and on the other is search for a share of the global economic pie.

These are not specifically racialized issues, though race does remain as a key player in the field. In this section I explore the work of thinkers who have addressed questions of immigration, borders, sovereignty and humanitarian crises. While they do not locate their discourse within CRS, I propose that their contributions have something to offer by way of theoretical paradigms to understand race-determined issues of borders, nations, communities and the human itself.

I have termed them 'new theories of difference' because they are concerned with how difference is instituted and executed. Jacques Derrida, Roberto Esposito and Aihwa Ong develop genealogies in which particular forms of thought (bio-politics, cosmopolitanism) and structures (immigration, exile) *define difference* and how juridical, social and political measures (for example, welfare measures or voting rights to immigrants, granting citizenship) with regard to particular ethnic groups, people and families are about *dealing with this difference*.

JACQUES DERRIDA, HOSPITALITY AND COSMOPOLITANISM

In his work on the question of the foreigner and the politics of cosmopolitanism, Jacques Derrida outlines a series of problems and propositions that resonate with the concerns of CRS, especially in the matter of immigration and refugees.

When the foreigner arrives, say at the port of entry, or the immigration office, he is asked questions about his identity and intentions. Derrida opens with the *language* in which these questions are posed (because, as we know in the case of several countries, a language criterion exists for citizenship):

> Must we ask the foreigner to understand us, to speak our language, in all senses of this term, in all its possible extensions, before being able and so as to be able to welcome him into our country? If he was already speaking our language, with all that that implies, if we already shared everything that is shared with a language, would the foreigner still be a foreigner and could we speak of asylum or hospitality in regard to him? (2000: 15)

Further, to offer hospitality to the foreigner is to offer hospitality and citizenship to her/his family to the descendants. This is a genealogical right and Derrida points out that the right to hospitality commits a household, a line of descent, a family, a familial or ethnic group receiving a familial or ethnic group. The point Derrida raises can be extended to include race (since he does mention ethnicity):

the offer of and demand for hospitality is not just between *individuals*. We offer hospitality *as a family* to another *family*.

Derrida then pushes the limits of hospitality further. The law of absolute hospitality demands, he argues, that we offer the place to the other without asking her/his name. We open up the home to the other to the foreigner (25). Playing with the etymology of hospitality and host ('hostis', the roots of 'foreigner', means both enemy and guest) Derrida calls into question the problem of language: who is the guest and who is the enemy?

The question of hospitality becomes, he points out, the question of borders and thresholds: 'between the familial and the non-familial, between the foreign and the non-foreign, between the citizen and the non-citizen' (49). And it is here that Derrida's explication of 'hospitality' coincides with the biopolitics of Esposito (see below). Derrida notes that to offer hospitality we need to be sovereign in our home ('invite whomever I wish to come into my home', 51). This means 'inviolable immunity remains the condition of hospitality' (51). The very integrity of the self is the precondition of hospitality but one can 'become virtually xenophobic in order to protect or claim one's own hospitality, the own home that makes possible one's own hospitality' (53).

This question of sovereignty opens up a different debate – one that occurs in a different form in political thought and nation-state immigration policies: how does one keep 'open doors'? Derrida (2001) calls for cities of refuge that would 'reorient the politics of the state' (4). He calls for a 'free city' that, in offering absolute hospitality to the exile, the nomad, the displaced and the refugee might, even free itself from the state (9). But what is more significant in Derrida's reading of cities of refuge is the condition he places even on unconditional hospitality (by which he means offering hospitality to everyone and anyone). He asks, 'how can a purely political refugee claim to have been truly welcomed into a new settlement without that entailing some form of economic gain?' (12) Derrida notes that the 'experimentation', as he calls it, would be to test how the conditions of offering hospitality (sovereignty over one's house) and right of residence might be worked at (22–23).

Derrida's relevance to CRS is his unrelenting emphasis on both the *language* (of hospitality, of the law, even of the name) and the *ethical* dimensions of the very idea and the institution of borders, identities and people. His careful negotiation of the laws of hospitality and the 'identity' of the foreigner are—despite his obsessive wordplay—matter of serious concern for, it is in the very *naming* of a category ('refugee', 'asylum seeker', 'illegal alien', 'exile', 'displaced') that a future lies. To initiate a name, to institute a discourse is to decide upon, adjudicate on a person's life or death. Just as once the naming of a slave decided his/her life for several generations, the classificatory paradigms of cities ('cities of refuge') and people could decide family destinies. The irreducible fact is that laws of hospitality and definitions of various types of exiles affect specific races the most. The question of the foreigner, as Derrida poses it, is, therefore, a question of race.

ROBERTO ESPOSITO AND *BÍOS*

In the colonial period, the white administrators in Africa, South America and Asia prepared detailed census reports about the native subjects. They identified particular tribes and castes in India as 'criminal' and placed these people under constant police surveillance. The Nazis perpetrated one of the worst race–and ethnicity-related genocides in modern history when they set out to exterminate the Jews during World War II. Technology, politics, economics and culture were all directed, during the Nazi regime, to show how the Jews were inferior, wicked, evil and deserved to be killed. They were initially placed under surveillance, marked out as a separate group and then, of course, killed in the concentration camps. What is important is that an entire apparatus was created to target a different race. In the twentieth century such technologies of surveillance as cameras, metal detectors, ID-scanners, often categorized as 'security measures', have become common in public places. Biometric scans for visas, genetic testing and biometric IDs (recently introduced in the UK, for 'immigrants', usually people from a different race) are more sophisticated common features in advanced nations.

What these examples go to show is that the body is the subject of constant monitoring, surveillance and control. We can perceive a *politics* based on the body, on its biology, when entire castes/tribes or groups are monitored simply by virtue of belonging to a particular group. Commonly referred to as biopolitics, this new politics has become the new technology of control, surveillance and oppression. After 9/11 the racial prejudices merged with national and territorial ones (seen in terms like 'Islamic fundamentalists', 'Muslim terrorists', 'Afghanistan as a "rogue state"', etc). Biopolitics is a new form of racialized discourse and racism too.

Roberto Esposito's work on biopolitics—first becoming available in English translation in 2006—constitutes a significant contribution to this new technology. Esposito suggests that the immunity paradigm has become the dominant over the community one within politics. The immunity paradigm favours and privileges the individual. The community is what begins where 'me' and 'my own' ends. The individual has a certain responsibility of exchange with this community. When an individual is freed of this responsibility and obligation to the community he is said to be 'immune'. Thus, immunity and community are antagonistic to each other. Esposito writes:

> If *communitas* is that relation, which in binding its members to an obligation of reciprocal donation, jeopardizes individual identity, *immunitas* is the condition of dispensation from such an obligation and therefore the defense against the expropriating features of *communitas*. (50)

Esposito reads modernity as a steady progression towards the immunity model where the responsibility towards the community is negated by encouraging the individual to be 'immune'. To be immune is to close off exchange, to guard *away*, to protect and contain. Immune is to not have anything in common (51). Immunization is the sealing off of borders in an act of self-preservation.

As an extreme example, Esposito takes Nazi Germany. Here, Esposito argues, the law (*nomos*) is biologized (i.e., rooted in the body) and *bíos* becomes a juridical concept and category. When Nazi doctors had to legitimize the Third Reich's political decisions, Esposito argues, we see a juridicalization of *bíos*. Then, first, the self is incorporated within the body and, second, the biological body is incorporated into the body of the nation. 'Every corporeal body', argues Esposito, was 'incorporated into a larger body that constitutes the organic totality of the German people' (142). Finally, sterilization and euthanasia were a form of biopolitics that suppressed life itself (the law on sterilization was the first legislative measure enacted after the Nazis came to power, 144).

Esposito's affirmative *bíos*, in contrast to the immunization paradigm, is the condition where the individual is not definable outside the political relationship with those that share the condition of life. This *bíos* is the living common to all beings. This affirmative *bíos* is a communal form of life where we see that our life is connected to, indeed dependent upon, others. For this, Esposito invests the process of individuation with something more. Esposito argues that the individual will be the site or space in which individuation takes place *thanks to other living forms*. The human body is to be seen in a series of relations with the bodies of others.

Esposito is speaking of a political category—though he does not mention race, it is significant that he begins with Nazis and the Holocaust which was a racial discourse leading to the horror—when he speaks of immunity and *bíos*.[3] By proposing a linkage and a community rather than a differentiating order, Esposito is redefining the relation—and proposing an ethical relation—between self and Other, individual and community.

In a work that parallels Esposito's, David Napier discussing the 'age of immunology'—the twentieth century—argues that immunology as a dominant cultural paradigm informs human relations now. This paradigm asks for the self, individual, community and nation, to be sealed off from the non-self.

Esposito's work points to the question of human relations in the age of biopolitics and offers us a new vision—and a politics—for the late twentieth century and the next one.

AIHWA ONG AND THE REFUGEE

Immigration and border crossings have been integral to the history of humanity. In the twentieth century the volume, demands and consequences of immigration, both legal and illegal, have been severe, testing humanitarian organizations, legal systems, health authorities and nation-states as never before. Extreme consequences of migration and the resultant multiculturalization of societies/nations include genocides and ethnic cleansing (Bosnia is a recent case). Images of ethnic groups fleeing across national borders to escape genocide, the conditions of refugee camps and stories of racial hatred towards refugees circulate with agonizingly frequency in global media. Countries seek to screen refugees and enact requirements for allowing them in (the Baltic states introducing language as a criterion for citizenship, for instance).

In such a context, critical race studies must turn—and it has, in the work of select thinkers—to the figure of the ethnic minority, the exile and the refugee.

Aihwa Ong's work on refugees (2003) is integral to CRS for it foregrounds racial and ethnic identities as well social policy and the role of the state. Ong detects three 'technologies of subject-making' (70).

(i) The USA has always worked on a logic of racial bipolarity and 'orientalism' (here Ong takes recourse to Said's iconic work). Whiteness becomes established as an identity through the contrast with African slaves, and fear and longing have influenced American interactions with and attitudes towards Chinese and Asian immigrants. Slaves and immigrants were 'cleansed' of ethnic tendencies through technologies of paternalism, care, welfare capitalism's 'reform' and disciplining.

(ii) The attempts to 'normalize' and assimilate ethnic groups into standardized American moulds were accompanied by the 'moral politics of poor relief' (74). Reforms aimed at the poor immigrant and the urban poor (usually migrants from the country to the industrial city) and the rise of the welfare mode were crucial in aligning poverty, race and morality in the discourse of 'deserving/undeserving' and citizenship.

(iii) The refugee's resettlement and return to citizenship has been a major project for most First World nation-states. The state and the refugee are often, Ong argues, situated as polarized positions. But, she notes, different kinds of refugees have also been differently perceived and received by peoples. National policies about refugees have often changed the 'moral status of the refugee' (79).

Ong's key argument is that the refugee and the citizen are not irreconcilable opposites. Rather, she writes, 'the refugee and the citizen are the political effects of institutional processes that are deeply imbued with sociocultural values' (79). For CRS this is a crucial argument (and one that recalls for us the work of Foucault and poststructuralism) on the following grounds:

- The category of the refugee and citizen are constructions within discourses.
- These discourses are informed and are controlled by social contexts of receiving societies, cultures and states.
- These social contexts encode particular values and ideas about family, duty, responsibility and individual.

- The refugee becomes the subject of these discourses and, to be accepted as citizen, might require to fulfill what the receiving society/culture perceives as the markers of a 'true' citizen.

That is, once the refugee has been instituted as refugee (in opposition to the citizen) then mechanisms and technologies that change her/his status will come into play. Here racialized discourses about the refugees' health, welfare, economic means come into force. As Ong notes:

> The legacy of racializing expectations with regard to market potential, intelligence, mental health, and moral worthiness came to influence at the practical, everyday level the experiences and understanding of both the newcomers and the long-term residents who assisted them. (82–83)

Ong's work demonstrates how racial discourses merge with discourses of health, economy, nationalism, morality and welfare in order to position the refugee in particular ways. These discourses determine the ease or difficulty of the refugee becoming a citizen.

*

CRS, as we can see, centres race as an analytic category. Even as the 'end of racism' debates rage across the world, the condition of refugees, exiles and victims of ethnic cleansing worsens as more and more places in the world erupt in ethnic strife. CRS is arguably one of the most significant and politically relevant pedagogic practices for such times.

FURTHER READING

Essed, Philomena and David Theo Goldberg (eds). 2002. *Race Critical Theories: Text and Context*. Oxford: Blackwell.

Owusu, Kwesi (ed.). 2000. *Black British Culture and Society: A Text Reader*. London and New York: Routledge.

Watson, G. W. 2002. *Multiculturalism*. New Delhi: Viva.

NOTES

1. Morrison wrote in 1995 that focusing on race by the public intellectual was a social responsibility and a cog in the larger democratic wheel of the USA (cited in Giroux 2002: 391).

2. Anzaldúa also, of course, foregrounds the gendered aspects of writing: the woman's forms of expressions, her connection with the earth, sisterhood and spirituality.

3. Esposito situates *bíos* as the Giorgio Agamben (1998) does: the opposite of 'bare life' or *zōē*. *Bíos* is not just biological life, it is individuated life within a community.

10 Ecocriticism

We live in a world increasingly lost to pollution, contamination and industry-sponsored bio-disaster. It is now a truism to say that mankind is efficiently committing ecocide, making the planet inhospitable for life of any kind. In such a context does esoteric and text-oriented theory have any role to play? Does ecological disaster require a theory to recognize pollution or to warn students of the dangers of that plastic wrapper or electromagnetic radiation? What is the role of theory in a time and context that demands praxis?

Ecocriticism originates in a bio-social context of unrestrained capitalism, excessive exploitation of nature, worrying definitions and shapes of 'development' and environmental hazard. While it does not seek to alter the course of any of these very real factors, its task is to see how theoretically informed readings of cultural texts can contribute not only to consciousness raising but also look into the politics of development and the construction of 'nature'.

Theory, as we have seen in the preceding chapters, is not empty textual reading. By paying attention to the rhetoric of the times—by which I mean discourses, such as those of war, development, the family, education, health and sickness, nation, sexuality—it shows how rhetoric codes actual material practices. Theory is, therefore, the analytic practice that shows us various contours of the real world.

Ecocriticism focuses on the material contexts of industrialization, development, pollution and ecocide while developing a frame for reading.

OPENING MOVES

THE ECOLOGICAL TURN

Raymond Williams in his elegantly argued *The Country and the City* (1973) showed how English literature contributed to specific notions of nature, the countryside, poverty, seasons and the city. Williams was not trying to explore the environmental aspects of the eighteenth-century literature. Rather, he was trying to demonstrate how the age worked with particular notions of 'nature' and 'culture'. In a sense, this is the starting point for an ecocritical theory. Ecocriticism begins with the assumption that cultural texts construct particular notions of 'nature', which then tie into material practices. As we have noted in the chapter on New Historicism and Cultural Materialism, cultural texts are not simply reflections of material and social conditions, they actively construct the conditions. Thus, ecocriticism believes that literary, visual and other representations of nature are very much to do with an age's views and treatment of nature. Further, it seeks links between literary studies and environmental activism, between human and social sciences and environmental discourse. It appropriates the rhetoric of environmentalism while looking at the effects such discourses have on the culture.

Early writers on nature in the twentieth century—Aldo Leopold, John Muir and Rachel Carson are the most famous—suggested different ways of looking at the environment. Their texts have become, justly, the inspirational moments of ecocriticism. Ironically, ecocriticism as a 'theory' arrived much after the emergence of the activists and the legal cases about pollution and development all over the world.

A basic definition of ecocriticism was provided by an early anthology, *The Ecocriticism Reader* (1996), which calls it 'the study of the relationship between literature and the environment' (xix). With its attempted links with activism,

Ecocriticism is a critical mode that looks at the representation of nature and landscape in cultural texts, paying particular attention to attitudes towards 'nature' and the rhetoric employed when speaking about it. It aligns itself with ecological activism and social theory with the assumption that the rhetoric of cultural texts reflects and informs material practices towards the environment, while seeking to increase awareness about it and linking itself (and literary texts) with other ecological sciences and approaches.

ecocriticism establishes itself as a more political approach to texts. In fact, ecocriticism is, as we shall see, resolutely interdisciplinary, as embodied in the title of one of its more significant journals, *Interdisciplinary Studies in Literature and the Environment* (ISLE).

Ecocriticism has been influenced by insights from philosophy, development studies in sociology, ecology (in science), feminism, Marxism and other disciplines and approaches. Ecocriticism thus works at the level of

- *Discourse*: drawing together a culture's ecological approaches/problems and its cultural texts that address or ignore the same.
- *Praxis*: contributing to ecological awareness by re-reading canonical cultural texts.

In this second dimension, it works in the manner of Cultural Materialism. It shows how, in literature classrooms, for instance, canonical 'Eng. Lit.' texts can be used to highlight the attitudes to nature *then*, but also to provide sources for highlighting and rethinking our *contemporary ecological problems*.

In dual focus mentioned above the question ecocriticism asks is (as summarized by Glotfelty): 'In what ways has literacy itself affected humankind's relationship to the natural world?' (1996: xix).

Ecocriticism seeks to study, explore and analyse

- nature-writing texts to add to the canon in literary and cultural studies,
- the role of *place*—physical, topographical, built—in literature and other cultural texts (it sees the 'world' in texts—routinely studied as social worlds by other theoretical approaches—as the *natural* world),
- environmental awareness in canonical texts,
- everyperiod's attitudes to non-human life and the depiction of the human–non-human relationship in them,
- the subtexts of literary works that reveal anthropomorphic, patriarchal and capitalist attitudes towards the non-human, women, nature and landscape,
- the assumptions of rationality as superior and emotions as inferior and other such discourses within texts, arguing that these beliefs lead to particular visions of the environment,
- a socio-political framework (from Marxist, ecofeminist and other approaches) for reading literary and cultural texts,
- literary examples within social discourses and acts of development, modernity, urbanization, demography,
- literary studies' links to environmental activism.

As we can see the programme is to locate literary themes within discourses and practices of biology and the natural world. It is a 'literary ecology', a term coined by Joseph Meeker in 1972 (qtd. in Glotfelty and Fromm: xix).

Cheryll Glotfelty isolates three main phases in ecocriticism (she models this consciously on the three stages in feminism, as identified by Elaine Showalter):

1. The study of nature representation in literature. Looks at stereotypes (the Arcadia, the virgin land, frontiers, savage wilderness)
2. Recovery of nature-writing texts
3. Analyses the symbolic construction of species, the discourses that construct the human and the genders, and develops theoretical frames (especially the ecofeminist variety) for reading texts

(Glotfelty 1996: xxiv)

The backgrounds to ecocriticism might be traced to Western environmentalist thought in general, the philosophy of 'deep ecology', the rise of a feminist ecological movement and theory known as ecofeminism.

'NATURE' IN WESTERN THOUGHT

Thomas Hobbes in the seventeenth century believed that the 'state of nature' was a primitive one, and that human community-formation constituted comfort and safety. John Locke suggested that humans must treat the land as their private property. He believed that the non-human world was valueless. Later thinkers, however, had a less instrumentalist perception of nature.

If we look at the Enlightenment period (mid- to late-eighteenth century) in Europe, a period that we usually see as marking the origins of 'modernity', we see some rigorous critical responses to industries.[1] Modern environmentalism draws upon some of these responses as the originary moment in environmentalist thought. For example, the ideology of 'improvement' in England and Europe (studied by people like Asa Briggs 1959) believed that you could improve yourself by improving nature. There was an intrinsic connection between the health and prosperity of the individual and the country. Romanticism in literature was a definite reaction to industrialization. The glorification of nature and landscapes in English and European poetry and paintings highlighted the delicate balance between man and the environment. The movement against cities in Wordsworth and others was a response to the grime, smoke and pollution of the city by gigantic machinery and profiteering industry.

Jean Jacques Rousseau argued that the state of nature was the purest and best form of human existence. His was one of the first critiques of the Enlightenment, arguing against the established notions of 'progress'. Rousseau believed that the 'natural' was innocent and that civilization was 'artificial' and corrupt.

During the eighteenth and nineteenth centuries, this 'civilization' was tied up with two other 'movements', colonialism and capitalism. Both regarded nature as something to be exploited by humans. In the case of colonialism, a further angle developed. Natives in the colonies were seen as a part of nature: savage, primitive, meant to be improved by European influence. Thomas Malthus in his theory of population (published in 1798) proposed that progress was difficult to achieve because food production increased in arithmetic progression (1–2–3–4) while human population increased in geometric progression (2–4–6–8). He also expressed concern over the biological–sexual aspect of the poor, arguing that more food will lead to less sexual restraint among the poor, resulting in more reproduction. Malthus was for the first time linking the world of economics with that of biology and nature in this argument.

With Charles Darwin's epochal work on evolution, the link between human and non-human life forms was altered in Western thought. By proposing that humans were also animals, Darwin provoked a different conceptualization of nature itself. By arguing that only those adapted to, suited to nature, will survive, Darwin called for a greater understanding of the human *dependence* on nature.

Karl Marx and Friedrich Engels in their materialist conception of nature and society also believed, like the Enlightenment thinkers, that human progress was based upon a careful exploitation of the nature and the non-human. Marxism's focus was on the kind of capitalist production and industrialization rather than on the consequences of these two on the non-human world.

In England, the utilitarian thinker J. S. Mill marked a departure from Enlightenment thought. In his essay 'Nature' Mill argued that all human actions are 'irrational' because they try to alter or change the course of nature. Mill was also against the idea that economy must always 'grow'. In classical economic theory—to which Mill was responding—the constant state of wealth, capital and population was seen as a negative type of 'progress'. Mill argued, in contrast, that a quiet static economy where people did not always want to get ahead and improve would leave scope for the improvements of the mind. Mill's precursor in the liberal–utilitarian tradition, Jeremy Bentham was one of the first to argue that cruelty to animals was completely unacceptable. These two might well be the primer movers behind Western green thought.

In the twentieth century critics writing on modernity have frequently looked at the question of development and the related issue of the nonhuman, natural world.

Jürgen Habermas, while deploring the excessively instrumental approach to nature is also against romanticizing it. However, he believes that the rise of the environmentalist movement constitutes a 'new social movement'. The focus here, for Habermas, is the very nature of life and life forms. He sees the movement as aligned with gay and lesbian and women's movements because they all express their dissatisfaction with the present institutional order.

Anthony Giddens sees environmental politics as 'lifestyle politics'. It is about the reorganization of society itself in a more moral manner. Giddens accepts that with increasing modernization greater and greater parts of the natural world—and he includes 'wilderness' within this—become subject to human control. This calls for a moral approach, argues Giddens, and proposes a more caring attitude to the environment (which, in a way, returns to the older idea of the human as steward of nature.).

> Western thought has often taken an instrumentalist view of nature—nature is there to serve human needs. After the eighteenth century more revisionary views have suggested that we need to rethink: the human–nature relationship as one of care (by humans of nature), the kind of exploitative capitalist development and the value of wilderness.

DEEP ECOLOGY

Deep Ecology has been perhaps the single most influential philosophy for environmental activism worldwide. Organizations like Earth First! represent this form of thinking about the environment. Deep Ecology's central premise can be described as follows:

> Our world view, thinking, responses and action are human-centric (technically called 'anthropocentrism'), but in order to ensure a safer planet we need to become eco- or biocentric.

Arne Naess formulated the key concerns of this philosophy. His major ideas are as follows:

- Human life forms are an integral part of the earth.
- Human forms must expand to include more of the others (this gestures at a certain spiritual tendency in Deep Ecology).
- There has to be an emotional relation with and response to nature and not merely a rational–intellectual one.
- Both human and non-human life forms have intrinsic values.
- The value of non-human life is not dependent upon the usefulness of these life forms for humans.
- While human life can flourish with smaller numbers of humans, for non-human forms to flourish, it requires smaller numbers of humans. That is, ecosystems in nature can only tolerate a certain level of human activity or interference.
- The emphasis should be on appreciating the quality of life.

> Deep Ecology believes in the fundamental interconnectedness of all life forms and natural features. It believes that anthropocentric thinking has alienated humans from their natural environment and caused them to exploit it.

Deep Ecology proposes a respect not only for all life forms but also towards landscapes such as rivers and mountains.

MARXIST ENVIRONMENTALISM

Adapting the Marxist formulation that production must be geared to meeting the real needs of the people rather than for wealth accumulation, thinkers like Peter Dickens and Ted Benton argue that 'species being' is central. Species-life or species-being is based on the fact that man lives from nature, nature is his body, and he has to maintain a proper relationship with it or die. Further, labour and production are always geared towards profit generation, and hence the environment is exploited.

Marxist ecologists argue that nature has become a *commodity* with capitalist production. Nature is, therefore, internal to capitalist mechanisms as a source of profits.

David Pepper (1996) suggests that man and nature are engaged in a dialectic. Man changes nature as much as it changes man. With globalization, sites of production move to poorer (Third World) nations, and both labour and nature are over-exploited.

Another dimension to Marxist environmentalism is their attention to social inequalities and its relation with nature. Eco-socialists argue that class inequalities influence the experience of the environment. As an example we can think of air pollution. The wealthier class escapes air pollution through the extensive use of (non–eco-friendly) air conditioning. The experience of polluted air is, therefore, restricted to the less wealthy classes who cannot afford rarified environments in their homes, vehicles or offices. Eco-socialism suggests that the difference in the distribution of wealth is at the base of such an experience of environments. Social exclusion leads to environmental exclusion, where the poorer classes do have the same access to clean air or water. This approach to the environment based on social structures and inequalities is particularly relevant to an understanding of Third World environmentalism (see below).

APOCALYPTICISM

Paul Ehrlich's *The Population Bomb* (1972) has the reputation of being one of the most popular environmentalist books ever. He builds on Malthusian theory about population to argue that global famine was imminent. Ehrlich's gloomy prognosis was the first of many. In 1995 Lawrence Buell's path-breaking work on American culture, *The Environmental Imagination*, declared: 'apocalypse is the single most powerful metaphor that the contemporary environmental imagination has at its disposal' (93). The spate of literary and cinematic works dealing with 'end-of-the-world' scenarios—from Nevil Shute's *On the Beach* (1957) to Margaret Atwood's

Oryx and Crake (2003)—showcase global ecological disaster, man-made or natural. Rachel Carson's classic *Silent Spring* (1962) highlighted the dangers of pesticide, and set off the great environmental debates of the twentieth century. Nuclear war, tidal waves, bio-engineering gone awry—the list is enormously diverse.

In most cases, these works of the apocalyptic (environmental) imagination see little hope for the earth. The rhetoric clearly distinguishes between good and bad (technology is bad, nature is good, humans are bad, animals are good). In some cases a more practical environmentalism is suggested.

Earth First!, the powerful environmental organization, has adopted the basic assumptions of apocalyptic environmentalism, seeing species death as unavoidable. Hence, they called for radical measures to save the earth, arguing that humans have no interest in, or role to play in, changing the course of disaster. Their opposition—humans versus the wilderness—situated humans almost entirely on the side of evil.

THIRD WORLD ENVIRONMENTALISM

Ramachandra Guha and Juan Martinez-Alier (1998) focus on the different environmentalism open to the Third World. They suggest that there is a strong link between poverty and ecological degradation, especially in Asian and African countries. Thus, the debates around development in these nations are far more complex, since they involve related issues of social equality, world funding policies, land use pattern by the poor and subsistence agriculture. Their argument against Deep Ecology is based on a simple yet convincing premise: Deep Ecology works in the West (it is more dominant in Scandinavian nations, Canada, the USA and Australia) because there are large tracts of wildernesses and tracts of land unused by or unaffected by human use. In Third World nations where there is a dearth of land for the poor, protection of wildernesses makes little sense.

This leads to what some critics have called 'liberation ecologism'. Linked to questions of environmental justice, liberation ecologism suggests, in Erika Cudworth's terms, that 'struggles for intra-human justice are closely bound up with those to prevent environmental exploitation' (2005: 34). It is based on a postcolonial take on ecology and environmental movement: the IMF–World Bank (or First World) policies on development affect the Third World in ways that are

(i) exploitative of the environment (an example would be genetically engineered seeds, the use of fertilizers, mining and patents), and

(ii) unequal in terms of human access to and enjoyment of resources.

That is, First World notions of development, trade agreements, free market economy, subsidy policies and patent rights adversely affect agricultural practices and social justice in the Third World. Further waste dumping and mining practices often have a racial dimension to them: wastes move from First World towards the Third World.

Ramachandra Guha (1989), a widely respected thinker and historian, has pointed out that notions of development in Third World countries like India are based on Western models of modernity. Similarly, ecological ideas about conservation come from the West and ignore the ancient social and cultural practices of local areas. People are evicted from lands they have occupied for centuries under the project of conserving wildlife (the debate about tiger conservation in Amitav Ghosh's *The Hungry Tide* is a good literary example here).

Guha and Martinez-Alier develop the idea of an 'environmentalism of the poor' (1998). They propose a basic framework: environmentalism in poorer nations cannot be de-linked from the issue of livelihood, distribution of resources and social justice. The poor tribals in jungles survive by cutting wood for fuel: to argue that this is deforestation and should be prohibited is to ignore the very basic inequality of the social structures. Further, environmental justice movements (India's Chipko is the best-known example, and more controversially, Narmada) are about the preservation of eco-systems that help the poorer sections of society survive. In contrast, First World environmentalism is often that of the wealthier classes seeking to preserve wilderness, when their basic needs are already taken care of. Adoption of either First World agricultural practices or environmental approaches is to ignore very local inequalities, forms of knowledge and practices.

Closely aligned with liberation ecologism, this 'environmentalism of the poor' asserts the

- strong links of local communities with their environment, and
- their right (a claim, it must be noted, *prior* to any development or modernization) to use nature for *survival* without (First World) intervention on behalf of animals or nature.

A significant feature of the 'environmentalism of the poor', notes Guha (2000), is the large part played by women. The connection of women to the everyday work and environment being more intimate, they are the ones most affected by changes in the ecosystem (for example, death of fowl, lack of firewood, shortage of water). Their stake in the environment is, therefore, greater.

ECOFEMINISM

Ecofeminists argue that patriarchal society's values and beliefs have resulted in the oppression of both women and nature. It ignores women's work, knowledge and 'situatedness' (her immediate location in nature, where the relationship with the environment is far more intimate than that of a man's).

Perhaps the most important approach within ecocriticism and ecological activism is that of the ecofeminists. The work of Vandana Shiva, Mary Mellor, Ariel Salleh and others has generated nuanced readings of the relationship between gender and nature.

GENDER AND NATURE

In Western thought and literature, one of the oldest binaries has been nature versus culture (see Raymond Williams 1973, 1981). Further, the two sides of the binary carry gendered values: Nature is feminine and culture masculine. A whole series of such gendered binaries can be seen proceeding from this primary one:

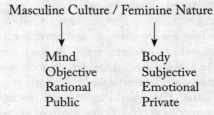

Masculine Culture / Feminine Nature

Mind	Body
Objective	Subjective
Rational	Emotional
Public	Private

Images like 'mother nature' achieve two things:

- They *naturalize* women
- They *feminize* nature

What this means is that nature is imaged as a woman whose basic tasks include reproduction and nurture. Then, women's functions are seen as 'natural' to her. Together, these two dimensions ignore the role of culture and society in imposing functions on the woman. By arguing that women are *like* nature because of their biology is to ascribe qualities to the woman. Likewise to say that nature *is* 'mother' is to assume that the basic task of nature is to sustain and provide for the human race.

Feminists suggest that these qualities of women and nature are both attributes given by males. As a result

  i. men dominate both women and nature,
  ii. men assume and act as though both women and nature are to be exploited by men.

Ecofeminist thought emerges from this basic assumption: both women and nature are equally oppressed by male ways of thinking and action.

MATERIALIST/SOCIALIST ECOFEMINISM

Keeping in line with the Marxist emphases on labour and production, materialist or socialists ecofeminists argue that

- labour and productive capacities of both women and nature are harnessed to *serve* men;
- men dominate the production and labour processes of both women and nature, whether it is women's domestic work or mining nature for various ores and metals;
- women's work is deemed to possess lesser value. Therefore, even *real* work like child rearing/care and domestic chores (food preparation, children's education, care of the old and sick) are devalued and not treated as *economic* even though they contribute to the economy of the household;
- nature's products and services are also, like women's work, deemed to be free and available.

What is needed is a reappraisal of what we understand as nature's economy and domestic economy. Ecofeminists also argue that all political economy is interdependent.

The sphere of production (represented by the factory) depends on the sphere of reproduction (represented by the home, family, nurture) both of which depend on nature's economy (natural resources like wind, water, minerals, plants).

Materialist ecofeminism, therefore, shows how we cannot treat the sphere of production (traditionally associated with the male) as being independent of the sphere of reproduction (traditionally associated with the woman). It is the woman's unrecognized labour in the domestic sphere that enables the man's work to take place. Both, in turn, depend upon the natural resources available. Materialist ecofeminists call for a greater quality in labour distribution, the recognition of the contribution of women's work, the centrality of nature's economy to any economic system. They suggest that

- the very definition of 'work' has to expand to include women's work,
- the notion of 'economy' cannot be restricted to the public sphere but must include the domestic,
- there is an urgent need for the recognition of the dependence of all economy on nature.

ECOFEMINIST SPIRITUALITY

An important strand of ecofeminism retrieves older myths and religious beliefs in which nature is revered. The reasons are obvious:

- They argue that pre-modern cultures have always treated nature with respect (their deification of nature is an index of this),
- They learnt that all human and non-human lives are embedded in nature,
- They legitimize female power, female bodies and female sexuality,
- They give importance to women's knowledge.

The spiritualist strand within ecofeminism, therefore, turned to Native American religions, goddess worship in Hinduism and other native cultures. The debate around the efficacy of introducing the spiritual within ecofeminism has been widespread, where the materialist ecofeminists see the turn to myth and theology as 'derail[ing] the ecofeminist engagement with social conditions and political decisions that tolerate environmental exploitation, encourage unbridled consumerism, and fail to rein in military spending', as Carol Adams put it in her Introduction to *Ecofeminism and the Sacred* (Adams 1993: 4).

Vandana Shiva, whose *Staying Alive* (1989) became a cult text for ecologists and ecofeminists, for instance, saw ancient India as possessing a more environment-friendly culture. Her depiction of this era as a 'golden age', however, attracted criticism because she had ignored ancient India's very real problems of caste hierarchy and gender inequality. Others like Ynestra King have seen the spiritual strand within ecofeminism as enabling social and collective action among women. Noël Sturgeon also notes that there is a preponderance of Celtic and European-Goddess worshipping traditions in many ecofeminist texts. However, Sturgeon sees these moments of 'oppositional spirituality' as rejecting the traditional thinking and heritage of Judeo-Christianity (1997: 129–30).

LITERARY ECOLOGY

Lawrence Buell suggests four criteria for evaluating a text as embodying an environmental consciousness:

   (i) The non-human dimension is an actual presence in the text and not merely a façade – thus implying that human and non-human worlds are integrated.

  (ii) The human interest is not privileged over everything else.

 (iii) The text shows humans as accountable to the environment and any actions they perform that damages the ecosystem.

 (iv) Environment is a process rather than a static condition.

(Buell 1995: 7–8)

Nature writing often privileges wilderness as an authentic, pure form of the landscape. It is the very opposite of a corrupted human condition and man-made landscape. Ecocriticism places a high premium on texts that situate nature as authentic and pure. Wilderness becomes, as Greg Garrard puts it, the 'touchstone' in the 'poetics of authenticity' (71). Texts like Thoreau's *Walden* or John Muir's writings are seen as good eco-texts.

Ecocriticism also looks closely at the human culture–nature interaction in texts. It assumes that nature and human culture are mutually influential. Texts that explore this mutual influence are supposed to embody an ecological consciousness.

In the case of Third World nations, postcolonial studies and ethnic studies are invariably based on local cultures. However, as William Howarth has pointed out, they focus on social and political spaces rather than the actual physical environs (1996: 81).[2] What is called for is a critical practice that links socio-cultural spaces to the physical environment.

William Rueckart proposes specific ecological concepts that can be used to read poetry.

(i) A poem is stored energy, and reading is a process of energy transfer, and classroom work must tap into the poem's energy to develop creativity and community, where all are interlinked by the pathways of energy (not unlike that in nature).

(ii) As readers, just as we ask questions of pedagogy, history and social justice, we need to ask questions like: how are we carrying out our responsibility towards the planet when we read literature? Is there an ecological vision here?

(iii) Literature has to be seen *within* an ecological vision.

(Rueckert 1996: 105–23)

Ecocritical reading also asks us to focus on the state of animals worldwide. Animals for biomedical research, the increased global demand and circulation of meat, the loss of habitats for a variety of animals worldwide, conservation, transgenic animals are some of the issues taken up by activists. Jody Emel and Jennifer Wolch speak of the invisibility of animals in the processes of globalization, modernity and industrialization and call for feminist-inspired notions of 'progress' and a more open attitude to animals (1998: 1–24).

*

Ecocriticism thus focuses on the link between literature and nature. Its emphasis on a practice of reading that pays attention to social inequalities as linked to gender oppression and environmental exploitation turns theory into praxis, locating 'reading' within an activist framework.

FURTHER READING

Barry, John. 1999. *Environment and Social Theory*. London and New York: Routledge.

Garrard, Greg. 2004. *Ecocriticism*. London and New York: Routledge.

Guha, Ramachandra. 2000. *Environmentalism: A Global History*. New Delhi: Oxford University Press.

NOTES

1. In the pre-modern era, in the Judeo-Christian tradition, there were three major approaches to nature: nature to be dominated by man; man to be stewards of nature;

man as obliged to perfect or improve nature. See Barry (1999), Chapter 3 for a useful summary.

2. A conscious ecocritical approach is seen in some novels from India today. Notable among them would be Arundhati Roy's *The God of Small Things* (1997), Alan Sealy's *The Everest Hotel* (1998) and Sohaila Abdulali's *The Madwoman of Jogare* (1998). However, ecocriticism as a critical method has not yet taken off here. Earlier writers like Raja Rao (*Kanthapura*), Narayan (in his Malgudi works) and Kamala Markandaya (*The Coffer Dams*) did locate people and events in local physical settings.

Bibliography

Adams, Carol. 1993. 'Introduction'. In *Ecofeminism and the Sacred*, ed. Carol Adams. New York: Continuum.

Adorno, Theodor. 2006. *The Culture Industry: Selected Essays on Mass Culture*. London and New York: Routledge.

Adorno, Theodor and Max W. Horkheimer. 1995. *Dialectic of Enlightenment*. Trans. John Cumming. London and New York: Verso.

Agamben, Giorgio. 1998. *Homo Sacer: Sovereign Power and Bare Life*. Trans. Daniel Heller-Roazen. Stanford, CA: Stanford University Press.

Alexander, Meena. 1993. *Fault Lines: A Memoir*. New York: The Feminist Press.

Allen, Paula Gunn. 1991. *The Sacred Hoop: Recovering the Feminine in American Indian Traditions*. Boston, MA: Beacon.

Anzaldúa, Gloria. 1999. *Borderlands/La Frontera: The New Mestiza*. San Francisco, CA: Aunt Lute.

Appadurai, Arjun. 1993. 'Patriotism and Its Futures'. *Public Culture* 5 (3): 411–29.

———. 1996. 'Sovereignty Without Territoriality: Notes for a Postnational Geography'. In *The Geography of Identity*, ed. Patricia Yaeger, 40–58. Ann Arbor, MI: The University of Michigan Press.

Arizpe, Lourdes. 1999. 'Freedom to Create: Women's Agenda for Cyberspace'. In *Women@ Internet: Creating New Cultures in Cyberspace*, ed. Wendy Harcourt, xii–xvi. London: Zed Books.

Arteaga, Alfred. 1997. *Chicano Poetics: Heterotexts and Hybridities*. Cambridge, UK: Cambridge University Press.

Back, Les. 2002. 'The Fact of Hybridity: Youth, Ethnicity, and Racism'. In Goldberg and Solomos 2002, 439–54.

Back, Les and John Solomos, eds. 2000. *Theories of Race and Racism: A Reader*. London and New York: Routledge.

Ballhatchet, Kenneth. 1980. *Race, Sex and Class Under the Raj: Imperial Attitudes and Policies and Their Critics, 1793–1905*. London: Weidenfeld and Nicholson.

Balsamo, Anne. 1998. 'Forms of Technological Embodiment: Reading the Body in Contemporary Culture'. In, *Cyberspace/Cyberbodies/Cyberpunk*, ed. Mike Featherstone and Roger Burrows, 215–38. London: Sage.

Banton, Michael. 2000. 'The Idiom of Race: A Critique of Presentism'. In Back and Solomos 2000, 51–63.

Barbour, Richmond. 2003. *Before Orientalism: London's Theatre of the East 1576–1626*. Cambridge: Cambridge University Press.

Barnard, Ian. 2003. *Queer Race: Cultural Interventions in the Racial Politics of Queer Theory*. New York: Peter Lang.

Barthes, Roland. 1978. 'From Work to Text'. In *Image, Music, Text*. Trans. Stephen Heath. 154–64. New York: Hill and Wang.

———. 2003. 'The Death of the Author'. In Lodge and Wood 2003, 145–60.

Baudrillard, Jean. 2003. 'Simulacra and Simulation'. In Lodge and Wood 2003, 403–12.

Belsey, Catharine. 1985. *The Subject of Tragedy: Identity and Difference in Renaissance Drama*. London: Methuen.

Bennett, Tony. 2003. *Formalism and Marxism*. London and New York: Routledge.

Bennington, Geoffrey. 1989. 'Deconstruction Is Not What You Think'. In *Deconstruction: A Reader*, ed. Martin McQuillan, 217–19. London: Taylor and Francis.

Benton, Ted. 1993. *Natural Relations: Ecology, Animals and Social Justice*. London: Verso.

Bhabha, Homi K. 2007a. 'Of Mimicry and Man: The Ambivalence of Colonial Discourse'. In *The Location of Culture*, 121–31. New Delhi: Viva.

———. 2007b. 'Articulating the Archaic: Cultural Difference and Colonial Nonsense'. In *The Location of Culture*, 175–98. New Delhi: Viva.

Bhaskaran, Suparna. 2004. *Made in India: Decolonizations, Queer Sexualities, Trans/National Projects*. London: Palgrave-Macmillan.

Bhatt, Chetan. 2000. 'The Lore of the Homeland: Hindu Nationalism and Indigenist "Neoracism"'. In Back and Solomos 2000, 573–93.

Bhattacharya, Rinki. 2004. *Behind Closed Doors: Domestic Violence in India*. New Delhi: Sage.

Bhavnani, Kum-Kum and Meg Coulson. 1986. 'Transforming Socialist Feminism: The Challenge of Racism'. *Feminist Review* 23: 81–93.

Bloom, Harold. 1975. *A Map of Misreading*. New York: Oxford University Press.

———. 1983. *Agon: Towards a Theory of Revisionism*. Oxford: Oxford University Press.

———. 1984. *The Anxiety of Influence: A Theory of Poetry*. New York and Oxford: Oxford University Press.

Blunt, Alison. 2000a. 'Embodying War: British Women and Domestic Defilement in the Indian "Mutiny", 1857–8'. *Journal of Historical Geography* 26 (3): 412–14.

———. 2000b. 'Spatial Stories Under Siege: British Women Writing from Lucknow in 1857'. *Space, Place and Culture* 7 (3): 229–46.

Boehmer, Elleke. 2005. *Stories of Women: Gender and Narrative in the Postcolonial Nation*. Manchester and New York: Manchester University Press.

Bourdieu, Pierre. 1984. *Distinction: A Social Critique of the Judgment of Taste*. Trans. Richard Nice. Cambridge, MA: Harvard University Press.

Braidotti, Rosi. 1996. 'Cyberfeminism with a Difference'. http://www.let.uu.nl/womens_studies/rosi/cyberfem.htm (accessed 18 November 2007).

Briggs, Asa. 1971. *The Age of Improvement, 1783–1867*. London: Longman.

Brooker, Will. 2000. *Batman Unmasked: Analyzing a Cultural Icon*. London: Continuum.

Buell, Lawrence. 1995. *The Environmental Imagination: Thoreau, Nature Writing and the Formation of American Culture*. London: Princeton University Press.

Burton, Antoinette. 1994. *Burdens of History: British Feminists, Indian Women, and Imperial Culture, 1865–1915*. Chapel Hill, NC: University of North Carolina Press.

———. 1996. 'Contesting the Zenana: The Mission to Make "Lady Doctors" for India'. *Journal of British Studies* 35 (3): 368–97.

———. 2003. *Dwelling in the Archive: Women Writing House, Home and History in Late Colonial India*. New York: Oxford University Press.

Butler, Judith. 1990. *Gender Trouble: Feminism and the Subversion of Identity*. London: Routledge.

Carby, Hazel V. 2000. 'White Women Listen! Black Feminism and the Boundaries of Sisterhood'. In Back and Solomos 2000, 389–403.

Carrington, Ben. 2000. 'Double Consciousness and the Black British Athlete'. In *Black British Culture and Society: A Text Reader*, ed. Kwesi Owusu, 133–56. London and New York: Routledge.

Castells, Manuel. 1996. *The Rise of the Network Society*. Oxford: Blackwell.

Chakrabarty, Dipesh. 2000. *Provincializing Europe*. New Delhi: Oxford University Press.

Chandler, Daniel. 2003. *Semiotics: The Basics*. London: Routledge.

Chatterjee, Partha. 1993. *The Nation and Its Fragments*. New Delhi: Oxford University Press.

Chattopadhyay, Swati. 2002. '"Goods, Chattels and Sundry Items": Constructing 19th-Century Anglo-Indian Domestic Life'. *Journal of Material Culture* 7(3): 243–71.

Childs, Peter, ed. 1999. *Post-colonial Theory and English Literature: A Reader*. Edinburgh: Edinburgh University Press.

Chodorow, Nancy J. 1997. 'Freud on Women'. In *The Cambridge Companion to Freud*, ed. Jerome Neu, 224–48. Cambridge, UK: Cambridge University Press.

Chow, Rey. 2003. 'Sexuality'. In Eagleton, M. 2003, 93–110.

Cobley, Paul. 2001. *Narrative*. London and New York: Routledge.

Cockburn, Cynthia. 1985. *Machinery of Dominance: Women, Men and Technical Know-How*. London: Pluto.

Cohen, Robin. 2001. *Global Diasporas: An Introduction*. London: Routledge.

Colley, Linda. 1992. *Britons: Forging the Nation, 1701–1837*. New Haven, CT: Yale University Press.

Cruikshank, Margaret. 1982. 'Introduction'. In *Lesbian Studies: Present and Future*, ed. Margaret Cruikshank, ix–xviii. New York: The Feminist Press.

Cruz-Malavé, Arnldo and Martin F. Manalansan IV, eds. 2002. *Queer Globalizations: Citizenship and the Afterlife of Colonialism*. New York and London: New York University Press.

Cudworth, Erica. 2005. *Developing Ecofeminist Theory: The Complexity of Difference*. London: Palgrave-Macmillan.

Culler, Jonathan. 1990. *Barthes*. London: Fontana.

———. 1994. *Structuralist Poetics: Structuralism, Linguistics and the Study of Literature*. London: Routledge.

———. 2000. *Literary Theory: A Very Short Introduction*. Oxford: Oxford University Press.

Davis, Caroline. 2005. 'The Politics of Postcolonial Publishing: Oxford University Press's Three Crowns Series 1962–1976'. *Book History* 8: 227–44.

De Beauvoir, Simone. 1984. *The Second Sex*. Trans. H. M. Parshley. Harmondsworth: Penguin.

De Man, Paul. 1982. 'Semiology and Rhetoric'. In *Allegories of Reading: Figural Language in Rousseau, Nietzsche, Rilke and Proust*, 3–19. New Haven, CT: Yale University Press.

Deb, Siddhartha. 2001. 'Fragments from a Folder'. In *People Unlike Us: The India That Is Invisible*, by Muzamil Jaleel et al. New Delhi: HarperCollins.

Deleuze, Gilles. 1994. *Difference and Repetition*. Trans. Paul Patton. New York: Columbia University Press.

Deleuze, Gilles and Felix Guattari. 2004. *Anti-Oedipus: Capitalism and Schizophrenia*. Trans. Robert Hurley, Mark Seem and Helen R. Lane. New York and London: Continuum.

———. 2004. *A Thousand Plateaus: Capitalism and Schizophrenia*. Trans. Brian Massumi. London and New York: Continuum.

Dennis, Helen May. 2007. *Native American Literature: Towards a Spatialized Reading*. London and New York: Routledge.

Derrida, Jacques. 1979. 'Living On/Border Lines'. Trans. James Hulbert. In *Deconstruction and Criticism*, by Harold Bloom, Paul de Man, Jacques Derrida, Geoffrey H. Hartman and J. Hillis Miller, 75–176. London: Routledge.

———. 1982. *Margins of Philosophy*. Trans. Alan Bass. Chicago, IL and London: University of Chicago Press.

———. 1985. 'Racism's Last Word'. Trans. Peggy Kamuf. In Gates and Appiah 1985, 329–38.

———. 1989. 'Biodegradables: Seven Diary Fragments'. Trans. Peggy Kamuf. *Critical Inquiry* 15 (4): 812–73.

———. 2001. *On Cosmopolitanism and Forgiveness*. Trans. Mark Dooley and Michael Hughes. London: Routledge.

———. 2002. *Of Grammatology*. Trans. Gayatri Chakravorty Spivak. New Delhi: Motilal Banarsidass.

———. 2004. 'Outwork'. In *Dissemination*. Trans. Barbara Johnson. 3–65. New York: Continuum.

Derrida, Jacques and Anne Dufourmantelle. 2000. *Of Hospitality*. Trans. Rachel Bowlby. Stanford, CA: Stanford University Press.

Desai, Jigna. 2002. 'Homo on the Range: Mobile and Global Sexualities'. *Social Text* 20 (4): 65–89.

Diesel, Alleyn. 2002. 'Tales of Women's Suffering: Draupadi and Other Amman Goddesses as Role Models for Women'. *Journal of Contemporary Religion* 17 (1): 5–20.

Dollimore, Jonathan and Alan Sinfield, eds. 1985. *Political Shakespeare: New Essays in Cultural Materialism*. Manchester: Manchester University Press.

Du Bois, W. E. B. 2000. 'The Conservation of Races'. In Back and Solomos 2000, 79–86.

Du Gay, Paul, Stuart Hall, Linda Janes, Hugh Mackay and Keith Negus. 1997. *Doing Cultural Studies: The Story of the Sony Walkman*. London: Sage.

Eagleton, Mary, ed. 2003. *A Concise Companion to Feminist Theory*. Oxford: Blackwell.

Eagleton, Terry. 1985. *Criticism and Ideology: A Study in Marxist Literary Theory*. London: Verso.

————. 1991a. *Ideology: An Introduction*. London: Verso.

————. 1991b. *The Ideology of the Aesthetic*. Oxford: Basil Blackwell.

————. 1996. *The Illusions of Postmodernism*. Oxford: Blackwell.

Ekins, Richard and Dave King, eds. 1996. *Blending Genders: Social Aspects of Cross-dressing and Sex-changing*. London and New York: Routledge.

Ellmann, Maud, ed. 1994. *Psychoanalytic Literary Criticism*. London: Longman.

Emel, Jody and Jennifer Wolch. 1998. 'Witnessing the Animal Moment'. In *Animal Geographies: Place, Politics, and Identity in the Nature-Culture Borderlands*, 1–24. London: Verso.

Esposito, Roberto. 2008. *Bíos: Biopolitics and Philosophy*. Trans. Timothy Campbell. Minneapolis, MN: Minnesota University Press.

Felman, Shoshana. 2000. 'The Originality of Jacques Lacan'. In *Postmodernism: Critical Concepts*, ed. Victor E. Taylor and Charles E. Winquist, 86–101. Vol. IV. London and New York: Routledge.

Firestone, Shulamith. 1970. *The Dialectic of Sex: The Case of Feminist Revolution*. New York: Bantam.

Fish, Stanley. 1980. *Is There a Text in This Class? The Authority of Interpretive Communities*. Cambridge, MA: Harvard University Press.

Fisher, Michael H. 2004. *Counterflows to Colonialism: Indian Travellers and Settlers in Britain, 1600–1857*. New Delhi: Permanent Black.

Franklin, Sarah. 1997. *Embodied Progress: A Cultural Account of Assisted Reproduction*. London and New York: Routledge.

Frye, Northrop. 1957. *Anatomy of Criticism: Four Essays*. Princeton: Princeton University Press.

Gallagher, Catharine and Stephen Greenblatt. 2000. *Practicing New Historicism*. Chicago and London: Chicago University Press.

Gandhi, Leela. 2006. *Affective Communities: Anticolonial Thought and the Politics of Friendship*. Delhi: Permanent Black.

Gandhi, M. K. 1909. *Hind Swaraj, or The Indian Home Rule*. http://www.mkgandhi.org/swarajya/coverpage.htm (accessed 24 April 2009).

Garber, Marjorie. 1993. *Vested Interests: Cross-dressing and Cultural Anxiety*. London: Penguin.

Garrard, Greg. 2004. *Ecocriticism*. London and New York: Routledge.

Gates, Henry Louis, Jr. 1985. 'Writing "Race" and the Difference It Makes'. In Gates and Appiah 1985, 1–20.

————. 1987. *Figures in Black: Words, Signs, and the 'Racial' Self*. New York: Oxford University Press.

————. 1988. *The Signifying Monkey: A Theory of Afro-American Literary Criticism*. New York: Oxford University Press.

Gates, Henry Louis, Jr and Kwame Anthony Appiah, eds. 1985. *"Race," Writing, and Difference*, Chicago and London: Chicago University Press.

Genette, Gérard. 1988. *Narrative Discourse Revisited*. Ithaca, NY: Cornell University Press.

———. 1997. *Paratexts: Thresholds of Interpretation*. Trans. Jane E. Lewin. Cambridge, UK: Cambridge University Press.

Ghose, Indira. 1998. *Women Travellers in Colonial India: The Power of the Female Gaze*. New Delhi: Oxford University Press.

Gibson, Andrew. 1996. *Towards a Postmodern Theory of Narrative*. Edinburgh: Edinburgh University Press.

Gilroy, Paul. 1993. *The Black Atlantic: Modernity and Double Consciousness*. London: Verso.

———. 2002. *There Ain't No Black in the Union Jack: The Cultural Politics of Race and Nation*. London and New York: Routledge.

Giroux, Henry A. 1997. 'White Squall: Resistance and the Pedagogy of Whiteness'. *Cultural Studies* 11 (3): 376–89.

———. 2002. 'Public Intellectuals, Race, and Public Space'. In Goldberg and Solomos 2002, 383–404.

Glotfelty, Cheryll and Harold Fromm, eds. 1996. *The Ecocriticism Reader: Landmarks in Literary Ecology*. Athens and London: University of Georgia Press.

Glover, David and Cora Kaplan. 2000. *Genders*. London and New York: Routledge.

Goldberg, David Theo and John Solomos, eds. 2002. *A Companion to Racial and Ethnic Studies*. Oxford: Blackwell.

Gopalan, S. n.d. 'Role of NCTs in Enhancing Women's Political Awareness'. In *Asian Women in the Information Age: New Communication Technology, Democracy and Women*, ed. Ira Joshi, 61–64. Singapore: Asian Media Information and Communication Centre.

Gopinath, Gayatri. 1996. 'Funny Boys and Girls: Notes on a Queer South Asian Planet'. In Leong 1996, 119–27.

———. 2002. 'Local Sites/Global Contexts: The Transnational Trajectories of Deepa Mehta's *Fire*'. In Cruz-Malavé and Manalansan 2002, 149–61.

Greenblatt, Stephen. 1988. 'Invisible Bullets'. In *Shakespeare Negotiations*. 21–65. Oxford: Clarendon Press.

———. 1992. *Marvelous Possessions: The Wonder of the New World*. Oxford: Clarendon Press.

———. 2003. 'The Circulation of Social Energy'. In Lodge and Wood 2003, 495–511.

Grewal, Inderpal and Caren Kaplan. 2001. 'Global Identities Theorizing Transnational Studies of Sexuality'. *GLQ* 7 (4): 663–79.

Groover, Kristina. 1999. *The Wilderness Within: American Women Writers and Spiritual Quest*. Fayetteville, AR: University of Arkansas Press.

Guerrero, M. A. Jaimes. 2003. '"Patriarchal Colonialism" and Indigenism: Implications for Native Feminist Spirituality and Native Womanism'. *Hypatia* 18 (2): 58–69.

Guha, Ramachandra. 1989. *The Unquiet Woods: Ecological Change and Peasant Resistance in the Himalayas*. New Delhi: Oxford University Press.

———. 2000. *Environmentalism: A Global History*. New Delhi: Oxford University Press.

Guha, Ramachandra and Juan Martinez-Alier. 1998. *Varieties of Environmentalism: Essays North and South*. New Delhi: Oxford University Press.

Gurko, Jane. 1982. 'Sexual Energy in the Classroom'. In *Lesbian Studies: Present and Future*, ed. Margaret Cruikshank, 25–31. New York: The Feminist Press.

Habermas, J. 2001. *The Postnational Constellation: Political Essays*. Trans. and ed. Max Pinsky. Cambridge, UK: Polity Press.

Hall, Catherine. 2002. *Civilising Subjects: Metropole and Colony in the English Imagination, 1830–1867*. Chicago, IL and London: Chicago University Press.

Hall, John. 1977. *The Sociology of Literature*. London: Longman.

Hall, Stuart. 1992. 'The Question of Cultural Identity'. In *Modernity and Its Futures*, ed. Stuart Hall, David Held and Tony McGrew, 274–316. Cambridge, UK: Polity Press.

———. 1996. 'On Postmodernism and Articulation: An Interview with Stuart Hall'. In *Stuart Hall: Critical Dialogues in Cultural Studies*, ed. David Morley and Kuan-Hsing Chen, 131–50. London: Routledge.

———. 2000. 'Old and New Identities, Old and New Ethnicities'. In Back and Solomos 2000, 144–53.

Hammonds, Evelyn. 1994. 'Black (W)holes and the Geometry of Black Female Sexuality'. *Differences* 6 (2–3): 126–45.

Hansen, Karen V. and Ilene Philipson, eds. 1990. *Women, Class and the Feminist Imagination: A Socialist Feminist Reader*. Philadelphia, PA: Temple University Press.

Haraway, Donna. 1991. 'A Manifesto for Cyborgs: Science, Technology and Socialist Feminism in the 1980s'. In *Simians, Cyborgs and Women: The Reinvention of Nature*, 149–81. New York: Routledge.

Harris, J. G. 2004. *Sick Economies: Drama, Mercantilism, and Disease in Shakespeare's England*. Philadelphia, PA: University of Pennsylvania Press.

Hartouni, Valerie. 1991. 'Containing Women: Reproductive Discourse in the 1980s'. In *Technoculture*, eds. Constance Penley and Andrew Ross, 27–56. Minneapolis, MN: University of Minnesota Press.

Hartsock, Nancy. 1990. 'Foucault on Power: A Theory for Women?'. In *Feminism/Postmodernism*, ed. Linda Nicholson, 157–75. New York: Routledge.

Hawkes, David. 1996. *Ideology*. London and New York: Routledge.

Hayles, N. Katherine. 1999. *How We Became Posthuman: Virtual Bodies in Cybernetics, Literature, and Informatics*. Chicago and London: University of Chicago Press.

Hennessy, Rosemary. 2003. 'Class'. In Eagleton, M. 2003, 53–72.

Hoerder, D. 2002. *Cultures in Contact: World Migrations in the Second Millennium*. Durham: Duke University Press.

Hoggart, Richard. 1958. *The Uses of Literacy: Aspects of Working Class Life*. Harmondsworth: Penguin.

Holland, Norman. 1968. *The Dynamics of Literary Response*. Oxford: Oxford University Press.

———. 1975. *5 Readers Reading*. New Haven: Yale University Press.

———. 1979. 'Reading and Identity'. http://www.clas.ufl.edu/users/nholland/online.htm#rdgident (accessed 8 January 2009).

Holquist, Michael. 1994. *Dialogism: Bakhtin and His World*. London and New York: Routledge.

Hooks, Bell. 1981. *Ain't I a Woman: Black Women and Feminism*. Boston, MA: South End Press.

Howarth, William. 1996. 'Some Principles of Ecocriticism'. In Glotfelty and Fromm 1996, 69–91.

Hubbard, Ruth. 1992. *The Politics of Women's Biology*. New Brunswick, NJ: Rutgers University Press.

Hulme, Peter. 1986. *Colonial Encounters: Europe and the Native Caribbean, 1492–1797*. London: Routledge.

———. 1999. 'Robinson Crusoe and Friday'. In Childs 1999, 108–19.

Humm, Maggie. 1998. 'Feminist Literary Theory'. In Jackson and Jones 1998, 194–212.

Hutcheon, Linda. 1995. *A Poetics of Postmodernism: History, Theory, Fiction*. London and New York: Routledge.

Hyam, Ronald. 1990. *Empire and Sexuality: The British Experience*. Manchester: Manchester University Press.

Ifekwunigwe, Jayne O. 2004. 'Rethinking "Mixed Race" Studies'. In *Mixed Race' Studies: A Reader*, ed. Jayne O. Ifekwunigwe, 1–29. London: Routledge.

Ilaiah, Kancha. 1999. 'Towards the Dalitization of the Nation'. In *Wages of Freedom*, ed. Partha Chatterjee, 267–91. New Delhi: Oxford University Press.

Innes, C. L. 2002. *A History of Black and Asian Writing in Britain, 1700–2000*. Cambridge, UK: Cambridge University Press.

Iser, Wolfgang. 2003. 'The Reading Process: A Phenomenological Approach'. In Lodge and Wood 2003, 189–205.

Jackson, Stevi and Jackie Jones, eds. 1998. *Contemporary Feminist Theories*. Edinburgh: Edinburgh University Press.

Jameson, Fredric. 1991. *Postmodernism, or The Cultural Logic of Late Capitalism*. Durham and London: Duke University Press.

Jayawardene, Kumari. 1995. *The White Woman's Other Burden: Western Women and South Asia During British Colonial Rule*. New York: Routledge.

Johnson, Barbara. 2004. 'Translator's Introduction'. In *Dissemination*, by Jacques Derrida. New York: Continuum.

Johnston, Anna. 2003. *Missionary Writing and Empire, 1800–1860*. Cambridge, UK: Cambridge University Press.

Joseph, Betty. 2004. *Reading the East India Company, 1720–1840: Colonial Currencies of Gender*. Chicago and London: Chicago University Press.

Kamps, Ivo. 1995. 'Materialist Shakespeare: An Introduction'. In, *Materialist Shakespeare: A History*, ed. Ivo Kamps, 1–19 . London: Verso.

Kanneh, Kadiatu. 1998. 'Black Feminisms'. In Jackson and Jones 1998, 86–97.

Kaur, Raminder and Ajay J. Sinha, eds. 2005. *Bollyworld: Popular Indian Cinema Through a Transnational Lens*. New Delhi: Sage.

Knudsen, Eva Rask. 1991. 'Fringe Finds Focus: Developments and Strategies in Aboriginal Writing in English'. *Australian Literary Studies* 15 (2): 32–44.

Kolodny, Annette. 1985. 'Dancing Through the Minefield: Some Observations on the Theory, Practice and Politics of a Feminist Literary Criticism'. In *The New Feminist Criticism: Essays on Women, Literature and Theory*, ed. Elaine Showalter, 144–67. New York: Pantheon.

Kristeva, Julia. 1984. *Revolution in Poetic Language*. Trans. Margaret Waller. New York: Columbia University Press.

———. 1980. *Desire in Language: A Semiotic Approach to Literature*. Ed. Léon Roudiez. Trans. Thomas Gora, Alice Jardine and Léon Roudiez. New York: Columbia University Press.

Krupat, Arnold. 1996. *The Turn to the Native: Studies in Criticism and Culture*. Lincoln, NE: University of Nebraska Press.

———. 2002. *Red Matters: Native American Studies*. Philadelphia, PA: University of Pennsylvania Press.

Lacan, Jacques. 1981. *The Four Fundamental Concepts of Psycho-Analysis*. Ed. Jacques Alain-Miller. Trans. Alan Sheridan. New York: W. W. Norton.

———. 2003. *Écrits: A Selection*. Trans. Alan Sheridan. London and New York: Routledge.

Leask, Nigel. 1993. *British Romantic Writers and the East: Anxieties of Empire*. Cambridge: Cambridge University Press.

———. 2002. *Curiosity and the Aesthetics of Travel Writing, 1770–1840: 'From an Antique Land'*. New York: Oxford University Press.

Leong, Russel, ed. 1996. *Asian American Sexualities: Dimensions of the Gay and Lesbian Experience*. New York and London: Routledge.

Lindstrom, Naomi. 2005. 'The Nineteenth-century Latin American Novel'. In *The Cambridge Companion to the Latin American Novel*, ed. Efraín Kristal, 23–43. Cambridge, MA: Cambridge University Press.

Lodge, David and Nigel Wood, eds. 2003. *Modern Criticism and Theory: A Reader*. 2nd ed. Delhi: Longman.

Loomba, Ania, Suvir Kaul, Matti Bunzl, Antoinette Burton and Jed Esty, eds. 2005. *Postcolonial Studies and Beyond*. Durham and London: Duke University Press.

Lorde, Audre. 1984. 'Age, Race, Class, and Sex: Women Redefining Difference'. In *Sister/Outsider: Essays and Speeches*, 114–23. California: Crossing Press.

———. 1984. 'Uses of the Erotic: The Erotic as Power'. In *Sister/Outsider: Essays and Speeches*, 53–59. California: Crossing Press.

———. 1997. *The Collected Poems*. New York: W. W. Norton.

Lovell, Terry, ed. 1991. *British Feminist Thought: A Reader*. Oxford: Blackwell.

Lowe, Lisa. 1991. *Critical Terrains: British and French Orientalism*. Ithaca, NY: Cornell University Press.

Lyotard, Jean-François. 2004. *The Postmodern Condition: A Report on Knowledge*. Trans. Geoff Bennington. Minneapolis, MN: Minnesota University Press.

Macherey, Pierre. 1978. *A Theory of Literary Production*. Trans. Geoffrey Wall. London: RKP.

Maynard, Mary. 1998. 'Women's Studies'. In Jackson and Jones 1998, 247–58.

McHale, Brian. 1992. *Constructing Postmodernism*. London: Routledge.

McIntosh, Mary. 1981. 'The Homosexual Role'. In *The Making of the Modern Homosexual*, ed. Ken Plummer, 30–49. London: Hutchinson.

Merchant, Hoshang, ed. 1999. *Yaraana: Gay Writing from India*. New Delhi: Penguin.

Mignolo, Walter D. 2003. *The Darker Side of the Renaissance: Literacy, Territoriality, and Colonization*. 2nd ed. Ann Arbor, MI: University of Michigan Press.

Miller, J. Hillis. 2003. 'The Critic as Host'. 1979. In Lodge and Wood 2003, 254–62.

Mills, Sara. 1995. *Feminist Stylistics*. London: Routledge.

———. 2003. 'Language'. In Eagleton, M. 2003, 133–52.

Mitchell, Juliet. 1974. *Psychoanalysis and Feminism: Freud, Reich, Laing, and Women*. New York: Pantheon.

———. 2003. 'Femininity, Narrative and Psychoanalysis'. In Lodge and Wood 2003, 387–92.

———. 1983. 'Introduction – I'. In *Feminine Sexuality: Jacques Lacan and the École Freudienne*, ed. Juliet Mitchell and Jacqueline Rose, 1–26. London: Macmillan.

Mohanty, Chandra Talpade. 2003. 'Under Western Eyes: Feminist Scholarship and Colonial Discourses'. In *Feminism Without Borders: Decolonizing Theory, Practicing Solidarity*, 17–42. New Delhi: Zubaan.

Moi, Toril. 1987. *Sexual/Textual Politics: Feminist Literary Theory* London: Methuen.

Mojab, Shaharzad. 2001. 'Theorizing the Politics of "Islamic Feminism"'. *Feminist Review* 69: 124–46.

Moraga, Cherríe. 1983. *Loving in the War Years*. Boston, MA: South End Press.

———. 1993. 'Queer Aztlán: The Re-formation of Chicano Tribe'. In *The Last Generation*, 145–74. Boston, MA: South End Press.

———. 1997. *Waiting in the Wings: Portrait of a Queer Motherhood*. Ithaca: Firebrand.

Moraga, Cherríe L. and Gloria E. Anzaldúa, eds. 2002. *This Bridge Called My Back: Writings by Radical Women of Color*. 3rd ed. Berkeley, CA: Third Woman Press.

Mukhopadhyay, Anindita. 2006. *Behind the Mask: The Cultural Definition of the Legal Subject in Colonial Bengal (1715–1911)*. New Delhi: Oxford University Press.

Murray, Jocelyn. 2000. 'The Role of Women in the Church Missionary Society, 1799–1917'. In *The Church Missionary Society and World Christianity, 1799–1999*, ed. K. Ward and Brian Stanley, 66–90. Grand Rapids, MI and Cambridge, UK: William B. Eerdmans.

Nagel, Joane. 2003. *Race, Ethnicity, and Sexuality: Intimate Intersections, Forbidden Frontiers*. New York and Oxford: Oxford University Press.

Namjoshi, Suniti. 1989. *The Mothers of Maya Diip*. London: The Women's Press.

Nandy, Ashis. 1983. *The Intimate Enemy: Loss and Recovery of Self Under Colonialism*. New Delhi: Oxford University Press.

———. 1998. 'A New Cosmopolitanism: Toward a Dialogue of Asian Civilizations'. In *Trajectories: Inter-Asia Cultural Studies*, ed. Kuan-Hsing Chen, 142–49. London and New York: Routledge.

———. 2004. 'Towards a Third World Utopia'. 1987. In *Bonfire of Creeds: The Essential Ashis Nandy*, 440–69. New Delhi: Oxford University Press.

Napier, A. David. 2003. *The Age of Immunology: Conceiving a Future in an Alienating World*. Chicago and London: University of Chicago Press.

Nayar, Pramod K. 2006. 'Bodies and Spaces: Women in/and Cyberspace'. *In-Between* 15 (1): 3–21.

———. 2007. 'Queering Culture Studies: Notes Towards a Framework'. In *The Phobic and the Erotic: The Politics of Sexualities in Contemporary India*, eds. Brinda Bose and Subhabrata Bhattacharya, 117–48. Kolkata: Seagull.

———. 2008a. 'New Media, Digitextuality and Public Space: Reading "Cybermohalla"'. *Postcolonial Text* 4(1). http://journals.sfu.ca/ pocol/index.php/pct/article/view/786/521.

———. 2008b. *Postcolonial Literature: An Introduction*. Delhi: Pearson Longman.

———. 2008c. 'Affective Cosmopolitanisms: Ashis Nandy's Utopia'. *E-Social Sciences Working Papers*. October 2008.

———. 2009a. 'African American Travel Writing and the Politics of Mobility: The Narrative of Nancy Prince'. *Indian Journal of Gender Studies* 16(1): 1–20.

———. 2009b. (forthcoming). *An Introduction to Cybercultures*. Malden, MA: Wiley-Blackwell.

Noghadam, Valentine M. 1997. 'Natonalist Agendas and Women's Rights: Conflicts in Afghanistan in the Twentieth Century'. In *Feminist Nationalism*, ed. Lois A. West, 75–100. London: Routledge.

Ong, Aihwa. 2003. *Buddha in Hiding: Refugees, Citizenship, and the New America*. Berkeley, CA and London: University of California Press.

Pepper, David. 1996. *Modern Environmentalism: An Introduction*. London: Routledge.

Petersen, Kirsten Holst and Anna Rutherford. 1986. 'Foreword'. In *A Double Colonisation: Colonial and Post-colonial Women's Writing*, eds. Petersen and Rutherford. Aarhus: Dangaroo.

Plant, Sadie. 1995. 'The Future Looms: Weaving Women and Cybernetics'. In *Cyberspace/Cyberbodies/Cyberpunk*, eds. Mike Featherstone and Roger Burrows, 45–64. London: Sage.

Paranjape, Makarand, ed. 1997. *Nativism: Essays in Criticism*. New Delhi: Sahitya Akademi.

Prasad, M. Madhava. 1998. *Ideology of the Hindi Film: A Historical Construction*. New Delhi: Oxford University Press.

Pratt, Mary Louise. 1995. *Imperial Eyes: Travel Writing and Transculturation*. London and New York: Routledge.

Rao, Raja. 1963. *Kanthapura*. New York: New Directions.

Rich, Adrienne. 1986. 'Compulsory Heterosexuality and Lesbian Existence'. In *Blood, Bread and Poetry, Selected Prose, 1978–1985*, 23–75. New York: W. W. Norton.

Rose, Jacqueline. 1991. *Sexuality in the Field of Vision*. London and New York: Verso.

Royle, Nicholas. 2000. 'What Is Deconstruction?' In *Deconstructions: A User's Guide*, ed. Nicholas Royle, 1–13. London: Palgrave-Macmillan.

Rueckert, William. 1996. 'Literature and Ecology: An Experiment in Ecocriticism'. In *The Ecocriticism Reader: Landmarks in Literary Ecology*, eds. Cheryll Glotfelty and Harold Fromm, 105–23. Athens and London: University of Georgia Press.

Rushbrook, Dereka. 2002. 'Cities, Queer Space, and the Cosmopolitan Tourist'. *GLQ* 8 (1–2): 183–206.

Rushdie, Salman. 1991. '"Commonwealth Literature" Does Not Exist'. In *Imaginary Homelands: Essays and Criticism, 1981–1991*, 61–70. London: Granta.

Ruthven, K. K. 1986. *Feminist Literary Studies: An Introduction*. Cambridge, MA: Cambridge University Press.

Ryan, Michael. 2002. *Literary Theory: A Practical Introduction*. Oxford: Blackwell.

Said, Edward W. 1978a. *Orientalism*. Harmondsworth: Penguin.

———. 1978b. 'The Problem of Textuality: Two Exemplary Positions'. *Critical Inquiry* 4 (4): 673–714.

———. 1993. *Culture and Imperialism*. New York: Vintage.

Sandfort, Theo, Judith Schuyf, Jan Willem Duyvendak and Jeffrey Weeks, eds. 2000. *Lesbian and Gay Studies: An Introductory, Interdisciplinary Approach*. London: Sage.

Sandfort, Theo. 2000. 'Homosexuality, Psychology, and Gay and Lesbian Studies'. In Sandfort et al. 2000, 14–15.

Sandoval, Chela. 1991. 'US Third World Feminism: The Theory and Method of Oppositional Consciousness in the Postmodern World'. *Genders* 10: 1–24.

———. 2002. 'Dissident Globalizations, Emancipatory Methods, Social-Erotics'. In Cruz-Malavé and Manalansan 2002, 20–32.

Sassen, Saskia. 2002 'Mediating Practices: Women With/In Cyberspace'. In *Living with Cyberspace: Technology & Society in the 21st Century*, ed. John Armitage and Joanne Roberts, 109–19. New York: Continuum.

Schueller, Malini Johar. 2005. 'Analogy and (White) Feminist Theory: Thinking Race and the Color of the Cyborg Body'. *Signs* 31 (1): 63–92.

Sen, Indrani. 2002. *Woman and Empire: Representations in the Writings of British India, 1858–1900*. Hyderabad: Orient Longman.

Senna, Danzy. 2004. 'The Mulatto Millennium'. In *'Mixed Race' Studies: A Reader*, ed. Jayne O. Ifekwunigwe, 205–8. London: Routledge.

Sessions, George, ed. 1995. *Deep Ecology for the Twenty-first Century: Readings on the Philosophy and Practice of the New Environmentalism*. London: Shambala.

Shiva, Vandana. 1995. *Staying Alive. Women, Ecology and Development in India*. New Delhi: Kali for Women.

Showalter, Elaine. 2003. 'Feminist Criticism in the Wilderness'. In Lodge and Wood 2003, 308–30.

Simmonds, Felly Nkweto. 1991. 'She's Gotta Have It: The Representation of Black Female Sexuality on Film'. In Lovell 1991, 314–24.

Sinfield, Alan. 1986. *Alfred Tennyson*. Oxford: Blackwell.

———. 1992. *Faultlines: Cultural Materialism and the Politics of Dissent*. Oxford: Clarendon Press.

Singh, J. G. 1996. *Colonial Narratives, Cultural Dialogues: "Discoveries" of India in the Language of Colonialism*. London and New York: Routledge.

Sinha, Mrinalini. 1995. *Colonial Masculinity: The 'Manly Englishman' and the 'Effeminate Bengali' in the Late Nineteenth Century*. Manchester: Manchester University Press.

Sisson, Jeffrey. 2005. *First Peoples: Indigenous Cultures and Their Futures*. London: Reaktion.

Spender, Dale. 1986. *Mothers of the Novel: 100 Good Women Writers Before Jane Austen*. New York: Pandora.

Spivak, Gayatri Chakravorty. 1999. 'Three Women's Texts and a Critique of Imperialism'. In *The Post-colonial Studies Reader*, eds. Bill Ashcroft, Gareth Griffiths and Helen Tiffin, 269–72. London and New York: Routledge.

Stein, Arlene and Ken Plummer. 1996. '"I Can't Even Think Straight": "Queer" Theory and the Missing Sexual Revolution in Sociology'. In *Queer Theory/Sociology*, ed. Steven Seidman, 129–44. Oxford: Blackwell.

Sturgeon, Noël. 1997. *Ecofeminist Natures: Race, Gender, Feminist Theory and Political Action*. New York and London: Routledge.

Sukthankar, Ashwini, ed. 1999. *Facing the Mirror: Lesbian Writing from India*. New Delhi: Penguin.

Suleri, Sara. 1999. 'The Adolescence of Kim'. In Childs 1999, 251–63.

Sunder Rajan, Rajeswari. 2000. 'Women Between Community and State: Some Implications of the Uniform Civil Code Debates in India'. *Social Text* 18 (4): 55–82.

———. 2003. *The Scandal of the State: Women, Law, and Citizenship in Postcolonial India*. Durham and London: Duke University Press.

Takagi, Dana. 1996. 'Maiden Voyage: Excursion into Sexuality and Identity Politics in Asian America'. In Leong 1996, 21–35.

Thompson, E. P. 1977. *The Making of the English Working Class*. Harmondsworth: Penguin.

Thompson, John B. 1984. *Studies in the Theory of Ideology*. Cambridge, UK: Polity Press.

Toorn, Penny Van. 2001. 'Transactions on the Borderlands of Aboriginal Writing'. *Social Semiotics* 11 (2): 209–27.

Traub, Valerie. 1992. *Desire and Anxiety: Circulation of Sexual Energy in Shakespearean Drama*. London: Routledge.

Travers, Ann. 2003. 'Parallel Subaltern Feminist Counterpublics in Cyberspace'. *Sociological Perspectives* 46 (2): 223–37.

Trivedi, Harish. 1996. 'India and Post-colonial Discourse'. In *Interrogating Post-colonialism: Theory, Text and Context*, ed. Harish Trivedi and Meenakshi Mukherjee, 231–47. Shimla: Indian Institute of Advanced Study.

Vanita, Ruth. 1997. '"What Sort of Beast Was I?" Thinking Beyond Gender in India'. *Trikone* 12 (4): 16.

————, ed. 2002. *Queering India: Same-Sex Love and Eroticism in Indian Culture and Society*. New York and London: Routledge.

Virani, Pinki. 2000. *Bitter Chocolate: Child Sexual Abuse in India*. New Delhi: Penguin.

Visram, Rozina. 1986. *Ayahs, Lascars and Princes: Indians in Britain, 1700–1947*. London: Pluto.

————. 2002. *Asians in Britain: 400 Years of History*. London: Pluto.

Wajcman, J. 1993. *Feminism Confronts Technology*. 1991. Cambridge, UK: Polity Press.

Wake, Paul. 2006. 'Narrative and Narratology'. In *The Routledge Companion to Critical Theory*, ed. Simon Malpas and Paul Wake, 14–27. London: Routledge.

Walcott, D. 1986. 'A Far Cry from Africa'. In *Collected Poems, 1948–1984*, 17–18. New York: Farrar, Straus and Giroux.

Walker, Alice. 1983. *In Search of Our Mothers' Gardens: Womanist Prose*. San Diego: Harcourt Brace Jovanovich.

Warrior, Robert Allen. 1992. 'Reading American Indian Intellectual Traditions'. *World Literature Today* 66 (2): 236–40.

————. 1997. *Tribal Secrets: Recovering American Indian Intellectual Traditions*. Minneapolis, MN and London: University of Minnesota Press.

Weaver, Jace. 2000. 'Indigenousness and Indigeneity'. In *A Companion to Postcolonial Studies*, ed. Henry Schwarz and Sangeeta Ray, 221–35. Cambridge, MA: Blackwell.

Weedon, Chris. 1987. *Feminist Practice and Poststructuralist Theory*. Oxford: Blackwell.

Weeks, Jeffrey. 1997. *Sexuality*. London: Routledge.

————. 2000. 'The Challenge of Lesbian and Gay Studies'. In Sandfort et al. 2000, 1–13.

West, Cornel. 2002. 'A Genealogy of Modern Racism'. In *Race Critical Theories: Text and Context*, ed. Philomena Essed and David Theo Goldberg, 90–112. Oxford: Blackwell.

West, Lois A. 1992. 'Feminist Nationalist Social Movements: Beyond Universalism and Towards a Gendered Cultural Relativism'. *Women's Studies International* 15 (5–6): 563–79.

————. 1997. 'Introduction: Feminism Constructs Nationalism'. In *Feminist Nationalism*, ed. Lois A. West, xi–xxxvi. London: Routledge.

Williams, Raymond. 1973. *The Country and the City*. New York: Oxford University Press.

————. 1974. *Television: Technology and Cultural Form*. London: Fontana.

————. 1981. *Culture*. London: Fontana.

————. 1983. *Keywords*. New York: Oxford University Press.

————. 1986. *Marxism and Literature*. Oxford: Oxford University Press.

Wilson, Elizabeth. 1991. 'Psychoanalysis: Psychic Law and Order?'. In Lovell 1991, 211–26.

Wilson, Richard and Richard Dutton, eds. 1992. *New Historicism and Renaissance Drama*. London: Longman.

Wing, Adrien Katherine. 2002. 'Critical Race Feminism: Legal Reform for the Twenty-first Century'. In Goldberg and Solomos 2002, 160–69.

Womack, Craig S. 1999. *Red on Red: Native American Literary Separatism*. Minneapolis, MN and London: University of Minnesota Press.

Woolf, Virginia. 2006. *A Room of One's Own*. New Delhi: Cambridge University Press.

Wright, Elizabeth. 1999. *Speaking Desires Can Be Dangerous: The Poetics of the Unconscious*. Cambridge, UK: Polity Press.

Young, Robert J. C. 2000. *Postcolonialism: An Historical Introduction*. Oxford: Blackwell.

Youngs, Tim. 1994. *Travellers in Africa: British Travelogues, 1850–1900*. Manchester: Manchester University Press.

Yuval-Davis, Nira. 1997. *Gender and Nation*. London: Sage.

Zimmerman, Bonnie. 1990. *The Safe Sea of Women: Lesbian Fiction, 1969–1989*. Boston, MA: Beacon.

About the Author

Pramod K. Nayar teaches at the Department of English, University of Hyderabad, India. He was Fulbright Senior Fellow at Cornell University (USA) in 2005–2006; Charles Wallace India Trust–British Council Visiting Fellow at the University of Kent at Canterbury (UK) in 2001; and the Smuts Visiting Fellow in Commonwealth Studies, University of Cambridge (UK) in 2000–2001.

Among his interests are English colonial writing on India, literary and cultural theory, postcolonial literature, and cultural studies. His published books include *English Writing and India, 1600–1920: Colonizing Aesthetics* (2008); *The Trial of Bahadur Shah Zafar* (2007); *The Great Uprising: India, 1857* (2007); *The Penguin 1857 Reader* (2007); *Reading Culture: Theory, Praxis, Politics* (2006); *Virtual Worlds: Culture and Politics in the Age of Cybertechnology* (2004); *Literary Theory Today* (2002); etc.

Index